Brigadier-General H. B. KENNEDY, C.M.G., D.S.O.,
King's Royal Rifle Corps,
Honorary Colonel, 21st London Regiment (First Surrey Rifles).

A WAR RECORD

OF THE

21st LONDON REGIMENT

(FIRST SURREY RIFLES),

1914—1919.

Dedicated

to

All who fought with the

First Surrey Rifles

in the Great War, 1914=1918,

and

In Grateful Memory

of those who fell

For King and Country.

FOREWORD.

TO ALL FIRST SURREY RIFLEMEN:

These few pages, put together, form only a slight history of the many vicissitudes which the 1st and 2nd Battalions of the First Surrey Rifles went through in the Great War, but I hope they will help to refresh memories of many happy times, as well as dangerous ones, spent in the regiment, surrounded as we were by our best pals.

I hope, too, they will form a lasting link between past, present, and future Riflemen.

I must heartily thank Capt. W. G. Pidsley, Lieut.-Col. G. Dawes, Capt. H. R. S. Coldicott, Major C. W. B. Heslop, as well as all the others who have taken so much trouble to make the book a success.

In conclusion, I want you all to always remember our motto, *"Concordia Victrix,"* which I translate liberally to mean, "As long as we stick together we shall win through."

December 25th, 1927.

CONTENTS.

PAGE

Foreword by Brigadier-General H. B. Kennedy, C.M.G., D.S.O. 7

PART I.

CHAPTER I.

August 2nd, 1914, to March 15th, 1915.—Camberwell, St. Albans, Braintree, Luton, Harpenden, Southampton 13–18

CHAPTER II.

March 16th, to June 6th, 1915.—Le Hâvre, Arques, Oblinghem, Richebourg Sector, Indian Village, Labeuvrière, Cuinchy, Béthune, Givenchy, Beuvry 19–32

CHAPTER III.

June 7th, 1915, to March 7th, 1916.—Maroc Sector, Les Brebis, Mazingarbe, Philosophe, Marles-les-Mines, Houchin, Allouagne, Loos, Noeux-les-Mines, Lone Tree Sector, Hulluch Road, Allouagne, Labourse, Vermelles, Manœuvre Area and Army Reserve 33–47

CHAPTER IV.

March 8th to July 27th, 1916.—Hersin and Souchez Sector, Villers-au-Bois, Carency and Vimy Ridge, Fosse 10 and the Bully-Grenay Line 48–57

CHAPTER V.

July 28th to October 16th, 1916.—Operations on the Somme 58–64

CHAPTER VI.

October 16th, 1916, to September 23rd, 1917.—The Ypres Salient 65–78

CHAPTER VII.

September 24th to December 31st, 1917.—Oppy, Hindenburg Line, Bourlon Wood 79–93

CHAPTER VIII.

	PAGE
January 1st to July 11th, 1918.—The Cambrai Salient and the German Advance	94–107

CHAPTER IX.

July 12th to September 7th, 1918.—The "Hundred Days"	108–118

CHAPTER X.

September 8th to November 26th, 1918.—The "Hundred Days" (continued)	119–123

CHAPTER XI.

November 27th, 1918, to July 5th, 1919.—The End	124–126
Changes of Battle Position, 1st Btn. F.S.R., 1915–1918	127

PART II.

Introduction	131

CHAPTER I.

England: 1. At Flodden Road. 2. Redhill. 3. St. Albans and Sawbridgeworth. 4. The Last Stages	132–145

CHAPTER II.

France: 1. We go to Louez. 2. The Trenches...	146–162

CHAPTER III.

Macedonia: 1. The Arrival. 2. To the Line. 3. At Dover Tepé. 4. The Vardar Valley...	163–185

CHAPTER IV.

Palestine: 1. Before Beersheba. 2. To Jerusalem. 3. The Jordan Valley. 4. Last Days ...	186–218

APPENDICES AND INDEX.

Battle Honours of the First Surrey Rifles ...	221
Honours List, 1915–1919	223
Roll of Honour of the First Surrey Rifles, 1914–1918	231
Index	269

PART I.

A WAR RECORD
OF THE
FIRST SURREY RIFLES
(FIRST BATTALION).

CHAPTER I.

August 2nd, 1914, to March 15th, 1915.

Camberwell, St. Albans, Braintree, Luton, Harpenden, Southampton.

The story of the Great War, so far as the First Surrey Rifles is concerned, begins at 10 a.m. on Sunday, August 2nd, 1914, for it was at this hour that the Battalion, as it existed in those days before the war, paraded under Lieut.-Col. Morton Tomlin for its Annual Training. The camp was to have been at Perham Down on Salisbury Plain, but as our commanding officer had prophesied when we met in the Mess before leaving Camberwell, its duration was limited to less than twenty-four hours.

Events followed each other rapidly and within four days we had returned from camp, gone to our homes, received our telegrams to mobilize immediately and paraded again at Head-quarters, this time not having the vaguest idea of what the future might have in store for us, or how long it might be before we again put on "civvies."

Mobilization was soon accomplished, not the least remarkable feature of this time being the wonderful response of the men of London to our appeal for recruits, so that within four days we had enlisted our full number of eager and stalwart citizens and were turning away long queues of disappointed applicants.

After a brief but exciting existence at Head-quarters in Flodden Road, we set out on the great advance, our first objective being the ancient city of St. Albans, which as we soon found out lay some twenty-five miles to the north of our Head-quarters.

The trek was interesting and included an inspection by the G.O.C. London District in Hyde Park and a bivouac on the outskirts of London (in the neighbourhood of

Edgware). The march was a severe test for the Battalion, but in spite of adverse circumstances it was accomplished in splendid style; our hastily requisitioned transport encountered some difficulty on the steep hills of the Shenley Ridge, but these were soon overcome and served to teach useful lessons for the future. It was towards the close of a hot August afternoon that the First Surreys, dusty but very pleased with themselves, entered St. Albans to the tune of the famous Regimental March, and those of us who had not previously realized the value of a regimental band did so on that occasion. Of the part played by the bandsmen under Bandmaster King we hope to speak later, but even at this early stage we cannot refrain from mentioning the premier march of its répertoire, the Regimental March—"Lutzow's Wild Hunt."

Billets had been arranged by the advance party (under Capt. S. F. Corby) and after giving "Eyes Right" to the C.O. a bee line was made for our respective quarters, and, greetings having been exchanged with our hosts, we proceeded to make ourselves at home in a way which in later years became almost mechanical through constant repetition. We cannot attempt to describe life at St. Albans without immediate mention of the hospitality and kindness of the citizens in general, and of our billet-owners in particular. Thanks to their public spirit and splendid arrangements, every possible facility for our military training and our general comfort was offered, and by their ceaseless private efforts many joys were added for the benefit of men, numbers of whom were, alas, destined to taste them there for the last time. To proceed, however, with our story: we had realized, of course, that we had not been put into uniform and cheered in the streets for the fun of the thing, and that before we could take part in war a certain amount of training lay in front of us. But we had not imagined how great were the energies and activities of our adjutant—Capt. H. B. Kennedy, of the 60th Rifles—(afterwards so well known by us all as General Kennedy) to whom the subsequent efficiency and fame of our regiment were so largely due. This officer, encouraged by divisional and brigade confederates and aided and abetted by our "R.S.M." (Sergt.-Major F. C. Jackson) had been quietly working out a system whereby life in the Battalion was to be made about as busy as a season in town running concurrently with a 60-hour week, nor was he long in putting his plans into operation. So rapidly did we progress that most of us were of the opinion that we should probably be in France in about two months, but it was at about the end of that time that we realized we were only at the beginning of military training. And so things went on.

We often look back and wonder whether we could accomplish to-day some of the feats which then formed our everyday routine—up at 5 o'clock, physical drill in a dewy field followed by a two-mile run along the hard high road in column of fours, a cold bath and a bolted breakfast, a hasty buckling on of numerous bulky articles of equipment, another rush to parade and wait in the roadway, a march of some six or seven miles to a place indicated by a "map reference" and then—and not till then, mind you!—training would begin! This included such choice items as "short sharp rushes" with the continued throwing of one's body heavily on the ground; this practice, vulgarly known as "belly-flopping," was all right in its way, for we had been shown the art of doing it, that is, by "holding-the-rifle-firmly-at-the-point-of-balance-in-the-right-hand-at-the-same-time extending-the-left-arm-to-the-front-simultaneously-bending-both-knees-and-letting-the-body-fall-forward-on-the-left-hand," &c., &c. But one must remember that all this was done on a hastily bolted lump of bacon, a can of tea, and some bread and jam.

The exercises mentioned above were intermingled with such items as extending in open order, advancing under shell fire (imaginary!), and various operations concerned with attack and defence. We certainly attacked—and probably defended also—very nearly all the farms, woods, ridges, and even villages in the vicinity of St. Albans; the attacks being generally planned to bring us towards the town and our dinners, though sometimes the fortunes of war were against us and we were forced to retire—away from our waiting dinners—only to march home victorious later in the day. If, however, we were back early there were always pleasant little lectures, musketry practices, or squad drill displays arranged for us in the afternoon, so we were "for it" either way.

On September 18th the F.S.R., together with other units of our division (the 2nd London as it was then called) had the honour of marching past His Majesty the King, and on the 29th of the same month the Secretary of State for War (Lord Kitchener) inspected the division in Gorhambury Park. That fine old soldier, Lord Roberts, also visited the troops in the St. Albans neighbourhood and came to our parade-ground on Hollywell Hill not long before his departure for France—to end there his life of devoted service to his country.

Our training was next varied by a move to Braintree, Essex, where we were to have an opportunity of learning to use that implement of war second only to the rifle in usefulness to the infantryman, the spade (or shovel as it was more correctly termed), and its first cousin the pick. The trenches we were to dig formed part of a general scheme for the defence of London in case of an enemy landing on our island. Whether or not our efforts would have saved the capital is not for us to say, but we learned one of the most useful lessons of all, and one which stood us in good stead when later on we many times relied on our digging powers to save our lives. Our stay at Braintree lasted only a couple of weeks, and after bidding farewell to our friends in that town we returned to St. Albans.

Christmas, 1914, was now approaching, and probable ways of celebrating this festival were discussed on all sides. Many knowing ones prophesied that we should by that time be having our first taste of war, presumably in Flanders, and at least one prominent commander hinted at the possibility of our being in contact with the foe "somewhere in Essex": this suggestion amused the battalion hugely and was the subject of many jokes and topical songs. The more sober-minded were naturally looking forward to a day or two with their families either in their own homes or perhaps in their billets; this would have been possible but for a sudden inspiration of the higher command as to the best way of spending Boxing Day. Of that more later, but meanwhile Christmas leave was practically cancelled, so we determined to make the best of things in St. Albans. The feast day itself, the first of many Christmas Days we were to spend together, was celebrated in right good style. The whole Battalion sat down together to the recognized dinner at midday in the spacious premises lent to us for the occasion by Messrs. Ryders (of seed fame), and after the poultry, the pork, the puddings, and the pies had been annihilated and while still some of the beer and sweets were holding out, toasts were proposed and drunk, and speeches cheerful and laudatory were showered on us from above, in lieu possibly of Christmas leave! The afternoon was spent in the only way suitable to such an occasion—in rest and meditation, but towards evening movement was more apparent and games and music held sway in most billets and halls. The officers, who in October had established their mess in the Red Lion Hotel, reserved their festivities for the evening, when in that very pleasant hostel each one, including Santa Claus, joined in the evening's stunts. Only a hazy recollection remains of the evening as a whole, although some of the incidents stand out in one's mind and will never be forgotten. It was a great night, and when at last we turned in and joined the rest of the Battalion in the arms of Morpheus, the "Higher Command" again stepped in and marched us all away.

At 4 a.m. on Boxing morning we were aroused somewhat rudely, ordered to pack up everything we had and load it all on our wagons preparatory to entraining; blankets in "bundles of ten," rations, Christmas presents, and all were to be packed into the wagons and to follow the companies on a march of some ten miles to the railway sidings of a distant village. It was cold, bitterly cold, on turning out, but after an hour's struggle with kit and blankets we were all pretty warm and by dawn were well away on our march. There had been a hard frost during the night and the roads after the recent rain were covered with ice; but we kept our feet somehow, and as the morning wore on and a thaw set in, the ice was turned to mud. By the time we reached the station and had seated ourselves in the train it was, as one might have expected, pouring with rain and we had visions of saying good-bye to England in a deluge. Not so, however, for having soaked us to the skin the rain ceased, and we "marched back to St. Albans again" to carry on.

We were by now, as might be expected, becoming pretty efficient, and our type of training involved bigger and more complicated schemes, the intervals between these being principally occupied in firing practices on the range which had been constructed in Gorhambury Park. This gave us more time and energy for recreation and excellent programmes were arranged for the evenings, these being shared by our comrades in other battalions and by our friends of the neighbourhood; many artistes and friends also came down from London. Amongst the entertainments we cannot forget the Christmas pantomine at the County Hall, entitled "Mary and her Little Lamb," "Mary" being the fascinating daughter of a lady on whom the "Lamb" (a rifleman in a certain battalion) was billeted. This little show was full of topical allusions, and many well-known and important personalities were introduced, much to their own amusement and the joy of the general audience.

Boxing shows were a great attraction under the management of our able and expert quarter-master, Capt. J. Fowles; so also were the numerous concerts and variety shows which were arranged at intervals during our stay.

Sundays were heartily welcomed by all ranks (including the adjutant) and gave us just that weekly rest which we needed to prevent any feeling of staleness creeping in. Our church parades at the beautiful old Abbey or one of the neighbouring churches were always impressive, as were also the drumhead services held on the battalion parade ground when weather permitted. Often in Flanders when attending divine service in a barn, a stable, or even an *estaminet,* one thought of the services at St. Albans, of the splendid organ and of our own band, which then, as always, was ever ready to give us its brightness and encouragement, whether on the march, in the public square, at mess, or at divine service.

But all good things must come to an end, and during the latter part of January the First Surreys again packed up their possessions and marched out of St. Albans—this time to take up new billets in Luton, and continue training, with more useful digging exercises. After some three weeks here, we moved nearer to St. Albans, to that charming little town of Harpenden, and it was whilst quartered in its cosy billets that we saw unmistakable signs of the "real thing" in our preparations for France. To most of us the first indication of coming events was the arrival of brand new transport vehicles of service pattern complete with harness, to replace the old ginger-beer carts and carrier's vans which we had commandeered on mobilization and used since. No time was lost in practising the men and animals in the arts of driving and drawing respectively, and while this was being done the rest of the Battalion, headed by the quarter-master, was having a busy time.

Our hopes were confirmed on March 14th (1915), and at midnight on that date we were down at the little sidings at Harpenden, bundling into the trucks and carriages which were to take us to Southampton.

The following day was spent at the docks loading up, and this completed, the First Surrey Rifles bade farewell to England to win fame on the battlefields of France and Flanders.

CHAPTER II.

March 16th to June 6th, 1915.

Le Hâvre, Arques, Oblinghem, Richebourg Sector, Indian Village, Lapugnoy, Labeuvrière, Cuinchy, Béthune, Givenchy, Beuvry.

The spring of 1915 brought reinforcements to the fighting lines of all armies engaged in the Great War; the opening onslaught of the Central Powers having been arrested, both sides were preparing for the second round with an eagerness hardly less energetic than that displayed during the preceding autumn.

The 1st Battalion of the First Surrey Rifles, as one of the reinforcing units, disembarked at Havre on March 16th in good time for that "Spring Offensive," which proved to be the first of several such annual events. The manner of disembarkation, the night's rest in a camp pitched for that purpose, the entrainment and journey to a village well behind the lines, and the subsequent settling into billets, were experiences similar to those of nearly every unit which joined the British Expeditionary Force in normal circumstances, and are so well known as to need no description. There are, however, many incidents which stand out in this and the following period, and a brief reference to them here may prove not uninteresting.

The first thing which seemed to strike everyone was the composition of the troop train which was to convey us from the coast to a siding in Flanders, a distance of some 150 miles; there were one or two passenger coaches of the usual Continental type provided for the officers, but the remainder of the Battalion was accommodated in cattle trucks which, as could be gleaned from the inscription on them, were intended to hold "Hommes 40. Chevaux (en long) 8." A kind of stove was allowed in each truck to keep the occupants warm, or alternatively a supply of straw, but, for obvious reasons, not both. We cannot tell exactly what the horses thought of this means of travel, nor can the precise thoughts of the men be placed on record, but judging from the guarded correspondence on the subject which one has seen since, one gathers that conditions were not all that could be desired : it is, however, possible that in later years of the war many a man would have given all his pay for quarters half as cosy.

The detraining was carried out at Arques, a small village near St. Omer (at that time General French's Head-quarters); thence a short march was made to billets at Wizernes, and during this march we learned some details as to our immediate future. The 2nd London Territorial Division (afterwards renumbered the 47th Division) of which the Battalion formed a part, was to join the 1st Corps, which was in turn part of the 1st Army; that the Division was thus placed was, we believe, the result of a request made by our former divisional commander, General Sir Charles Monro, at that time commanding the 1st Corps. We further gathered that after a brief period in reserve, during which just sufficient training to keep up our high standard of efficiency was to be indulged in, we were to go into the trenches.

Parading in the snow at Wizernes on the morning of March 19th, we marched that day to St. Hilare, and on the following day retraced our steps a mile or so to the village of Norrent-Fontes, where we remained for a week. On the 27th a long morning's march brought us to Oblinghem, about four miles from Béthune. Here, for a further six days, we were sufficiently near the firing line to hear the guns, and at night to see the gun flashes, as well as the flares sent up from the front line by each side whenever cause for anxiety, real or imaginary, existed.

We had a pleasant time in this little scattered village, and made good friends with the other occupants, both military and civilian, learning from them all the local gossip on such varied topics as the likelihood of an offensive in that particular sector, the best *estaminets* to visit in Béthune, the latest estimate of the duration of the war, or the best farm at which to purchase eggs. At length orders were received for a move towards the line, and when we were fairly on our way news reached the head of the column to the effect that we were to march straight on that evening (April 2nd) and go into the trenches as pupils in the art of trench warfare, or, to be more explicit, to be attached to regular battalions which were holding front line sectors.

The Battalion was accordingly rapidly split up into companies, half-companies, and platoons, and committed to the safe keeping of the battalions of the 1st Brigade, which was then composed of the 1st Coldstream Guards, 1st Scots Guards, 1st Black Watch, 1st Cameron Highlanders, and the London Scottish. The Coldstream being in Brigade

Reserve, our companies, "A" (Captain Walford), "B" (Captain Hutchence), "C" (Captain Heslop), "D" (Major Richards), were attached respectively to the other battalions in the order named, and joined them in the positions they were occupying. Darkness had fallen, and it was well into the night before we had settled down into our posts. Our officers, non-commissioned officers, and riflemen, were distributed evenly throughout the units to which they were allotted, and were thus enabled quickly to become acquainted with the many practical details of trench organization and warfare, which, without this initiation, would have been learned only by a longer and more costly experience.

Though one was thrilled at the time, these early days in the trenches were, for the Battalion as a whole, uneventful in the light of later events: that it bore itself well and proudly was only to be expected when one considers the material we had, the training we underwent, and the excellent company in which we found ourselves. Our hosts, or instructors, whichever seems the more appropriate term, realized exactly our position and treated us magnificently: not only did those splendid fellows, who had already gone through so much, teach us all the various little "tricks of the trade" of trench warfare, but they also helped with our domestic arrangements, and gave us many tips invaluable for our future health and comfort. We appreciated especially the way in which the Regular Army received the first Division of Territorials in France as brothers—younger, perhaps, but brothers none the less—a manner which showed that the "Saturday afternoon soldiering" idea was past and done with.

The particular piece of the line in which the Battalion was placed was situated between Givenchy and Neuve-Chapelle, and was immediately south and in front of Richebourg-St. Vaast. The country in this locality is all as flat as a board and intersected by ditches intended to carry away surface water and at the same time to act as boundaries between properties. They may have been quite useful and efficient in their original state, but artillery fire had spoilt all their good qualities and they naturally proved a constant source of discomfort. The water-level in these miniature canals was only about eighteen inches below ground-level, and it can therefore be readily understood that anything in the nature of trenches was quite impossible unless they were to be filled immediately with water; cover from fire was therefore obtained by means of breastworks or walls of earth sufficiently high to give shelter, and sufficiently thick to stop a bullet.

These breastworks were constructed either of filled sandbags or of earth piled behind hurdles, boards, corrugated iron, or any other suitable material which might be available. Additional protection from bursting shells was often afforded by the construction of a second wall (known as a parados) some three feet behind the first, the two walls forming what was in effect a trench raised above ground.

In those early days of the war elaborate dugouts for protection from shell-fire or weather were unknown, and front line troops were exposed to both unless in the fortunate position of being able to rig up some sort of shelter with the the help of a ground-sheet and some old bits of iron or timber.

Of interest to us during this period was an event which gave us some idea of the meaning of the term "minor operation." At dawn one day a move forward was made by a detachment of infantry to the north of our sector for the purpose of occupying a more advanced position and thus lessening the distance between the hostile lines. By way of retaliation the enemy's guns distributed for an hour or two showers of shrapnel up and down our line. There was fair shelter from fire of this kind, but casualties occurred, though not, during that episode, among our own men. The first man of the First Surreys to fall in action was Rifleman H. R. Jameson, who was mortally wounded by a German rifle bullet on Easter Eve, April 4th, 1915.

Our stay in this sector was varied by moves into support positions in what remained of houses just behind the line, where we slept by day and emerged under cover of darkness to perform one or other of the duties appertaining to this kind of campaign—carrying rations, ammunition, or materials, constructing breastworks, filling sandbags, or erecting barbed-wire entanglements! The houses referred to were, for the most part, situated along or near the roadway (known as the Rue du Bois) which ran parallel to and some two hundred yards in rear of our line, and being intermittently swept by machine-gun fire during the nights, was not a pleasant highway on which to linger! We have often thought we should like to see those billets, trenches, and shelters again, but this is impossible, for a visit to the neighbourhood early in 1919 revealed that the destruction of war and the restoration of peace had combined to sweep away the old landmarks, and had rendered their exact location impossible.

Our period of instruction lasted nine days and cost us four men killed—Riflemen Jameson, Manson, Martin, and Sherlock—and nine wounded; it was terminated on

April 10th, when we bade farewell to our friends of the 1st Division, and on the following day marched back from Richebourg-St. Vaast to "peace" and all the beauties of spring in the delightful little hillside village of Lapugnoy, near Béthune. Here we spent a week or so whilst some of the other battalions of our Brigade—the 22nd and 24th (Queen's), and the 23rd—underwent their initiation. This rest passed all too quickly, for we had much to do; first of all the cleaning of arms, equipment, and clothing, and the removal of all signs of "war"; then further training in the way of marching and exercises to keep us fit, and lastly, our private correspondence with those at home and our discourses in French(?) with the pleasant ladies of our billets, whom we found abounding in good "spirits"; some, alas, occasionally treated us to a very inferior brand, though it wasn't so bad when taken in coffee!

By the middle of April, 1915, the 47th Division had served its apprenticeship in trench warfare, and was ready to take its place in the line side by side with those regular divisions which had been battling throughout the autumn and winter; other Territorial Divisions were also arriving and taking up their positions in various sectors of the Western Front, whilst Kitchener's Army and the 2nd line units of the departed Territorials were training hard at home to join in the conflict at the earliest possible moment.

The particular bit of line allotted to our Division ran in front of Festubert and Richebourg-St. Vaast, the latter being the portion taken over by our Brigade (the 142nd). The First Surrey Rifles soon found themselves back in the old bit of trench in which they had already spent a week, but this time Lieut.-Colonel Morton Tomlin was in command of the sector: at last our ambition was realized, and we were really "doing our bit in the Great War." This sector, at the period to which we refer, was not excessively unpleasant, although various localities became "unhealthy" at times. It is, of course, a recognized and natural understanding in trench war that where the shells are thickest there must also be the best protection—an adaptation, in fact, of the law of "supply and demand"—and a very sound idea, too! What we should have done in that exposed Richebourg sector had there been anything like a serious bombardment, as we knew them in after days, we do not know; but nature again steps in by laying down the law that where cover cannot be obtained for her mortals, neither is it forthcoming for their opponents' guns. It remains, therefore, for those responsible to select, and if necessary fight for, the positions that will both give protection to their own men and also provide lurking places from which their guns can harass their unhappy foes.

In our present situation there seemed little to choose between the ground held by us and that in which our enemy was living, the whole district being entirely flat; as, however, we had our backs to the sea it followed as a general principle that water from his trenches ran into ours, where it was *most* unwelcome, as we had far too much already! When we were on higher ground than the enemy one used sometimes to think that the law of gravity (like many a law in the Army!) had been cancelled, and really at times our work seemed more suited to the Navy, or, at any rate, the London County Council, than the Army, and we would have given anything for some of the later-day motor-boats in which to get round our "trenches." But it was all in the day's work, and our spells in these liquid quarters were generally short, billets in barns or stables being really comfortable as an alternative.

In every part of the line at all stages of the war, there were certain landmarks which stood out either in connection with the defence of the sector or to meet the needs of those engaged in administration or communication; these were generally given popular names, easily remembered by all concerned; and chosen in special reference to some action, regiment, or leader, or, more often still, by reason of some local association. Many names were, in addition, selected as a compliment to spots dear to our hearts, much in the same way as places in the Colonies were named by their founders. For instance, in this particular locality we had "Indian Village," a small collection of farm dwellings and buildings in which, prior to our arrival, a gallant action had been fought by Indian troops—to which the many graves bore testimony: then there was the well-known "Dead Cow Farm"; the derivation of the name we could not definitely ascertain, but the spot, nevertheless, periodically produced irrefutable aromatic claims to its title! "The Orchard," though less romantic, had its compensations in its never-ending attractions for the Germans, both infantry and artillery, as a result of which, many of our people viewed it only from a distance. We had a very welcome "Burlington Arcade" close at hand, which ran straight from the Rue du Bois to our front line, and was constructed by knocking openings in the party walls of a row of labourers' cottages, thus giving a passage from end to end entirely screened from observation. Needless to say, one could not obtain there such a variety of goods, or goods of such a pleasing nature, as are displayed in the London prototype, but still, S.A.A., bombs, rubber wading boots, shovels, and other useful and necessary articles were always kept there, in addition to the nucleus of a chemist's shop, this being administered by our beloved M.O., Capt. H. H. Robinson. Place-names of this nature will crop up in succeeding chapters, and although the derivation may not be recorded, or may, perhaps, not be known, it may be interesting to speculate on the reasons why some humble spot in France or Flanders received a name uncommon, and perhaps amusing or imposing.

The duration of a company's tour in the line depended upon more circumstances than come within the scope of a book of this nature, but in those early days of the war, and during the winter months, generally lasted from four to six days, at the end of which a similar period was spent in support or reserve; these positions were occupied in turn until the battalion or brigade was due to be relieved, when we marched back to billets for a time. Whilst the division was holding this part of the line, the First Surreys alternated between the trenches and the villages of Essars, Les Facons, Le Touret, and Le Quesnoy, and it was during this period that we received the news of the impending retirement of our commanding officer. Col. Tomlin, who had commanded the Battalion since August, 1911, and had worked without sparing himself during the whole period of mobilization and training, was now, after having shared our first experiences of active service, compelled, under doctor's urgent orders, to return to England. We were all sorry to lose him, but the M.O.'s orders had to be obeyed, and Col. Tomlin, therefore, undertook fresh duties at home, which included the training of new units and drafts for the field. The command of our Battalion passed therefore to our second in command, Major Wm. F. Morris, and to him fell the honour of carrying on the good work and of guiding our fortunes in the Great War.

For a time the normal routine of billets and trenches remained undisturbed, and it was not until the second week in May that we had our first experience of active operations on a large scale. The Battalion, although not actually taking part in the attack of May 9th, was ordered to hold the trenches on the right of the positions selected for the offensive, and to be ready to co-operate in any way considered necessary. Battalion Head-quarters was therefore moved forward to "Indian Village," where it was in close touch with the two companies in the line, and also within easy reach of the support and reserve companies. At 6 a.m. on Sunday morning the attack was launched, and heavy fire was opened on our front; throughout that day and the next heavy fighting was in progress on our left, our own works were badly damaged by shell-fire, and we suffered many casualties in consequence. Our orders were to assist our attacking troops by bursts of rifle and machine-gun fire on the trenches to our immediate front, and further, to be ready to oppose any counter-attack or any attempt on the part of the enemy to leave his trenches. It was a hot and tiring time, and news of the progress of the attack only reached us slowly and in fragments, but the outcome of the fighting is well known, and as we were not directly concerned, further details are hardly necessary here; we will therefore turn to the events which led up to our next offensive operations.

Immediately after the battle, arrangements were made for the relief of the Battalion by the 2nd Bedfordshire Regiment, and after a march of some five or six miles we arrived at the village of Le Quesnoy to snatch a few hours' rest before going farther back the following day. The artillery fire of May 9th, although insignificant in the light of later operations, seemed terrific to our unaccustomed ears, and it was in fact the largest concentration of guns which had been heard of up to that time. In wonderful contrast to the fighting and the bombardment was our lying down to sleep in this peaceful village, serenaded by the nightingales for which the gardens of the Château at Gorre have long been noted, the distant booming of a few tired guns sounding rather in the nature of an echo of the past. Another attempt to break through the line of trenches had failed!

The first taste of Corps Reserve enjoyed by the First Surrey Rifles was at the village of Labeuvrière, and although of short duration, was much appreciated after our fill of the trenches in the neighbourhood of "Indian Village"; this opportunity for a rest was brought about by the division's changing its sector for one farther South, and no time was lost in preparing for our new venture.

First of all, everyone enjoyed a hot bath—a luxury not possible whilst in the line—and that particular district was certainly well able to help us in this little matter. There were, it appeared, other people besides soldiers whose work ncessitated their taking frequent baths and changes of attire —to wit, the coal miners—and at nearly every large pit-head an elaborate system of hot shower baths had been installed, of which most of those at a safe distance from the line were in working order. Arrangements were accordingly made with the mine authorities for our troops to make use of these baths at convenient times—the fact that this in some cases involved a march of five or six miles did not matter, although nowadays it seems a long way to have to go for a bath!

Other little domestic affairs, such as mending uniforms and boots, replacing unserviceable articles of equipment, and a thorough cleaning of arms, held our attention whilst out of the line, and the time we found was all too short, especially as physical exercises and route marches were necessarily included in our daily routine.

After spending a few days at Labeuvrière, the Battalion again marched eastwards, and at the end of the first day's march we billeted in Beuvry (not many miles from our previous stepping stone on our way out of the line), but the next day brought us to Annequin, where we spent a couple of days before taking over another system of trenches.

The brickfields of Cuinchy proved an interesting sector, and their associations with the battles of the previous five months were recalled with interest; these excellent trenches, paved throughout with bricks obtained from the stacks nearby, bore testimony to the ingenuity and hard work of their former occupants, whilst the dugouts, also made of brick and earth, seemed very cosy after the inferior shelters we had left at "Indian Village." We had now settled down to the normal routine of trench warfare, and were ready for any excitements which might come our way—our day had not yet come, but in the meantime our hopes (and fears!) were raised by rumours of mining and countermining. These naturally put everyone on the *qui vive,* and listening-posts were established along our front to report any suspicious sounds. One officer soon had a "case," and reported it to head-quarters, who straightway summoned the expert to listen and take what steps he considered necessary. The only steps taken were towards a large shell hole in No Man's Land, which was found to be inhabited by a family of lusty frogs, whose continuous croaking had sounded to strained ears at a distance not unlike a pick-axe at work— thus was our first mine scare exploded! Subsequently our Engineers gave us a chance of seeing a mine "go up," and we were able to realize what an important part in trench warfare such methods could play. It may be added that our later dealings with mines were on a larger scale, and it is hoped to describe them in some detail.

Battalion Head-quarters in the line at Cuinchy were comfortably ensconced in the cellar of a house at the Pont Fixe (a bridge over the La Bassée Canal) and were next door to what had once been a large distillery, but which had long ceased to function; what was useful, however, was the kitchen garden, from which supplies of spring vegetables were procured, not the least among these being some very tasty asparagus! After a few days spent in these trenches the Battalion did its turn in Brigade Reserve some few hundred yards back, during which a chance presented itself for refitting—this was immediately taken advantage of, especially as we heard rumours of our going back for a few days to civilization in the only important town in that area.

Béthune — pronounced during the war as Bethoon, Bethuen, Betune, or Baytoon—may have been a place of little interest to the average young man in peace time, but to the First Surreys, after two months of trench warfare, it teemed with life and excitement in each one of its dirty little cobbled streets. Eight enjoyable days were spent in this little metropolis—eight days of perfect May sunshine, which filled us with new life and hope, and brought such treats as a daily swim in the open-air baths, shopping excursions to replenish our small stock-in-trade, and new forms of refreshment in the shape of *pâtisseries* and *confiseries,* ices, fruits, and drinks, and such luxuries as hair-cutting, shampoos, and cigars!

It is doubtful whether the average soldier would care to stand a longer period in these surroundings under such circumstances—a small income, tempting extravagances, and no responsibilities—but, be that as it may, our own particular case was settled for us in a way which made every heart beat fast with excitement, for we were to fight our first battle with the Germans in their own trenches.

Our attack at Givenchy on May 25th, 1915, formed part of the general offensive which was being undertaken by our 1st Army in conjunction with the French Armies immediately south of us, and was directed against the town of La Bassée, which formed a prominent salient in the German front. For some days prior to this, many troops, including those of the Canadian Corps on our immediate left, had been engaged in the operations, and when the time came for our attack to be made on the German trenches immediately north of the La Bassée Canal, the G.O.C., 47th Division (which was holding the sector at the time) selected the 142nd Infantry Brigade to carry it into effect. The enemy's trenches to be assaulted consisted of his front and support lines running in a northerly direction from the Canal. The attack was planned to be carried out on a front of two battalions—the 24th supported by the 22nd on the right, and the 23rd supported by the 21st on the left—and the actual assault was timed for 6.30 in the evening.

An artillery bombardment, of such intensity as our supplies of ammunition at the time would permit, was kept up prior to the attack, and much damage was thereby done to the German barbed-wire entanglement and trenches; we had, in addition to our own field guns, two brigades of French gunners equipped with the famous 75 mm. guns. It is difficult now to recall exactly the circumstances under which the First Surreys made their assault—still harder is it to record all those gallant deeds which, taken individually, would occupy volumes and, as a whole enabled those at home to read in their daily papers that London Territorial troops had successfully attacked and held a strong enemy position east of Givenchy. At the hour appointed our comrades of the 23rd and 24th Battalions swarmed over the parapet and made for the trenches opposite—a distance varying from 100 to 300 yards—but were met by a storm of bullets from every German rifle and machine-gun in the vicinity; weakened in numbers but undaunted, they rushed on and entered the German trenches. Two companies of the 21st Battalion, "D" Coy. (Major H. P. Richards) on the right, and "B" Coy. (Captain A. Hutchence) on the left, were now holding our original front line, and their leading platoons were ordered to advance and take part in the capture and consolidation of the enemy support trenches—thus the time had now come to prove that the weeks spent in training had not been spent in vain. Our trenches were practically battered out of existence, and we had already suffered many casualties from shell fire, but, undisturbed by their losses, the leading platoons of "B" Coy., under Captain A. Hamilton Moberly, proceeded to get into their assaulting position in front of our trenches, as they had done many and many a time during training. No. 6 Platoon (Lieutenant Savel) was on the right of No. 5 (Lieutenant Hull), and both platoons advanced to the attack as one man, but the enemy was by now thoroughly aroused, and brought every available gun and rifle to bear on this fresh advance. We lost heavily from the beginning—Lieutenants Savel and Hull, both fearlessly directing and encouraging their men, were killed soon after leaving our lines. Captain Moberly, who was in command of the half-company, managed to reach what had once been a German position, where he was severely wounded by a bullet in the chest. The company had lost heavily in all ranks, and by the time Lieutenant G. M. McKay came along with No. 7 Platoon the actual strength of the company had been reduced by about one-half. This officer, however, with his well-known cheerfulness and fighting spirit, reorganized the position and carried on until he himself was wounded in both legs and fell amongst the German wire in front of their support line.

The state of affairs in the captured trenches was now indescribable, and such men as were left set to work to build up the defences so as to be able to ward off any counter-attack which might develop. The men of "D" Company on the right had received a little better treatment than their comrades of "B," and their two leading platoons (Lieutenants N. A. Taylor and Tooth) were fighting, together with the 23rd Battalion, to frustrate the frequent attempts of the German bombers to regain possession of their old trenches. Lieutenant Tooth was wounded whilst taking part in the assault, and both these platoons were badly knocked about, particularly by the enemy enfilade fire, against which the shallow and battered trenches gave but little protection.

Soon after midnight Captain Hutchence received orders to advance with the rest of his company to reinforce our forward men, and with Lieutenant Persse, his sole remaining officer, he set about reorganizing the sections and repairing as far as possible the damage done by shell fire. What our men went through that night can only be realized by those who have had similar experiences—it cannot be imagined, still less described. The work of getting up ammunition, bombs, and water, and of dressing and sending back the wounded, was carried on unremittingly, and platoons from both "A" and "C" Companies (originally in reserve) were engaged in this. Two platoons of "C" Company had also been sent up early in the evening to dig a communication trench from our front line to the captured position, and these suffered heavily in consequence, but stuck to their work until daylight broke.

The dawn of May 26th revealed the exact nature of the situation to those who were holding on. The left of the position held by the Battalion was entirely "in the air," and a similar state of affairs seems to have existed on the right flank of the 24th Battalion. In conjunction, therefore, with this battalion, it was decided to throw back our lines so as to gain touch with the units on either flank, and that this was the only practical course will be realized when it is stated that both flanks were already unsupported (and, therefore, exceedingly vulnerable), that the position held offered no protection from the very heavy and continuous artillery bombardment, and that our ammunition, both rifle and artillery, was running short, without any possibility of replenishing the former during daylight. Finally it was discovered that a body of the enemy was still holding out on our left flank (and in rear of us) and that this party was inflicting heavy casualties on us! In carrying out this adjustment of our line, Lieutenant Taylor and his men had first to overcome the resistance of this body of the enemy, forcing them to retire on to a section of the 8th London Battalion, with whom we thus gained touch on our left.

This line was held throughout the day, during which the garrison made every endeavour to improve the conditions of tenancy as much as possible. No time was lost in building up the parapets, so that when the Battalion was relieved on the following day and marched back to billets, a position worthy of the name might be handed over to the new garrison. The casualties suffered during this action at Givenchy included two officers and thirty-two N.C.O.'s and men killed, and three officers and 120 N.C.O.'s and men wounded. That the enemy suffered heavily also, there can be no doubt, for, in addition to the killed remaining in his trenches, many wounded and unwounded prisoners were taken.

The first message of congratulation received on this very successful operation was from our former divisional commander, but then G.O.C. 1st Corps, and it ran as follows:—"Lieut.-General Sir Charles Monro sends his congratulations to his gallant old comrades of the 6th London Infantry Brigade on their achievements of last night." This was followed by a special Order of the Day from Divisional Head-quarters in the following words:—"The General Officer Commanding wishes to express to the Brigadier-General and all ranks of the 6th London Infantry Brigade his great appreciation of their behaviour during the operations of the 25th and 26th May. They may be sure that the news of their achievement, which was worthy of veteran regular troops, will be received with pride at home.—C. Barter, *Major-General.*"

A short paragraph appeared in the London newspapers the day following the attack, and later on the official casualty lists told their own story, but many deeds of individual bravery passed unnoticed by the public eye. One instance of devotion to duty received official recognition, and earned for the regiment its first decoration in the Great War: Rifleman Shellard was awarded the Distinguished Conduct Medal for personal bravery in endeavouring to help his officer when mortally wounded, and afterwards in performing acts of gallantry both by way of rescuing wounded who were lying in the open and in carrying out his duties as a defender of the captured trenches. For a few days after the affair at

Givenchy, the Battalion was left to its own devices in the little town of Beuvry, about four miles from Béthune. Times such as these must necessarily provide food for thought—memories of fallen comrades—hopes and fears for the recovery of the wounded—and longings for another chance to add glories to the records of the regiment. But active service gives but little time for such musings, and after writing home to one's own people to relieve their anxious minds, and giving what tidings and comfort one could to the relatives of the fallen, we turned aside to re-equip and repair so as to be ready for future effort.

CHAPTER III.

June 7th, 1915, to March 7th, 1916.

Maroc Sector, Les Brebis, Mazingarbe, Philosophe, Marles-les-Mines, Houchin, Allouagne, Loos, Noeux-les-Mines, Lone Tree Sector, Hulluch Road, Allouagne, Labourse, Vermelles, Manœuvre Area, and Army Reserve.

During the war there were many people who thought the end was bound to come before a certain period had elapsed, this period varying from three months to three years; a large number of prophets foresaw the signing of peace by the early summer of 1915, and these were joined in their prophecies by many in the ranks of our ever-increasing army in the field. We may, indeed, be thankful that the curtain did not fall at such an early date, as the last act of the world's greatest drama, had it been staged in 1915, would surely have produced a very unsatisfactory "curtain" for the Allies.

Those of us who were engaged in the operations which lasted throughout the spring and summer of 1915 may have realized by now what a huge bluff they were; what little backing they had behind them in the way of ammunition and trained battalions, and to what a momentous issue their success or failure led! However, the majority of fighting soldiers were too busily occupied to indulge in such reflections in those days, and the First Surreys were certainly no exception to this rule.

After the attack at Givenchy a bare fortnight sufficed for our re-equipment and reorganization, and the second week in June saw the Battalion taking over that part of the line which was then the southernmost part of the British front. The trenches at Maroc were indeed a pleasant change after those in Flanders, for in addition to being provided with excellent shelters they were so substantially built as to afford good protection from shell fire, and were at such a distance from the enemy's lines as to preclude all attempts at bombing. To regiments which had suffered in action and needed a less strenuous life they were a godsend, and with the coming of more favourable weather and shorter nights our standard of health and happiness rose by leaps and bounds.

The Battalion was privileged to spend two months in this sector without any disturbances, not that these sixty days were spent continuously in trenches, though even that would have been possible in this particular section; the time was divided into periods of from eight to twelve days during which we were either holding our front system, or being quite near in what was known as Brigade or Divisional Reserve. In order that these expressions may be understood, and as they must frequently be made use of in a record such as this, the writer may be permitted to explain them briefly. A division, composed of three infantry brigades, when holding a section of the line, generally placed two of these brigades actually in the forward zone and kept the third in reserve (Divisional Reserve) in case of emergency; similarly each of the brigades in the forward zone would keep one or two of its four battalions out of the front line system as a local reserve (Brigade Reserve) for use on the front of that brigade. The units in reserve were thus resting and available to act as reliefs for, and to change places with, those in the front line from time to time. For the battalions in reserve, villages or camps were set apart and billets were earmarked, so that no time should be lost in having to select suitable accommodation, and so that the best possible use should be made of the all too short periods out of the trenches.

The principal village which fell to our lot whilst in the sector of which we are now writing was Mazingarbe, and whilst resting here many memorable incidents occurred in the life of our Battalion. Mazingarbe is a village very typical of this particular part of France; its population in normal times might have been somewhere about 1,000 souls, and these consisted principally of holders of small farms, and their assistants, together with the necessary shopkeepers and *estaminet* proprietors; the proportion of the latter (as in all such villages) appeared to us to be distinctly high. We were glad, however, that such was the case, for these humble cafés provided a welcome retreat from the labours of war, and although the refreshment obtainable at them was limited and, at times, somewhat poor in quality, the company was always cheery. A description of a typical *estaminet* scene borrowed from the "First Surrey Rifles Magazine" (which was published about this time) is reprinted here, and having been written on the spot seems eminently suitable, as affording just that local "atmosphere" so necessary to a description of this nature :—

"As one has read, it is good to be on the hill-tops—to be near the sun, but the wine is in the little valleys. So, in war, is glory to be found in the trenches and between them, but the romance of war is hidden amidst the little hamlets which nestle deep in the shaded lanes of Northern France. The agony of fighting, the frightfulness of killing, crushes from the field of battle all semblance of beauty. And without beauty there can be little romance—that full-throated, flamboyant romance which appeals to the multitude and lifts even the soberest imagination to flights of almost drunken greatness.

"True romance there is of course—where death, the glorious death of the soldier is, there romance must always be—but that is romance so supreme that it is above interpretation in words. Certainly such art is beyond me.

"It is enough for me to find war romance—bizarre, picturesque and glorious war romance—amidst the little hamlets of Northern France. In those little rooms, rough, sometimes unclean places, where fighting men foregather and drink and talk, sometimes to the lilt of the music of tin whistle or mouth organ, sometimes to the accompaniment of no other noise than that which comes from strong throats richly lubricated; in such places one finds romance—romance simple and comprehensible.

"There is a village some five miles behind the firing-line, a place so small and obscure that so far it has escaped the mad-dog rage of the Huns. Even its tiny church is untouched by shell fire, and in the little house of Madam Adair one can for a moment forget that there is a war. Madam herself is large and fat, a little ugly perhaps, but infinitely good-natured; also, being of the prosperous farm worker class she is, especially when heated, in appearance somewhat oleaginous. But always, she is the good Adair, as her friends the four sergeants of French Artillery know, and as their friends—half-a-dozen English soldiers—also know. This good Adair—Madam of the Café au Lait. Rhum! Ah, rhum is forbidden; but there is wine—red or white. Well, well! It is cold to-night—or is it hot?—and perhaps in the bottom of one small bottle there is a tiny drop. She is a kindly soul, and even the vilest rhum is sweet—when it is forbidden.

"The fattest of the four fat sergeants sighs and smiles and accepts an English cigarette from an English corporal. He is English in his cigarette habit and is becoming English in his speech. So he says, 'In Inglees mush*e*room,' 'Très bon mush*e*room,' and then he slaps with one great paw his greater stomach, and contemplates with satisfaction the platter from which he has eaten. 'My Inglees is très bon good better, eh? Soon I say proper good morn, dam hot, eh? to

Monsieur ze Inglees Capitaine, quite proper, eh? Bon. Bon.'
At this moment he swings from his chair, stands erect—a pleasing mixture of solid muscle and quivering fatness—and salutes. 'Eh bon! Now for the mewsick—the flute. It must be the march of the premier regiment, please.'

"The English corporal draws from his pocket a yellow tin whistle. He is a serious looking man, this English corporal; he has a habit of looking down his nose and at the floor as he plays the stirring air. Silently the Frenchmen listen to the swinging music of 'The British Grenadiers.' Then a French sergeant performs a great and daring march on a small tooth-comb covered with paper. After this there is a duet—the English corporal and the French sergeant. Then someone bursts into a chorus; and in the midst of the chorus the good Madam comes in, and more bottles are opened. As she pours out the wine, Madam slaps the bald head of one of the sergeants with her chubby hand. The injured warrior jumps to his feet, seizes Madam in a fierce grip, and kisses her on either cheek.

"The serious-looking corporal instantly leads off with 'The Wedding Bells are pealing,' and there is a great chorus of English voices. The French sergeant and the good Madam seem to understand. Anyway she blushes a little, and her eyes seem to sparkle; while the sergeant shouts, 'No, no, no!' waving his hands and arms; finally he shrugs and, lighting a fresh cigarette, sinks into his chair again.

"Then an English soldier tells of an attack he has just been in—he had many narrow escapes from death, and the fighting was terrible. From the story one gathers that practically the whole of the British Army was blown into nothingness, and only the sergeant escaped.

"Presently a French artilleryman, who has long shown signs of great uneasiness, tells of a shell he has fired. First, of course, he loads the gun. In that little room he loads the gun, fires it, follows the shell in its flight and becomes the shell itself as it strikes its object and explodes. Then he is the explosion; and after the explosion the wrecked building, the wounded, and the dead; finally he becomes the harassed German Army itself. It is all good acting. This sergeant of artillery is an all-round man, quite apart from his fatness. His weakness—and it is a weakness, I think—is that invariably, after he has finished his yarn, while the applause is not yet dead, he starts on it afresh and tells the same story again from the very beginning; the second time in greater detail.

'But this is scarcely wearisome, as one need not listen. There are other things—some men in a corner are singing an attractive chorus; a French and English soldier are cockfighting in the centre of the great table, and Madam is flirting in her cheery fashion with three sergeants at once.

"In the distance is the noise of heavy firing. We can even distinguish the prolonged crackle of rifle music. Night has fallen; through the window one sees flares and flashes—the flaming tongues of battle. There comes a silence in the little room. One thinks of yesterdays and to-morrows. Of those things we have seen, and those others we have yet to live—God send it may be LIVE—through. And then naturally there comes a longing, a great full-hearted longing for the end; for the homeland; for those hands we are longing to touch; those lips we are burning to kiss. We leave the little room and wander forth to that bare patch of earth we call our bed.

"Yes, it is war—the shells and the flashes and the noise of fighting tell us so. It is romantic in its way. In our way *we* are romantic—a part of the great romantic whole. But oh, for the homeland ! For England and home; for the sight and touch of those we love.

"Ah, well ! Meanwhile we are on the hill-tops and near the sun."

Our visits to Mazingarbe and other such villages lasted usually from four to eight days. During this time we were part of the brigade in Divisional Reserve; the other battalions of the brigade would be either in the same village or quite near, and the head-quarters of the brigade was generally situated so as to be in the midst of its battalions. Near Mazingarbe were the mining hamlets of Les Brebis, Maroc, and Philosophe, and at each of these we were privileged to spend long periods on more than one occasion—in fact, the garden city of Les Brebis became quite a familiar resort and we made many friends amongst the inhabitants. The billets in the immediate vicinity of the pit-heads we found far more comfortable than those in purely agricultural districts. It can readily be understood that the parlour or spare bedroom of a modern house would be preferable to a dilapidated barn or a leaky poultry house, and so we came to look forward to our turn at Les Brebis, where in addition to the attractions of the billets the hot baths at the mine building were most welcome.

The trenches held by our division during the summer of 1915 were, as previously stated, very pleasant when compared with those of the other sectors, and our life whilst occupying the forward area was by no means uncomfortable; in fact, there were many who preferred it to the more strenuous times in reserve, when parades and strict training were the order of the day. The principal hardship of trench life at this time was the difficulty of obtaining water in the front line; every drop had to be carried through long communication trenches. Most of the water which reached that line was naturally for drinking, and what little there was available for washing or shaving was often used over and over again before being finally given to the favourite pinks or poppies which adorned practically every dug-out and trench. The story is told of a platoon of an Irish regiment attached to the First Surrey Rifles which brewed some excellent tea by using the solution of hyposulphite of soda which was stored in the trenches as an emergency against a gas attack; the beverage produced no apparent effect on the constitutions of the drinkers and no gas, luckily, made its appearance before the stock of solution could be renewed. No damage was done, therefore, although the M.O. had a few anxious moments.

The means by which water was carried at this time were as primitive as they were varied; many types of receptacle were used, of which the stone rum jar, the wooden wine cask, and the iron tanks borrowed from the mines are fair examples. That most useful of containers, the two gallon petrol tin—which afterwards became a universal liquid-carrier—had as yet scarcely made its appearance, though its counterpart for solids—the sandbag—was already in general use. What these two articles meant to the soldier in the field may be gathered from the following account of some of their uses: large numbers of petrol tins, after supplying the needs of the motor transport, found their way yearly to the trenches, where for weeks on end they might be used for carrying water, soup, or even oil; after removal of the top, and fitting a wire handle, a serviceable bucket for use in case of fire was formed, and this as time wore on was often placed bodily on a camp fire and used as a saucepan or frying-pan. If carefully cut in half lengthways a substitute for a wash basin, or even a bath (!) was formed—horses have fed out of similar contrivances, and the cooks have even been known to use them for baking cakes or puddings. There were other uses, but these will suffice as samples. The sandbag was made of loose canvas and was some 28-in. long by 9-in. wide, being intended primarily to be filled with sand or earth and used in the erection of protective earthworks. But a great number of those used during the war never reached this glorious ideal, although like many human beings they performed duties no less necessary. A very convenient method of sending tea to the men in the trenches was to half-fill a sandbag with it and then tie the bag with cord tightly round the middle, the remaining half being similarly filled with sugar; this, with the tins of water previously mentioned, formed an easily portable supply of drink for a thirsty company. Loaves of bread, biscuits, bully beef, in fact all kinds of rations have been at some time or another thrown into sandbags, as well as parcels and letters from home. Of course, the bags sent up to the line in this way could be, and were, put later to their strictly legitimate use, but in addition to this they were often required as protectors from the weather for rifles, bombs, legs and arms, and even heads. Moreover, as the parapets themselves were more often than not constructed of sandbags, these same bags formed a really useful means of camouflaging heads and shoulders, periscopes, helmets, and rifles.

In the particular sector in which we are for the moment interested, there was little artillery fire and the damage to our trenches was in consequence slight, especially as the subsoil was good hard chalk and the summer was fairly dry. Nevertheless, there was plenty of work to be done by way of building shelters and strong points and erecting barbed-wire entanglements in front of our lines, and we were glad therefore to learn that we were to be relieved early in August, when the whole division was to go into Corps Reserve for a month's training.

On August 3rd we cheerfully handed over these trenches to a battalion of the 15th Division. Men of this formation, which was one of the New (or Kitchener) Army Divisions, had been attached to us for instruction in trench warfare during July (in the same way that we had been to the 1st Division in the previous April), so having given them all information about their new sector and made them as comfortable as we could, we started off on a trek to one of the pleasanter places of Northern France. After assembling at Mazingarbe the battalion marched to Marles-les-Mines, a distance of some sixteen or seventeen miles, where we found good billets and many comforts awaiting us, and the time passed all too quickly.

While out of the line each brigade in turn was ordered to spend a week in digging defensive works some seven or eight miles behind the front line, and we did our share of this about eight days after reaching Marles. The trenches to be dug were situated close to the village of Houchin, where our stores and transport lines had been whilst we were in the line and the Battalion now moved to this place so as to be near the work. We were favoured with good weather and no "false alarms" whilst in Corps Reserve, and as leave to England lasting seven days at a time had now begun and was being enjoyed by those whose turn came early for such a privilege, life seemed to be worth living; especially when, after completing our digging at Houchin, we made our first acquaintance with Allouagne, with which village the Battalion was later so closely connected.

At Allouagne we had a thoroughly good time, and although two weeks out of our four had already gone, we made the most of our remaining days. The mornings were normally taken up with parades, inspections, exercises, or marches, but in the afternoons and evenings sports, games, concerts, and joy-rides contributed to our general well-being. Before returning to the firing line the command of the Battalion changed hands for the second time since mobilization. Colonel Morris, who had commanded us for five months in the field, was offered an appointment on the Staff of the 47th Divisional Head-quarters and this he accepted after taking counsel with his comrades in the First Surrey Rifles. Regrets at the severance of Colonel Morris's connection with the battalion were keen on both sides, but such is war. Captain H. B. Kennedy, of the 60th Rifles, who had been our adjutant since 1913, and who, as a Regular Officer, had done so much in training and guiding the Battalion, was now promoted to the command. Captain Kennedy's record in France was such that he was already overdue for promotion, and there can be no doubt that had he not been appointed our C.O. he would very shortly have been promoted elsewhere, and (though this is unthinkable) would have been lost to the First Surreys. This fact was well realized by all of us, and greatly to Colonel Morris's credit, it influenced him strongly in accepting the staff appointment already referred to, and thus securing in the command of the Battalion so efficient and popular a successor to himself.

On September 1st we said "au revoir" to Allouagne and marched back to the firing line, spending one night at Haillicourt on the way to our previous sector; we found the trenches much the same as we left them a month before and soon settled down to our well-known posts. September seemed to be slipping away, and with it the summer weather and light nights, and we began to wonder whether any further operations were to be undertaken before the winter—rumours had been current to the effect that some form of "stunt" was being arranged, but no definite orders had been received. Days passed, and we remained in the front line without relief, our artillery increased its number of guns and volume of fire, and was further reinforced by batteries of French "seventy fives." Captain Corby, our assistant adjutant, now undertook a special and "secret" duty in an improvised workshop at Les Brebis, in which he was assisted by carpenters and painters from all battalions of the brigade. Actually they were all engaged in making "dummy" khaki figures which, when placed in position, could, by means of a string, be made to represent men firing from the prone position, but no matter how we racked our brains over them we could not imagine the purpose for which they were intended.

It was, however, now apparent that operations on a large scale were contemplated by the Higher Command, though what part we were to play in the future battle of Loos we did not yet know. Our immediate duty was to remain in occupation of the front line till further orders, and it thus came about that the Battalion spent a full month in the front line system without relief.

The battle of Loos (in which are included the actions which immediately followed the taking of Loos itself) was the third operation in which the First Surreys took part, and from a general point of view was the most successful attack carried out during the year 1915. On September 19th the British and French artillery began a heavy and continuous bombardment of the enemy's lines and rest areas from Lens to La Bassée; this bombardment was continued with increasing intensity for five days, culminating at dawn on September 25th, when the fire was concentrated on the front line trenches. At the same time quantities of smoke and gas were discharged from our trenches and carried on the breeze across to the German lines, the former to act as a screen from observation and the latter to asphyxiate and demoralize the enemy. At 6 a.m. our infantry made its attack along a front of some five or six miles, the 47th Division being on the right, or southern flank of the attack. Our Battalion had from the commencement of the bombardment formed, with the 22nd Battalion, the garrison for the trenches on the right of the divisional front, and this entailed a great deal more work and responsibility than would appear from the simple statement of the fact. In the first place there was all the work connected with the preparation of the trenches and shelters for an attack and carrying up all manner of reserve stores, including ammunition for all kinds of weapons, rations and water, engineering materials and tools, and the heavy cast-iron cylinders containing the compressed gases, for which specially constructed emplacements had to be prepared. This and other preparatory works, such as the laying of telephone lines, making trenches, and preparing roads and bridges, kept the garrison busy until the eve of the attack when an additional duty fell to us in connection with Captain Corby's dummy soldiers to which reference has already been made. The figures were carried up during the hours of darkness and hidden in the long grass in "No Man's Land" where, under their creator's supervision, they were connected by strings to suitable positions in our lines.

Our Battalion's rôle in the scheme of operations was to form part of the right defensive flank of the main attack and to hold the junction of the British and French lines, a position naturally particularly open to counter-attack and one which must be held at all costs; whilst effecting this it was also our duty to keep the enemy opposite us on the *qui vive* and divert his attention from the main attack on our left. It was here that the dummies were to prove useful, for by the skilful manipulation of the strings they appeared to the "nervy" and excited Germans to be live men making a real attack, and thus they drew heavy fire which would otherwise undoubtedly have been directed against the troops on our left who were really attacking under cover of the smoke screen. This illusion, known as a "Chinese" attack, was heightened by showing in our trenches scaling ladders and flashing bayonets, by excited blowing of whistles and by rapid covering fire from selected positions; and that the ruses were successful was subsequently proved, when an examination of our poor dummies showed them to be literally riddled with bullets.

On September 26th our sister battalion in the trenches—the 23rd London—was ordered up to reinforce the 141st Brigade, and on the 27th a company of this battalion, under the command of Captain H. Ruthven of the First Surreys—for the heavy loss in officers which the 23rd had sustained earlier in the year had been partly met by an attachment of officers from the First Surrey Rifles—took part in a daring and successful attack on a position known as "The Copse."

The main attack, so far as the 47th Division was concerned, had been completely successful, all objectives being gained and held throughout the battle in spite of the enemy's counter attacks. The troops advancing on the left of the division made great progress at first, but the Germans were quickly reinforced, and for some days the opposing lines swung to and fro in a fluctuating battle. The Guards, who had entered the fight on September 27th, and had suffered terrible losses from the now rapidly increasing hostile artillery, were on the following evening holding a line which included Hill 70, immediately on the left of the 141st Brigade of our Division. That night (September 28th) our Brigade (142nd) relieved the 141st, and on the night of September 29th the First Surrey Rifles found itself in supporting positions in the western outskirts of the town, between the cemetery and a trench work known as Fort Glatz. On the 30th, two of our companies ("B" and "C") took over part of the Hill 70 line, "A" and "D" being posted on the other side of the "Loos crassier," a slag-heap running out southeastward on to the shoulder of the hill. The head-workings of the mine from which this *crassier* was thrown up were famous among us for the twin towers which had for months stood out as a landmark in the enemy's lines and had become known to all as the "Tower Bridge."

On the night of October 1st we were in our turn relieved by a magnificent battalion of French troops, and marched to a bivouac near Mazingarbe, going on in the morning to Fouquières, where, and at Noeux-les-Mines, we spent ten days resting and preparing for the next stage of the battle. On October 12th we moved up into some old trenches northwest of Loos and a day or two later relieved troops in some captured trenches, lying a mile or so to the north of Loos and running alongside the Loos-Hulluch road. These trenches were in a very exposed position, though the only landmark was the remains of a small oak tree, known as "Lone Tree." This spot will always be remembered by everyone then in the Battalion, as it was the point to which rations and water were brought each night after dark, and was, as a consequence, subjected to periodical outbursts of shelling (otherwise known as "strafes") by the German gunners. Altogether this sector was by no means pleasant, as the trenches having only recently been bombarded, assaulted, and captured, were not exactly in a good state of repair, and dug-outs (or "splinter proof shelters" as they were officially termed) did not exist. In addition to all this the weather throughout our stay was vile, and even when the rain permitted, no fires were allowed to be lighted as our position rendered the slightest sign of smoke visible to the enemy and was certain to call down vengeance on our heads. Food for the men in the line had therefore to be cooked back at the quarter-master's store at Mazingarbe and brought up under cover of darkness in the company cookers, and it was in the delivery of these precious meals in the neighbourhood of Lone Tree that many risks were run and untold numbers of dixies of army stew were roughly dealt with by enemy "whizz-bangs."

Very illustrative of the Hulluch sector as we experienced it is the following anecdote :—

It was a perfectly filthy night—deluges of rain overhead, and oceans of mud, with exasperatingly frequent patches of derelict wire and other débris underfoot. We were on our way up to the trenches and had ploughed on for mile after mile, hour after hour, when one Sergeant said to another, "I say, Arthur, where do you think we are now?" "Don't know," said the other, "somewhere about the second 'g' in beggary, *I* should think."

In these circumstances we were not sorry to learn of a scheme for a further advance, and when we went back to Mazingarbe for a few days in order to practise the attack on Hulluch (a "course" had been laid out with white tape and flags on a piece of ground more or less resembling the actual site) we were full of enthusiasm. The attack as originally planned did not take place, however, and although several minor enterprises were undertaken in order to make local adjustments in our line, our time for another Corps Reserve came round before any large attack was made from our front.

The first fortnight of November, 1915, was spent in Divisional Reserve at Mazingarbe, whence large parties went to work in the forward area each night; these were much more strenuous and fatiguing than the actual holding of the trenches, and we were unfeignedly glad when on the 11th we entrained at Noeux-les-Mines for Lillers, and marched thence to our former comfortable billets at Allouagne.

With the prospect of a clear month of freedom from fighting and trench work, the Battalion was able to take a fresh lease of life and to make up arrears of training, interior economy, and personal appearance generally, with which a prolonged spell in an unpleasant sector plays such havoc. Strenuous and strict training in the mornings, and well-organized sports, concerts, and other recreations in the afternoons and evenings were the order of the day, and with Colonel Kennedy in command it will readily be understood that there were not many wasted hours. Competitions and inspections led to a healthy spirit of rivalry between companies and sections, so that by the time we were due to "face the foe" again, we were once more the spick and span fighting force which had left England exactly nine months before.

By the middle of December, 1915, practically all fighting resulting from the battle of Loos had ceased; what little activity existed was confined to mining and bombing in the sector immediately in front of Vermelles, and it was in this part of the line that the Battalion was engaged until the middle of January, 1916. This period, lasting but a bare month, proved, with the exception of a couple of days at Christmas, one of the most uncomfortable times we had during the early part of the war. The trenches were even worse than those in the Lone Tree sector, and the bombing raids and trench-mortar fire were very trying, especially in the neighbourhood of the famous Hohenzollern Redoubt—this work was shared by us with the Germans, and one was never quite sure how much actually belonged to either side. We were lucky in being able to spend our first Christmas abroad in the comparatively comfortable village of Labourse (being at the time in Divisional Reserve) and still luckier in that we were not called out during the festivities to support those of our people who had to spend the time in the trenches. We wondered whether this was possibly due to the fact that even the Hun celebrates Christmas Day.

It is difficult to imagine, and even more so to describe, the marvellous transformation that can be worked on eight hundred soldiers within the short space of twelve hours; arriving from the trenches at, say, midnight, covered with mud and slime and carrying anything up to 70-lb. of kit and trench stores, one is not exactly seen to the best advantage, but, given a few hours sleep, breakfast, and a wash (possibly even a bath !) and brush up, and a morning in the sun—well, to say the least of it a very different figure is presented. Thus it was that on Christmas Eve, 1915, the Battalion, having enjoyed the aforesaid luxuries, was able to settle down to a good night's rest in readiness for the morrow. We don't think any "stockings" were hung up, but if they were it was in order that they might dry rather than in the expectation of any presents being dropped into them. We had had enough of "presents" being dropped in our vicinity whilst in the line, and all we desired at Christmas was peace—and plenty to eat. We were not disappointed, for at dinner next day every little *estaminet* in Sailly-Labourse was crowded with healthy, ruddy faces ranged round every available table, on which, through the steam, or smoke, could be discerned "sausages and mashed," joints, pork pies, vegetables, apples, champagne, beer (*English* beer), nuts, and crackers—yes ! even crackers in a few cases. Healths were drunk, speeches made, songs sung, cheers given on the slightest provocation. Everything but the moment was forgotten—even the noise of the distant guns was drowned and forgotten. And when bedtime came again, we all turned in full and contented and ready for anything. Boxing Day by comparison was uneventful—the usual football matches, and the usual orders for moving up to the line again. We learned, whilst pushing along in the darkness (4 o'clock in the morning), that our friends in the 22nd Battalion had had a rough time, and as they expected further trouble we went up to reserve trenches in front of Vermelles. Our suspicions of German mining operations were confirmed on the 29th, when a projecting bit of trench, garrisoned by the 22nd Battalion on our right (it was known as the "Hairpin") was blown up, causing many casualties and necessitating the construction and holding of a new trench.

New Year's Day, 1916, found us moving up into that horrid bit of front line where we had been so uncomfortable just before Christmas, but it was only for a few days, and we were glad then to be relieved by a regiment of dismounted cavalry, and to march back to huts and tents at Houchin. This move was part and parcel of a welcome "side-slip" to a more salubrious part of the line, which when completed, brought us back again in front of Loos and to the little mining villages of Les Brebis and Maroc. Neither the rest billets nor the trench system east of Loos had changed much during the winter months, but early in the New Year various minor operations were undertaken. One of these enterprises, in which C. Coy. (Captain Walford) took a leading part, was carried out at 2 a.m. on January 23rd, and consisted of the exploding of a large land mine and subsequent consolidation of the crater so formed.

At one point (known as the "Cow's Ear") a line, running very close to that of the enemy, was a constant source of anxiety. It was decided to tunnel under the enemy trenches and by means of a heavy charge to form a large mine crater as a sort of safety gap.

The operation was entirely successful; the mine was exploded, and whilst C. Coy.'s bombers were holding the enemy edge of the crater, the rest of the company, assisted by a field company of Royal Engineers (under Major Blogg) made good our front line. Heavy artillery and machine gun fire ensued throughout the night and following morning, but the work was pushed on, and by the time the Battalion was relieved, a good trench had been constructed. Our casualties during the operation were very slight. Here we spent four more weeks, alternating between trenches and reserve, until our time came round again for Corps Reserve and we were relieved by troops of the 16th Division.

The last few days of February were spent in quite a novel way, being devoted to a divisional route march to the First Army training area, in which we were allotted billets at Enquin-les-Mines. We did really serious training here, including outpost schemes and advanced and rear-guards—subjects on which we had become somewhat rusty since leaving St. Albans. But the day we enjoyed most was that on which we engaged in a pitched battle, with snowballs as ammunition, all round the village, finishing up in a big field in a sort of "set-piece," with Major Richards and his company nobly trying, but in the end failing, to hold the fort against the three other companies of the Battalion. It was great sport, and revealed initiative on the part of those whom we had hitherto suspected of being quite innocent of that quality. Our Brigadier (General F. G. Lewis) watched the finish of the fight, but one never quite knew whether he appreciated the instructional side of the game!

After this glorious spot, where we had the free run of every field in the neighbourhood, it was quite a change to get back to our pet village of Allouagne, where we spent the last week of our Corps Reserve. The elements at this time were against us, and little could be done—we pondered on our new trenches, wondering what they would be like and hoping that their present tenants were paying due attention to the "drains," for although it was now nearly a month since we had been in the trenches, the memory of flooded sections and moist and slimy shelters was still fresh, and our feet still tingled at the bare thought.

But such reflections as these could never be allowed to mar our present life of luxury 'and ease, so with the usual round of sport and enjoyment we made the most of what remained of our "rest" of the winter of 1915-16, and on March 7th we packed up and were bundled into the familiar old cattle trucks which were to take us back to the war.

CHAPTER IV.

March 8th to July 27th, 1916.

Hersin and Souchez Sector, Villers-au-Bois, Carency and Vimy Ridge, Fosse 10 and the Bully-Grenay line.

What would the Territorials have said if in the spring of 1915 they had been told that twelve months hence they would be still marching in and out of trenches? The answer is given in the song which was so popular at that time, and ran, "They wouldn't believe it!" Or possibly they might, in the words of another song, have said, "Marching, marching, marching, always blooming well marching"! Nevertheless, March, 1916, saw the First Surreys, after a month's training, again marching eastwards to take up its position in the front line immediately opposite the town of Lens. The trenches in this sector between Souchez and Maroc were somewhat like those at Loos, a little to the north, but being on lower ground they were wetter, and consequently less comfortable; a good deal of work was necessary to repair the damage done by the winter rains and frosts, and spades and pumps were more in demand than rifles or bombs. Luckily, active operations, or artillery preparation for such, were not contemplated, although, of course, the usual rumours of a "push" were current. But poison gas, which had first been used by the enemy in the winter of 1914-15, and had later assisted us in our attack at Loos, was now a constant source of danger, and the possibility of its discharge by the Germans whenever the wind was favourable, necessitated yet another bundle of precautionary measures. Before coming into this sector we had, therefore, been provided with the then most up-to-date gas mask (or smoke helmet) and had, of course, been frequently trained in its use and adjustment. This helmet, known as the "P.H.," consisted of a flannelette bag, which was placed right over the head, the lower part being then tucked safely beneath the jacket; eye-pieces, similar to motorists' goggles, were provided, and breath was inhaled through the chemically treated material and exhaled through a tin mouthpiece fitted with a rubber valve. This type of protector (which, incidentally, was horribly uncomfortable!) replaced numerous even more primitive patterns, and remained in use until the winter of 1916-17. In dealing with "gas" we were not acting only on the defensive, for, during our tour in this sector, we spent many weary nights trudging along with cylinders of compressed gas, which we carefully installed in selected positions in our front line. They were discharged by another brigade after we had left the neighbourhood, and from all reports produced excellent results!

The line we were now holding offered no special opportunities for excitement, the only unusual feature being a post on our extreme right, which was completely isolated from the rest of the line. It should be mentioned that the Souchez River ran through our lines (between us and the troops on our right) and the valley for some 200 yards on either bank was so boggy as to render trenches impossible; besides this, they were quite unnecessary by day, as the ground was completely commanded from either side. Along this valley the railway also used to run, and it was in a large dug-out under the little station of Souchez that a complete company was quartered for use in case of necessity. The enemy was unaware of its presence, and the greatest care was necessary to keep the secret, especially during daylight. By night this garrison awoke and had to work hard at all the duties necessary both for its protection and sustenance—patrols, ration parties, working parties for repairs and drainage, to say nothing of sentries to watch the ground between us and the river. It was a trying post, and reliefs were consequently frequent, but a change soon came for the whole Battalion, for we once more marched south, and, after a fortnight or so in reserve around Villers-au-Bois, we made our first acquaintance with the now famous Vimy Ridge. This was quite a new situation, and the change in our methods of life and work occasioned by the altered geographical and geological conditions was refreshing, if not wholly pleasing.

The British position in front of Carency in April, 1916, ran along the crest of the Vimy Ridge, from north of Arras to just east of Souchez, where the Ridge ended and the ground dropped steeply to the river, and it was at the Souchez end that the First Surrey now took up its position; the German trenches were also on the high ground, and were some 80 to 100 yards away. Behind us ran a deep valley (named by the French the "Zouave Valley"), and behind this again there was a sharp rise to the "Cabaret Rouge" and the rolling plains which stretch between Arras and Béthune. This description is somewhat involved, but perhaps it will be possible to gather from it some vague idea of the unique sector which we were destined to hold intermittently for five months, during which many exciting incidents occurred.

The month of April passed uneventfully, the Battalion alternating between the trenches and the villages of Villers-au-Bois, Maisnil Bouché, and Carency—in the line we performed the usual duties, and when billeted in the villages named, each company in turn had to find working or carrying parties. It was whilst engaged on these unpopular (but very necessary) trips to the front line that we made our first acquaintance with the steel helmet—or, as it was more generally called, "tin hat." It was, of course, intended that each one of us should ultimately possess his own "tin hat," but at this stage the Battalion was given first 50, and then 100, for the use of men in specially dangerous positions, and they were handed over from party to party as required. Unpopular as they were at first, it was not many months before the majority of us felt quite unsafe, or, to use a more expressive word, "naked," if we had not a good old tin hat on when bits were flying about.

Before the Battalion had been long in this sector it became apparent even to the latest arrival from the Base that there was trouble ahead; ever since the French attack of 1915 had subsided, and whilst our Allies were still holding these very trenches, the tunnellers on both sides had been working furiously in attempt after attempt to blow up the other man's trenches, but nothing on a big scale had yet been accomplished. Towards the end of April we were engaged night after night in carrying up bulky boxes of explosives, and as these reached the front line they were tucked safely away in the forward end of mine galleries running out into No Man's Land, some 40 or 50 feet below the surface of the ground. We soon learned what was to happen, and which Battalion had been chosen to share with the Tunnelling Company and the R.E.'s the honour of carrying out the largest mining operation that had yet taken place—and, needless to say, it was the First Surreys. On a certain bright, sunny afternoon in May, the front line trenches on Vimy Ridge appeared as quiet as, or quieter than usual, at least as far as the surface was concerned; but below ground men were working like ants in order to complete by 4 p.m. all preparations for "blowing" three large land mines under the German lines, destroying not only their trenches, but all their mining works in the neighbourhood.

Our share in the business was, as soon as the mines had been exploded, to rush forward and seize the more advanced points of the craters and the surrounding ridges of débris, and whilst these were held, others were to dig a new system of trenches and construct firing points and machine-gun emplacements in the most advantageous and commanding positions that could be hurriedly found; the new front line was to be dug and occupied, and the "covering parties" having been withdrawn, trench warfare was once more to settle down to its usual routine. The advantages we hoped to reap were, a better position for ourselves, and a worse one for the enemy, and, what was far more important, freedom from the danger of the German mines until he had been able to construct fresh tunnels! The whole operation was known to be a fight against time, and we knew quite well that, unless we were ready first, the Germans would blow their mines, and we should all go sky-high.

It was decided that 4 o'clock on the afternoon of May 3rd was the latest moment up to which we could safely afford to wait, and consequently that hour was chosen for the simultaneous exploding of our three giant collections of high explosive.

After almost superhuman efforts, the 176th Tunnelling Company, under Major Momber, reported all ready at about 3.55 p.m., and at the same time the wires were connected at Battalion Head-quarters with the electric apparatus which was to give life to the nineteen tons of explosive packed tightly away under No Man's Land. At the same moment Major Love, commanding the Field Company of Engineers attached to the Brigade, reported his men as in position and ready to "lay out" and supervise the construction of the proposed new trenches. The infantry taking part in the show had been organized into small groups, each with a definite object—the bombers and Lewis-gunners to seize and hold specially selected points, and the riflemen to seize and hold the enemy's side of the craters, and in addition to dig and build as quickly as possible. Our field artillery had special orders to pour a heavy fire into the enemy's lines to prevent him from daring to hinder our men at their work, and the "heavies" were to do their best to prevent the German batteries from opening fire on our trenches. The schemes had been very carefully prepared, and great care had been taken that there should be no delay in putting them into operation.

The thoroughness with which all the arrangements for this operation were made was in itself wonderful, but the pluck, energy, and determination displayed by the officers and men who actually took part in the work are beyond mere words. The work of the bombers was especially praiseworthy, and as a result, one of their number was rewarded with the Military Medal—one of the first ever awarded.

Everything went like clockwork, from the moment when Colonel Kennedy pressed the plunger which detonated the explosives, till the time when the Battalion, very pleased with its exploits, handed the trenches over on relief five days later. The actual blowing of the mines produced a truly remarkable spectacle. As already mentioned, there were three mines, and simultaneously three enormous eruptions occurred; vast masses of chalk, clay, and smoke, rose from the ridge to a height of some 60 to 70 feet, seemed to hang there momentarily like giant mushrooms, and then subsided to the ground in a terrible jumbled mass.

The havoc that had been wrought in these few seconds was astounding—tunnels and dug-outs blown, trenches wrecked, timber and iron tossed about like matchsticks, and the whole face of the ground in the immediate neighbourhood changed beyond recognition, whilst the trembles from the concussion were felt for miles around. Three enormous pits or "craters" were discovered in front of our trenches, with great mounds of chalk, earth, and débris thrown up all round them—and over these our parties scrambled to carry out their allotted tasks. The Germans, although taken by surprise, quickly appreciated the situation, and commenced to harass our working parties; they even attempted once or twice to drive us back from the craters, but our covering parties of bombers, Lewis-gunners, and riflemen, dealt with these gentlemen so successfully that within forty minutes we had the beginnings of a carefully planned trench system running along the edge of each crater, and the trenches between (or what was left of them) having been cleared and repaired, we were able again to present a continuous front line. This line was at the same time improved, and every opportunity taken to secure all commanding ground. The craters were immediately christened with the names of the Commanding Officers concerned respectively in their creation, capture, and consolidation, namely, "Momber," "Kennedy," and "Love" (i.e., Tunnellers, Infantry, and Royal Engineers), and they are, so far as we are aware, known by these names to this day. Kennedy Crater was the largest, being some 50 feet deep and 100 feet in diameter, whilst the ridge blown up around it varied from 10 to 25 feet above the original ground level. The highest point was eventually made into a very useful observation post known as the "Crow's Nest."

It was near this spot that some few days later the Battalion had the misfortune to lose its second-in-command,

Major H. P. Richards. This popular and gallant officer, who had done so much for the First Surreys in pre-war days, and whose influence had been so great and so helpful during his war service, was called to make the supreme sacrifice whilst visiting the advanced sentries in the crater on a bright moonlight night. It was risky work, but so persistently did Major Richards stick to his duty that he fell the victim of a German sniper. Major Richards' death was a great blow to the Battalion, and especially to his own company ("D") : he will always be remembered as one of the "Old Brigade" who, first as a Volunteer and later as a Territorial, gave in peacetime so much, and in war gave himself, to the service of his beloved country. He set a fine example to his comrades, which many followed not only in life, but also in death. Major Richards was buried at Cabaret Rouge Cemetery, where lie many other First Surrey men who fell on Vimy Ridge.

After this little crater "show" we were given six days' rest, and then came back to complete the work we had begun, but things seemed more unpleasant than ever, and it appeared obvious to anyone who noticed anything at all, that the enemy's artillery in this neighbourhood had been strongly reinforced; whether he expected us to follow up our mining successes with a further attack, or whether he proposed making one himself we did not then know, so, having duly reported the enemy's unpleasant attitude and completed our tour of duty, we again went back to rest at Estrée Couché.

The country was now looking most delightful, and all the freshness of early summer was in evidence, but *we* were not to enjoy it in peace. The day after our relief we heard a heavy bombardment from the direction of the Ridge, and at 6.30 p.m. the Battalion was ordered to "stand to" in battle order, and to be ready to move within half an hour. Two hours later we paraded and marched up to a supporting position in Villers-au-Bois, where we learned that the Germans, after one of the heaviest concentrated bombardments known up to that time, had launched his attack and driven the British troops off a part of the Ridge on the immediate right of our old sector, and had captured our old front and support line trenches. We consequently expected to have to make a counter attack, and to this end got into fighting trim, equipping ourselves with extra ammunition, bombs, and "emergency rations." This was, indeed, barely completed when we were ordered to move still further towards the front, and take up a position of readiness in reserve trenches behind Cabaret Rouge, known as the Maestre line. The Battalion arrived in this position at 3 a.m. on May 22nd, and anxiously awaited further orders; throughout the day men lay about in the sun wondering what the next move would be, whilst some of the officers and the scouts were busy attending conferences and reconnoitring the ground. Towards evening orders for our counter attack were received, and at 8 o'clock we relieved the 20th Battalion in our old reserve line, which was now the foremost position remaining in our hands! Turning for a moment to our old friends, the three craters, we found that in spite of the enemy's numerous assaults they still remained ours, this being doubtless due in no small degree to the excellence of their defences and the careful siting of our fire positions thereon.

The attack was to be carried out in conjunction with the 24th Battalion on our right, and we were ordered to recapture our old support line and, if possible, the front line as well, so as to regain as far as might be our old position on the Ridge. The nearest of the craters was to act as a pivot for the attack, and was to be held at all costs by "B" Company, some of the bombers being told off to assist in the capture of our old trenches by advancing along them from the crater, and the riflemen by enfilading the Germans in their trenches during our advance. "A" Company was detailed for the attack, and "C" and "D" were to support, one platoon from each being kept as a reserve for use in case of emergency.

The attack as carried out by "A" Company was probably one of the finest of the many assaults for which the Battalion was responsible. They swept all before them, and although losing heavily, gained our original front line during the evening, and began consolidating against its recapture by the enemy. Ammunition and bombs were carried up and communication established, but it was more difficult to hold the position than had been anticipated. To begin with, the troops of another division on our right had been less fortunate than ourselves, and their misfortune, as must always be the case, made our position all the more difficult. Time after time we were attacked both from our front and from our right flank, and at last, weakened by heavy losses and running short of ammunition, our platoons, although reinforced by "C" and "D" Companies, had to retire to our support line. It was during this operation that the true spirit of the Battalion manifested itself in the numerous instances in which wounded men were brought back to safety by their comrades; one of the most notable being the case of Company-Sergeant-Major O. Laing. Seeing one of his N.C.O.'s (Sergeant Miller) lying severely wounded and in peril of being killed or captured by the Germans, Sergeant-Major Laing nobly went to his rescue, and in spite of the very heavy rifle and shell fire, succeeded in bringing him safely back to our lines. For this act Sergeant-Major Laing was afterwards awarded the Military Cross.

The enemy now having been reinforced by some of his numerous reserves, repeatedly attacked our depleted garrison, driving us out of our position, but failing to take his real objective, which was our last remaining line of trenches on the Ridge.

The Battalion had suffered so heavily that it was decided to send a Company of the 22nd Battalion to reinforce our front line, and with their welcome aid, and by means of various feint attacks, the Germans were kept at bay until they finally gave up their attempts to dislodge us. By this time we were pretty nearly at the end of our resources; the bombardment had been tremendous, and all communication between the Ridge where the Battalion was hanging on and the positions in rear had long since been cut. Our only means of letting Brigade Head-quarters know what we were doing was by our marvellous runners, who, now as ever, both before and afterwards, did their duty in a manner almost beyond conception; our signallers, too, stuck to their work marvellously, and, impossible as it may seem, telephonic communication between Company and Battalion Head-quarters was kept up throughout the attack! In our front line men of the 21st and 22nd Battalions, Pioneers, R.E.'s, and Tunnellers, stood side by side, and there they remained, keeping the enemy in hand until comparative quiet was restored and the tired garrison was relieved at 4 a.m. on May 24th by the 23rd Battalion who, although nominally in reserve, had spent the night in carrying ammunition and other stores up to the Ridge. The casualties in this action were the heaviest the Battalion had as yet suffered, amounting to 187, inclusive of seven officers; amongst them were many pre-war members of the Battalion, and their influence and experience were tremendously missed. The Battalion was rewarded with a personal letter of congratulation and thanks from Sir Henry Wilson, and received seven Military Crosses for the one operation—surely a record!

We spent a day back at "Extra Cushy" (Estrée Couché) refitting and reorganizing, and then marched back to Corps Reserve at Divion on May 25th, exactly one year after our first action at Givenchy. At Divion we remained for three weeks, resting, training, and enjoying the air and wine of the district!

Leave to England (U.K. it was officially termed) was now a regular institution, and, although of not very frequent occurrence, was, nevertheless, the most discussed topic of the day. The original period of seven days had by now been increased to ten days, so that those whose turn had been put off till now actually gained by the delay. Those of us who went away on leave from Divion found on our return that the First Surrey Rifles was once more taking its place in the firing line—still in the area of the First Army but on another corps' front.

The new trenches which we held from June 21st, were in the Bully-Grenay Sector, being immediately east of that village and a little to the left of our previous battlefield. The line here was well defended, and the enemy was some 120 to 130 yards from us; mining was not indulged in, but artillery duels and sniping were prevalent. It was whilst in this sector that we gave our third course of instruction to troops newly landed in France, our pupils on this occasion being the lads of the Naval Division, most of whom had already been in action in Gallipoli. The Battalion remained in this sector throughout June and most of July, and during this time it enjoyed good trenches and ultra-comfortable rest billets. The reserve area consisted entirely of mining villages belonging to the famous Lens coalfield—they were designed for the most part on garden city lines, and it was in these snug *petits corons* that we slept so comfortably and enjoyed our *petits Coronas* without interruption from the enemy or the elements !

Whilst in these comfortable quarters (at Fosse No. 10) we received news of the beginning of the great Battle of the Somme on July 1st. This operation was, of course, the biggest offensive which had yet been undertaken by the Allies, and so large was the scale on which it was carried out that within a few days fresh troops were being sent south to take the place of Divisions either exhausted or depleted. Such movements were noticed in the neighbourhood of the 47th Division, and it became a matter for speculation as to when we, too, should be sent off to have our "whack." We were not kept long in suspense, for while holding the line on Vimy Ridge on July 27th, the Battalion was relieved by the survivors of *three* battalions of Tyneside troops who had just returned from Fricourt, and from whom we learned a good deal about the Somme fighting.

These North-country men had been in the thick of the fray and had distinguished themselves by their gallant attack, but at what cost was apparent to us all. In the early days of the Somme fighting it had been usual for all ranks of a battalion to go into action on each occasion on which it was engaged, but it was found that with such enormous casualties the resulting confusion was indescribable. It was accordingly ordained that "understudies" for certain individuals (e.g., C.O., Adjutant, R.S.M., and Sergeants) should be trained, and that either they or their principals should remain with the depôt when the Battalion went into action.

The Battalion, having bidden farewell to the famous Ridge, was given twelve hours in which to prepare for the journey to the Somme, but we had yet to learn what particular form that journey was to take.

Looking back on our four and a half months' experience of Vimy Ridge and the Lens Sector, with its billeting areas of Villers-au-Bois, Carency, Ablain, Maisnil Bouché, Estrée Couché, and the mining *corons,* one cannot help being struck by the contrast between the violent fighting in the former and the comparative quiet and luxury of the latter. The First Surrey had here, as ever, lived up to its motto of *Concordia Victrix,* and although many of our dearest and most gallant comrades lay buried in the Pas-de-Calais, the spirit of the regiment went with it to the battlefields of Picardy, there to watch over it and urge it on to whatever duty fate might hold for it.

CHAPTER V.

July 28th to October 16th, 1916.

Operations on the Somme.

The British advance in the region of the Somme, which began on July 1st, 1916, was, as is well known, one of the most important links in the chain of major operations calculated to lead to final victory. The Battles of the Marne, the Aisne, La Bassée, Neuve Chapelle, and Loos, although they had loosened the enemy's hold in France and Flanders, had by no means induced him to abandon his original plans, and now the Allies were to make another attempt which, if successful, might conceivably prevent the horrors of another winter campaign.

Division followed division in sustaining the effort of the prolonged attack, and each withdrew from the fray badly hammered, but not without having wrested another slice of desolate and devastated France from the hands of the invader. The turn of the 47th (London) Division to take its part in the Somme battle was not long in coming, and the First Surreys, with the rest of the division, started to

"Pack its grip and take a trip
To a good old Southern Town,"

marching out on July 28th from Maisnil Bouché (behind Vimy Ridge) to the tune of the song quoted above. After a march of some ten miles we arrived at the little village of Bajus; here a halt was made for two days before beginning the long trek southwards.

Everybody in the Battalion (especially those whom duty caused to sit astride a horse or mule) looked forward to the novel experience of a real long march by easy stages. The weather was ideal—a trifle on the warm side at times—and the roads, being mostly bye-ways, were good and, generally speaking, not paved with those objectionable stone blocks so common on the Routes Nationales. Our immediate destination we soon discovered was St. Riquier, and the journey to this townlet was divided into five stages, halts (for one or two nights in each case) being made at Bajus, Maizières, Barly, and St. Acheul. The march, which was uneventful, was carried out as a rule in the early part of each day, the Battalion parading between 4 and 5 o'clock each morning and dismissing to billets well before noon. This arrangement allowed plenty of time for dinners, a siesta, and generally a bathe in some refreshing stream during the afternoon; a concert or "gaff" of some description after teas, and an early retirement to "bed." (Note the word "bed" is here guarded by inverted commas to warn all concerned that it is the state of sleep that is referred to, rather than the particular piece of furniture which the word implies. Throughout the war soldiers never saw a completely equipped bedstead except in hospital, or in one or two cases in the snug little mining villages of the north.)

The march from Maizières to Barly was not carried out in the early morning, but at the other cool end of the day, that is between 6.30 and 11.30 p.m., and a remarkable march it was—principally on account of the impromptu efforts of the band, which having no lanterns by which to read its parts, and having exhausted all the tunes which it knew by heart, proceeded to vamp out such airs (both classical and otherwise) as came into its combined head. Much to the gratification of the troops, the horror of the sergeant-major, and the amusement of the adjutant's horse.

St. Riquier, which we reached on August 5th, proved a charming town to us, and although our fortnight's stay there was spent in intensive training, we had an opportunity of making friends with our hosts and hostesses and generally entering into the life of the neighbourhood. Abbéville was only about twelve miles west of us, and a few fortunate folk were able to get leave to visit the city, which, untouched as yet by bombs from the air, boasted a gay life, and had much to be proud of in the nature of architecture, commerce, and *estaminets*. From St. Riquier we marched eastwards by stages, Buigny L'Abbaye, Vignacourt, Villers Bocage to Lahoussoye, where special training and manœuvres were to take place. This trek was similar to the first, the Battalion parading daily at an early hour in the old familiar order: band and buglers leading, then the scouts and signallers, followed by the C.O., adjutant, sergeant-major, and the four fighting companies. Each company, led by its commander, took its turn at being nearest to the band and farthest from the dust, but the second-in-command and the M.O. were destined always to ride behind the last company. The regimental transport, with ammunition, baggage, and the steaming field-cookers, generally followed in rear, but on some occasions they were sent off on a route of their own.

In this fashion the days soon passed; Lahoussoye was a busy little village, and being on the Amiens-Albert road, was full of life. Training here was both realistic and serious, and from it we caught glimpses of what was in store for us on the Somme battlefields.

On September 10th the battalion left the training area. We marched nearly to Albert with band and bugles playing, and as we passed the many camps which lay alongside the roadway, we had a wonderful reception from the thousands of troops occupying them. They crowded up on to the road to cheer us and wish us luck, and at one time the crowd was so dense that Sergeant Dew, of the scouts, who was leading, had his work cut out to force his way through. A real good send-off those men gave us—most of them had already had their turn "on the Somme" and they knew what we were going up to. We went straight through poor battered Albert to a little bivouac in the wood at Bécourt, and leaving this at dawn next day, we went at once into the firing line behind High Wood, in relief of troops of the First Division.

The position we now held had been captured only a few weeks previously, so that little had been done to elaborate the trenches or shelters; the signs of recent fighting were everywhere evident, and within a few days signs of future strife also became apparent. We here recognized the actual German position an imitation of which we had, whilst at Lahoussoye, attacked, captured, and consolidated. Orders for an attack on High Wood were soon received and from them we learned that whilst the other two brigades of our Division were to attack the wood and the trenches beyond it, the 142nd was to be in reserve for use as and when required. We were accordingly moved back during the night of September 14th and 15th to a bivouac in the Bois de Fricourt, meeting on our way the troops of the brigades which were to make the attack next day. Such a move as this was always full of interest, for all roads and tracks were crowded with men, horses, guns, and ammunition; but in this particular case the presence of many unfamiliar pieces of heavy machinery, noisily grinding their way eastwards, aroused additional interest. These mysterious contrivances, which revealed themselves later as the now familiar tanks, were here used for the first time, and, imperfect as they were, struck terror into the hearts of the astounded Germans. Throughout the night we rested, and some of us slept, but at dawn on the 15th we were roused by the heavy gun fire, and knew that the attack had been launched. At 6.30 a.m. the fighting portion of the Battalion moved to Mametz Wood to be nearer the line, and at noon we were placed at the disposal of the Brigadier-General commanding the 140th

Brigade. It now transpired that the wood had been captured, but not without some difficulty, and that both the other brigades had lost heavily; exactly how far the line had advanced beyond the wood, or whether the two brigades were in touch with each other, we could not ascertain. From such news as we could get it appeared that the final objectives had not been gained, at any rate on the particular piece of front that we were supporting.

Time, we know, heals old wounds, but it also dims our memories, and it is difficult now to recall the minute details or exact sequence of the deeds of the First Surrey Rifles on the afternoon of September 15th, 1916; the main features, though, cannot be forgotten by any man who went safely through that remarkable action. Words are not ours to convey the spirit of times like these, and the account which follows must serve purely as a record of events rather than as a pen-picture of one of the many glorious sacrifices which have been made in the world's history.

The heavy fighting around High Wood died down somewhat towards mid-day, when it was found that the remnants of the 140th and 141st Brigades were holding isolated portions of what had been the German support line. These brigades were not in touch with one another, and between them lay some 300- to 400-yds. of trench strongly held by the enemy. The First Surreys received orders at 3.30 p.m. to turn the enemy out of this position and restore communication between the advanced troops of the division, with a view to making a further attack on the final objective, and after a short meeting of company commanders, at which plans were discussed and orders issued by Colonel Kennedy, the Battalion moved off to the attack exactly as it had done so many times during training. The first part of the advance was not visible from the enemy's position owing to high ground intervening, and under cover of this ground companies rapidly shook out into the familiar "artillery formation," with "B" Company on the right and "C," "A," and "D" in this order to their left.

All went well until the leading platoons reached the ridge immediately to the east of High Wood, when at 4 o'clock on a brilliant autumn afternoon, they came into full view of all the enemy's gunners within range; this was probably in the circumstances inevitable, but the results would certainly have been less disastrous had our own artillery been able to support us by harassing the enemy's, or if our attack could have been made at dusk; as it was, however, the Battalion was received with a veritable tornado of shells from guns of all calibres. Whole platoons were wiped out by direct hits, but in spite of this, and in spite of the heavy rifle and machine gun fire under which they now came, the other platoons shook out into extended order and held steadily on, until the remnants were able at last to make a united and determined assault on the German trenches in face of a murderous fire. The assault was partially successful, and we succeeded in capturing a section of battered trenches, where touch was afterwards gained with troops of the 140th Brigade; this position was consolidated, but further advance was impossible owing to our losses and consequent weakness. Of the 19 officers and 550 men who had gone into the attack, only 2 officers and 60 men now remained, 17 officers and 490 men having been either killed or wounded in that one gallant, but ill-fated venture. The actual operation had not lasted more than an hour or so, and the ground covered was not more than one mile, but in this short space the First Surreys suffered more heavily than in our months of previous fighting. Many of the world's historic battles fought against fearful odds have been immortalized in verse and remembered proudly by generations of young Britons; would that it were in our power thus to perpetuate the memory of those of our men who, in a fight no less glorious, fell that day at High Wood. (Major Lord Gorell, of the Gunners, who was in a forward observation post, telephoned back the message, "The First Surreys have gone over just as if they were on parade"; this was after we had come under the fire described above and were actually engaged in shaking out into our extended line.)

Throughout the night which followed shells continued to fall thick and fast, making doubly difficult the work of the stretcher-bearers under Captain H. H. Robinson, R.A.M.C. Few probably realize what this gallant little band went through that night, nor does the immediate award of the Military Cross to the officer named adequately convey it; there must be some living, though, who owe their lives to the gallantry and thoroughness displayed by Captain Robinson and his bearers in searching the shell-pitted battlefield and tending and bring back the wounded who must otherwise have perished.

At 7.30 on the following morning we were ordered to withdraw and reorganize at Mametz Wood. It was a melancholy process, and the few who answered their names at the Roll Call could not but be thinking of the many who would never parade with the First Surreys again. We had a simple but impressive Church Parade, and one looked from this tiny gathering back to the days when we filled the customary three sides of a square, and when the singing of "Onward, Christian Soldiers" could have been heard a mile away. But this was not a time for reflections, and our immediate business was to march back to the little village of Millencourt to pick up a draft of some three hundred men from the 2/5th East Surrey Regiment. Refilling and reorganization proceeded apace, and on September 27th we again marched up to High Wood and bivouacked there in reserve.

On October 7th the brigade again went into the line, which had been advanced about half a mile since our last attack, and on the following day the Battalion went into the front line with the object of delivering another attack. This operation was to be one of the many minor enterprises which were undertaken to keep the enemy on the move, and from consolidating his positions, by pushing forward our line whenever possible, and although on a smaller scale than our last "show," it presented many difficulties which were accentuated by short notice, unknown ground, and a combination of some tired, and many inexperienced men. A rapid reconnaissance on the morning of the 8th showed us that we were expected to capture an enemy position some 400-yds. away from our line, so that we might have a good "jumping off" mark for a subsequent assault on the famous Butte de Warlencourt. Our present position consisted of rough trenches immediately north of the monastery of Eaucourt L'Abbaye; on the right we were supported by the 24th Battalion whilst the 23rd were to attack with us on our left.

The attack was originally to have been in the nature of a surprise, no artillery being employed prior to our advance, but this plan was subsequently modified and an intense bombardment was carried out for one minute before we left our trenches. The enemy, whether alarmed by the bombardment or previously expecting an attack, was found to be thoroughly on the alert, and so heavy was his fire and so stubborn his resistance that we were unable to advance more than an average distance of 200- to 300-yds. Here, roughly 200-yds. from our objective, we were compelled to dig ourselves in and, forming a chain of small posts, wait for a more favourable opportunity of completing the advance.

Events moved quickly on the Somme, and at this moment the 47th Division, already exhausted with heavy fighting and weak from its enormous losses, was ordered out of the line. Our Battalion was relieved by troops of the 1st South African

Brigade, and during the early hours of October 9th we made our way back to our old shacks in Mametz Wood, there to snatch a few hours of well-earned rest before leaving the region of the Somme for more healthy surroundings.

The immediate subsequent movements were uneventful and swiftly carried out; a move back to Laviéville on the next day followed by four days in which to clean and polish ourselves and pack up generally. We listened to complimentary words from our Corps Commander and a farewell speech from our Divisional General (he had commanded us since 1914 and was now proceeding to an appointment at home), and at last we entrained at Albert on our way north again.

Our railway journey was not exactly carried out at "express" speed, unless you can thus describe a journey of twenty-six miles in twenty-eight hours! Be that as it may, we eventually reached the quiet little town of Pont Rémy, where we spent one night (five hours to be exact) in luxurious billets, and in the morning "caught" another train, which speedily and comparatively comfortably conveyed the First Surreys from the battle area of the Somme to the training area immediately behind the Ypres Salient—"The" Salient it was called in those days. October 16th was thus spent rolling northwards through Abbéville, Boulogne, Calais, Hazebrouck, to the Salient.

CHAPTER VI.

October 16th, 1916, to September 23rd, 1917.

The Ypres Salient.

The part of the Western Front most closely associated with the British Armies throughout the War was undoubtedly the country round Ypres. This district, which was once the most prosperous in Flanders, and had until recently been both picturesque and peaceful, lay then a tract of devastated and ruined country laid desolate by the unceasing ravages of two years of modern warfare—known to the world simply as "The Salient." What memories are awakened by that term, which literally means merely a projecting curve in our line of defence, but is in this instance associated with years of hardship, adventure, and discomfort for vast numbers of British soldiers. "The Salient," preserving as it does the graves of many thousands of our bravest, means as much to us as it does to those brave Belgians who were fighting with us in our endeavour to preserve some part at least of their historic little country.

The First Surrey arrived in the reserve area, behind the Salient, on the evening of October 16th, 1916, detraining at a little station which rejoiced in the huge name of Godewaersvelde, under the shadow of the famous Mont des Cats, and marching at once to a group of huts known as Connaught Camp, near Boeschepe. Three days sufficed for refitting, reorganizing, and brushing off the mud of the Somme, after which our division took over a part of the line just south-east of Ypres, the 142nd Brigade being at first in divisional reserve. The Battalion during these six days was quartered in a weird collection of wooden huts dignified by the name of Halifax Camp, which, with Scottish Camp (famous for its mud!) shared the honour of sheltering us from the subsequent gales and frosts whenever our turn came for a rest from the front line. These hutted camps, situated some four miles west-south-west of Ypres, and adjoining the road to Reninghelst, were comparatively comfortable, and although the gaiety and camaraderie of Flemish village life were lacking, there was compensation in the shape of dry billets, wooden floors, watertight roofs, and comparative freedom from uninvited and unwanted little

E

visitors at night! Each group of camps generally possessed its church, canteen, baths, and theatre, and many were the comforts, joys and pleasures provided thereby.

Our brigade went into the line on October 24th, leaving us quartered in reserve at a partially ruined country house known as Belgian Château, some two miles behind the line. It was here that we received our supplies of the new and final pattern "box respirator," the *dernier cri* in protection from poison gases, replacing the now insufficient "smoke helmets." The box respirator consisted of a mask, with goggles, fitting lightly over the face, and provided with a mouthpiece and flexible tube through which air (filtered through a tin containing chemicals) could be drawn: the tin (and the mask when not actually worn) was kept in a small haversack, this being always carried when within range of German gas shells. We practised with and tested these respirators at Belgian Château, so that we might be able to use them with confidence and certainty if and when necessary, for it should be remembered that it was at Ypres that gas was first used in 1915, and since then it had been an ever present menace to both sides.

Our first association with trench warfare in the Salient dated from October 29th, when we took over our allotted section immediately opposite the famous Hill 60 (so called on account of its height in metres being 60, and being thus shown on all maps). Fighting here was not heavy, the very simple reason being that the enemy, like ourselves, was relieving his divisions exhausted by the Somme fighting, and sending them to "quiet" sectors such as this; consequently both sides were none too anxious to stir up strife, and so, for the moment, we were able to get our breath in preparation for the next round.

The chief consideration in all trenches in Belgium was the efficient drainage of water and mud, and as the country is notoriously flat, the difficulty was not easily overcome; much time and labour were necessary to keep our line intact, and even then conditions were not exactly comfortable. This matter of efficient drainage systems exercised not a little the minds of certain staff officers, and one, who shall be nameless, made a special hobby of mud disposal. His special labour-saving scheme was to use the earth, removed in the construction of drains, for filling sand-bags for earthworks, and with this end in view he in one particular place had a line of drain marked on the ground with a white tape. One morning it was discovered, to everyone's horror, that the night digging-party, instead of digging carefully along the taped-out line, had obtained the filling of their sand-bags from places some ten yards away, and as the drainage specialist was due to pass by during the day, there was nothing for it but to shift the tape and make it follow the line of pits—instead of vice versa! This was actually done by a resourceful platoon commander, and the position was saved—the higher command, not noticing the change, was delighted with the work, but whether the water and mud subsequently played their part in the little deception by flowing up-hill as well as down, is not so certain!

It is probably safe to say that it was in the Salient that one felt, more strongly than anywhere else, the real spirit (the hopeless and helpless spirit) of trench warfare. Ever since the first winter there had been but little open fighting, and now, towards the end of 1916, trench systems had become very complicated—all around the ground was merely a mass of shell holes, and the artillery positions and other likely targets on both sides were so well known that a nearer approach to a state of permanent siege could hardly be imagined. To give an illustration of what this meant, it is only necessary to refer to the colossal system of underground tunnels that existed wherever the ground was, or could be made, suitable, some for purposes of shelter, others for mine galleries under the enemy's lines; of the former we were glad to take advantage, and of the latter we gleaned news—mysterious and thrilling—from time to time. But some months were to elapse before the full significance of these underground "powder magazines" was to be revealed to us.

November passed, with little or nothing to vary the dull monotony of trenches and reserve camps; in the former we were harassed principally by large trench mortars (*minenwerfer* or "Minnies") and in the latter by aeroplane bombs or long range guns, but no matter where we dwelt there existed an ever pressing need for work with shovel and pump to keep ourselves and our shelters from being submerged or washed away. December brought no relief in the depressing weather conditions, but thoughts of Christmas festivities once again cheered us up. According to the usual routine of trench reliefs (ten days in and ten days out) the battalion would be due to eat its turkey (or bully beef "in lieu") within sixty yards of a Bavarian regiment munching sausages—in other words, we should be holding front line trenches. This calculation proved to be correct, for daybreak on December 25th found us standing to arms (as on any other day in the front line) in the trenches at Verbrandenmolen, or rather at the place where Verbrandenmolen had once stood! The day passed quietly, and the First Surrey enjoyed its second Christmas on the Continent, notwithstanding the fact that we were within sight of the famous Hill 60, and were immediately on top of many tons of explosive. Feasting and foregathering were, of course, out of the question owing to the "exigencies of the service," but such activities as harassing fire, sniping and bombing were, by mutual consent, reduced to a minimum, and it was commonly rumoured (truthfully or otherwise) that such firing as the Germans did indulge in was effected with blank ammunition!

But to a good many of us there remains one outstanding memory of Christmas Day, 1916—the celebrations of the Holy Communion which were held by our padre (familiarly but lovingly known as "Little" Plumptre) in a dug-out near Battalion Head-quarters in Strong Point 9, which was normally used as a drying-room for gumboots. It was small and stuffy, and although we overflowed into the trench outside, it would not accommodate all who wished to attend (nor, of course, could all be spared from their posts at one time) so we came down in relays, and the padre held services accordingly. This observance, and some slight additions to the usual rations supplied by our gem of a quarter-master, were all that marked the actual Day, but we didn't worry, as we were due to be relieved on the 29th, and were then to celebrate the Feast in a manner worthy of the occasion and of the First Surrey, in our old quarters at Halifax Camp.

Whilst the rest of us were in the line, the quarter-master and his highly efficient staff had been utilising their spare moments in accumulating suitable stores (such as "live" pork, fruit, nuts, and even crackers) and the transport section had been likewise busy in fetching and carrying from railhead, or from the neighbouring farms and towns, such as Poperinghe, so that by the time we came out everything was ready, and we decided to declare New Year's Eve as a complete holiday for the Battalion, and hold our feast on that day.

It was bitterly cold, and wetter than ever in Halifax Camp, but, church parade being over, each mess adjourned to its own hut, specially decorated for the occasion, and there partook of a really worthy Christmas dinner, with a due accompaniment of toasts and greetings, which were drunk in a variety of more or less alcoholic liquors. One or two of us visited every mess in turn, riding from one to the other—there were about fifteen of them!—and we know what drinks there were, for we sampled them. They ranged from whisky (neat) through Port and Malaga to beer! Mounting our horses wasn't so easy after the fifteenth mess as after "D" Company's at Pioneer Farm, which was the first we visited.

The divisional "Follies" (The Quarante Se(p)t), most of whom belonged to us, excelled themselves in the "pantomime" which they gave us in the evening. The title, "——— and Halifax," conveyed nothing of the variety and talent which were following, and the audience for its part was fully appreciative from long before the curtain rose till sometime after it fell. During the last few minutes of 1916 the battalion again became busy—this time mixing a "Loving Cup" of hot rum punch, by means of which, with the customary musical accompaniment, we saw the New Year in. "All present and correct" we retired to sleep the sleep of just and well satisfied mortals!

The first four months of 1917 were not (comparatively, at any rate) teeming with excitement or adventure, and in fact the New Year seemed to be keeping us out of harm's way, as though in return for the riotous welcome we had given him on his "Eve." We remained in Halifax Camp and Scottish Lines until January 18th, and then, after doing the usual tour in trenches not too uncomfortable, we were again relieved and came in for our turn of divisional "Works Battalion." This was a new idea, consequent on the large amount of trench repair, digging, draining, and other forms of labour required in this region at this time of the year, which necessitated a whole battalion at a time being placed at the disposal of the R.E.'s to assist them in keeping pace with their work on the divisional front. The First Surrey took its turn at this from January 29th till February 20th, during which time all but specially selected men, who were sent away on various forms of training courses, were employed on constructing light railways and any other of the jobs mentioned above. This duty, of course, involved long hours and hard work, but there was always the satisfaction of knowing that one had a dry billet to go back to for food and sleep!

During the next few weeks the Battalion participated in the usual routine of winter warfare, doing its tour of duty in one or other of the sectors for which the division was responsible between the Canal and Hill 60. The weather proved the most interesting topic of this period, for never before had we suffered such intense cold; the frost held for several weeks, and many and curious were the effects of this on our battalion life. In the first place, so hard was the ground that digging was quite out of the question for any purpose—a certain amount was done with the help of explosives, but this was of necessity difficult. Other features were the freezing of all water points save one, for some distance round Ypres, with the result that it took several hours to obtain even one cart full; freezing of the water in the cooling chambers of machine-guns, and the destruction by fire of a large number of shelters owing to the over-strenuous attempts of the occupants to get warm. More than one such fire occurred in Halifax Camp, much to the inconvenience of one or two individuals, who lost every scrap of their belongings except such as they actually had on them at the time. Night after night at this time, whole hutfuls of men were out and about at 2 or 3 a.m. in a vain effort to get warm: sleep was out of the question, and movement was the only possible way to keep the circulation going. Really the only redeeming feature was the fact that we actually had some sliding and skating in the very front line —this was at the head of "Petticoat Lane," where a large pool was frozen solid, and one sportsman had a brain-wave, and wrote home for his skates, which arrived in due course.

But with the warmer weather came a change in the programme for the battalion, for on March 24th the division was relieved, and we started on a march, extending over three days, which landed us in picturesque little Moulle, near St. Omer. We marched by way of Steenvoorde and Arneke, and very trying it was to the feet, after the winter of mud and frost in waterlogged and ice-bound trenches and camps: the change, nevertheless, was most welcome, and we looked forward to the training, no matter how strenuous, for were there not prospects of afternoon outings to St. Omer, and little gatherings at the Café Vincent, or some other such favourite rendezvous?

It was at Arneke that we first experienced summer time. Arriving late, after a long and dusty march, at our billets in scattered farm-houses, we failed to get our orders for the following morning's move till well after midnight. After the usual preamble, "The Battalion will form up facing North . . . . at 6.15 a.m."—we gave a groan even at this, but there was worse to follow—the end of orders introduced a G.R.O. : "In consequence of the coming into force of Summer Time, all clocks will be put forward one hour!" The net result was that we retired about 2 a.m. (Summer Time) and had to be up at 5—and *some* of us had sheets for the first time for months!

Although training and drills and all the rest of it started in earnest the day after we arrived at Moulle, we were not permitted to continue them for long; once again it was the weather which prevented an intelligent interest being taken in the work, and for the whole of that first week in April it seemed as though the rain and snow would never stop. However, our brief period away from the line was not to be wasted, for amongst other things there were all sorts of sports and competitions, in which the four companies competed for various championships. With these events and the usual inspections and entertainments, our stay at Moulle ended all too soon, and we again moved eastwards, halting for a couple of nights at Steenvoorde. By April 15th we were back again at Dickebusch, and on the following night relieved the 15th Battalion in our old front line trenches at Ravine Wood, where we spent an uneventful week working hard to keep the trenches in repair.

On being relieved in the front line, a pleasant surprise awaited us in the form of an unexpected journey by train back to Moulle for the special purpose of firing a musketry course—this was a specially cheery prospect, as we were one and all anticipating a somewhat wearisome tour in the trenches. Although our week at musketry was a pretty busy one, it was generally on occasions like this that one had time in which to think and, looking around, to realize what changes two years on active service could bring about in a battalion. Comparatively few of the officers and men who had embarked at Southampton were now with us—possibly about three officers and 100 other ranks. Casualties and sickness, of course, accounted for most of the missing ones, but there were other causes. The employment of men with special qualifications at one or other of the various headquarters in France, the granting of commissions to many of our N.C.O.'s, and the promotion and staff appointments which came to many of our officers were some of the other reasons for the changes.

It was about this time that the battalion sustained a great loss owing to the last-named reason. Lieut.-Colonel H. B. Kennedy, who had commanded us since the days of Loos, and had on many occasions deputised for the brigade commander, was now selected for the command of the 140th Infantry Brigade (one of the other brigades in our division). The First Surrey's love of and admiration for General Kennedy, who came to us as our adjutant in 1913, from the 60th Rifles, are too well known and too sincere to need description here, and the sorrow of losing him as our C.O., particularly as he was going to another brigade, was beyond words. All ranks realised that it was "K.K." who had made us the really efficient fighting machine which we undoubtedly were at this time, but beyond this he had in everything studied the comfort and welfare of his officers and men, and was never too busy to give his advice or help when they were sought (as they very often were). We all felt we were losing a personal friend, but there was one bright side to the picture that was apparent to us all, and that was the fact that General Kennedy had at last won the promotion we all knew he so richly deserved.

The new C.O. was one of the most senior and keenest of the old-time pre-war First Surrey officers, Major A. Hutchence, M.C., who, although wounded with the battalion at High Wood, was back again with us, and now realized what was probably the dream of his life. Many other changes had taken place in the personnel since we came to France, but to record them is obviously beyond the scope of a work like this.

To turn again to the current affairs of the time: it must not be forgotten that with the coming of the spring and the better weather, there always sprang up in those days of strife a wonderful crop of rumours about a "spring offensive." Our rapid departure for a course of rifle practice and thorough training in musketry had almost the effect of a patent manure on these "seedlings," and when, later on, we again came away from the trenches to practise an attack over a "flagged course," it was realized that this time it was truth, not rumour, and that we were "for it"! All this happened during the early part of the month of May, the end of which saw us back again in our old sector—a rejuvenated fighting unit truly thirsting for blood! We had not long to wait, for on the last day of May we again went back to spend a few days preparing for battle, it being known that our next tour of duty would include an attack on a large scale.

The battle of Messines, June 7th, 1917, in which General Plumer's Army (the 2nd) drove the Germans from the high ground south-east of Ypres in so short a time, is now generally recognized as one of the most highly organized and successful engagements of the War, and here again the First Surrey was privileged to take its share. The 47th Division, attacking with the 41st on its right and the 23rd on the left, was ordered to advance along the north bank of the Comines Canal, and swinging across the water north of Hollebeke, to take up a position commanding that village.

For this purpose the 140th Brigade was given the right of the line and our brigade (142nd) the left, the 141st being held in reserve. The attack of our brigade was divided into two phases, the 24th and 22nd Battalions taking the first phase, the 23rd and ourselves passing through them and going on to the final objective. The general character of the battle is well known—a five days' artillery bombardment of the enemy's trench system preceded the attack, and at zero hour (3.10 a.m. on the 7th) the colossal land mines at Hill 60, The Caterpillar, and St. Eloi (sixteen others went up at the same moment along the battle front) were exploded, and our infantry swarmed across No Man's Land. Stunned by the explosion of the mines and by the terrific barrage put down by our artillery, the Germans were not in a position to offer a very effectual resistance, and so far as our particular section of the front was concerned, the first phase went absolutely according to plan, and was a complete success. The First Surrey now took up the advance, and by 6.15 a.m. we had assumed our "jumping off" position in the newly captured trenches, with only sixteen casualties, which, considering the exposed nature of the advance and its length, was indeed light. From this position it was necessary for our men to make a half-right-wheel so that we might cross the canal along the left of which we had hitherto been advancing, but before we could do this we had to seize the enormous spoil-bank thrown up during the cutting of the canal : this was honeycombed with tunnels and concrete machine-gun emplacements, and as the artillery had unfortunately not been able to deal very effectively with these, the bank naturally formed a very formidable obstacle. The task with which the First Surrey was confronted was hardly an easy one, and still less will it appear so when one realizes that the troops on our left, in Battle Wood, had met with a very stiff resistance, and being unable to advance as fast as we had done, were now some distance behind us. This, of course, meant that the enemy machine-gun posts in Battle Wood were free to devote their attentions to us, and to fire into our flank and rear as we advanced.

Our first objective was a line of German trenches, somewhat irregular in alignment, known as Oaf Lane; this was captured and consolidated by A and C Companies within fifteen minutes, and Battalion advanced head-quarters were established in a former German command-post in this line. The advance was now to be continued by B and D Companies, and the spoil-bank mentioned above was to be seized by them. Accordingly, at 7.30 a.m., our leading platoons pushed forward in the face of heavy rifle and machine-gun fire to the nearest point of this objective, which was reached only after we had suffered heavy casualties. Here fighting continued throughout the morning, but it was impossible to seize the whole of the position, and it seemed only a matter of time before the enemy would, by bringing up reinforcements, be able to turn us off the small part we actually held. The situation at 9.30 seemed to be that our advanced platoons were holding the spoil-bank, and one party of about three officers and twenty men had succeeded in crossing the canal and establishing themselves in shell holes on the south bank, but so exposed were they, and so little good could they do there, that after waiting for possible developments they were compelled to withdraw again to the north bank. It was now forced in upon us that our left flank was dangerously exposed, and that to complete the capture of the spoil-bank was in the circumstances an impossibility. The divisional commander, in view of this and of the general situation on our flanks, decided to withdraw all our troops from the spoil-bank itself and to subject it to an intense artillery bombardment, this to be followed by a further attack by the First Surrey with reinforcements from the reserve brigade. The bombardment began at 2 p.m. and lasted till 7 in the evening, when our leading men, having been reinforced by two companies of the 20th London, were prepared for the further effort, but at the precise moment that we were to jump off, the Germans also put down an intensely heavy barrage, rendering any movement on our part absolutely out of the question. It was believed at the time that this barrage was the prelude to a heavy counter-attack on the enemy's part, but, however this may have been (and the point has not, so far as we know yet, been settled), no such counter-attack developed, being effectually quashed by *our* barrage—the effect being that both we and the Germans were forced to remain where we were!

During the night of the 7th/8th the Battalion was ordered to withdraw from the advanced positions it then held to the original German support line (i.e., Oaf Lane) and reorganize, at the same time putting this line in a thorough state of defence against possible counter-attack. That this was necessary was soon proved, for at 4 p.m. on the afternoon of the 8th, the Germans made a desperate attempt to retake our system and Battle Wood on our left; but this attempt failed, as did a further one some four hours later, and our new positions were then finally consolidated. Two points in these two days' fighting are worth recalling—our runners, who were always wonderful, simply surpassed themselves in this action, crossing and re-crossing without question long and exposed tracks (often there were no tracks at all) to our forward positions, or back to brigade under heavy artillery and rifle fire, and never once failing to carry out their job; the signallers, too, whilst it was humanly possible, kept their lines going in an almost incredible way. The other special feature was that a party of our Lewis gunners who had established themselves on the spoil-bank, and whom we failed to find when the withdrawal was ordered, remained in their position during the whole of our second bombardment, and it was not until after nightfall on the 7th that they were able to rejoin us. Poor Captain Perkins was badly wounded early on the 7th, on the far side of the canal, and we were unable to get him back till late that night; his death from his wounds (on the 8th) was a real loss to the Battalion. Our losses in this fighting were again heavy—seven officers and 237 men killed or wounded in the action itself, in addition to thirteen men killed and eleven wounded by one shell which, in Ypres, made a direct hit on the lorry which was bringing the party up to the forward area.

After holding the captured positions for another forty-eight hours, we handed over to the 19th London and returned to reserve positions in Old French Trench, to recuperate and snatch a few hours' rest. Two days later (June 12th) the division was relieved, and the First Surrey, after a three days' march, went into rest billets at Sercus to train and re-equip before taking further part in the fighting. The fortnight here was spent in early morning training, lasting from about 5.30 to 10 a.m., early dinners, and then sports or other amusements in the afternoon—small wonder that most of us were ready for "lights out" before the said lights had even been lit ! It was while resting at Sercus that we lost one of the best friends and the most popular officers the First Surrey ever had—"Doc." Robinson, who had been with us ever since we mobilized, and was respected and loved by us all, was at last selected for promotion, and left us to join a Field Ambulance. He had richly earned his promotion, but we hated losing him.

The Battalion next went into the line a little to the right of its previous trenches, and immediately south of the Ypres-Comines Canal, marching by way of Meteren and Ridge Wood, spending a night at the former place in billets, and at the latter in bivouac. Between July 1st and 25th the Battalion wavered between front line trenches immediately north and south of the canal, and support positions, or reserve billets at Ontario Camp, close by the village of Ouderdom. It was during this period that we (and we were one of the first units in the British Army to come across this new horror) experienced a new form of poisonous gas—known as "mustard gas"—the after-effects of which were worse and more painful than those of the gases hitherto used. On July 18th sixty-six men went down with this particular form of poisoning! There was but little artillery fire, and practically no infantry fighting in this sector, yet, such are the ways of war, it was in this comparatively quiet spot that our padre, the Rev. B. P. Plumptre, was killed by a stray shell whilst visiting one of our companies in the line in front of "White Château." His death robbed the Battalion of a character and personality not easily replaced, and there was not one of us who did not feel that he had lost a real and personal friend. His bravery and unselfishness were remarkable, but his outstanding characteristic was undoubtedly his faith in his religion—a faith which very many of us felt *must* bring him safely through everything. He is gone, but we look back with pride and respect to his unfailing cheeriness, his gallant deeds on many battlefields, his untiring efforts and ready help in billets or on the march, and to his real and true friendship to all ranks under all conditions throughout his sojourn with the First Surrey. A service to our padre's memory, held a few days after we got out of the trenches, was attended by the whole Battalion, as well as by many men from other units of the brigade and division.

August 1st, 1917, found us comfortably encamped in the little Flemish village named Heksken—the term "comfortably" is used in a merely comparative sense of course, for during this month there were certainly many discomforts. Even *occasional* air raids are generally admitted to be annoying, but when these annoyances occur nightly, and the only protection one possesses is that afforded by the canvas of a bell tent, the effect is increased somewhat! Then to add to our troubles the weather was distinctly wet, with the result that very little military training of any real value was possible. A move on August 8th took us to a camp at Dickebusch, much nearer the line, where the conditons, both as to bombing and the weather, were worse than at Heksken. Our transport and stores were stationed in a hutted camp near Reninghelst, which suffered even more than we did from the attentions of enemy aircraft. It was in this camp on August 10th that we lost another of our old friends in the person of our quarter-master, Lieut. F. C. Jackson, better remembered by old members of the First Surrey as our regimental sergeant-major. He came to us from the East Surrey Regiment in pre-war days, went through our mobilized training and two and a half years' active service with us, and now, whilst asleep, fell a victim to a German air bomb, which smashed up the hut in which he lay, wounding at the same time Lieut. S. Persse, our transport officer. A perfect gentleman, a gallant soldier, and a wonderful quartermaster (what he couldn't get for the Battalion might almost be said not to exist!) Lieut. Jackson was yet another of the little band which, in spite of heavy losses and the consequent new blood, had kept going throughout the years of fighting, and had handed on to newcomers the genuine First Surrey traditions and spirit. We buried him in the military cemetery behind the church in Reninghelst.

The dislocation of battalion services which might easily have resulted from the bombing of Ontario Camp was entirely avoided by the splendid work of Regimental Quartermaster-Sergeant R. Martin, and his promotion and appointment as quartermaster was a source of very great satisfaction to us all.

On August 12th the Battalion was relieved by the 14th Hants, and marched to York Camp, which it left on the 17th, and entrained at Abeele for St. Omer. From St. Omer we marched to Moringhem, where we remained in billets for about a week.

The latter part of August and early September were marked by further changes at battalion head-quarters. In the first place we lost Lieut.-Colonel Hutchence. He was, as has already been noted, one of those officers of the Battalion who had been wounded in the action at High Wood on the Somme: he had strenuously (and successfully) opposed being "evacuated" to England, rejoining the Battalion at the earliest possible moment after being discharged from hospital in France. The actual physical trials of service in the Salient were by no means salutary for anyone, and Colonel Hutchence's health had for some time been suffering; an opportunity for giving him some well-earned rest was therefore being sought. His orders arrived on August 23rd, when he left us at Moringhem, being shortly afterwards appointed to the command of a battalion in Ireland.

The Battalion was parading to move "up" again when this loss fell upon it, leaving Major Heslop in command, with Major Walford as second-in-command, and on August 27th it found itself in the front line on Westhoek

Ridge, battalion head-quarters occupying an old German "pill-box," which had somehow acquired the curious name of "Kit and Kat."

On the 29th Major Walford was ordered away to take over as second-in-command to another unit, and on the following day his place with us was taken by Major Tolerton of the 23rd London, an old and popular friend of the First Surrey Rifles.

It could scarcely be said that there were any pleasant positions in the whole Salient, especially in wet weather, but Westhoek Ridge was generally voted to be "the limit" for discomfort, though the very excess of mud and water, and the attentions bestowed mutually by the enemy and ourselves brought at times their own "light relief."

We were not sorry to be moved to dry quarters in Ypres on the night of September 1st. On the 4th we came to billets at Steenvoorde, where Major Heslop fell sick on the 7th, and was removed to hospital at Poperinghe.

On September 16th a welcome change came for the Battalion: it was to leave the Salient. So, after eleven months in that abomination of desolation, we made our preparations in common with other units of the division for a journey to another part of the fighting line, on being transferred to the First Army once again.

The transfer of a complete division from the command of one army to that of another was not always without difficuty, but now, after our years of practice, it had become a mere matter of routine, although, looked at from the view-point of the private soldier, it was hardly the same manœuvre as in the eyes of the higher command! In this instance probably few of the fighting men knew what was happening, where we were going, or what the move meant—it was just another series of marches, billets, inspections, cleaning up, and then marching again. Three days of this brought us from Château Segard (just outside Ypres) via Wippenhoek and Eecke to Bavinchove, where, on September 23rd, we entrained for the billeting area of the First Army.

CHAPTER VII.

September 24th, 1917, to December 31st, 1917.

Oppy, Hindenburg Line, Bourlon Wood.

The turn of the wheel, or the machinations of G.H.Q., brought us back to the neighbourhood of Arras, which, to those who knew it, seemed even more battered than they had known it before. The line ahead of us, which was to occupy our attention for the next two months, had come into our hands during the aftermath of the Easter offensive; Gavrelle on the right had fallen on St. George's Day, and on the left the strenuous efforts of the 2nd, and later the 5th, Divisions had secured a position half in and half out of Oppy Wood.

On September 24th we took over in the Red (reserve) line, and reconciled ourselves to heavy calls for working parties; at this duty we were unfortunate two days later in losing Lieuts. Squibb and Roberts, wounded, the latter succumbing to his wounds. On the 28th Major Heslop came back and resumed command. October 2nd found us in the front line on the left, and we made acquaintance with the post system prevailing in the sector. Once there, the ideal thing was to stay there. The communication trenches, especially on the left, were more like half-set toffee than anything man was meant to walk in, and the lateral connecting trenches were either broken down or non-existent—an ideal playground for people like Lieut. Gilkes and Corporal Tidmarsh, who excelled in practising the Napoleonic maxim of moving on their stomachs—but a source of anxiety to Battalion head-quarters, when they had to take General Gorringe round; he *would* see all there was to be seen, and appeared to be reversing the former's methods of securing identifications by putting his head well up and having a sniff at the opposing lines. As ever, he was indefatigable, and no persuasion would prevent him from making his way up the stickiest communication trenches.

Relief by the 8th Battalion sent us back to Maroeuil on the 10th. Disturbances in a neighbouring Chinese labour camp called for an armed guard; this and cable parties helped to lessen our chances of training, which was carried on, however, with the available men. We managed, nevertheless, to get in some football in the afternoons, and the mill buildings provided a theatre for the "Follies."

It had been obvious for some time that Major Heslop was working himself to a standstill, and that his health would not bear the strain much longer. Of those suggested by G.H.Q. for the command, the only name which was known by any of the staff was that of Major G. Dawes (S. Staffordshire Regt.) whom Colonel Turner (the G.1) had known as a company officer in Cameroons. Since leaving that campaign he had spent nearly a year in France with the 2nd Division, during which time he had commanded the 2nd Battalion of his own regiment for about nine months. Having been hit on the head in the early morning before the taking of Gavrelle, he had just returned to France, and on being posted to us, came back to the line in the very sector in which he had been hit. He arrived on October 13th.

There were performances of the "Follies" during our stay in reserve, and a boxing show, at which Riflemen Scoggins and Hardy distinguished themselves. Captain Stickland was at this time answering for both the transport officer and the quartermaster, and carried on their good work on brick-floored horse standings and an up-to-date cookhouse at the transport lines. Lieut. Martin got back from leave in time for the Major-General's inspection, when the work was highly commended.

The immediate necessity was to settle on the personnel of the new battalion head-quarters; a relief had to be found for Major Heslop, who was destined for work at divisional head-quarters, and there was no permanent adjutant. When Major Dawes arrived, Major Tolerton had been acting second-in-command to Major Heslop, and Captain Turner, who had been acting adjutant, had handed over to the assistant-adjutant, Lieut. Hollands, on going to Brigade. Fortunately we were able to retain the services of both Major Tolerton and Captain Turner, who took up the duties of their appointments at once. Both were old friends of the Battalion, though belonging to the 23rd. Later Lieut. Hollands took over transport officer, after Captain Eastwood went on a staff course, and was brigade and battalion transport officer until he left to go to the Indian Army.

The winter programme had now come fairly into force, and between the post scheme in the line and camp improvements behind, we began to feel a proprietary interest in the sector. While we were in at Gavrelle the 23rd and 24th Battalions carried out a most successful evening raid, taking fifteen prisoners and inflicting many casualties. During the raid we withdrew on one company front from the front line, and put up an assortment of fireworks. Lieut. Chambers was very slightly hit in the face, and was extremely indignant at being reported "wounded and at duty" as he protested that he had often hurt himself worse shaving. We now had eight days in reserve at Wakefield camp, and before going in on the left (November 13th) the officers beat the sergeants at football by two goals to one.

In the Oppy sector there was much work to be done on the posts, and the tour was conspicuous for continuous patrolling of No Man's Land. Lieut. Gilkes and his satellites sported in the German front line by day. On one occasion he was advancing in snake formation towards the enemy wire when he looked round and became aware of Corporal Tidmarsh's conspicuous head, with no hat on, just behind him; resourceful as ever, he at once crowned him king of No Man's Land with a huge tussock of grass. In the night, patrolling usually included an inspection of the "Willows," on our left front, and one such visit must be recorded, as it afterwards supplied a war song and dance for "B" and "D" Companies' officers. Lieut. Elkington, who was not in the front line at the time, was to command the patrol, and as it was a pitchy night, he went ahead to get the exact direction of the "Willows" from the front line company commander. This was Captain Wilson of "D," who, jaded with digging in his portion of the "winter garden," peremptorily ordered the nearest sentry to fire Vérey lights in the required direction, and to go on firing them till the officer expressed himself satisfied. The verse was sung to the tune of the "Queen's" march past, and after wishing "jolly good luck" to the patrol commander, ended up—

"Where are the weelows?
Put up a Vérey light and see,
A light and see-e-e-e,
Elkie ——————."

(the last note could only be achieved by skilled vocalists!)

On relief by the 31st Division we returned to Wakefield camp to criticize the improvements made during our absence, but not for long. We were for a move again. The cooker, the aid post, the sanitary squad, and the church, alike agreed that it must, and should, be Italy. Not us! Following the 2nd Division, who followed the Guards, we made our way by march route, through the filthy weather from which we had suffered for weeks, to the Cambrai front. On the 25th we were badly held up at Bapaume, as the three divisions

F

apparently converged on the railway crossing, by two different roads and the railway. During the long wait, however, we were cheered up by the appearance of General Kennedy, who had not seen the Battalion for some weeks, and who rode past chaffing old friends. It was here that Colonel Dawes made his acquaintance, having only met him previously in conversation on the telephone, and the fact that the General's horse presented one of its shoes (complete with foot) to Colonel Dawes, could only be taken as a token of good luck!

We got into Barastre eventually, settled down as night fell, and prepared to see the last of the "battle surplus." The officers' messes met up in a single hut at a late hour of night, and before closing down there were several minutes' intense noise. Conducted by Captain Stickland, "B" and "D" officers gave the "Elkie" chorus many times over, and "A" and "C" replied no less indefatigably with a new turn, sung to the tune of "A perfect day," which began—

> "We are the boys from Camberwell,
> Who come from the Flodden Road . . ."

After everybody had sung both choruses several times, to say nothing of sundry others, the party broke up to avoid an official complaint from our neighbours. Anyone less forbearing than Colonel Greenwood, of the 22nd, would not have stood it.

Next morning the battle surplus, under Major Tolerton, left for Mailly-Maillet, and on the following morning the Battalion moved forward again to Beaumetz, and the final preparations for taking part in the battle were made.

On the night of the 28th we made our way through the battery positions to the sector allotted to us in the Hindenburg support line. It was a strange position, and "pick and shovel" immediately became the order of the day. Except round the entrances of the dug-out workings—many of them incomplete—the trench was non-existent, being merely cut out to the depth of a few inches. There were also several deep square excavations, already fitted with reinforcing iron, ready to become concrete dug-outs.

It was an amazingly interesting position, with the marks of battle fresh upon it. The scene on our right showed us the perils of the tank, when favourably placed artillery could get its range, and we sympathized with the newest arm for the bad time it had had round Flesquières. But around us in our own sector were the tracks of the tank triumphant. Wide easy roadways, a joy to assaulting infantry, were crushed through the tremendous wire belts of the Hindenburg line. If a fillip were needed to moral, the evidence of the enormous assistance given by this auxiliary arm would have supplied it. None such was required, however; the Battalion was on the top of its form, and in the best possible condition to meet the strenuous doings of the next three weeks.

That the time ahead of us *would* be strenuous there could be no doubt. From our position in the Hindenburg support line we could see all the battle past Graincourt and Anneux to Bourlon Wood. The fighting of the 30th was terrific, and it was only too obvious from the preparations to withdraw the artillery from the plain if necessary, that our tenure of the line in the Bourlon salient was far from certain, and also that the attacks from Moeuvres to Bourlon were of the heaviest. These attacks were meant to turn into a disaster the reverse we suffered that day at Gouzeaucourt—a reverse which was checked, and in great measure retrieved, mainly by the Guards, supported by our own artillery. We were fortunately unaware that the divisional commander was affectionately examining his revolver, as an aeroplane message dropped at his head-quarters had informed him that the enemy was advancing *behind him* on Metz-en-Couture.

Although the recapture of Gouzeaucourt relieved the division of the most pressing danger of being cut off altogether, the position in the Bourlon salient was still critical. There was every prospect of a repetition of the attempts to regain the wood, which had been frustrated to a great extent by the gallantry of Colonel Segrave and the Civil Service Rifles. This battalion, though hanging on determinedly to the positions in and on the left of the wood, which it had maintained, was hardly strong enough numerically—not to mention its fatigue—to stand a further assault on such a scale. Its relief by the First Surrey Rifles on the evening of December 1st had accordingly been provided for, and the necessary orders had been issued, when a further complication arose.

It was considered essential to provide against a possible resumption of the German counter attack, which might occur before the relief could be carried out. The C.O. went forward to the advanced brigade head-quarters, and saw Generals Erskine and Kennedy, and it was decided that he should arrange for the reconnaissance of two positions, one in the right rear, and one in the left rear, of Bourlon Wood; either of the positions was to be taken up in accordance with the requirements of the moment, and it was to be arranged later whether the position was to serve as a jumping-off place for a counter attack to re-establish the line, should it be pierced, or as a defensive flank to protect the retirement of the garrison of the wood should either flank be irretrievably broken. Positions were to be taken up on receipt of orders, "reinforce right," or "reinforce left."

The reconnaissances were carried out under Lieut. Jackman, who brought back to head-quarters gloomy accounts of the two positions, which, from the state of the ground, were obviously marks for the enemy artillery. Of two bad positions, that on the right was far the worse.

The First Surrey Rifles was to leave its positions in the Hindenburg support line immediately after dark, and to pick up its guides from the 15th at the head-quarters of the front brigades. The company commanders had assembled at battalion head-quarters to get the last news about conditions in the wood, at about 4 o'clock, and there had been report of a disturbance in the front line in the direction of Fontaine. Before they dispersed, a cancellation of the relief order arrived and no surprise was felt when "reinforce right" followed, but the atmosphere was brightened by some lurid language.

The colonel and adjutant set off at once for the brigade head-quarters, and the companies followed. On his arrival the C.O. was told by General Erskine that the S.O.S. in Fontaine had turned out to be a false alarm, that he could consider the "reinforce right" order cancelled, and had better go and see General Kennedy about carrying on with the relief of the 15th. It was a great "let off," as no one looked forward with pleasure to the other job. The 15th guides were found and attached to our companies as they arrived; even then all was not plain sailing, as the night was very dark, the guides very tired, and the ground not very familiar to them. However, the left-hand corner of the wood served as a land mark, and was frequently visible by the light of bursting shells and Vérey lights. The relief was carried out without much incident, and none too soon; the casualties had been most severe, and Colonel Segrave—himself badly gassed—was the only officer left who had gone in with head-quarters; a corporal was answering for his regimental sergeant-major.

The position was about as unpleasant as had been described. Most of the time it stank of gas, and the enemy periodically put down a gas and high explosive barrage on the line of battalion head-quarters and the reserve company. Great activity was essential in the front line, as the Germans were constantly feeling forward from Bourlon village, and our front was only kept clear by constant patrolling. It was very difficult to get to and from the front line by day, and a great deal of responsibility devolved upon Captain Stickland—the senior company commander in front—who established a great reputation during the time that followed, particularly the next night, when the battalion on our left carried out a small operation to improve its positions. Captain Stickland gave valuable assistance in the consolidation of the new line, so much so, that when the 8th were relieved, the C.O. sent his adjutant across to say he could not leave the front line without formally thanking the Battalion for the assistance rendered during the operation. To everybody's satisfaction, Captain Stickland was subsequently given the Military Cross.

During this period the transport took the opportunity of distinguishing themselves. Sergeant Reid brought up his limbers through the "evening hate," which happened to be unusually unpleasant, drew up at battalion head-quarters, unloaded his rations, reloaded with empty water tins, and got clear in three minutes. One horse was slightly wounded on the return journey, close to the Cambrai-Bapaume road. After something of a tussle with the corps commander, the Military Medal was secured for Sergeant Reid and two of the drivers.

The story of this great fight, in which the Battalion took part, was written and issued officially, and full credit given to the magnificent efforts of the 2nd, 47th, and 56th Divisions, and while the county regiments in the 2nd Division were not forgotten, it was felt to have been, to a great extent, a "London" achievement.

Meanwhile, the position on December 4th was still very precarious, and it was obvious that unless very considerable reinforcements could be provided, it could not be improved, or indeed even maintained, without heavy loss. The very pronounced salient was kept continually under a heavy bombardment of high explosive and gas; twice, if not three times, the front entrance of battalion head-quarters was seriously knocked about, and some of the head-quarters staff, who went about their daily occupations at the bottom of the stairs, suffered considerably in health. Dyer, the cook, was badly upset by the fumes of the explosion, and it was weeks, if not months, before Tidy could announce the C.O.'s bath in anything but a hoarse croak. Another casualty from a similar cause was Captain Wilson of "D" company, who, in addition to ordinary gas, was choked by the fumes of an erratic Vérey light which is said to have chased him round his head-quarters ! That company, as well as head-quarters, spent practically the whole period from the 1st to the 4th in an atmosphere more or less charged with di-phosgene. So it happened that early in the afternoon on the 4th, orders came for the C.O. to attend a conference at Brigade. Here instructions were issued for a withdrawal from the Bourlon salient. The First Surrey Rifles was to evacuate its position at mid-night, leaving such a party as was considered necessary in the front line to deceive the enemy as to our movements.

On the way back to head-quarters, Sergeant Dew of the runners began to display a propensity for falling about, which later became most unfortunate. About a quarter of a mile from head-quarters the party, consisting of the C.O., Sergeant Dew, and a couple of runners who were returning from duty at brigade head-quarters, had put on their gas masks. Suddenly the C.O. discovered that he was alone, and on further investigation, found himself standing on the edge of an enormous shell crater, with the rest of the party tied in knots at the bottom. When they had extricated themselves they all committed the irregularity—in which the C.O. joined them—of taking off their masks, and the party raced for head-quarters. It was justified. The Bosche was putting down a most intensive hate, and that part of the country-side was no place to linger in, and to pick one's way amongst the shell holes was too slow to be safe. Sergeant Dew eventually, during the evacuation, tripped half-way down the steep side of the sunken road near Anneux chapel, and broke his leg on arrival at the bottom.

The salvage of ammunition and materials before leaving the wood was principally in the hands of Captain Turner; it was a necessary but arduous duty, and for the able and energetic manner in which it was carried out, together with the acts of gallantry and devotion to duty performed while the Battalion held this most dangerous position, Captain Turner received a well merited award of the M.C. Two others were granted, to the younger Lieut. Edmunds and Lieut. Crowther, to whose platoons was allotted the dangerous task of remaining for three hours in the front line, after the Battalion had been withdrawn, as a screen to hide our movements from the enemy. The normal duties of the front line garrison were carried out by these two platoons, and the enemy was completely deceived—indeed, it was some time before the men of the platoons themselves realized the true state of affairs.

Meanwhile, the line, with the four companies in depth, had been re-established in the Hindenburg support line, and outpost positions. After a short period for necessary rest, the men were turned on by reliefs to put the new line in a proper state of defence. It was a great relief when the last of the Bourlon garrison were reported in. The period from December 1st had been a trying one, and we had suffered many casualties from gas and high explosive, as well as those inseparable from front line work where patrolling was incessant and the enemy active. Shortly before the bulk of the Battalion left the wood, Lieut. Hunt was mortally wounded and succumbed almost immediately; Captain Stickland, reporting his death at battalion head-quarters before the retirement, stated that it was uncertain whether he had not been shot from our own lines. Hunt was, at the time, commanding a patrol between our lines and the enemy, and returned to our front line at a time when firing was going on from both sides, and the patrol was thus exposed to a double danger. Space has been given to the details of this casualty because what was described and reported at the time as a matter of doubt was spoken of later in England as a matter of fact; whatever doubt may have existed, one thing is certain : the risks run by this patrol were identical with those to which all patrols were exposed : the duty it performed was an essential one : and an officer who met his death by being exposed to our fire died in defence of the line as surely as if he had been killed in an encounter with an enemy patrol, or by a chance shot from the German lines.

December 5th was spent in consolidation, and at night the C.O. went back to the transport to get over a mixed attack of malaria and gas, and until his return on the 7th the command devolved on Major Tolerton, who had come up from the battle surplus. When the C.O. got back Captain Turner was sent down for a rest, and Major Tolerton took over his duties. The enemy meantime had occupied Graincourt, and was pushing along the Hindenburg support on our left towards our point of junction with the 23rd Battalion. The 8th was comparatively quiet, and our work little interrupted. One difficulty recurred nightly at this time, and that was the guiding of the ration parties of "A" Company to the post held by that company in the old double-brigade head-quarters. These parties were continually going astray, and always Lieut. Gilkes was appealed to when other guides had failed to find the post.

On the 9th the enemy at last made up his mind to test the strength of the positions we had been consolidating since the morning of the 5th. The brunt of the attack was borne by the 23rd Battalion oupost on our left front, known afterwards, from the name of its gallant defender, as Durrant's post.

At 7 a.m. the enemy succeeded in occupying part of the post, but touch was shortly re-established. It was very difficult to gather from our lines what was happening to our left front, as the enemy had taken advantage of the unoccupied sunken road and trenches to our front, and after the original assault, attacks, which succeeded in cutting off our advanced parties from the post, were made by these channels, and not "over the top."

About 11 o'clock a scheme was drawn up at brigade headquarters by Captain Peel, the Brigade Major, Colonel Dawes, and the artillery liaison officer at Brigade, by which a party of the First Surrey Rifles was to try to ease the situation. The scheme was then put before the Brigadier, who approved of the attempt being made. A heavy crash was to be put down on the sunken road, and under covering artillery fire, an attempt was to be made to seize this and to set up a post to cover it. It was felt that at the best this move might restore the line, and that at the worst such a diversion would reduce the pressure on Durrant's post, and render possible a reconstruction of the line under more favourable conditions. When the advance was made two hours later, the latter event was practically what occurred. Unfortunately, several of our own shells fell actually in the post, and Captain Durrant had no alternative but to evacuate his wounded and relinquish the post.

Meanwhile, the attacking party had actually reached the sunken road, but the artillery fire had not succeeded in knocking out the machine guns there, and the party, receiving heavy casualties, was forced to retire, without being able to set up the new post. A position was, however, established for a time, half-way between the sunken road and our front line, which undoubtedly assisted the 23rd in their retirement to their own front. It was a costly attempt, and one of the officers killed was Lieut. Richmond of the First Surrey.

At the same time an incident occurred which must be recorded. Sergeant Alexander, who had been wounded in the thigh, had gone back to the aid post to be dressed; he was waiting with other casualties to be sent down the line, when he heard of the operation which was taking place. He could not be away from his company at such a time, and slipped away to the front line. He arrived in time to see our repulse from the objective, and observing some of the enemy who, confident with success, were following up over the open, he called on a few men close by to follow him, and charged with the bayonet. The charge was a complete success and the enemy party was routed, but the brave sergeant was killed, his name appearing in the next despatch. The act, however, was a wonderful example; it had the most inspiriting effect on men already tired out with their long tour in the line and the fatigues and hardships of their tenure of Bourlon Wood, and disappointed, too, at their lack of success in this operation.

The loss of Durrant's post made it necessary to withdraw our distant outposts, and concentrate on our main line, which was by now in a fair state of defence, after five nights of digging and wiring. Orders were received that Lieut. Edmunds should evacuate the post in the old brigade headquarters in the early hours of the following morning, and later that a party of sappers was to go out that night and arrange for the destruction of the post. It was not known then that the dug-outs had already been prepared for demolition.

Some hitch occurred in the despatch of the demolition party, and it was only after the garrison got back that they learned that such a party should have arrived, and reported that it had not done so. The men of the post were laden with S.A.A. and grenades, but even so a fairly large amount had had to be left behind.

The failure to demolish the post left us in a very awkward position. We could not hand over the sector with the dug-outs in so strong a post left intact; it seemed almost certain that the Germans would lose no time in establishing themselves there, and the brigadier insisted that it must be raided and destroyed. As the men were very tired, and suffering from their long gassing and exposure, he agreed to gamble on the chance of the evacuation not having been observed, and to let us first attempt the destruction with a small patrol. The chances of success seemed slender, as enemy planes, flying low, had been over the post that morning.

It was arranged for Lieut. Gilkes to pick a small party, and to take out a supply of phosphorous bombs immediately after dusk. He went out early in the evening with Corporal Tidmarsh, Lance-Corporal Browett, and Rifleman Chivers. They carried thirty-six "P" bombs between them.

Success was complete; the woodwork of the dug-outs was well alight before the patrol left, and subsequently the front line sentries reported an explosion and clouds of smoke from the direction of the post. Fortune favoured us at two points. As Lieut. Gilkes's party was setting about the work of destruction, two men of the front line company appeared and reported themselves. They had got separated from a ration party the previous night, had crossed the front line without realizing where they were, had wandered about in the direction of Graincourt till just before dawn, when they found themselves at the post with its signs of recent occupation, and being overtaken by daylight, had found out where they had got to, and made up their minds to stay there till night. No doubt they had been spotted by the German airmen, who had taken them for sentries, and reported the post still occupied.

The second piece of luck was that the post had already been prepared for demolition, and when the woodwork blazed up, the destruction was rendered more complete.

Nevertheless, it was a dangerous undertaking, daringly carried out, and the awards given were well deserved. Lieut. Gilkes got a bar to his M.C., the two N.C.O.s bars to their M.M.s, and the rifleman a Military Medal.

At last, on the 12th, we were relieved, the 23rd Royal Fusiliers of the 2nd Division taking over the left portion of the line.

On withdrawing to brigade reserve, we were bivouacked beside the 23rd Battalion, sharing a head-quarters with them for three days, until we were relieved by the 7th Battalion and marched to Bertincourt, where we were one night in divisional reserve. Early next morning we marched to Velu, where we entrained and proceeded to Aveluy. Thence we marched to Laviéville, through the snow for the last two or three miles, and got into billets at dusk. The next few days were spent in completing, to our satisfaction, a degree of cleaning up which it was impossible to achieve in bivouac, and in getting as comfortable as possible in billets. But, of course, the most important thing in the near future was the proper celebration of Christmas, and as we were now in corps reserve we were even able to allow our minds to run on this vital question to some purpose.

To make the Christmas dinner a success a fund had been started in London to supplement our ordinary fare, and to provide decorations and so on; gifts from many generous friends of the regiment had been received by Miss Dawes, a cousin of the C.O., who had kindly undertaken to acknowledge these donations and pay them into the bank. The result was a dinner worthy of the occasion, and surroundings worthy of the dinner. On Christmas Eve the band toured the village, beginning at brigade head-quarters as dinner started, going on to the head-quarters of the Battalion a few doors away, and enlivening each officers' mess in turn with their well-known répertoire, interlarded with Christmas carols. After the band had retired, a rival party turned out about midnight, and serenaded battalion head-quarters, singing what they supposed to be carols. Either the education of the singers was incomplete, or they had forgotten most of what they knew. However, a good will and plenty of "la la" made up for deficiencies. One sentence, not specially applicable to the festive season was plainly heard; it was, "He's deaf ear up; sing well into the window." After which it was no good the victim pretending to be asleep any longer!

So much for the Christmas holiday, which was generally voted a success.

We got in as much training as we could in the inclement weather, and after a divisional conference at Baisieux, at which the change of situation caused by the collapse of Russia was explained by the divisional commander, a counter-attack scheme was carried out. The scheme was very valuable in view of the fact that everyone was inclined to get obsessed with the rather artificial tactics of position warfare; it was of special interest to the signallers and runners, and proved that they had not got out of touch with open warfare routine during a phase of operations in which their work was confined almost entirely to telephone and running. At the same time a hint was received that we could not be always holiday-making, as we were put on four hours' notice to move.

The blow fell on the 30th; in the evening orders arrived to entrain at Albert at 9.30 p.m. We had a rush for it. The roads were distressing for infantry and the next thing to impossible for transport. Just the right amount of traffic over just the right amount of snow had rendered the roads so slippery that it was a case of two paces forward to one and a half back. Still, we reached the gates of Albert station —closed against us, by the way—at exactly 9.30 p.m.—we just did it. It was not the same as being ready to entrain at that hour—it was not really up to time—but it was so much better than some of our neighbours that we felt there was no need for complaint. Nor was there, for at best our trains were not ready, and we had time to be reduced to chilled meat before starting a nightmare-cold journey that landed us at Etricourt just before dawn. What a journey! and what an arrival!

Our new billets were tents that had been bombed by enemy aircraft. Every one had holes in it, and every one had had the door flaps left open—with the snow nearly a foot deep on the ground, many of the tents contained drifts to the height of thirty inches. One thing we were thankful for—we had not got astray from our rations. Later in the morning, when the head-quarter mess had breakfasted, the colonel and second-in-command met General Bailey in Etricourt; the brigade mess-carts had gone astray, and the staff had spent the night in an empty hut with no beds, and nothing but their overcoats, and no breakfast. He was led protesting up to our hill-side, to finish off the breakfast bacon, and first walked through the camp, discreetly and mercifully looking the other way when he passed things being broken up for the fire which had no business to be burned by any well-ordered battalion. However, the one necessary which was hopelessly lacking was fuel, and it was better to court censure than to freeze.

Two new-comers to the Battalion felt they had joined us at an unlucky time; one was Dr. Pollard, an American M.O., who had just come, and the other was the Rev. Mr. Sillitoe, the padre, who had replaced Marshall on Christmas Eve. The former left us invalided from the Ribécourt line, and the later was with us until, at the re-shuffle on reduction, we went to the 140th Brigade and the Rev. A. R. Browne-Wilkinson joined us. Perhaps Padre Sillitoe will forgive the repetition of a story sometimes told by the C.O. on his behalf: On cold, dark evenings, when we were out of the line, the C.O. would sometimes while away the long half hour before we dined by what he called "shaking a cocktail." It was a succulent but innocuous mixture that resulted; the only harm it was ever known to do was when the cork came out suddenly and scattered sticky whiteness on the shaker's clothes! On one such occasion at Lechelle the C.O. summoned Sergeant Huish and demanded gin, angostura, soda, ideal milk, sugar, perhaps just a glass of Cointreau, and one empty bottle with cork. The shaking had been going on for some time and most of the ingredients were in, the gramophone was playing the tune of the moment, and the padre, apparently taking no interest in the proceedings, was discoursing on "Why big guns go bang," or "What the Oxford movement means to Putney." He suddenly broke off and remarked, "Now you want the gin," and stretching out for the bottle, handed over the one missing ingredient. "Good heavens, padre," said the C.O., "when did *you* give up being a bar-tender?" and Sillitoe had the grace to look abashed at the indignant reproof he received from the assembled party.

We never knew what it was to have a "dud" padre. Every one we had was out to do his job or help with other people's, always and anywhere. During the last year or so all the chaplains actually living with the Battalion were Church of England, but there were others who will not readily be forgotten; amongst them was Williamson, who, if the Church knows him as "Father Benedict," cannot conceivably be known in military history as anything but "Old Happy Days."

So ended a momentous year. After giving us in the Cambrai show as hot a time as the division ever had, it offered us a distinctly chilly farewell.

CHAPTER VIII.

January 1st, 1918, to July 11th, 1918.

The Cambrai Salient and the German Advance.

New Year's Day found us still on our snowy hillside. It was an enemy attack on the 23rd Division on the Welsh Ridge that had caused us to be pulled from our billets, and though the more important ground lost had been regained, it was thought necessary to have another reserve brigade nearer the line. On January 1st the battalion commanders reconnoitred possible counter-attack routes over the Highland Ridge in the direction of Villers Plouich. Once in the forward area we did not expect to be long out of the line, and sure enough, on the 3rd we moved up into shelters and bivouacs in Havrincourt Wood, reconnoitred the front line on the following day, and at night took over in the line at Ribécourt.

The front line, with detached posts in front of it, gave fine observation to the right and left of Orival Wood. There was an extensive No Man's Land, which necessitated constant and vigorous patrolling, though the enemy was rarely encountered. Works consisted for the the most part in the construction of a trench which was to join our forward posts with the Flesquières line on the left through Beetroot Factory. Work on the trenches was very difficult. They were deep in snow, and in front trenchboards were lacking. As long as it froze we were all right, but constant short thaws made it impossible to keep clean or dry. It was the kind of weather when "trench foot" was hard to combat. Constant applications of whale oil and mustard, daily changes of socks, and as much hot food as it was possible to get up to the front line during the night did a little, but only a little, to make the conditions tolerable. Fortunately, as far as food was concerned, there were facilities for preparing and heating it at Ribécourt village. The battalion head-quarters unit was housed in the brewery, and the officers had a little room leading off the main cellar. Near by was a tumble-down house which made an excellent soup kitchen, and there was a good water supply handy. We had a visit from the corps commander, one result of which was that the awards for the transport men for Bourlon Wood were secured.

The alarms and excursions which were to trouble us until our advance in August now began, and early one morning, an attack being expected, our guns filled Orival Wood with gas in case it was being used as a forming-up position. All things considered we were not sorry to be relieved by the 6th Battalion and to get back to some degree of warmth at Lechelle, where we had a chance to get clean.

On January 18th we went back to the line, further left, in Flesquières. Posts—somewhat detached—were in the village and in the low ground to its left and front. We had an uneventful tour, the principal feature being careful reconnaissances with a view to raiding some old gun pits in front of our left sector, which the enemy had occupied and was consolidating. Most of the patrol work was done by Lieut. J. M. Alison, but the raid was never carried out. There was a very good soup kitchen and gumboot store in the cellars of the Red Château, which was a great aid to comfort for front line troops and working parties. We went out of the line on the 24th, and that day Major Bury came from the Royal Welsh Fusiliers to take command while the C.O. went on leave. This was necessary, as at Lechelle Major Tolerton had left us for the senior officers' school in England, and no second-in-command had been appointed. Major Tolerton was a great loss, but it could not be expected that an officer of his ability, with all the experience he had gained at the front, would remain a second-in-command for ever.

Training for counter-attack, and work on the rear defensive lines now occupied most of our time, and with the exception of twelve days in the line, from February 2nd to the 14th, we were constantly employed on these duties, being housed in huts at Barastre, Bertincourt, and Equancourt.

Meantime the Battalion had changed its master owing to the reduction of divisions, which was necessitated by the dearth of recruits from England. We were sorry to leave our old brigade and General Bailey, but it was a great consolation that the change brought us under the command of General Kennedy, always a firm friend of the Battalion. We received, as a reinforcement, a company of the 2nd/11th Battalion, under Captain R. R. Tidd; with them also was Lieut. T. Newton Hannay, who later became adjutant during the Somme offensive. On March 17th a divisional field-day to practise for counter-attack took place over the ground near Saillisel and St. Pierre Vaast. That evening General Kennedy and his brigade-major dined at Battalion Headquarters to celebrate the arrival of the Battalion in France in 1915. He went round all the N.C.O.'s messes after dinner, and as a close to the evening, Captain Stickland and his "Society Improved Entertainers," whose programme had grown in volume and power since the first days of the "Elkie" chorus, gave an excellent programme, concluding with a very amusing and good-natured skit on some phases of the "pow-wow" which had taken place after the morning's field-day.

We now heard that we were to relieve the 2nd Division in the line owing to the very heavy gas casualties they had suffered. On the 18th Colonel Dawes got in touch with Colonel Alban, who had commanded the 2nd South Staffords since Colonel Dawes was hit eleven months earlier, and from him learned the condition of the support and reserve companies' areas in the Villers Plouich sector which we were to take over. They were described as absolute gas traps, which indeed they were. The G.O.C. 2nd Division was consulted, and he pointed out the impossibility of altering the defence scheme now that the German offensive seemed imminent, but undertook, if it were decided to hold the line with only two companies, to house the remaining half battalion in the huts they then occupied. This arrangement was agreed upon, and no doubt saved many unnecessary casualties when the storm broke two days later.

We took over on the night of March 19th from the 23rd Royal Fusilers, under Colonel Winter; this was the same officer who took over the left of our front sector in the Hindenburg line after Bourlon. His meetings with the Battalion always seemed to be unlucky to him. On the former occasion he had sprained his ankle at the entrance of the aid-post dug-out while on his taking-over inspection of the line; on this occasion he was almost speechless with gas.

The 20th was spent in reconnoitring the sector and salving arms and equipment which had had to be abandoned by the gas casualties of the units which had recently held that part of the line.

On the morning of March 21st, the enemy taking the initiative, the first great battle of the year began. Under an intense trench mortar and artillery bombardment he approached our lines, though not with the masses that hurled themselves through on our flanks. On the left he got a footing in our sap-heads, and on the extreme left, in a portion of the front line which connected them; for a time, too, but not for long, we were out of touch with the 17th Battalion on our left. After a while, and when it had changed hands several times, the area described above became practically No Man's Land; the Hun found we made the saps too hot to hold, and for our part, when we were assured of this, we saw no point—with our reduced garrison—in putting men into these exposed places, especially as there was more important work to do with the men available. Captain Stickland made a defensive flank to connect with the 17th, and with great skill and daring, and ably supported by Sergeants Charman and Sylvester, resumed and maintained touch with that unit. By the time Captain Stickland left the Battalion at noon, to go back to Brigade, the worst was over.

Towards evening the C.O. went to see the 17th H.Q., and met Colonel Parish coming to call on him. The latter introduced himself by saying, "I am sure you must be Dawes of the 21st; I am Parish, and have just taken over the 17th. May I introduce myself by saying we are very much indebted to your battalion; for hours we have been unable to get anyone to or from our front line companies, and all the news I have had of my battalion has been through your H.Q." The 17th had indeed suffered more severely than we, and it was an achievement that their line held at all.

Our right company was practically untouched, but even so, was not without its troubles and anxieties. With only the immediate support sections of the front line company to do it with, touch had been kept for some time with our neighbours on our right. Before evening, however, this became impossible, and the posts which had been put out to our right rear merely kept a look out in case of an attempt to roll up that flank. About five, Brigade was asked to relieve our hard-worked left company with one of the fresh ones, and was told that if that were done, and our right secured, we were prepared to go on holding the line with two companies indefinitely. Brigade answered that orders had been received that no reinforcements were to cross the Couillet Valley, and we sat down to wait for orders to retire, hoping that nothing untoward would happen in the meantime on our now exposed right flank.

The orders to go back to the Highland Ridge came eventually, and in the small hours of the morning the retirement was carried out without mishap, except that one of

G

our water-carts passed along the Villers Plouich road at a time when no one happened to be there to stop it, and drove to Germany.

The Highland Ridge position seemed almost as strong as that we had just vacated, but it was some time before this was tested. Indeed, only on our left flank, where an attack was repulsed just before we were again withdrawn on the evening of the 22nd, was there any fighting for the line itself. But in front of the line a fine delaying action was fought against the enemy advancing to and through Villers Plouich by Lieut. Chambers, the Lewis gun officer, with an independent detachment of four Lewis gun teams. The enemy finally made it too hot for him, and he "reported in" nearly twelve hours after we had vacated the Welsh Ridge line.

The effect of the break through on our right now began to make itself felt in the receipt of contradictory orders as to where we were to go. The higher commands were continually finding the state of affairs changed as soon as orders were fairly issued to cope with the last situation. Eventually, however, we found ourselves in line in the Metz switch. The First Surrey Rifles were on the left of the brigade, with two companies of the 4th Royal Welsh Fusiliers—covering the cemetery—between us and the 23rd Battalion (142nd Brigade). The 17th and 15th held the line to Dessart Wood. About 8.30 a.m. battalion head-quarters in the quarry in Metz received orders for a retire-ment to Equancourt; across the end of the order was written "time later." Warning orders were issued to companies accordingly, and just as the C.O. and adjutant were leaving for the line the 4th Royal Welsh Fusiliers were ordered to take their two companies away to the right of the brigade. Verbal orders were given to cover the cemetery with two platoons of the left company as the Royal Welsh Fusiliers went out, and then to re-distribute the companies to cover the extra length of line. As the head-quarters party reached the right of the line, Corporal Sexton, the runner with the party, was wounded. There was nothing to be done now but to hold on until the message arrived giving the time for the move detailed in the warning order.

A reserve position was taken up above the quarry by the head-quarter party of four extra Lewis guns, which had been organized by Lieut. Chambers from guns salved in the Villers Plouich sector. There was a good deal of rifle fire from the front line about 11 o'clock, and ammunition, which was asked for by Captain Barker, was sent up, the runner bringing back word that it had been duly delivered, that the enemy had tried to advance in force, but that the situation was satisfactory. Shortly afterwards it was learned that Colonel Maxwell, commanding the 23rd Battalion on our left, had his head-quarters in Metz. As it had also been heard that the brigade on our left was going to retire, the C.O. went in search of him, leaving instructions with Major Walford, now again with the Battalion as second-in-command, that if the confirmation of the warning order arrived in his absence, the companies were to be instructed accordingly, and he himself was to take the head-quarters party back to the new line and establish Lewis gun posts so that the Battalion would have something definite to fall back on. It was not known that Equancourt was already in the hands of the enemy and that our own transport had got out of the village just in time to avoid capture.

Colonel Maxwell was found eventually, and his information was that the 142nd Brigade had begun withdrawing about noon, starting with the left battalion, that the last of his own battalion was to leave at 1 o'clock, and that he himself was leaving shortly to set up his new head-quarters. He was as ignorant as we were of the altered position on our right rear. The C.O. undertook to hold on, if possible, for a quarter of an hour, and then to echelon back behind him, little thinking that he was in no position to carry out the undertaking. On returning to the quarry he found that no further orders had been received; in fact, as already suspected, the despatch rider with the confirmation of the warning order had been captured.

Major Walford now got his detachment drawn up on the Metz-Fins road ready to move, and the necessary orders were sent off to the companies, with additional instructions to warn the 15th and 17th of the altered conditions. The right company of the 23rd Battalion was now seen retiring in excellent order, but obviously under heavy pressure. When Captain Brett came out with the last of the company he brought the news that he had, for a considerable time, had the enemy on his immediate right, and that repeated attempts to eject them and to get in touch with our left company had been unsuccessful. (Captain Brett was later wounded and captured at Vallulart Wood, but the C.O., who knew the circumstances of his fight at Metz switch, was able to recommend his action to Colonel Maxwell, and he was subsequently awarded the D.S.O.)

At the same time, the runners sent up with the orders to withdraw got back with the information that on getting to the left company positions they had found the enemy in possession, and had barely escaped. As the order affected the whole brigade the runners were sent back with orders to go to the right of the original line and deliver the orders. After seeing away the last of the 23rd and Major Walford's party, the C.O., with Captain Newton and Corporal Ley, set off slowly towards Fins to join the companies as they came out. There was no sign of the runners, nor, indeed, were they heard of again, and after waiting a short time, the C.O.'s party started up the ridge themselves by a shallow communicating trench.

Looking for the Battalion, they were soon pleased to see troops coming towards them in good order, but, if anything, too slowly; a man was seen trying to call up from the top of the ridge, and Corporal Ley got on the side of the trench to reply; as he did so the attitude of the nearest sections became suspicious, and a further look assured the party, from the shape of the approaching helmets, that the battalion was not the First Surrey Rifles, but the enemy. There was, nothing for it but a hasty and ignominious retreat, which was carried out under a generous but very "third-class shot" rifle fire.

On their way to Equancourt Colonel Winter, of the 23rd Royal Fusiliers, stopped the party and told them that the village was already in the hands of the enemy and that Major Walford had been wounded trying to get his party into it. So much for what battalion head-quarters knew. We must return to the companies in the Metz switch.

When the 4th Royal Welsh Fusiliers had left the position near the cemetery the enemy had succeeded in getting a footing there; soon after the C.O. had left the line the enemy had attempted a general advance, which, as we heard, was driven back. Strenuous attempts were made to prevent him from exploiting his footing at the cemetery, and casualties here were very heavy. He succeeded, however, in improving his position, and it was from here that his next attempt was made. With strong attacks he extended his hold in Metz switch, and eventually forced the Battalion back towards the remainder of the brigade. At the same time the troops responsible for stopping the gap on the right of the brigade had failed to do so, the gap being too great and their numbers insufficient to hold up the enemy, who had pushed through. With both flanks of the brigade hopelessly gone, and no reserves, Colonels Segrave and Parish extricated their battalions as best they could, and took the First Surrey with them. The report of what had occurred, however, never reached the head-quarters in the quarry. Meanwhile, the position mentioned in the warning order for the withdrawal, was already in the hands of the enemy. Thus the Battalion again became divided : a part, including the head-quarters party, was got into position and dug in on the Four Winds Farm aerodrome above Lechelle, the remainder fought their way back further south, and later came under General Kennedy's orders in Rocquigny.

At the aerodrome Colonel Dawes and Captain Dubs, the brigade-major, got the mixed details of the brigade into some sort of position, with its right continued by the 1st Royal Berks. Here Captain Saumarez, the staff-captain, was killed while distributing S.A.A., which he had succeeded in getting to the line. The brigadier sent for the battalion commanders to attend a conference about 6.30, and Colonel Dawes was told to take over the brigade troops in the front line. Just as the conference ended the line was broken by an enemy advance under a heavy bombardment from guns which had been brought up on the high ground above Ytres. The force had just re-formed in the valley behind the aerodrome, and a fresh position on the next rise was being sought, when an officer of the 63rd Division arrived, and said that he was bringing up a detachment from a battalion of his division to dig in on a line in that part covering Bus, and at his request our mixed force took up a line between Bus and Le Mesnil, with its left on Bus. It was eventually withdrawn at about 3 a.m. to Rocquigny by General Kennedy, who was organizing a very mixed force of 47th and 2nd Division troops, with details from our right, at that place.

In the morning the Battalion was again divided. Two companies which had not rejoined at Rocquigny till late the previous night, were kept under the brigadier's own hand, and were eventually posted between us at Rocquigny and Le Transloy. The men of the 15th, who had been with us on the 23rd, were withdrawn to their own battalion, and that unit went into brigade reserve. Colonel Dawes was ordered, with the head-quarters and the now depleted remnants of two companies of the First Surrey, a slightly larger party of the 17th and the remains of two companies of the 1st Royal Berks (99th Brigade, 2nd Division) to form the front line of the brigade and to proceed to take over from the outposts near Bus. In addition to the above, the 140th Brigade detachments had with them men from the division on our right who had become detached from their own units.

The party set out with the First Surrey Rifles leading, and the detachments Royal Berks in reserve. A few hundred yards out a party was met marching to Rocquigny in fours. The officer in charge said they had been on outpost duty, and had been ordered to withdraw at dawn. He knew nothing about waiting for us to relieve him: he had seen the Germans advancing, and thought they must have reached the position he had left. Sergeant Charman was sent hurriedly forward with a party of scouts, and the force pushed on. Sergeant Charman came back all too soon, and reported that the enemy were not only in, but past the position we were making for, and, moreover, in numbers too great for us to counter-attack with any hope of success. There was just time to get a party of the First Surrey into position in a detached piece of trench on the left of the road, while the remainder, with the 17th, were put into the main trench covering Rocquigny (held by the 141st Brigade) and filled up a gap about the road, with the 20th (Colonel Grimwood) on their left. The Royal Berks detachment was placed in reserve near the Rocquigny water-point, lining a bank on the road running east of the camp.

The forward party broke up the enemy's advance till about 9.30, and then, beginning to be enfiladed from the right, was withdrawn into the main line. During the rest of the morning the enemy was steadily building up a line opposite our positions, but suffered heavily from our rifle fire in doing so.

About 11.30 the C.O. was asked if he could supply reinforcements for the right, which was in difficulties. He ordered one company of the Royal Berks to that flank, and, as the main line was now very crowded, he sent our headquarter section to join the other Royal Berks company at the water-point, subsequently joining them there. Shortly afterwards, news came back that though this party had succeeded in helping to check the enemy it had suffered heavy casualties, including the officer. About this time a warning order was received for a withdrawal to Le Transloy; this was soon contradicted by orders to form a new line at Les Boeufs. No definite time was given for this move, but it was to be carried out covered by the 141st Brigade, when the situation on the right, which was now becoming dangerous, rendered it necessary. About 12.30 British tanks were sent over on our left, and, from the top of the water-point were seen to be dealing very effectively with the enemy there.

The feeling of optimism which this produced was soon damped by the complete collapse of the troops on our right, who, when the enemy had got round behind them, came pouring down the road towards battalion head-quarters.

The head-quarter section and company of the Royal Berks were moved to a position at right angles to that they were occupying, to form a defensive flank facing south; orders for an immediate withdrawal to the Les Boeufs position were sent to the front line, and then attention was paid to the troops coming from the right.

These consisted of men of all sorts of units, and in the confusion even section organization had been lost. There were very few officers among them, and the only thing to do was to form them into parties of ten and a dozen and send them under the available N.C.O.'s to the Les Boeufs position. Most of these were clear when the enemy began to follow up; two machine-guns were brought to bear on the defensive flank party at the cross roads, but this party gave such a good account of itself that the machine-guns decided to give Rocquigny best, and retired to join the force that was pushing through the gap on Le Transloy. A party of the Royal Berks, who were cleverly posted by the regimental sergeant-major, did excellent work at this time, and a report of the sergeant-major's action was sent to his battalion later.

The remains of the Royal Berks detachment was next sent back, and the First Surrey Rifles party was about to withdraw when a verbal message came from Colonel Grimwood asking for help, as his right flank was in trouble. Apparently the 141st Brigade orders had gone astray, as ours had the day before. Although it was necessary for headquarters to get back to Les Boeufs, and for the C.O. to take command of the force he had sent to the new position there, he replied that he would hold Rocquigny while the 20th withdrew. Receiving a message that the 20th were going to stay where they were, he sent back most of the head-quarters men, told Captain Newton to hold the Rocquigny crossroads with a small party for twenty-five minutes, and went to see Colonel Grimwood, whom, however, he did not find. Colonel Grimwood was with the battalion on his left, but Colonel Dawes discovered that the reason the 20th were not withdrawing was that in the absence of orders from the 141st Brigade, Colonel Grimwood had given an undertaking to the unit on his left that he would not uncover its flank. This unit had had no orders for withdrawal, and was sure that, as tanks had been sent over, a counter-attack was contemplated. Colonel Dawes arranged with Major Reed of the 20th, that he would try to get in touch with the two companies which had been between Rocquigny and Le Transloy, and that if he could get hold of them he would make a strong point at Rocquigny to secure the right flank of the 20th. He found in the line Captain Tidd, Regimental Sergeant-Major Laing, and Sergeant-Drummer Clark, who had been with the 20th when the order for our force to withdraw had got to the line, and leaving with Major Reed a runner, Rifleman Hardy, who would know where to find him, he took the others back to the cross-roads.

Meanwhile, Captain Newton had remained at the cross-roads for the prescribed twenty-five minutes and a further five, had seen the rest of the party on its way towards Les Boeufs, and had then returned for ten minutes on the chance of meeting the C.O., before going after his party. Consequently the C.O.'s party found the cross-roads empty, but the enemy was past and round it, and apparently in possession of Le Transloy, and the companies had been withdrawn to the new line. He sent back a note to the 20th that what he had suggested was now out of the question, described the general situation, and told his runner, Lance-Corporal Appleford, to bring Hardy back with him, striking north and west, and rejoin as best he could. The party passed through the north edge of Rocquigny, which was then being shelled by the enemy, and made off across country at the double, being pursued by machine-gun fire from the south. The head-quarter section was caught up close to Beaulencourt, and just before this heavy firing was heard from the 20th's line; the unit on the left of the 20th, having now got orders to withdraw, Colonel Grimwood had started sending back his companies one at a time, but the second had just left when the enemy rushed the position and overwhelmed the remainder of the battalion.

At Beaulencourt an R.A.M.C. sergeant was delivering instructions to men of various units, and told our party that he had seen the brigade-major, and that a concentration on Gueudecourt had been ordered in place of the withdrawal to the Les Boeufs line. Near Gueudecourt General Kennedy was met, and he pointed out the Battalion disappearing in the direction of Eaucourt L'Abbaye, on their way to Bazentin, where the concentration was now to take place. The Battalion was soon caught up, and being now all together again, arrived at Bazentin Wood late at night, and after the brigadier had arrived and held a conference, positions were taken up in and in front of the wood.

Among the casualties this day, Captain Barker and Lieut. Chambers were wounded before the withdrawal from

Rocquigny : the latter, who had been hit in the leg, got back to a dressing station where his wound was dressed, and then, with a lift on a lorry part of the way, attempted to rejoin the Battalion at Les Boeufs. There, however, he found the Germans, and was very lucky to get away.

Soon after daylight on the 25th, the Battalion was ordered to occupy and hold the old trench in front of the Contalmaison-Pozières road, and we started deepening and clearing and putting the trench in a state of defence. The front companies had not got away without a fight, and Captain N. A. Taylor was mortally wounded; he had not long been back with the Battalion, and was sadly missed by everybody. The enemy provided wonderful targets all day, and suffered heavily as he pushed across the front of the wood in the direction of Pozières. Towards evening we began to be enfiladed from our right, and though on the whole, the day had been quiet on the battalion front, the troops just on our left had had a close encounter, in which, at the point of the bayonet, they drove an advanced party of the enemy from a communication trench which ran back into their line. Beyond them again, in the next brigade front, enemy planes, flying low, had succeeded in covering an assault on the trench, but the line was reformed in a bank which successfully covered our flank.

During the morning Lieut. Hannay had taken advanced parties from each company to work on the old La Boisselle positions, but it was not until the small hours of the morning of the 26th that orders were given to get back across the Ancre and march to Bouzincourt. We were covered by a rear guard under Lieut. J. O. B. Hitch. The Pozières dumps were ablaze as we moved across country to Ovillers and took the main road to Aveluy, and just before reaching the Ancre we passed troops of the 37th Division in position, and ceased to be the front line troops for the first time since the 19th. We passed through Aveluy in the early dawn, and after a rest of some hours at Bouzincourt, marched to Louvencourt, where we spent the night. The 27th was spent in digging trenches for a reserve line covering the Louvencourt—Lealvillers road, and in the evening we moved to Toutencourt, and billeted there; on the 28th we moved to Warloy, and on the 29th back to Bouzincourt in reserve.

On the 31st we took over from the 17th in the front line, and steady digging, assisted at night by parties of the 4th Royal Welsh Fusiliers, was our main duty. This was not carried out at our leisure, as the enemy was very active and threatening, though he never succeeded in reaching our lines.

He made continual attempts to do so, especially when he was attacking towards Aveluy Wood and Martinsart.

On the night of the 4th we changed over with the 15th, who came up from billets in Senlis; here we got a small draft of reinforcements, but we got little rest, being heavily shelled with H.E. and gas, and suffering many casualties, among whom was Lieut. Alison, who was badly gassed. He had been recently brought to head-quarters as assistant-adjutant. After one more short spell of digging in the line, we were relieved on the 8th by the 4th North Staffords, their divisional commander expressing to General Corringe great satisfaction with the work that had been done, and the handing over. On the 9th we moved to Beauval, which was so crowded we could hardly find billets. Here we met Captain Turner, who rejoined us for a time with a large batch of recruits from the "divisional wing."

We marched through St. Riquier to our billets in Lamotte-Buleux, where we settled down to steady training, especially in musketry and Lewis gun, but we were very much hampered by the stubborn reluctance of the farmers to place any ground at our disposal for either training or recreation. Not the least surprising part of our experiences in France was the extraordinary variety in the attitude of the inhabitants towards the troops; side by side with amazing kindness and sympathy was displayed apparently unreasoning obstruction. Almost invariably the least sympathy was displayed by those who were farthest from the line, and who seemed to have suffered least from the war, and to be, financially at least, making a very good thing out of it.

A welcome arrival at this time was Major Hutchence, while Captain Newton left to be second-in-command of the 19th, and Lieut. Hitch came to head-quarters as acting adjutant.

On the 29th we got a sudden order to "embus" for the line, and came back to Warloy, relieving an Australian battalion in support at Laviéville.

May was comparatively uneventful, although continual work and vigilance were necessary, as a fresh attempt at Amiens on the part of the enemy was constantly expected. Our reinforcements had been taken from us when we left Lamotte and were undergoing intensive training at the divisional reinforcement camp. They were seen there by the C.O. on his way to Boulogne for five days' dental treatment. During his absence Major Hutchence took over the Battalion.

On June 21st we went into corps reserve to Ferrières, in the Cavillon area, about five miles behind Amiens. We had good billets, fine weather, baths, and training and recreation grounds were available. If we had not had influenza at the same time, conditions would have been almost ideal : as it was, we had to take advantage of these good things by instalments as we became convalescent. We required a large training ground to map out a taped course for a projected minor operation ; this we obtained by helping the owners to cut and carry a large hayfield, which we afterwards used. During the period the 17th and ourselves were inspected on parade by the divisional commander, who presented medal ribbons to recent recipients of immediate awards. The Battalion had a very successful training and transport competition, and divisional water sports at Picquigny were a source of general satisfaction. If the 140th Brigade Head-quarters did not win the first prize for the best comic craft, they deserved to, if only on account of the trouble the staff-captain took to improve (with first field-dressings) the figures of the two "lovely ladies," who appeared from their burlesque bathing-machine.

During the last week in June, Captain Hannay took over the duties of adjutant, and at the end of the month the C.O. handed over to Major Hutchence and went on leave to England.

Now we had got rid of the influenza we had to begin thinking about a return to the line—so a chapter which was full of incidents and hardships, and at one time looked almost like including disaster, ended with about the pleasantest period of rest and training the Battalion ever enjoyed in France.

CHAPTER IX.

July 12th, 1918, to September 7th, 1918.
The "Hundred Days."

On leaving Ferrières we returned to familiar ground. On July 12th we went to Senlis for musketry, and on the 14th to Warloy; thence, on the 18th, to the front line in the "Nine Elms" sector, south of the Amiens-Albert road. The colonel came back from leave, and a party of American officers, N.C.O.'s, and sniping observers joined us to get an insight into the working and routine of an infantry battalion in the line. The senior officer was Lieut.-Colonel Rowell, a very pleasant visitor, keenly interested in all he saw, and combining firmness and enthusiasm with great personal charm. He was active and dapper—a typical soldier; he had seen service in the Philippines, the occupation of Cuba, and in Mexico. Both he and his officers were almost embarrassing in insisting on having an exact reason for details which had become so much a matter of routine that they were taken as a matter of course.

We were very sorry to lose a company commander of this party, Captain Williams, who was attached to "A" Company (Captain West). He was very keen to go out with a lance-corporal's post which took up an advanced position near the German wire at dawn and came in after dusk. This was forbidden, as not being the duty of an officer of his seniority, but he was told he could go out at night and see the work of a wiring party; a rifleman was attached to him as a runner and guide. Just as they were getting out of the trench there was a burst of fire from the enemy's lines; the runner was hit in the head and killed at once, and Captain Williams was hit in the body and succumbed a few hours later.

From now until the middle of July we were carrying out normal tours in the front line, support, and reserve. Major Hutchence, besides coming up daily to do a daylight tour of the line for the C.O., came up to command for one tour, the C.O., who had been detailed for a visit to the corps school, remaining at the transport lines. We got back to the front line north of the Amiens road in time to see, going on on our right, the great battle which opened on August 8th. This battle caused the enemy to draw back on our front, and at Albert on our left, and "D" Company, holding an outpost line on the railway, was able to push forward standing patrols.

On the 10th we handed over this forward line to the Americans, who were just on our right, and the following night the Battalion was relieved by a unit of the 18th Division, who had come from the battle to the south, and we went back to Baisieux. The following day a party of officers and other ranks, detailed by the divisional commander, had the honour of attending the parade held by His Majesty the King, on his visit to 4th Army Head-quarters, in recognition of their services in November, 1917, and during the March operations.

On the 15th a new front line sector was reconnoitred in the Bois de Tailles, and the same night the transport was very heavily bombed in Warloy, and we lost twenty horses. It was a bad time for the transport, for the following night when the Battalion went up to relieve the 24th, the limbers were caught on the way by a burst of shell fire, three drivers were wounded, and four more horses were killed.

We had a busy time in the line, and an uncomfortable one. Cover was scarce, though there was a fairly good dug-out in the wood, which was shared as company headquarters with some of the 15th; the men in the front line were distributed in detached posts. The enemy was strongly posted on the railway line, and constant patrolling was necessary to look out for any chance to improve our positions, and to keep an eye on enemy movements. He was obviously nervy, and used a great deal of gas, especially at night and in the early morning. It was a very interesting line from the intelligence point of view.

While we were in, the divisional commander went round the front, and on his way back through battalion headquarters, told the C.O., in confidence, that the units behind the line were already training for a special operation, and that when the Battalion was relieved it would only be for a short time, to make final preparations to participate. He also suggested that the operation was likely to be one of far greater importance than any of us imagined.

Accordingly, on the 20th, we were relieved by the 19th Battalion, and the following day came up into the old trench system south of Morlancourt. Here we received orders for the next day's operation. The 140th Brigade was to wait for the result of the attack by the remainder of the division, and when, after the capture of the "Happy Valley" (four miles south-east of Albert), whippet tanks and cavalry had gone over, was to be used to exploit the success.

Accordingly, on the morning of August 22nd, we got on the move, but it was not long before it was clear that all was not well with the advance. The enemy had succeeded in holding on to a strong point in the "green line"—the final objective—and had counter-attacked heavily after the cavalry had been repulsed with severe casualties. The line had been rolled back to our side of the Bray-Albert road, and only on the right were the 22nd holding on, defending the left flank of the Australians. During the afternoon, Lieut. Chambers, who was battalion intelligence officer, was sent up to try and find out the exact situation; he made a reconnaissance of the "Happy Valley," and furnished a valuable report, but unfortunately got into so much gas that he had to be sent back for a few days to recoup. He was awarded the Military Cross for his services.

In the evening orders were received at Brigade for the 140th Brigade to make a fresh attempt to take the green line; but General Kennedy, now in charge of the divisional troops in the front line, had already found it necessary to order up two battalions into close support, and as these were on the move, and one at least already involved in the battle, he was in no position to comply. Accordingly, it was decided to wait a day, and orders were received for an attack on the green line at 1 a.m. on the 24th. The 140th Infantry Brigade was to attack, with the First Surrey Rifles on the left, the 17th on the right, and the 15th in support, the latter having the special duty of mopping up the "Happy Valley." The strong point which had broken up the attack on the 22nd was just outside our northern boundary in the area of the 12th Division, and on our right was a brigade of our friends the 58th.

In brilliant moonlight, and with a splendid barrage, we went over, and were almost immediately in the trenches which formed our objective, Captain Pike's company being kept in reserve half-way between the green line and the Bray-Albert road.

The success, though rapid, had not been plain sailing, however. The strong point on our left had held out to good effect. The right battalion of the 12th Division had been so severely handled that it was unable to get in, and left scores of casualties in front of the German lines. Our own left company (Captain Hunter) suffered severely; half of it became casualties at once, and it lost all its officers. For this reason it was never quite clear what happened, but as Captain Hunter was found wounded well beyond the "green line" when the advance was resumed the following day, it was supposed that he realized the danger of the strong point, and endeavoured to get round it. He died of his wounds the day after he was brought in. It was a gallant but costly attempt. Captain Hunter had been a company commander so long, and with his quiet, determined manner, had filled the position in such a way that all who knew him felt he would be hard to replace. The others killed were Lieuts. Garner, Morton, and Sadler.

The danger flank now came under command of Lieut. Wray, who had gone up in command of "A" Company; he had been lightly wounded two days before, but had been able to remain at duty. He was ably backed up by C.-S.-M. Charman. This warrant officer was awarded the M.C. for this action, to add to the D.C.M. which he had won in the March retreat, and a M.M. already in his possession.

He was also recommended for a direct commission for gallantry in the field; this recommendation was strongly backed by the brigade and divisional commanders, and specially recommended to the Commander-in-Chief by General Birdwood. The Commander-in-Chief instructed that it be held over and sent up again in two months' time, when it was more certain what course the operations then in progress would take; when it was re-submitted, the Armistice had been signed, and he expressed his regret that circumstances rendered it impossible to deal favourably with the recommendation.

During the morning the remaining company commanders, Captains Tidd and Pike, were both wounded, though not dangerously. Sergeants Burley and Sylvester, acting for their C.-S.-M.'s, were both awarded the D.C.M. for this action; so also were Corporals Tidmarsh and Buss, who were promoted to the rank of sergeant in next day's orders.

For some hours after dawn it remained a morning of alarms. The strong point was a source of great danger, and its garrison withstood all attempts to bomb it out; it threatened us continually, and was made a pivot for attempted counter-attacks. At the same time a heavy minenwerfer in the post was able to enfilade our line, and this, with heavy shelling, reduced the captured trench to something like a shambles. It was difficult to reinforce it, as the ground back to the Bray-Albert road was kept under heavy shrapnel fire, and the road itself subjected to heavy crashes of high explosive. During one of the alarms we had got a message back by lamp to the 17th head-quarters, and thence by telephone to Brigade, describing the danger of the situation. This had elicited a note from the brigadier saying that any necessary use must be made of the 15th Battalion, and of all brigade machine-guns in that part, to secure the threatened flank; that the flank must not go, or that anyway if it did, the 21st Battalion was to be posted so as to make the 17th absolutely secure.

Meanwhile, the 15th Battalion had carried out their task with complete success, and were already working like niggers on the support trench, which they extended in such a way as to cover our left rear, and when the available machine-guns had been so placed as to prevent the exploitation of the enemy's success at the strong point, and the garrison of our front line had been reorganized with reinforcements from Captain Pike's company, it was at last possible to wire Brigade: "Sorry, false alarm. All objectives taken and held." During the afternoon the appearance of tanks decided the garrison of the strong point to give us best, and the 12th Division was able to come into line, but the casualties lying thick round the strong point showed how costly their initial attempt had been.

We were not given much time to consider the morning's events. In the afternoon the brigadier met battalion commanders at the head-quarters of the 17th, and orders were issued for a fresh advance. The First Surrey were to side-step to the right, and were given an objective some two miles distant. At 2.30 a.m. we started, and advanced behind a creeping barrage at the rate of 100-yds. in four minutes. There was practically no opposition, the only enemy met with on the way being demolition parties on the light railway who had been caught by the barrage.

It was a real walk-over, especially after our experience of the day before. The work really began when the objective was reached and the consolidation was put in hand. Soon after the Battalion was thoroughly settled in we had the satisfaction of seeing the troops of the 58th Division cross our front from right rear to left front in artillery formation; it looked as if the war of movement had begun at last. We thought so all the more when we were told that the time was past when troops in the attacking corps could be taken back into billets on being temporarily withdrawn from the battle, and that bivouacs on recently won ground would now be the rule. After congratulatory messages had been received from the corps, we were withdrawn, and unfortunately had a night of pouring rain.

During the next few days we had time for cleaning up. We had visits from the divisional and brigade commanders, and the latter inspected the Battalion. There was an openair performance by the "Follies," and the day before we got on the move again the corps commander visited brigade head-quarters and saw battalion commanders there. The colonel had a flattering message to bring back. When General Kennedy introduced the battalion commanders, he began to remind General Godley that it was the First Surrey Rifles who had been on the left on the 24th. General Godley interrupted him with : "You needn't tell me about that—that is a matter of history," and then added to the colonel, "and I cannot congratulate you too highly on the magnificent achievement of the battalion under your command."

On the 29th, the division being again on the move, we marched across country to the Carnoy area, where we settled in about 7.30 p.m. We crossed immediately over the ground we took on the 24th, and the C.O. and adjutant went forward during a halt, with our chaplain, Browne-Wilkinson, and the latter read the funeral service for those killed during the engagement, at the place where Garner was buried. It was surprising, and also rather amusing, to see the mortars and machine-guns lying in the very positions in which they had been captured, all marked with chalk as Australian trophies. The party responsible for the claiming of trophies must have strayed rather in their efforts to do their work efficiently, as there was a brigade of the 58th Division, as well as the 17th Battalion, between us and them.

On the 30th we continued the advance, in reserve, as far as Maurepas ravine, where we settled down into shelters and bivouacs. The next afternoon there was a conference at brigade head-quarters where the divisional commander communicated the plans for an attack which was to finish on the edge of St. Pierre Vaast Wood. The C.O. returned to the Battalion to fetch Lieut. Chambers, who was with us again after his gassing in "Happy Valley," and a reconnoitring party to go and see the forming-up positions in the line held by the 18th Battalion. On the way back, passing brigade head-quarters, it was learned from General Kennedy that he had sent for Major Hutchence, since operations were becoming so protracted that he thought the second-in-command should take a turn. As a matter of fact, the message took so long to reach Major Hutchence, that he was just able to get to Brigade as the Battalion was on its way up, so the colonel compromised by going with him, promising to hand over to him when it came to setting up

H

the new head-quarters after the advance had gone through, and undertaking not to go forward himself except to the advanced head-quarters to see Major Hutchence.

It was a fortunate arrangement, as a complication arose later which would have been puzzling to anyone who had come in at the last minute, and had not been in touch with the scheme from the start. On arrival at battle head-quarters we met the head-quarters of our neighbours of the 141st Brigade, who were attacking on our right; on the edge of St. Pierre Vaast Wood the map showed two jutting portions of wood of an exactly similar shape. The left-hand one had been given as the right boundary of the brigade, but the battalion on our right was working on the right-hand one as its left boundary. Luckily General Kennedy had impressed on Colonel Dawes that the objectives were wide for battalions now depleted by casualties, and that if gaps occurred it was better that they should be within the brigade (where the easier co-operation would tend to obviate dangers from this source), than on the flanks—suggesting also that he should keep his right strong. Two platoons had accordingly been earmarked to follow the right flank. These were now thrown into the front line, and told to keep in touch with the brigade on the right, the whole battalion being eased a little towards the same flank. There was no time to get in touch with the 15th on our left and tell them what had happened, and the 15th, finding none of our men at the point of junction, went over under the impression that we had not arrived. Many prisoners were taken, but casualties were heavy, too, and by the time the Battalion got forward to the edge of the wood, the assaulting parties were so small that the mopping up of the whole objective was out of the question; they could only hang on in a series of strong points which practically alternated along the line with German machine-gun and sniper posts. This made Major Hutchence's task an extremely difficult and dangerous one, but how ably it was carried out, and how little he spared himself, was proved by the very slight delay there was in getting back to Brigade the report on the positions of our posts.

During the afternoon Captain Hitch was hit through the right hand, and late in the evening Major Hutchence was brought back with a dangerous wound straight through the right side of his head, which resulted in his losing his right eye and the use of his right ear. On the same day Captain Stickland also received a dangerous wound through the head.

Shortly after dark we got orders to stand by for relief by the 141st Brigade, and later, close on midnight, Lieut. Gilkes arrived from brigade head-quarters with instructions to pull out as best we could, refit with ammunition and rations which were on their way to the original battle head-quarters, and proceed to Bouchavesnes. Here the brigade was to start at 5 a.m., in rear of a brigade of the 74th Division, in the following order : 15th left front, 17th right front, 21st behind the 15th. The brigade of the 74th was to capture Moislans, and then push on towards Nurlu, while the 140th Brigade was to pass through Moislans behind them, and then turn left to form a defensive flank with the 21st on the left in touch with the 142nd Brigade, and the 15th on the right in touch with the 74th Division; the 17th in support.

In addition to the head-quarters section and aid post, we had collected nearly one hundred men. These were formed into a company with Lieut. Jackman in charge of it, three of the platoons being commanded by officers, and the fourth by C.-S.-M. Charman. Rations and ammunition were issued, and with about ten minutes to spare we got to Bouchavesnes, and formed up in time to advance. The C.O. and adjutant, with their runners, kept in touch with Lieut.-Colonel Fielding of the 15th, Lieut. Jackman followed with the company; the head-quarters unit, with Lieut. Chambers as intelligence officer, and Lieut. Boughton in charge of signallers, came behind at a good distance.

As it afterwards turned out, it would have been safer if they had not been ordered to follow so far behind, for the enemy was very slow in opening up with his artillery. Most that came over was high explosive fired at long range, and containing blue cross gas ; one of these shells fell right on the head-quarters unit, and several were hit, including Rifleman Hardy, the runner who had been left with Major Reed on March 24th. Both the officers were hit, too, but they remained at duty until the following day, and rejoined after a few weeks at the corps rest camp.

Meanwhile, increasing daylight displayed the fact that between us and the barrage was no assaulting brigade. We came under heavy fire from Moislans, from the ground to its right, from a strong point covering Moislans on this side of the canal, and from far away on our left rear from machine-guns in St. Pierre Vaast Wood, which were subsequently mopped up by the 4th Royal Welsh Fusiliers. There was a dangerous gap also on the right of the 15th. The latter battalion checked to reorganize in the shell holes in front of the Moislans trench, and then party after party rushed the wire, suffering heavy casualties, but eventually gaining the trench. Lieut. Alexander, who succumbed afterwards, Captain Hannay, Lieut. Jackman, and C.-S.-M. Charman were wounded this side of the wire, but the C.O., with the remnants of the composite company—rather over forty men —joined the 15th in the trench.

They had not been in long when a party of Germans appeared behind the trench; we lined the parados and drove them off, and they retired on the strong point which held out this side of the canal, between ourselves and the 142nd Brigade.

We now proceeded to sort ourselves out, the First Surreys taking the left and forming a block in the trench between themselves and the Germans, and the 15th continuing on the right, where the gap on their flank was shortly afterwards covered by a detachment of machine-guns attached to the brigade. We suffered several further casualties on the left flank from bombs, but, as on the previous day, we were too few to extend our gains, and there was nothing to be done but sit it out. The head-quarters unit was out of touch for some time, but was eventually found in a communication trench running back from Moislans trench. It was the most convenient place for the runners and signallers, and further, was suitable in case they should have to be thrown in as a reserve to counter renewed activity on the part of the Germans on our left.

During the morning the enemy withdrew, from the high ground to our right front, two field guns which had been giving us much trouble, and the success of the 142nd Brigade and the 4th R.W.F. away on our left gave us some relief, but the enemy held on stubbornly in Moislans and on our side of the canal.

At about 1 o'clock a small alleviation occurred in the return of the C.O. and his runner, the latter with a large tin of bacon sandwiches, and the former with a tin of 250 Gold Flake cigarettes. The C.O. in an attempt to get into touch with advanced brigade head-quarters had come upon Sergeant Huish and the mess staff. Sergeant Huish had worked his way up to be provost-sergeant, and had taken over the duties of mess sergeant some months before. His tenure of the latter office was a brilliant one, punctuated by many a triumph in the shape of "No. 1 dinners," but the production of that large tin of cigarettes at a time of unusual stress and strain was perhaps the greatest triumph of all.

The process of sitting it out continued until 11 o'clock at night, when we were withdrawn, and the line taken over by a unit of the 74th Division. We came out through a cloud of gas, for the enemy put down a defensive barrage on the line of the canal at about midnight, and also shelled tracks and trenches between it and Bouchavesnes. Just as Bouchavesnes was passed, a burst of shell fell among us, principally among the head-quarters unit, and Corporal Newman of the runners, who had served with distinction throughout the war, was wounded, and afterwards died of wounds.

After a long rest on the road above Le Forest, we got back to Maurepas ravine about 7 o'clock on the morning of the 3rd. There were the colonel and three subalterns unwounded, about thirty-five men of the composite company, besides the head-quarters unit; this also had suffered casualties both on the way up at 5.30 a.m. and as we passed Bouchavesnes on the way out.

The situation was bad enough, but not quite as bad as it sounds, for we were rejoined during the day by 2nd-Lieut. Lowry and forty-one other ranks, who had been fighting in conjunction with the 141st Brigade on the 1st, and got out of touch with battalion head-quarters; we also got back two parties whom we had been reluctantly compelled to detach as "carriers" for the machine-guns during the recent actions. There were also one hundred men of the battle surplus, but these included the band. Lieut. Catlow acted as adjutant in place of Captain Hannay, and we were promised Major Newton, the former adjutant, as second-in-command when he returned from the senior officers' school in England. The 15th and 21st were so reduced that General Kennedy decided not to risk the trained specialists of two battalion head-quarters with so few men, and decided that Colonel Fielding and Colonel Dawes should relieve each other with their head-quarters, and that the battalion which had the head-quarters out should supply a composite company to the battalion that was in. Accordingly, a company, 150 strong, under Lieut. Wray, reported to Colonel Fielding the next day, and took part in the successful operations round Nurlu and Liéramont up to the 6th; they were withdrawn to Moislans, and "embussed" for Heilly on the 7th.

Head-quarters and the few remaining men had gone back meanwhile to the transport at Cléry, where we got a draft of old members who had got over their wounds of six months before; among them was Corporal Sexton who had been hit in the Metz switch on March 23rd. The party from Cléry joined the 'bus procession to Heilly, where we were billeted for a few days in something like comfort.

Thus ended our part in the great Somme offensive. General Godley told us that as the supply of reinforcements then available was too small to keep two London divisions in the line, and as we had been in continuously, with only one break in corps reserve (between August 24th and 29th), and were very much reduced in numbers, he must dispense with us and keep the 58th. We were promised that our lightly wounded should come back as reinforcements to us, and not be sent elsewhere. Our casualties had been heavy—heavier perhaps than in March—but what a different atmosphere! Victory was in the air.

CHAPTER X.

September 8th, 1918, to November 26th, 1918.

The "Hundred Days" (continued).

We were quite sorry to leave Heilly, and sorrier still to get to Choques, which had a dismal, deserted appearance. Even the weather was against us. It was a great relief when we moved on the 12th to Marles-les-Mines, where the Battalion had many old friends. On Sunday, September 15th, we marched to Auchel for a brigade church parade, which was attended by General Birdwood, into whose army we had now come. After the service he made a speech to the men. The speech was typical of him; after congratulating them on their recent successes, and commenting on the wonderful improvement in the general situation, he told a number of anecdotes which set everybody laughing. The men were very much impressed by the sincere and simple way in which his congratulations were offered. He had the battalions marched home under their sergeant-majors, and then all the officers were introduced to him.

A few days later we were visited on the range by Lieut.-General Morland. We now got definite orders that the often rumoured move to Italy was to be put into effect, and the brigadier went on leave, expecting to join us there. Colonel Dawes went to answer for him at Brigade, and as we were still without a second-in-command, Major Young, of the 15th Battalion, took over in his absence. Training of specialists was proceeded with, especially Lewis gunners, signallers, and scouts. On the 27th we moved to St. Michel to be ready to entrain at St. Pol; this we did on October 2nd, but not for Italy. Arriving at Merville at 3 o'clock in the morning of the 3rd, we marched to Lestrem and bivouacked, moving on to a camp at Rue de Tilleloy at 4 o'clock in the afternoon. We moved forward again on the 4th, and on the 5th took over in the front line from the 18th Battalion, with head-quarters in Radinghem.

The country we were passing through now was very low, and waterlogged in parts, so that we were sometimes in breastworks instead of trenches, and attempted short cuts across country landed one in streams and dykes. The companies were distributed in depth in old German trenches, the main one of which ran up to the railway just north of Erquinghem.

For the last fifty yards our side of the railway, it was unoccupied, and very much broken down, and it contained a blown-up concrete shelter. At the point where it reached the railway embankment there was a closed door with a tangle of wire in front of it. Major Young went up the embankment with Lieut. Chambers and Sergeant Tidmarsh, as he found they could approach it without drawing fire. He sent back the sergeant to "A" Company Head-quarters to say that if Colonel Dawes came up from Brigade he was to be asked to join him on the embankment. The colonel was at "A" Company when the message arrived, and went forward and joined Major Young.

All was quiet on the railway embankment, though a few Germans could be seen moving about the cottages at some distance away to the front. Major Young was anxious to put a post over on the far side of the railway and try to work forward at this point, but did not want to do so until he could get the door opened. The colonel told him Brigade was sending up a party of sappers for special work in his sector, and that they should be asked to help in forcing the gate; he suggested having a party of about twenty standing by with a Lewis gun in the trench to meet any eventuality. He was on his way to the 17th, and promised to direct the sappers straight to the spot if he met them on the way round, and Major Young sent a message back to battalion head-quarters to have them sent up in case the colonel missed them.

When the sappers eventually arrived, and the door was blown in, it was a case of "When the pie was opened, the birds began to sing"; a large party of Jaegers appeared on the railway embankment, and a machine-gun came into action, not against our party, but firing towards the left along the railway in the direction of the 17th Battalion. The Lewis gun opened up at once on the machine-gun, and knocked it out, and the enemy disappeared, leaving eight killed behind them. We had one man killed and two wounded. It was clear we were not likely to establish ourselves across the railway by peaceful penetration!

The rest of the tour was uneventful, and we went back to huts at Le Maisnil, where the C.O. rejoined from Brigade. With rumour of Italy renewed, we again went back, and after a few days on the move, were billeted in St. Hilaire. The truth of the postponement of the Italian move was that the advance was going so rapidly that railways were working at high pressure, and there was not the rolling stock to spare to move a division. As a matter of fact, the 7th Division, whom we were to relieve, were busy with operations which ended in the capitulation of Austria-Hungary.

At St. Hilaire we were informed that we were for the line again in France, and that on our way up to the front the division was to have the honour of carrying out the ceremonial relief of Lille. We arrived in Lomme, a suburb of that city, at dusk on the 26th, and marched to our billets through dense crowds of enthusiastic inhabitants.

All the town was out; women were among the ranks, tossing their children in the air—staff cars pushed their way past—crawling through the dense crowds, weighed down with excited children of the schoolboy age. We struggled through an enthusiastic mob to our luxurious billets.

The following day, Sunday, was spent in intensive cleaning and polishing, and it was a very smart division that marched through the city on Monday morning. Every house and shop was beflagged—every inhabitant appeared to be either in the street or at the window, cheering, clapping, and waving flags. Although the First Surrey Rifles was the last unit, except the pioneers, in the procession, there was apparently no abatement in the enthusiasm of our welcome; if there was, the ovation accorded to the leading troops must have been terrific. In the Grand Place we marched past the mayor and notables of the city, who occupied a platform with General Birdwood, Lieut.-General Haking, and the divisional commander and their staffs. After a short halt near corps head-quarters in La Madeleine, we marched through to our billets on the far side of the city. It was a most impressive day, and one that will be hard to forget.

Though Lille was a city *"en fête"* there were on all sides the marks of wanton Hun destruction, and in every mouth tales of harshness and oppression. In every house all metal of value had been commandeered; in the enormous barrack of a factory where we were billeted in Lomme every bit of machinery had been removed, and what could not be used had been ruthlessly destroyed: nothing was left but the cast iron beds on which the machinery had rested. And there are those who wonder why France insists on reparations and guarantees, though most of this destruction was deliberately carried out, not, as might have been justifiable, to bring about the military downfall of France, but to retard her post-war recovery!

In defeat, too, the Germans produced the manners and habits of the sty. The billets which we occupied after the procession through the city displayed a state of filth that from its absolute beastliness is best left to the imagination. General Kennedy could tell a story of his billet in Lomme which would appear to show that acts of dirty indecency were not confined to the billets of the rank and file, where they might have been attributed to ignorance, or to the slackness bred of a waning discipline.

On the evening of the 28th, General Kennedy was unexpectedly recalled to England on family affairs, and the colonel went back to Brigade; the command of the Battalion devolved upon Major Newton, who had joined us as second-in-command some days before we moved up to Lille. After another day in Lille we moved forward into Belgium, and spent a few days at Cornet, where successful sports were held. On November 4th we moved into Honnerain to relieve the 17th, who went forward into the front line on the Escault. Next night the colonel came back from Brigade, but, having got influenza at brigade head-quarters, left for hospital the next morning, and Major Newton commanded the Battalion during the closing days of the war.

These days saw the evacuation of Tournai, and we were actually beyond that city, the brigade, with the First Surrey Rifles leading, being in support to the 142nd, when, on November 11th, we were told that the advance was cancelled, the war was over, and we were to march back to billets in La Tombe.

Considering the talk there had been about "when the war is over," there was extraordinarily little enthusiasm. The end had been expected for some days, and actually the first week of peace was very little less eventful than the last week of war. If there were sighs of relief for a bad business well over, that was all the enthusiasm that bad weather and a certain amount of boredom could raise. No mafficking, no shouting—there was enough of that elsewhere—it was all rather flat and tame.

After being very busy for some days cleaning up the traces of German destruction on road and railway, we moved back to Willems on the 18th, where the officers took advantage of a billet with a suitable dining room to inaugurate a battalion mess on the 21st, and the same day Colonel Dawes, who had finished having influenza, and rejoined on the 15th, went on leave—and that was the last that was seen of him, except by an undemobilized portion of the Battalion to whom he paid a flying farewell visit at the end of January before returning to the warmer, sunnier skies of West Africa.

On November 24th was held a divisional church parade of all denominations, headed by their own clergy, a fitting if feeble acknowledgment that whatever we had suffered and whatever we had lost, we had very much more to be thankful for than our own unaided efforts could have attempted, much less attained. We left Belgium two days later, and returned to our old haunts in Auchel.

CHAPTER XI.

November 27th, 1918, to July 5th, 1919.

The End.

As soon as we got to Auchel there was one subject which became uppermost in our thoughts; one subject which, wherever there were two or three gathered together, you could be sure was the theme of conversation, and that was demobilization. And to keep us from thinking too hard on this subject, General Head-quarters devised and widely advertised its two counter-irritants, sport and education. Now, while all formations were maintaining their strength and no longer suffering daily casualties, football matches and athletic contests and horse shows fostered the rivalry which is the basis of self-respect and hence of discipline. Cup-ties were played to great audiences on the high and rather bleak hill-top dividing Auchel from Lozinghem, and there were few afternoons, save when the weather was too unpropitious, without some inter-company event. Nor was training of a more strictly military nature neglected. Guard discipline and ceremonial were made more of than had been possible in the fighting days, and route marches of a morning sweetened tempers without exhausting physique. And once a week there was always the luxury of hot baths for everyone at the mine buildings.

Education was made, and rightly, a matter of importance. So many had been snatched away to war almost straight from school, and were, in proportion to the keenness with which they had answered their country's call, by just so much the more unfitted to return to civilian occupations. So General Head-quarters took the matter in hand and issued a large number of pamphlets and regulations on the subject. Suggestions for classes ranged from higher mathematics to bee-keeping, and a general aspect of educational energy was soon attained. From the more intimate point of view of a battalion commander, education seemed to take on two phases; a period when there were many men but few teachers or text-books; and a second period when teachers and text-books were easier to find, but the men had gone. The experimental work done at this time proved a valuable experience for those about to organize similar training in the post-war Regular Army, where "education" became so important.

Speaking generally, minds and hands were fully occupied, and there were few opportunities anywhere for mischievous idleness. Indeed, the whole state of discipline remained creditable to the very end, and this is no small matter when we realize that here were 600 men all anxious to go home, all feeling that the war was over, and conscious of a gradual weakening of that sense of intimate cohesion which naturally unites men who will be going into the line again to-morrow against a common foe.

Nor were the intricacies of the demobilization regulations calculated to increase confidence, discipline, and goodwill. In the remoteness of St. James's Park it may have seemed the right national policy to release four "pivotal" men (teachers, farmers, fishermen, printers, carmen, builders, municipal employees, &c.) to every one long-service man, but to the fighting soldier it seemed unjust. And as few men went at once to work on getting home, the argument for this form of preference certainly broke down in practice. It is, however, generally possible slightly to misunderstand the complicated regulations of a very high and distant authority, and few long-service men in the Battalion had cause for complaint, while many of the indispensable W.O.'s and senior N.C.O.'s voluntarily offered to remain with the Battalion so long as their services were wanted.

Very few men in any case left us before Christmas, which was spent in the traditional way at Auchel. Morning service was held in the "Follies" theatre, and the afternoon was devoted to feasting and song in the ten separate rooms into which the companies were divided, mostly the large rooms of *estaminets,* but in one case a whole company was together in a barn, with its walls hung with army blankets and gay with Chinese lanterns. The C.O. visited all the companies in the course of the evening, and a week later drank the New Year in with the sergeants' mess.

Demobilization really began for the Battalion about the second week in January. Fifty men had left by the 13th, and 110 by January 18th, and over 400 by February 10th. On February 20th the depleted battalion moved to Ferfay to join the other two battalions of the brigade, the 15th and 17th, in quarters round the Château of Ferfay. By now we had ceased to be a battalion, either in numbers or organization, though we were still to linger till May 4th before the cadre, which had in the meanwhile shed its superfluities to the Army of Occupation or to the United Kingdom for re-enlistment, entrained at Pernes for Hâvre, Southampton, and Felixstowe, where, thanks to the efficiency of the quartermaster and transport officer, the final formalities of handing over stores were quickly disposed of, and by the middle of May we were once more civilians.

On the last Thursday of this same month of May, Camberwell gave an official welcome to the cadre of the Battalion. For this purpose a body of men was chosen more representative of the fighting record than was the actual cadre which was disembodied at Felixstowe, The mayor first entertained the officers and men to dinner at the Masonic Hall, when the health of the First Surreys was proposed by Dr. T. J. Macnamara, M.P., after which they marched to the Town Hall, where the mayor gave them an official welcome in the Council Chamber. Thence the march through the borough was resumed, and the parade dismissed at Brunswick Park, where a fête in aid of the Borough War Memorial was being held.

The final public act in which the Battalion took its part was the triumphal march of London troops through London on July 5th, 1919, five years all but a month from the day on which they had been embodied. In those days they were troops of whose prowess even their well-wishers could have no more than anxious hopes: now all were veterans in a battalion whose record from Givenchy to Moislains was second to that of none of its comrades on this historic march. Past the school-children on Constitution Hill, His Majesty King George V. in front of Buckingham Palace, and my Lord Mayor at the Mansion House they passed on that sunny July day. Their last triumphal march of the kind had been in October of the previous year, into Lille, a city very visibly delivered from a brutal enemy, whose foul traces everywhere remained about it. London, they had less obviously, but no less surely, helped to preserve from the same ruthless hands, and it was fitting that their last corporate act in the war should be to receive from their fellow-citizens a homage of this nature before dispersing finally to their several homes and becoming indistinguishable units of the crowd upon the pavement.

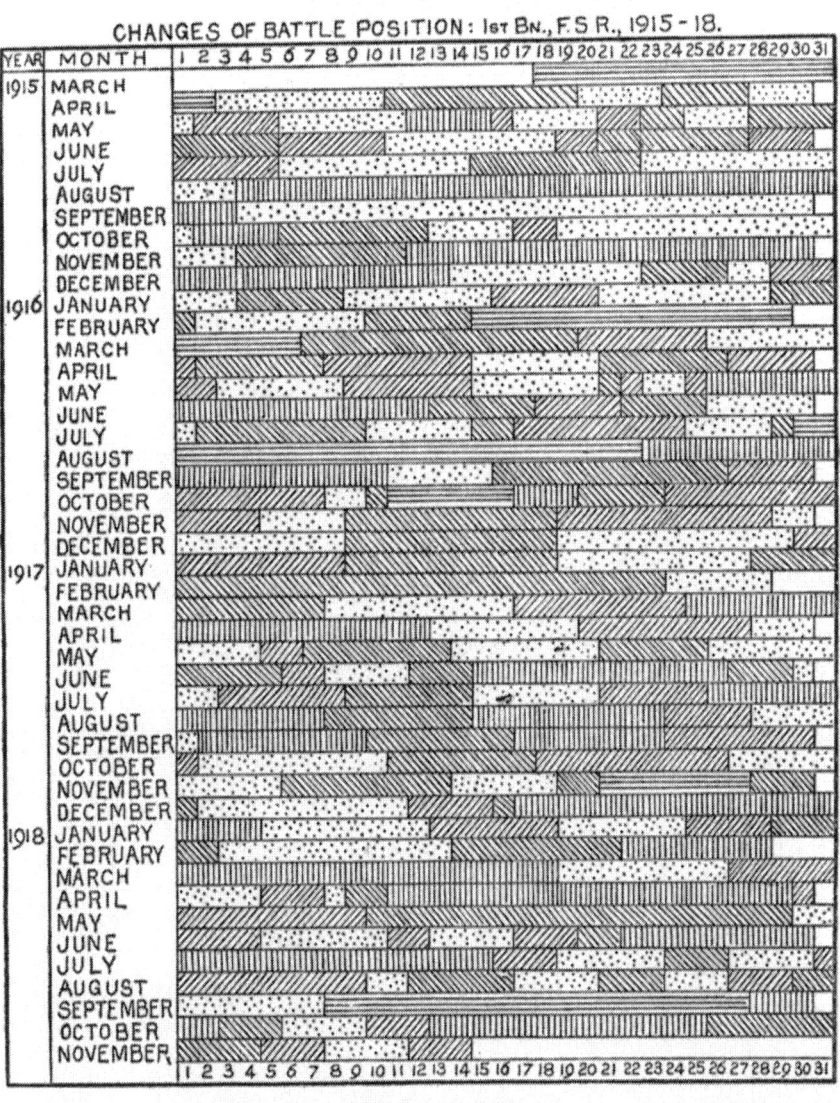

PART II.

A WAR RECORD

OF THE

FIRST SURREY RIFLES

(SECOND BATTALION).

INTRODUCTION.

The 2/21st Battalion, The London Regiment came into being in an unimportant side-street in Camberwell: it was disbanded in Palestine on a bare, rock-strewn hill-slope a few miles north of Jerusalem. Between these two places and the two points of time they represent lies the history of the unit. It is a record with which Destiny took some trouble. Most of her military charges went straight into the maelstrom to be engulfed, thrown out, re-engulfed, almost mechanically until the end. In those fearful processes of quick attrition units can hardly be said to have had a continuous history. The speed at which the personnel was destroyed left nothing sometimes but the label of the name to march under. How units in France or Gallipoli fought against this destruction is in their own histories the central theme. But for us, men of the 60th Division, another set of experiences was staged. Our drama was long and regular: its four acts were four countries, and its catastrophe the Jordan Valley. The Jordan Valley! No premonition of it, no hint of the volcanic splendours of that far region visited for a moment the half-companies now materializing for our first chapter in the drill field at Camberwell.

CHAPTER I.—ENGLAND.

"The Beverley Brook, and Ruskin Park:
(*Mutton pies on a rainy day*).
Half a tragedy, half a lark:
(*When do you think we are going away?*)
"To France! To France! ere the War be done!
(*List to the voice of the Great Untried*)
Don't you be in a hurry, my son!
(*Allah is good, and the world is wide*)."

1.
At Flodden Road.

When the 21st Battalion, The London Regiment, left Camberwell, it dropped at the depôt a certain number of officers to form the nucleus of a second battalion. This second battalion, the history of which now comes to be written, was not originally destined to have a history—it was to be quite simply a draft-finding unit, nothing more. For some considerable time during its life in England it bore this intention of the authorities in its official label—"21st (Reserve) Battalion." Against this view commanding officers strove, and at length, as the magnitude of the war began to be perceived, gained their point, and we, in conjunction with other units similarly placed, became known as "second battalions," and began to look forward to service overseas in a division of our own.

But this is looking forward. In September, 1914, all the rank and file, and most of the officers of our civilian-clothed unit, were only counting the weeks before, equipped and trained, we should be called upon to do important work. Enthusiasm, coupled with little knowledge, combined to telescope time. Long before September was over the ranks were full. Every morning of those first glorious days of late summer saw us marching off, bag-capped or bowler-hatted, to Ruskin or Brockwell Park to receive the elements of training. "We shall be all right when we know our job," one officer said to another as they marched together. That officer served with the Battalion from beginning to end. He certainly did not imagine that our formal training period would extend for close upon two years.

The history of these early months is one of progress in the teeth of many obstacles. We were lucky in having left to us a fine head-quarters with a large drill hall and adequate drill field. Nevertheless, we were much overcrowded. It had early been decided to give the men at least dinner and tea at head-quarters, and as the Battalion was too big to be accommodated in the hall, tents were erected on the field, and cook-houses near them. This was a great advantage, as we got more hold over the men and were able to arrange training programmes more effectively. Looking back, it is surprising to see how much in the way of training was actually accomplished. During the whole of the time no rifles were available, except a few which the Dulwich College authorities kindly allowed us to use when we visited their grounds. Colonel Coldicott, who had taken up the command early in September, took great pains to make this early training as interesting as possible. It was his theory that men who came, as ours did, from a good class, and were intelligent and quick to learn, would benefit from simple tactical exercises. These would also serve to give a purpose to route marches, which become monotonous when practised again and again over a small area. This idea of his, which was thoroughly popular, became in practice that ingenious series of exercises on Wimbledon Common, when White Force fought Brown Force in the neighbourhood of Beverley Brook. Many will long remember the humours of those field-days, the ovations the Battalion had from upper windows of houses, the excitement upon arrival, the schemings of Captain Harry to outwit Captain Crowe. There is no doubt that they did the Battalion a great deal of good.

These exercises stand out by themselves, but most of the events of those first months come now into one's mind as a series of little pictures—a series with no continuity. There is the daily morning assembly in the drill-field, and the adroit, or maladroit, evolutions of the eight companies as they moved into close column. There are those lectures in the dining tents, by officers who were not put more at their ease by seeing riflemen turn up with text-books in their hands. One can see Captain Harry on one of these occasions lecturing on map-reading, and Lieut. Mills, the geologist, annoying him by standing up and propounding difficult questions of a scientific nature. There is the cinder track at Ruskin Park, and men in shirt-sleeves hopping round it with their hands on their hips. One can remember the difficulty of obtaining silence when the orderly officer came round with his "any complaints" at meal-times—discipline did not come easily in those early days. Officers will recollect their first acquaintance with bayonet-fighting—evening attendances in the drill-hall under Captain Wright. N.C.O.'s looking back will think of the first promotion classes, those examinations in the drill-field, and Sergeant Fletcher. And the men will remember the dual lives they led, half at home and half at head-quarters, like day-boys, unsatisfactory to them and to the army.

Late summer had yielded to the attacks of an unusually rainy approach of winter before our Londoners were given any sign of a change of habitat. One abortive expedition had been made by a small party into Essex—the first billeting expedition—but the authorities destroyed their work at the last moment, and many months passed before a roundabout route led us to that county. Under the curtain of an almost incessant rainfall, life at Flodden Road had become only less miserable than the lot of our cousin battalions lodged in the jimcrack stucco palaces of the White City. Our enthusiasm was by this time changing its first gay coat for something of a more sober hue. By very slow degrees, and after many soakings of civilian clothes worn miserably shabby, odds and ends of outer and inner garments began to issue from the quartermaster's stores, until the time came when the officer, splendidly encased in a Church Lads' Brigade uniform, no longer enjoyed adventitious prestige on that account. This, at a time when our once green drill-field had become a mud-flat, gave an extraordinary fillip to a unit that had become heartily sick of Camberwell and all its surroundings. The news that everyone was to be bundled off to Redhill gave rise to excitement that made Christmas an almost unregarded festival.

Billeting preparations followed, developed on delightfully spacious lines by Captain Crowe. Days passed, and in due course the silver bugles of the 2/21st—a parting gift from the ladies of Dulwich—announced the end of the first stage of the Battalion's history, and the beginning of a long process of new development.

2.

Redhill.

Four outstanding events are engraven on the record of our sojourn at Redhill: the institution of "company feeding," the trench-digging at Merstham, the arrival of the Japanese rifles, and the hasty change from eight company to four company organization. Some would add a fifth—the famous march to Epsom in the snow, to be reviewed by Lord Kitchener. Still another event was the arrival of "the Brigade"—the establishment of our Brigade Head-quarters Staff in a house in Redhill.

The Brigade, however, attracted little notice amid the general awareness of the partial breakdown of the food supply, or, if not perhaps of the actual supply, of the means of turning it into meals. Our move had dislocated for the first time an excellent cook-house organization, and there was nothing immediately available to replace it. The quartermaster's stores were ill-suited for the purpose, and though the cooks worked hard, it was difficult to get the machine to run smoothly. Finally, the arrangements that had been made for central feeding were doubly bad, in that accommodation was both inadequate and only of a temporary nature, and that the billets were much scattered and men had to come a long distance for their meals. The trouble was solved by the action of the companies, which took upon themselves the responsibility of drawing rations and the entire feeding of their men. This sudden decentralization was, in the circumstances, justified, for the Battalion was scattered, and no suitable place for central feeding could be found. The immediate problem of finding eight company head-quarters, of sufficient size to house the men for meals, was solved by the almost simultaneous arrival of four company organization, and a few days saw the building up of four strongholds, jealous and highly critical of each other ! The financial support on which these fortresses rested was the allowance of fourpence per day per man for milk, butter, and vegetables. These small sums were drawn in bulk a month in arrears by the company commanders, and administered by them. Daily messing books were unknown or disregarded, and though some attempt at an audit was once made by head-quarters, there were in reality no checks on how the money went. In effect the result was good; better results were obtained, and large sums of money were actually saved and expended on extra food for special occasions. Enterprise even went as far as the then almost unheard of provision of recreation rooms for the men.

The general badness of the weather, coupled with extra work entailed by the new conditions under which the Battalion was working, caused a good deal of sickness, especially among the officers, and "Iodine Dick," as our doctor was popularly called, would have been kept busy had he not already acquired the art of dealing rapidly with his patients. In the prevailing wetness the usual difficulty was experienced of varying sufficiently the outdoor training, for no one can route march in the rain for ever, and army overcoats would not stand more than a light summer shower.

Affairs were in this posture when some high command grew fearful of the state of London's defences, and we were suddenly ordered to go and dig trenches on the top of Merstham Hill. Some hated this, but to others it was a welcome change. A few fine days lured us into thinking that we were making reasonably good progress. Tools were given out from a large barn, cocoa and soup conveyed thither by the companies. Officers fed adequately in a farmhouse. Everyone grew muddied almost to the neck. All went fairly well until the trenches filled with water! Then the snow came, and a thaw, and the Merstham trenches were little more than an expression on paper. But the training was real and valuable : the Battalion gained for the first time practice in the use of the spade—an implement which is often, in war, second only in value to the rifle. Officers were able to learn the importance of drainage problems, and the labouring side of war was here exhibited to us, a pale English reflection of what it might be : we had not yet seen a sand-bag.

About this time our long-expected rifles arrived, packed solid in mysterious-looking cases. It was the talk of the Battalion, but our feelings were of a mixed order when it was discovered that they hailed from Japan. Not a few realized more deeply than ever the inadequacy of our national resources. Examined critically, the rifle proved no toy or second-rate piece of mechanism, but a well-made weapon, and, as we shortly afterwards proved at Hythe, a remarkably accurate one. Two things militated against it : the number of delicate and easily lost accessories of the kind that accompany sewing machines, and the slimness of the bullet, which rendered it a less deadly weapon than ours. There was a simple device that made it impossible to close the bolt when the magazine was empty, in order to prevent men excited in action from clicking off without reloading. One of the small etceteras was known as a "jag." The first thing the 2/21st did was to lose most of them!

The Redhill period is mainly a record of bad weather, and training carried on in the teeth of it. When a battalion, whose members have only recently ceased to be civilians, is quartered at large upon a town in winter, progress becomes difficult and slow. Looking back, route marches, courses (just commencing) close order drill on sloppy fields and commons, even the excitements of mock attacks over a tumbled heath, have ceased to remain clear in the memory against a definite background. Perhaps it is something more than the vagary of an individual mind that keeps secure so many pictures of the domestic side of that life, details of billets, the interior of a company orderly room, a meeting of officers at Battalion Head-quarters (that cramped shop in the High Street), the fusty smell of dirty, knocked-about rooms overcrowded with men, the mixed smell of groceries and garments that hung in the quartermaster's stores. What survivor of "D" Company will, even in his ninetieth year, forget that first company head-quarters, "Ordnance House," the two dilapidated stucco mansions knocked into one, with its platoon dining-rooms crammed with mobs of hungry men, queues of mess orderlies formed up in the basements, cooks, stripped half-naked in the kitchens' sweltering heat, and sweating like stokers, hauling out great joints and masses of steaming vegetables? How easy, in a more deliberate history, to set forth the desperate financial straits into which "C" Company was rumoured to have fallen, and see those straits reflected in its miserable head-quarters at the top of the hill. "What did you give your men for dinner to-day?" one company commander would jealously ask another. "Our men had pies for breakfast yesterday and they won't touch them. Dainty brutes!"

"You're too well fed, that's what you are," said an officer once (it was in Spells' shop, Sawbridgeworth), and the startling remark became a byword. Indeed, in the light of after experiences, these early days were luxurious enough in spite of bad cooking and management. The food was better than that served to young guardsmen at Chelsea Barracks, and there was more of it, but many men had plenty of money to buy extra food at shops, and this made some despise army rations.

By the time Redhill had become well habituated to us we were gone. The inhabitants, not staled as some towns were by the continual passage of troops, had given us a very hearty welcome, and, what is far more difficult, had kept it up. One of the last acts of the Battalion shortly before its departure was the much-needed establishment of a mess. An empty house was taken and furniture hired, but the catering is memorable only for its badness. It was in this mess that several new officers made their first appearance, amongst them 2nd-Lieut. Bull, who had been in the ranks, and who afterwards made a reputation as signalling officer.

3.

St. Albans and Sawbridgeworth.

By the time the Battalion had arrived at St. Albans, winter was definitely over. Preliminary arrangements had taken a long time—over a fortnight—and billeting was a matter of extreme difficulty, for the town had been deluged with troops and (without any disrespect to our first battalion be it said!) had had enough of them. We got, on the whole, the worst area, which included a wretched district whose centre was Sopwell Lane. Central feeding was absolutely impossible, and company head-quarters not officially hireable. It ended in premises of a modified kind being taken for companies, while Battalion Head-quarters established itself at the "White Hart." The quartermaster had a large and excellent warehouse luckily secured for him, whence he could radiate his blessings without fear, favour, or undue confusion. The usual intense interest and strife of factions attended the making of these dispositions. The Battalion arrived, all curiosity, by train. After some minor grumbles it settled down.

By this time the Japanese rifles had been withdrawn, and musketry practice proper commenced at a range some miles out of the town. It was a week or two before winter's last rains were over, and this shooting was carried out in cold, wet weather. A new kind of "fatigue" appeared—that of building up the ranges, which were continually being destroyed. This most unpopular exercise used to be sprung upon companies suddenly on a Sunday morning, and was resented by the men, who still regarded that day as privileged. Another not very appreciated amusement was the "company run" before breakfast, an invention of Captain Wright, who, by dint of much persuasion and reiteration, got the colonel to set his seal to it. The enthusiastic ones put on sporting attire, the old and debilitated ambled painfully in trousers. All wore gym. shoes, bought out of the immense funds of the Battalion, fruits of economic management of the food supply at Flodden Road. There seems to be no doubt that this parade, though it was finally condemned by the doctors, was of great value to the Battalion. Run on generally sporting lines, it helped to improve good relationship between the most athletic of the officers and the men, and it got the men well-breathed, which most branches of military training fail to do. A very early start had been made in this direction at Flodden Road. The running parade, as it was called, continued throughout the St. Albans and Sawbridgeworth periods. Several isolated runs were held in the winter at Coggeshall, and there was an effort made at Sutton Veney.

After the first ten days the weather grew fine enough to have an influence on training. Everyone began to be enthusiastic about advancing in "short rushes." Small bodies of men would get up quickly, rush forward a few paces, and then fling themselves down again perfectly flat. These exercises took place in a series of grassy fields conveniently situated just out of the town, and here, too, an historic scene took place. Though now it seems unthinkable, the Battalion was then composed of two sorts of men—those who were willing to take the "Imperial Service Obligation," and those who were not. At Camberwell, when this question was put to the vote, over eighty per cent. volunteered for service abroad. But there were indications that now the proportion that had decided to remain "Home Service" had increased. After we had been a week or two at St. Albans, a number of green forms arrived, on which the men were asked to record their final decision. This sudden putting of the question stirred us like a general election. It came very hurriedly; the return was wanted at once. Officers went round to canvass their men; speeches were made that evening under lamp-posts. Next morning the Battalion was marched to the training field and an appeal was made by the colonel. Then the Home Service men and those who had signed on for Foreign Service were paraded separately. A "stand easy" was given, and the Foreign Service men called for individuals to come over. Some came, amid cheering, but a considerable number remained obstinate. No attempt at penalization was made, the question was regarded as an open one, to be settled by each man in his own heart.

About the same time—it was towards the end of our six weeks at St. Albans—Captain Harry and Captain Russell left us for Camberwell, where, with the assistance of the band, they hoped to raise enough men to start a third battalion. Few thought that they would have much chance, for in the spring of 1915 voluntary recruiting was at a very low ebb. But, mainly by Captain Harry's energetic adoption of popular tactics (a phrase covering not a few amusing incidents) the adventure was a complete success, nor did these two officers return to us.

It must not be supposed that the Battalion was divided at this time; the Home Service business had only assumed a temporary importance, and a few days after the memorable parade, programmes of training, sport, amusement, the weekly struggle for leave to London, made for individuals a life so busy and complete, that few bothered about anything but the immediate present. Soon everyone was talking about the Battalion sports, and companies started training teams for a Marathon race, which was finally brought off as the culminating spectacle of a great day.

When the news came that we were to pack up and go on our travels again, and Sawbridgeworth was named as the Battalion's summer residence, everyone was highly delighted, for we were to have the whole of the village to ourselves and would be "on our own." The usual billeting party made the usual lavish arrangements, and in due course the Battalion arrived, this time by "march route."

These were rural billets. The quartermaster's stores were lodged in a very old empty inn, with ranges of tumble-down stables. Many of the men were billeted some distance out in old cottages. Head-quarters were in an old empty house called "Hatter's Croft." When we left St. Albans the quartermaster's stores, which, like the rich young man in the Bible, "had great possessions," abandoned a quantity of its belongings, and amongst them a wooden hut built for the doctor at Flodden Road, and known as "Iodine Villa." Our history would not be complete without mention of this famous structure, but what finally happened to it the historian cannot tell. Perhaps it went the same way as our forms and tables, our band instruments, and our cash surplus!

At Sawbridgeworth we spent the summer—our golden time. All old members of the Battalion will agree that here we were at our very best. Had the summons come now for us to go to France we should have cried that we were ready. We were not ready, for the training of those days was not sufficiently technical to fit anyone for France, but for spirit, discipline, enterprise, knowledge of open order warfare, steadiness on parade, general intelligence, smartness, the Battalion here, by general consent, reached its high-water mark. We had become excellent peace-time troops. In the summer night our bugles would sound perfectly the "Last Post," and with pride the colonel loved to listen to them, standing outside "The Red House." R.S.M. Jennings, always in the prime of professional competence, would be heard at Sawbridgeworth sometimes to say that he was almost a little pleased, though, even now, his "Ho, no! that won't do for the Sergeant-Major," echoed at least once a day. But here, without doubt, the Battalion had its chance, and took it. Companies were given opportunities as never before, and ran little tactical exercises. One night "D" Company ("God's Own," as they were called) went up to a lonely rabbit-warren and by dawn completely dug themselves in. One awful night the Battalion went out and bivouacked —in the rain. It is easy to laugh at such enthusiasm, but where is the like of it now?

It all came to an end suddenly with the news that the Home Service men were to be sent away. Some four hundred, they paraded with their kit-bags and marched to the station. It was a blow to the unit, but it settled at last a vexing and troublesome question.

4.

The Last Stages.

Early in September the Battalion moved into camp at Hockerill, on the high ground outside Bishops Stortford. Here we found ourselves for the first time in company with the other battalions of the brigade, the 2/22nd, 2/23rd, 2/24th. Drafts came to us, field-kitchens arrived, a battalion mess was started. Everyone settled down to still more training. Rumours ran round, and were duly confirmed, that everyone was to fire a course at the ranges. A school of bombing and trench digging began on a hill on the other side of the town.

Over these new activities a new chief presided— Brigadier-General Watts, who added to our lives a new liveliness, and certainly made the brigade move more quickly.

Hockerill Camp, if not altogether a dream of delight, was pleasant enough until the weather broke. A sketch of it, together with much other matter relating to this period, is to be found in the Battalion magazine, the first of whose two numbers was published in that camp in October. Before the end came and the mud overwhelmed us, a picturesque event took place—what was long known as "The Essex trek." This was an operation of some magnitude in which, for the first time, all arms of the division were engaged. It lasted several days, and then we had to do it again because the artillery (so it was said) had played us up! At the close of the manœuvre it was found that far too little consideration had been given to the billeting scheme and arrangements. Darkness came: the country was unknown. Battalion transport, which had lately come into existence, had a memorable time. We realized suddenly the tremendous importance of *staff* : the experience of ours in the movements of large formations was as yet only in its infancy.

Nevertheless, like the muddy times we had spent on Merstham Hill, these two great expeditions benefited us. It was good to leave the camp at Hockerill, with its dull routine and small company outings, which, however realistic enthusiastic officers might make them, were curbed remorselessly by tea or by the mid-day meal. As the year advanced and the weather broke, our camp became first unpleasant, then intolerable. No one had been allowed to drain it; the tents had been pitched much too close together; soon it was a sea of mud, where anyone who attempted to salute promptly fell prone. In the middle of these storms, on a day when a cataract of rain was pouring down, the Battalion struggled out *en route* for winter billets at Coggeshall. "Soldiers! that's what they call 'em. Soldiers!" said the regimental-sergeant-major, as he watched the strings of sodden wretches plunging singly on to the road, and fell straightway into recollection of some far-away Dublin adventure, when tents, packs, fodder, and thousands of pounds' worth of Government stores floated away down the Liffey. He could always go one better by fishing something out of the past. Now we are his past, and those older adventures probably lie forgotten.

The march to Coggeshall was like other marches when long columns of troops move on roads—irregularly and unpleasantly punctuated with untimely checks and hurries : but Coggeshall was like nothing else we had ever seen. A remote Essex village, guiltless of troops, to which, as a community, the war seemed nothing but the echo of a tale. Much could be written of it, nothing can here, except that we filled the place. Here, in spite of very bad weather, the colonel led out his small army to many a tactical operation. Bridges were defended and captured, church towers disgracefully used as observation stations. Here were long route marches along winding lanes, past places with quaint names. Here, in a large field belonging to a fine old house a mile or so away, an effort was made to capture the realities of trench warfare with two opposing lines of trenches and quantities of old material. A truck-load of sand-bags, sent charitably from London from a private source, was lavished on this scheme. But the Brigade had heard of something new in trench fashions, and these of ours filled with water, and the snow came, and there was an end of it. It did not matter. The Battalion was not thinking about the present :

it speculated, in billets and out of billets, at crowded feeding-times, on the march, tramping in jolly parties to catch the London leave-train at Kelvedon, about its future. How entirely rumour held the stage can be seen by a glance into the second and last number of the Battalion magazine, a grand production of over fifty pages, crammed with illustrations. The existence of this store-house of information (those who seek to revive old memories can do so in a moment by turning to "Company Rhymes") makes a full description of Coggeshall days needless in this chronicle. It shows how full of life we were, how rich a personality the Battalion had developed, how eager the unit was to get abroad. 1914 had gone by; 1915 had come to an end; everyone felt that our continued presence in England was a disgrace. How any longer could men on leave face the girls? What explanations could they render?

The departure of our band for Clacton, where the Home Service men disported themselves, gave no clue to possible removals; but close on this came the transfer of Colonel Coldicott to the third line. No event in the history of the Battalion up to this date is of greater importance. His vacation of the command marks an epoch. To him the leaving of the Battalion was a most bitter disappointment; he had hoped that, despite his age, he would have been allowed to take it abroad.

Except for the final six months, which can be regarded as an epilogue, the creation and training of the Battalion was largely due to him. Whatever influences it came under in after-days, he unalterably formed it and made it. Members of the Battalion who date from its first year and who survived the war, will always remember his active figure and soldierly bearing, on horseback or marching at the column's head. He rammed home the importance of route marching and open order warfare : subsequent events proved he could not have made a better choice. He was a man who, since his early youth, had held a commission in the Volunteers and the Territorials. He had given the leisure hours of nearly half a century to preparation for the war he long expected, and which, at last, came a few years too late for him. His ambition to see active service in France was at last gratified, and he spent two strenuous years there, not without adventures. The Battalion throve under his command, and deeply regretted his departure.

This change was but a prelude to a greater. Towards the end of January, 1916, the Battalion moved to No. 1 Camp, Sutton Veney, a few miles from Warminster, on the edge of

Salisbury Plain. Just before we left Coggeshall a large draft of recruits arrived, for the defection of the Home Service men had left us much under strength. The train journey was long and miserable, and the march from Warminster left the road strewn with the recruits who, naturally enough, found they couldn't carry kit-bags as well as full marching order. Our new camp was at the further end of a world of hutments. On one side of us were green fields, and in front several hills, at some distance, marked the end of the plain; but behind us and to our left there was nothing but huts and camps and dumps—all the impedimenta of war.

Before a month had elapsed we had been reviewed by Lord French, had recognized a new divisional commander in General Bulfin, and had been bidden farewell by our brigadier. In his place came Brigadier-General Parsons : our brigade-major was Captain Horlick, and our staff-captain, Captain Bartle-Edwards, both very popular officers.

In a few days we had settled down to a humdrum, busy existence in much mud and discomfort. Very little leave was granted, with the result that "crime" increased, as more men stole their holidays. The Battalion gradually went through its last changes preparatory to going abroad. Major Fletcher, who from the beginning was second-in-command under Colonel Coldicott, had now succeeded him as commanding officer. Into his old place stepped Major Wright, not altogether happy to have to give up a company. Puckle, English, Coldicott, Walter, had finally come to the top as company commanders; Macdonald was settling into his permanent position as adjutant; Levy had taken the transport over from Bloy; Bull's time was entirely devoted to mysterious communings with the signallers. Regimental-Sergeant-Major Jennings was, as ever, absolute lord and master of a world of N.C.O.'s.

Slowly the months rolled by, crammed with incidents too numerous to be recorded here. January and February brought hosts of sick men, snow, discomfort, monotonous route marches and trench diggings. March saw some of our Home Service men compulsorily returned to us, soon to be swamped in a growing enthusiasm for musketry. In April the specialist sections lifted up their heads and drained the companies of men. This month, too, took Major Durham away, quartermaster since the Battalion had been formed, a familiar figure amongst us, and much missed. A host of small events belong to this time—the arrival of the short rifle (in boxes mysteriously labelled "Home Service"); the issue of new boots, and the oiling of same; the appearance (once or twice only) of Major Wright's pet drum and fife band, whose voice was as the twittering of young swallows; the visit of the 179th Brigade to Ireland. In May everyone was talking about battalion sports, but the real event was a brigade exercise designed to give us a foretaste of the trenches.

In many respects it was wonderfully realistic, but grotesque elements caused a hilarity few found in the real event. It should not have been possible, for example, to send from the front line to the battalion mess for plates of sandwiches! Lieut. Liddiatt, who was a great man in those days, had sole charge of all fireworks and bombs and ballistic apparatus, and it was during these mimic operations that he caused us to be shelled with tiny bags of sand propelled by one of his catapults. By night the discrepancies were not so apparent, and star shells, muddy trenches, and long strings of burdened men stumbling across mud flats might have caused a veteran to dream for a moment of rest billets and the next mail.

On May 30th the King reviewed the division. Then came "final leave": a longer farewell for most of the men than they ever dreamed. Just as we were making last preparations for departure a draft of eighty-six men came from the London Rifle Brigade to make us up to strength. These men were a very fine and smart contingent, and immediately became popular.

At length, on June 24th, after nearly two years in England, the minute of departure came. The Battalion was launched. It seemed to some of us that something must prevent it at the last moment—something that would decree the East Coast, or squad drill without arms. But there were the men—entrained! And, by gad! the train really is moving out of Warminster Station. Jump in, you officers! We are off to France!

CHAPTER II.—FRANCE.

1.

We go to Louez.

Do you remember old St. Pol
Where first the companies detrained?
The smear of far-off Verey-lights,
How tired we were and how it rained?
I've never seen the town by day
It may be empty of delight;
To us it was a journey's end:
France! and our second night!

The Battalion disembarked from *La Marguerite* early in the morning of June 25th. Hâvre, as representing France, did not look enticing; it was wet, and the passage from Southampton had been rough! The "Docks Rest Camp," also, held no attractions; but brilliant sunshine came at length, and it was a very lively battalion that was packed into the French troop train. We were going the way of a million troops before us, but we made jokes as if war were a new thing and we the first men eager for the first engagement. Darkness had fallen before we arrived in the dim-lit station of St. Pol, and there detrained. Lorries were at hand to take our packs, and we were soon marching packless in a moonless night up a straight avenue. It was not far, someone announced, to our billets. Time went on and still we marched, passed a crossing, and went on again. To our left, on the horizon, star-shells rose and quivered to a fall. It was raining; the road was bad and muddy. After a long time we turned to the right up a narrow, winding lane. The low out-buildings of a small farm showed dimly against the night. Our column's head ran into our billeting party. The lane split into tracks, and the Battalion vanished by companies into various selected darknesses. An hour after our entry into Ecoivres the whole of the Battalion was asleep except the transport, which, by dawn, was discovered to have arrived.

In the morning we sorted out our packs, and were engaged in cleaning up when orders came for us to move to Tinques. We arrived about 7.30 p.m. The inhabitants were anything but hospitable (with the exception of some girls in a café), but we got nearly a day's rest before setting out for Louez, our final destination, a place within a short distance of Arras. Our route, once clear of Tinques, lay for the most part along the Arras road, a fine causeway, straight and monotonous, with a track for horses on one side of it. There was nothing romantic about the road, nor were the villages we passed—Savy, Haute-Avesnes—of any particular interest, and yet that march to Louez claims a memorable place in this history. Quickly the daylight passed, and darkness swallowed us up as we pressed forward to we knew not what, a body of untried men, some excited, some eager, some apprehensive, but all mere children in a new world, with slates absolutely clean. "How much further?" was a question officers were continually being asked, as the hours wore on and packs grew heavier and heavier. Every shred of information was passed from man to man, dissected, commented on. At one point in the last three-quarters of an hour it looked doubtful if the Battalion would ever get to Louez. Several men fainted, probably from excitement: one or two of the officers were almost dead beat. The dead straight road seemed like a straight line projected into eternity; it went on and on—and then, suddenly, by a little white house we turned to the left, towards the fireworks on the far horizon and the intermittent rumble of guns. Men and officers pulled themselves together. There was a general unspoken wonder as to what would happen if a shell dropped into the middle of one of the platoons, and officers were thinking about the duties of stretcher-bearers, when a tremendous explosion took place and a great glare shot up into the sky. Then that moment followed, afterwards so familiar, when one wonders if one is wounded, and when the pain will begin. It passed, and the men started whistling. It turned out that the explosion had come from a heavy howitzer that fired once an hour during the night from the other side of a hedge on our left. Our training had not even prepared us for that. We felt a little more confident. We were no longer green.

This night we went to sleep, with the exception of the officers, in one building. It was a sugar refinery, knocked about in places by sporadic shelling. There was a gateway that opened into a courtyard, and factory buildings lay beyond. During our march we had eagerly looked out for smashed houses and had seen none, though the ruinous appearance of some of the French farmhouses had given rise to discussion as to whether they had been hit by shells. Now, on this dark night, after the long march, we had been plunged into the middle of the true débris of war—walls with irregular holes in them, buildings performing miracles of equilibrium, floors piled with masonry, multitudes of glassless windows. In shadowy outline only, wrapt in the black cloak of night, these were presented to us. Whispered stringent orders cautioned us of the dread results possibly sequent to the striking of matches—the shelling of the place —no less. Where that supreme excitement, "the line," was, no one knew: for many it existed only a few hundred yards away. Company by company, almost like blind men, the Battalion stumbled in to various totally unknown interiors, some into a great hall, some up an outside staircase into a chamber whose floor was a series of bricked domes, with intervals where there was no floor at all. It dawned dimly upon our Londoners that night how everyone must look after himself once out of England—no "Southern Command" here. The courtyard cleared of men without disaster, in came our field-cookers with their fires banked, one of them getting stuck in the gateway. The last scene is a little group of officers sitting on some steps in the courtyard—the colonel, the adjutant, and others—waiting for the billeting officer, who is lost. Without him, no billets. "Well, I suppose he'll turn up some time," one was remarking. "At any rate, we've got here."

2.

The Trenches.

Morning found a full Battalion full of curiosity, well tuned-up, and ready for all adventures. The night before was ages away, as thin and useless as a dream: the present had taken a double dose of reality. In the courtyard a military policeman stood. Three blasts of his whistle and we knew hostile aircraft were approaching. These interruptions were frequent, and the men regarded them as a game. Now that the element of danger had entered at last into their lives all went astonishingly well. From the ashes of our English military experience a blithe new joy in things was born, a seriousness covered by a humorous mask that augured the very best for the future. Rumours began to come to us about the line—it was not as near as imagination had placed it. There was a village called Anzin in front of us where very long communication trenches began. A day was given us to turn round in, and on the next, the last of the month, our formal introduction to trench life started. According to the custom at that time, the Battalion went out of Louez in little driblets, so that no one shell could hit more than a few. The officers had studied with great attention the information given to us, and the men were as eager as children to hear it. For the next few days we would barely exist as a unit, but would be the guests of two battalions of the 154th Brigade, 51st Division, the 4th Seaforth Highlanders, and the 9th Royal Scots. The way to Anzin lay over a tract of what had been a very prettily broken-up piece of country. As we approached the village, farmhouses and cottages became more and more desolate and ruinous. At length, after about a mile, no peasantry remained except the inmates of one of a row of cottages on the left of the road, which advertised "English beer." For the rest of the way stove-pipes sticking up unexpectedly out of gardens or amongst the débris of dwellings, showed that an underground population of soldiers inhabited these parts, mostly artillerymen, it seemed, and other specialists. There was no difficulty in finding Anzin church, as the road led straight up to it, and then branched left and right. On the left, in the angle made by the two roads, and a little way back from them, stood a substantial square country-house almost untouched. To the right lay an open space, with another larger mansion beyond it, fortified with sand-bags, and with a quantity of engineers' stores in its gardens. This became a very familiar scene to us, for we always went up to the trenches this way, and meetings generally took place at Anzin Church. The road that went to the left ran in the direction of St. Eloi, but the right hand arm of the T head was the beginning of Anzin's village street. The place itself looked as if an earthquake had destroyed it. The church steeple was intact, but the tower was three parts blown away. It looked as if it might fall down every minute, but several men were laughing and talking under its shadow. The church itself had been turned into a mortuary.

Beyond the village lay an expanse of farmlands now without a vestige of cover, and utterly desolate. This was pierced by trenches, chiefly communicating from Anzin with a complicated system of burrowings that ended in the line. Two were in common use, the "Avenue Anzin" for "up" traffic, and the "Génie" trench for "down." Both these important thoroughfares started in an unobtrusive way at their Anzin end. One began in the ruins of a house. Once the "Avenue Anzin" swallowed us up we found ourselves in a new world with a strip of sky to roof it, and eternal strings of unequal muddy duck-boards underfoot. Always winding and bending, never for more than a few yards dead straight, this wonderful trench led us on and on, past mysterious turnings, muddy culs-de-sac, and sudden drops and pitfalls, under a road, along a deep hollow, where the carcase of a smashed-up factory towered above us, past "the barricade," still on and on through a new series of twistings and turnings of the same old writhen trench, till finally at a T head it delivered us amazed and breathless (they've lost touch in rear!) at the very backmost portions of our main system of defences.

We now entered a veritable rabbit warren, where no inexperienced soldier could possibly find his way. Here trenches existed by the dozen, some used, some falling into disuse, some opening out into quite wide places, natural saucer-like depressions in the ground above. On sign-posts, never sufficiently frequent, we read the strange French names of the causeways of this underworld, soon to become as familiar as Clapham, or Tooting, or Peckham. There are hearts that may still beat faster at a recital of the old names now seen by our little piloted parties for the first time. Boyau Charles, Abri Centrale, Abri Mouton, the Bidot, the Chemin Creux, Sablier, Rippert, Grand Collecteur, Avenue des Mortices (an impassable trench), and lastly, the famous "Bonnal," our front line—what 2/21st man who served in France can ever in his life forget them? Here, when they look back, some know that the happiest period of their lives was spent. With plain duty in front and a common purpose, is not happiness bound to spring up, even in the most unlikely soil? What in civil life can ever be compared to the relish those meals had, taken in loathsome dug-outs under the front line? Whenever had expectancy been greater than just before the arrival of the mails? Or why, if these backward glances are false, did we go whistling and singing about our work in those unforgettable days?

Fitly enough our new life was heralded by the blowing up of two mines on our right, two tremendous explosions followed by night-long artillery unrest. Even in the snug reserve trenches at Abri Centrale hot fragments of metal whizzed about like humming bees. The next night the first casualty occurred. A large working-party of "C" Company was engaged on a long trench that led from the reserves to the supports, a deep trench and a very safe one. Here, in some extraordinary way a man was shot through the lung. A feeling ran through the party as if a street accident had occurred. After much wandering, the aid post was found in Sablier. Shortly afterwards the party knocked off for the night.

We stayed in the line for a week, the companies changing places with each other. All this time we were instructed by the Scottish troops in possession, fine battalions and most kindly hosts. Gradually the network of trenches became more familiar to us until at last we could find our way from the Bonnal to Sablier, and thence by Boyau Charles to Abri Centrale. Sablier was the centre of the whole organism. This was an open dell, a slight fold of the ground so situated that it was hardly ever hit by enemy guns. Here, in almost every direction, trenches radiated. It was a pleasant place, an oasis of bliss compared with the desperately kept ditches of the Bonnal. Here several little trees grew, secure from harm, looking pathetic in such surroundings. Near them were several carefully kept graves of French soldiers, with white crosses and inscriptions on them. In the middle was a small dump with stores of spare duck-boards, corkscrew irons, and bobbins of wire wound criss-cross on short sticks. The orderly room was here, and the aid-post and the head signal office and a place where the sergeant-major lived; here, too, was the commanding officer's dug-out and living places for all the numerous retainers that a battalion headquarters cannot do without in the trenches.

Going up from Sablier to the front line you crossed a wonderful trench known as "The Grand Collecteur." It was wide and of great depth, and ran right away out of the Battalion sector and on towards our left: no one had ever seen the end of Grand Collecteur. On the right of our right sector it went out into nothing, for our position was peculiar in being the extreme right of a divisional front. There was, in fact, in that direction a curious break in the line, low ground covered with the ruins of Roclincourt and threaded by trenches no one ever held. Beyond this again another system of trenches began, in advance of ours, and cut in the chalk. The gap was commanded by a very carefully concealed machine-gun emplacement on some tumbled ground where our responsibility ceased and no one bothered to go. There was a through connection by derelict trenches to the other division, and later on it became a duty to say "how-d'ye-do" to them at odd intervals. The Grand Collecteur was supposed to be the main line of resistance, though we did not much trouble about it. High up on the top of its front edge one of the original wire field fences of the farm in which all this confusion had happened just managed to stand upright, and there was a plough up there, too, just as the farmer had left it. Dotted along the forward face of the trench were a number of openings with or without doors.

Originally they had all led into a huge dug-out capable of sheltering half a battalion, but the place had been badly shelled when the French had it, and the dug-out had collapsed here and there, and now was subdivided. In that historical past of which we, the latest arrivals, knew nothing and could only see the signs, a number of French soldiers had been trapped in the big dug-out, and thus the central portion had become a grave, with crosses on the outside. This was only one of Grand Collecteur's many interests: the left portion of its passage along our system had other singularities.

There was a good space of ground between Grand Collecteur and the front line, and "Avenue G (up)," as the signboard called it, was not in a hurry to get there by any direct route. Gradually, as you stumbled up it, heavily weighted, like most who trod that trench during a relief, you could not help noticing a change in its appearance. So far, the trenches had shown signs of much peaceful labour bestowed on them: here every step took one deeper into surroundings that told of a perpetual struggle. The trench grew narrower: the duck-boards underfoot had settled immovably at odd angles, and even in the fine weather were foul with stagnant water. Here and there a portion of the side had been smashed by shell-fire or some stray aerial torpedo. Things were very quiet these days, the Scots told us, but somehow the last yards of Avenue G did not seem so deep and secluded as the first parts of it. Now, on the left, a square pit connected with the trench by a short passage, gave one a glimpse of a stumpy little trench mortar ("Toc Emma") squatting on its base like a toad; to the right the narrowest of slit-like trenches led away to somewhere unknown . . . . and, look out! this is the Bonnal, keep low and follow me.

A coat on the back of a beggar such as one rarely sees now, patched and ragged and torn till little of the original remains—that to ordinary coats is what our Bonnal was to Avenue Anzin or Boyau Charles. Poor old veteran trench, it had all the dignity of a scarred hero. By all the text-books dealing with such places it was entirely wrong; its traverses absurdly small, the upper parts of it too wide, its composition a mixture of everything. Under the parapet were numberless dug-outs—a place where dug-outs certainly should not have been. The wire that defended it was poor and inadequate: the saps that wandered out from it into No Man's Land veritable death-traps. It was sited wrongly—but could any front line trenches in France ever be said to have been definitely sited? As a matter of fact, the original French line, the Pantilotchi, lay in a partly obliterated condition half way across No Man's Land, and Bonnal evidently had begun life as a support trench, and these saps of ours were nothing but an old system of communications. Among all this again ran faint indications of a yet earlier conflict. The ground was like a palimpsest, written upon many times.

Coming into it for the first time at the heels of a guide, we saw little of this—only torn, sand-bagged walls, and the shock-headed Scots who squeezed up against the parados to let us go by. Many days passed before midnight adventures and surreptitious daylight peepings and explorations told us fully what sort of a place we were responsible for and what lay between us and the Hun. It then became evident that the companies that took it in turn to hold the right half of our sector had a No Man's Land to keep watch over very different from that of the corresponding companies on the left. The latter had craters in front of them with, at the extreme left, the remains of the Lille road. A rabbit-eared tree stump still marked the place where it ran across the Bonnal in a dead straight line towards the enemy trenches. In front of the right half there were no craters, and the ground was flat. Both portions were equally intersected with old trenches and strewn with old systems of wire. Somewhere in the centre lay the last remnants of a fallen aeroplane.

After seven days' introduction to these sights, the Battalion was "pulled out," and collected, not at Louez, but at a village near it called Maroueil. It presented a sorry spectacle! Ignorance mingled with keenness on the part of both officers and men had made most of us keep our boots on almost continuously for several days. The result was that it was only with the greatest difficulty that anyone could march. One or two wet days had made matters worse. This and the unaccustomed strain, and to us, new hardship of trench life, made the platoons look very miserable as they limped along slowly to Maroueil. It was expected that here we should be allowed to rest, but we received orders that on the following morning we were to march to Chelers, a village in a back area, beyond far distant Tinques. On the way men dropped out like flies. When we arrived, a company was almost immediately ordered off to Agniers to learn how to consolidate craters.

The fifth day saw us, refreshed in spirit, marching quite well along the now familiar road by Tinques, Savy, Haute-

Avesnes, to Etrun, our third resting-place behind the lines, this time the final village of our adoption. An issue of steel helmets had made us feel twice the men, and though on our arrival at Etrun they were taken away again, it was not long before they came to us for good. On July 16th we relieved the 2/23rd and went as a complete unit into the trenches.

From this time onward we fell into a routine which roughly worked out as follows : Seven days in reserve, seven days front line and support, seven days in Etrun. This was further sub-divided amongst the companies, no one of which ever spent longer than three days in the front line. The history of the months that followed can only be called back to life by enumerating numbers of small incidents, hundreds of experiences of individuals or small parties, a method too detailed to be attempted here. Every week enemy guns and mortars took small but regular toll of our men. To maintain the trench in this passive state called continually on all the energy of every man we had. We were in a sector where much of the fighting was carried on by short range trench-mortars. Every day the Hun battered the Bonnal to pieces with shells and aerial torpedoes, and we replied with our eighteen-pounders (firing from a valley at St. Catherine), mortars that fired round bombs like footballs that the men called "toffee-apples," and Stokes guns. Every night, as soon as darkness permitted and up to the coming of daylight, the Bonnal would be full of busy ants, filling bags with slime, putting up new stakes, or stealthily repairing wire. In the daytime activity would die down, but at night the whole area woke. Then light railways, idle and almost indiscernible by day, would emit grinding noises as trucks filled with wire and sand-bags and wood were lugged and pushed linewards by huge fatigue parties. There the post and rations would come up, and the dead go down. Every night when the Battalion was in the trenches the same scene would be enacted at the barricade—the nearest point to the line for wheeled transport. First the empty road, a whistle of machine-gun bullets passing over it from time to time, and strings of men in shadows, waiting. Then the arrival of the limbers, steel-helmeted drivers looking like Cromwellian soldiers in the faint, white glimmer of falling star-shells, or in the more dangerous radiance of the moon. They have come, but are anxious to be off again; they are afraid for their horses, eager to get the job over. There is excitement. Disputes arise. Rations are thrown out. Officers meet quartermaster-sergeants and pitch into them, and quartermaster-sergeants in a few tense words transform themselves into heroes, men of energy, wonderful workers on behalf of blind, ungrateful companies! Fatigue parties hurriedly endeavour to check their rations to see that they have not been "had." Someone finds a sack half-full of sugar: "Come along, Bill, this'll do fer us!" "Corporal, stop those two men over there with that bag." Our transport officer is dancing with impatience to get away. "You've got it all," he says, and begins to turn. There is an order that he is to take back three corpses stitched up in blankets. "It is a rotten game," he grumbles, "to push this sort of thing on to the transport." The transport officer hates taking them back, but they are lifted in, and off he goes.

There were summer days, too, when Avenue Anzin, old interminable trench, was red underfoot for yards with blown poppy leaves from the fields above, where acres of weeds and wild flowers luxuriated together. At this time it was strange to be out wiring in No Man's Land with the heavy scent of blossom around you. Birds sang in the early morning in that still hour when little columns of blue smoke rising lazily in the thin sunlight showed that the Hun, too, was early afoot, getting his breakfast. There was a good deal of tacit non-interference on our front; we were like adventurous parties picnicing on a volcano. When it did burst—and any day might see the signal—the transformation would be terrible enough. The artillery of either side had enemy O.P.'s carefully "taped," but each gave the other plenty of rope. Beneath us, though battalions knew very little about it, incessant mining and counter-mining went on, and it was said we could appear at any moment in the Hun support trenches. This lent to life a suppressed excitement, almost, though not quite, sufficient to carry off the tedium of constant work. Our chief discomfort was the irritating succession of reliefs and inter-reliefs. As in a lugubrious song, a stock item in the répertoire of one of our N.C.O.'s, we were ever being told to "move on there," always taking up our beds to walk. It was perhaps the boredom of it all that caused a man of "A" Company on October 8th, towards the end of the period, to walk over in broad daylight to the German lines. He could not have been a renegade, for no bombardment of our hidden emplacements followed, and our defences relied almost entirely on the fact that our dispositions were an unknown quantity to the enemy. An extraordinary act, and it caused much uneasiness at Sablier.

It was getting on towards the end of September, and the Battalion had been in and out of the trenches for nearly three months, when it began to be whispered that we were to make a raid. Higher commands have an insatiable desire for knowledge of enemy personnel, and raids were considered useful for keeping up the warlike spirit of the men—blooding them, as it were. Our warlike experiences had been confined so far to standing in T heads of saps in the daytime and being passively killed in them, or in creeping about No Man's Land by night. We knew as yet nothing about the German trenches except that they were in the chalk while we were in the clay, and that they were apparently in very bad condition. The Hun had done some funny things in the two and a half months we had been sitting watching him, chief among which were his poking up of several notice-boards with nothing on them. Latterly he had grown quieter—you could look over the parapet in the daytime and he didn't shoot—some credulous people began to wonder if most of him had not gone away. Others said that he must be there in some numbers because he always mended up his wire after our guns had cut it. It was in respect of wire that the defences of the opposing lines were so unequal. Ours was paltry stuff, a mere apology in most places, in some, little more than what in past time the French had left behind with their dead, and their picturesque names for trenches. But the Hun did not play with these matters. To right and left, as far as the eye could see at the dawn of a summer's day, ran a mighty belt of it, continuous, irregular, coloured deep rusty-brown, and as thick as gorse. Miles and miles of wire in every hundred yards, better barbed than ours, and double as thick.

Between September 11th and 15th our artillery undertook, in conjunction with the medium trench-mortars, a special programme of wire-cutting, and during the following week 2nd-Lieuts. Southin and Townend, the officers chosen to lead the raid, went out many times on patrol. With them went Sergeant Line, a charming fellow, brave as a lion, splendid at all work in connection with trenches. He shared with Lance-Sergeant Lash, who had been killed during a heavy bombardment of the right sector of the Bonnal on the night of September 11th, a genuine delight in war. Both loved what most of us undertook only as a duty—the joys of listening at dangerous posts and crawling about in strange parts of No Man's Land. Lieut. Southin, who comes into this history for the first time, was a highly nervous officer of great dash and daring. From now onwards he was given a disproportionate amount of dangerous work to do. Headquarters got into the habit of using him on all occasions, probably because he was in charge of our scouts. He was always brave, always willing, and it is an extraordinary fact that he was not killed in the service of the Battalion, but met his death in England in the Air Force. Townend, his companion in the raid, had not long been with us, but had already given proofs of an unusual competence and sense of responsibility.

The night was pitch dark. At 10.20 p.m. the raiding party went out. An intense suspense held the remainder of the Battalion : everyone felt that we were on our trial. By midnight all was over. Reconnaissance had shown that only one gap was possible in the enemy's wire. The enemy threw a shower of bombs among our waiting men. 2nd.-Lieut. Southin ordered the gap to be rushed. The enemy threw bombs into the gap, which filled with smoke. We were driven back, and returned through our covering party to sap 23. Our covering party threw all their bombs and retired. It was found that Townend and Line were missing. Search parties then went out three times in succession, and Townend was finally rescued from the further side of the enemy wire and taken to a shell-hole twenty yards back, where he was picked up by a stretcher-party. Sergeant Line's body had to be abandoned. Townend was past recovery, and died at the 42nd Casualty Clearing Station. 2nd-Lieut. Tiddy was wounded in helping to lead the search parties. Sergeant Hessey, who showed great courage, saved further casualties by picking up a bomb which fell amongst his party and throwing it instantly into the next shell-hole, where it exploded.

Such, in brief sentences, is the outline of a tragedy that plunged the Battalion in gloom. The brigadier-general, in his report to the division, said, "I consider that the operation failed chiefly owing to the want of dash and resolution amongst the men of the raiding party, though I do not think they were conscious of having left a wounded officer and N.C.O. behind them, owing to the pitch-black darkness of the night. The officers and some of the N.C.O.'s behaved with courage, as did also the covering party." It is impossible not to endorse this report, but outsiders are of opinion that the raid was badly planned. To attack at the one obvious place without even attempting to create a diversion, was to attempt something which could only succeed by the sudden rush of a body of determined men ready to chance great losses. But the men wavered for a moment, the enemy was waiting, the leaders were sacrificed.

Sad for the Battalion as a whole, this unhappy raid was bitter beyond words for the central figure in it. No one would have thought for a moment of accusing Southin of lack of courage, or making him responsible for the failure. Yet he, in the anguish of that night, telling his broken story at Sablier, or restlessly hurrying through the trenches, took everything upon himself—the deaths, the mishaps, the blame. It seemed to him then, in his overstrung and disillusioned state, that nothing was left on earth to be said, or done, or experienced. The Battalion had been let down; his own good name, everything that he stood for, snuffed out at the beginning. And yet, this young man was to learn that, far from being at the end of a career, he was only standing on the threshold, that fast-falling events would soon bury that terrible night under layers of fresh experiences, until, at the last, it would come to be the memory of a dream in which he had played some shadowy part. Even on the morrow it all seemed slightly different, and his mind, waking gradually, began to deliver a judgment on what was already becoming a part of the past.

As to the companies which had had no lot in the raid, or had only indirectly been concerned with it, they explained our lack of success quite simply—the operation had not been entrusted to them. Had only they been given a free hand in that affair they would have done this or that or the other . . . . Thus, in the dug-outs of men and officers the talk went on.

October brought a succession of wet days. We had only just come back into the trenches after the periodic "rest" at Etrun, when a "rum jar" fell in the left sector, killing two men of "D" Company and wounding two others. We were better off than the battalions on our left, who had their trenches and dug-outs smashed up by enormous trench-mortar projectiles which left behind them a trail of sparks like a rocket, bored their way into the sodden ground and then burst, scattering mud and sticks in all directions. Our worst enemy now—though the Hun's winged torpedoes arrived as regularly as ever—was the wet. We were on clay, and the Bonnal was on a slight forward slope. The foundation of this trench had been badly sand-bagged at the outset: then a mysterious gas corps had arrived and messed up the lower portions of the parapet with wooden frames for their detestable cylinders: finally, our field company of R.E.'s, not content with peacefully constructing duck-boards in the grounds of the mansion at Anzin, came up and further undermined us by piercing deep holes in the bottom. Under these malign influences poor Bonnal began to show signs of withdrawing her protection and becoming one of the forgotten trenches of No Man's Land. Those dug-outs, too, under the parapet, no one dreamed they were so thin on top until one night a sentry, seeing a candle shining just beneath him, scared everyone with tales of an enemy mine! All this spelt work, and repairs were in progress when the 35th Division, who had been hankering after a gas attack for some weeks, suddenly delivered themselves of it on October 8th, the night on which the 2/22nd Battalion made a successful raid. The inevitable result was that the Hun retaliated, not on the 2/22nd, nor on the 35th Division, but on our miserable Bonnal. The support trenches, too, even "Grand Collecteur," began to collapse in unexpected places. Like the parson's buggy of American legend, everything showed signs of wearing out simultaneously. Two days later we went into reserve, "A" Company to Abri Mouton, "B" to Ecurie Defences, "C" to Sunken Road, "D" to Abri Centrale. The old routine had us fast-locked in its embrace; our thoughts were of the condition of the trenches; we were steeling our minds against the approach of winter. We had come to know our area so well that it had somehow made friends with us in spite of its nastiness. Each appointed tarrying place, caravansary of a few days though it was, had for the company that visited and revisited it a special charm. "B" Company claimed to have made Sunken Road into a paradise. To the others it was a gruesome place, with its boots with legs in them sticking out of parapets—relics of an awful past. The immense amount of work we had done in these positions had endeared them to us, our interests had become bound up entirely with theirs. For us they existed now, not as a vague maze of foreign trenches, but as a labyrinth we might call our own. We had learnt it, we had improved it, some of us had given our lives for it. We knew intimately its pleasures and its pains, knew it in heat and frost, and under the midnight moon. There were the rats on the parados of the Bonnal, piebald ones some of them, making those muckheaps at the day-dawn one tremendous mass of movement. There were the currants in the shelled gardens of broken Roclincourt, worth getting though you chanced your lives for them. There were the dumps—Madagascar, Aryian, Minotaur—visited chiefly by night, wonderful store-places of expanded metal, wood, corrugated iron, sand-bags. For the signallers there was another world laid like a spider-web in this one, a world of wires, mended and pegged up, and altered over and over again, leading them into trenches where ordinary infantrymen seldom penetrated. There were, too, more dangerous places, T-heads in saps, sections of wall individuals had built up and looked upon as their own, fixed rifle batteries where great sport had been, stretches of wire in No Man's Land, the results of many nights of labour. It would not do for it all to slip into decay : in spite of frost and wet we must keep it going somehow.

We were in the line again, working away at the trenches and thinking of the week at Etrun that lay before us when a rumour came to us, first via the ration party, then more authoritatively from some hanger-on to the Brigade, that another division was coming to take over these trenches. Almost at the same time we learned of the arrival of a new chief at brigade head-quarters. Some of us had seen a tall man going round our various positions with the brigadier. They had stood together on a heap of mud at Sunken Road, and a remark to the stranger had been overheard, "This is the left of our front."

Our new commander, Brigadier-General E. C. Da Costa, was tall, imposing to look at, and took an almost embarrassing interest in everything and everybody in our trench system.

There was no doubt either, about the relief—the great change. A few days after the brigadier's visit, advance parties of the newcomers came to learn the trenches. We did the honours with some apologies for the condition of our cracking world, but to the 2nd Canadian Mounted Rifles it was evidently a paradise. They unaffectedly praised our dug-outs, our duck-boards, and our sanitary arrangements, and said they had never seen anything like it. Evidently, we began to think, there are many worse places not far off. The Canadians made light, too, of the work of reconstructing the Bonnal; their engineers would fix that up in no time. Long afterwards a stray letter told us that it fell to pieces and that they abandoned it. And very sensible, too !

The Battalion was relieved on October 25th. The brigade had held the sector close on four months. During the whole of this time the Battalion did not lose more than about fifty men killed and wounded, and half these casualties could have been avoided if the T-heads of saps had not been held as observation posts during the day—a custom rather than an advantage. It was unfortunate that only a few days before we left the line an officer named Ward should have been shot by a sniper while exploring a trench with Southin. Poor Ward! It was a warning to the whole Battalion. We had grown latterly very careless.

We moved, not to Etrun, but to Maroeuil, nor were we allowed to rest there for more than a single night. We marched on to Izel-les-Hameau, very ragged, and much in need of being pulled together. For four months the Battalion had not seen itself on the road, and now for the first time we realized how slack we had become. There had been a good deal of wastage through sickness, and there was an infusion of new men who had never fallen under the sway of Sergeant-Major Jennings, the great god of smartness, now rejoiced to be out of trenches where he had almost dwindled to a mere store-keeper, and find himself once more an important person at the head of a column of route. We were now under the command of Major Leman, an officer who had originally been in the 1st Battalion and had joined us from England early in July with immense seniority, after being wounded by accident at a bombing school. It is impossible to chronicle in a history of narrow compass the many vicissitudes that befell individual officers in the way of rank or appointment, nor are such details of general interest now. But one disappearance caused deep regret—the departure of Colonel Fletcher on leave some few days before we left the trenches, and the fact that he was going to another appointment. Colonel Fletcher had been universally popular; he had maintained in the Battalion a very good tone, and his only fault was that he was too kind. Naturally great speculation followed as to his successor, nor had we long to wait, for on the second day of our march, as we were entering Etrée-Wamin, a large man on a horse was noticed at a turning of the road watching us in. This was Lieut.-Col. F. D. Watney, the Queen's Regiment, our new commander.

It was now generally whispered that we were destined for the Somme, and a new spirit of seriousness spread over the Battalion. Officers, N.C.O.'s, and men combined to make great efforts to recover the smartness trench life had dulled and defaced, and even as we marched onwards discipline was tightened up, and many points of detail re-insisted on. The general sentiment ran that if we were to be decimated—and all knew what the Somme would have in store—we might at least die decently and put up a good last show. The effect was remarkable, and the change astonishingly rapid. We passed to Neuvillette and on to Autheuse as if to a triumph. So far the weather had been

L

fine, but at Autheuse it broke. Here we stayed for five days doing company drill and practising in a large field advancing behind a barrage. It was a melancholy business, walking at a funeral pace in anticipation of the deadly real event, but it was also irresistibly comic, for the barrage itself was represented by an officer who had a watch in his hand, and through various misunderstandings was not as automatic as a barrage is supposed to be. On November 3rd we were off to a village called Bermeuil, and thence to Villers-sous-Ailly, in the department of the Somme and not far distant from Abbéville. On our arrival, the astonishing news was circulated that we were to be diverted to Salonica for the Macedonian front. The news came at the last moment: certain engineer units of our division had already reached the Somme battle area and were engaged there. We stayed at Villers-sous-Ailly for nearly a month, training and devoting ourselves to that amusing occupation, "interior economy." The transport, to the great grief of that department, lost all except its riding horses. In Macedonia it was to find mules. Leather jerkins were issued to the men. Some of the officers, and a few N.C.O.'s and men, were given a never-to-be-forgotten leave to England. In some companies the men cast lots. Mixed feelings now reigned in the Battalion, but for the most part it was expected that we were going to have a very good time, and Salonica was popularly pictured as a city of white palaces where there were dancing halls and Chinese lanterns, and café chantants, and where everyone, including the soldiery, lived a life of relaxation and careless gaiety. Senior officers knew that they were doomed now to long eras of ceaseless supervision in a land where plenty was probably by no means rife. But we were in for it: the short life and the merry one with the glorious end was evidently not for this unit. Destiny had not done with us yet, she was only beginning to show her hand.

On November 23rd, after a pleasant march and a detestable wait, the Battalion entrained for Marseilles at Longpré Station. On the 26th it arrived and marched to Carcassone Camp. The train journey had been magnificently spectacular but in other respects was something of a torture. Sanitary arrangements were practically non-existent, and the men travelled, as usual, in trucks. At Marseilles we were separated from our transport, which went to Fournier Camp and travelled by a different boat. On the last day of November the Battalion embarked on the transport *Ivernia*.

CHAPTER III.—MACEDONIA.

1.

The Arrival.

On the slope of a hill a mud-paved town
To a glorious harbour crowding down :
A road that runs through a swampy plain
Then hills and valleys, and hills again
Till at last you come to the great divide,
To peaks that only the night can hide
Clad in a fleckless awful white ;
To rivers that roar in the plains by night
In chasms where never the sun has shone
At the end of the land called Macedon.

The Battalion was eight days at sea—on the blue Mediterranean in perfect weather. Already the Western Front—the Bonnal, Anzin with its ruined church, the maze of trenches—had fallen into one composed past, from which Memory traces us; first coming in cattle-trucks, next sojourning at Carcassone, and now here, in the live present, watching at night on deck the slow, balanced movement of the forward mast to and fro, a slender black spike that kept us in its care and seemed to know our fates. This wonderful sea—"the sea of civilization and of all history"—was presenting us with sunny days and lovely moon-lit nights which even the dullest could not but watch and wonder at. We passed Corsica and long Sardinia, and drew towards Malta, biscuit-coloured, delicate and bare, with its forts, and the guns, and a sentry just discernible, first motionless, then marching up and down. Later loomed the edge of Africa, shadowy grey cliffs very far away. Then, in the last stages of the voyage, any morning would discover some strange Greek island, come to us as if by enchantment, marvellous for a time, but presently lost in our wake and forgotten.

All felt the warmth and new sense of discovery of these days, but the men were very much taken up with "House," that strange gambling game permitted in the army. Our divisional general and his staff were with us, and Colonel Watney was "O.C. troops." There were the usual drills with life-belts and sudden practice alarms, but we were all so new to that sort of thing that no one worried much, though danger was nearer than we imagined. In fact, on this trip the submarines just failed to get the *Ivernia,* and on her next voyage out she was sunk.

On the morning of December 8th we steamed slowly into the harbour of Salonica—one of the finest in the world. The morning was cold, and there was a slight drizzle of rain. We all crowded on deck, and gazed silently at the city. The General himself, not pleased, apparently, to have left the Western Front, muttered gloomily, "It might have been worse," and turned away. Before us, backed by an amphitheatre of hills, with the long arms of the harbour stretching forward and away from it, lay a cascade of crowded houses, all tumbled together and coming down seemingly to the water's edge. Among them in the rearward of the city, where the tall plaster houses of merchandise gave place to a general mass of native residences, numbers of minarets shafted whitely upward. On the left the houses stopped abruptly, but to the right they spread for some distance along the shore, and were modern, European, and substantial-looking. Such was our first sight of a town that, third-rate and tawdry though it was, stood for us when we were up the line as our only link with civilization.

We disembarked early in the afternoon, and after a tedious wait on the quay, began to march to our camp, situate, we had been told, on a plain. That afternoon Salonica at close quarters showed herself in her worst colours. Hardly one of us had ever before seen a third-rate Eastern port, or realized the results of utter public incompetence. Here no one seemed to care for "the commonwealth"—the very expression in that setting was grotesquely out of place. Here someone in the past had had the energy to build houses, but no one for many years had made the slightest effort to keep them in repair. No one swept the streets or the disjointed fragmentary pavements; they were covered with a thick, dark, oily mud through which vehicles and passengers together painfully struggled. On every hand was squalor and lack of public conscience; broken houses, dirty shops, pavements full of holes, sheds with the corrugated iron flapping in the wind. The streets were crowded with very slow-moving oxen, bearing heavy, clumsy-looking yokes and dragging native carts. To the throng add many donkeys, loaded with huge panniers. Amongst this press, with feet unused lately to marching, we just contrived, by pushing, to keep our ranks, and so passed out of the city. A rough road lay before us. Native stone or mud-built hovels grew fewer and more wretched, till at length we were passing nothing but dumps and ordnance depôts, and base encampments of R.E., Transport, and A.S.C. The men grew very weary, and presently, just before the approach of twilight, Major Puckle drew the Battalion off on to an open space on the right of the road, to rest. It was quite dark when we had re-started. The road, cumbered by many lorries, was good; the weather, bad at the outset, grew colder and colder; finally, it began to rain. Mile followed mile, but at last we came to Ushanta Camp, an open plain, now very dark, with numberless tents. The position set apart for us—though we hardly seemed to have been expected so soon—proved the farthest of all. We broke off the road to the right, and scrambled over a ditch. In the wet and miserably cold weather and blackness of inhospitable night, sections of tents were hastily allotted to companies, and the men turned in. Even at that hour many of the tents were blown flat, for our camp lay low and the pegs would not hold in the mud. Without food, in the wet and cold, some may have slept for weariness, but in the morning there was scarce a tent upright. Such was our arrival at Salonica.

The days that followed were uneventful enough, monotonous, but not, on the whole, wretched. Lack of good rations, very serious for the first few days, became less acute, though everyone's money (we were paid in drachma notes) soon melted in the face of monstrous prices. For the men there was practically no amusement. Officers occasionally went to Salonica, where the French gave us welcome hospitality at their club, at the harbour side, a little way past the White Tower. That, with "Bottoms Buildings," where one descended into white-tiled baths, divided their time in the town.

What money remained easily went in a moment at the famous Emporium of Oresdi-Bak, "the Whiteley of the Balkans." Those who loved colour could get it at the harbour-side. At sunset the port was magnificent. You could see the Greek coasting vessels, laden with apples; the warships at anchor; the long-boats pushing off to them, English, French, Balkan; the motley land crowd—Greeks, Turks, Servians, French soldiers, Italian R.A.M.C.; all were composed, as the sun went down behind Olympus, into a fine spectacular drama.

Gradually the brigade came together in the wet, flat terrain seven weary miles back of Salonica. Not much military exercise was possible; learning to march in single file without straggling, and finding out how to pack and pitch the little bivouac tents now for the first time served out to the men, took up most of the time. To relieve the tedium one still lectured vainly on outposts. The transport had its hands full. Hundreds of untrained mules, fresh from South America, afforded huge amusement to those who did not have to deal with them. They escaped so frequently that it was a clever C.O. who knew how many his battalion owned at the end of every day.

From week to week cold winds would come, blowing for three days on end. Then the sun would reassume its magnificent but tiring sway. We were beginning to have some taste of the enchanting qualities of the East, but Christmas seemed unnatural in those surroundings. Rumours of an impending journey to the frontier grew wilder and more diverse as the New Year set in, and we had various practice alarums which reminded us of our old home training. At last, on January 10th, the ultimate orders came. That morning we left our uncomfortable camp, in clouds of white dust, and marching in single file. The mules had been passably tamed, the ambulances had absorbed their new equipment, the third stage in the history of the Battalion was set; our period of wandering was well begun.

2.

To the Line.

Discussions about "the line" had been frequent these last weeks amongst all ranks. On the *Ivernia* officers had unfolded large scale maps which showed unbelievably vast stretches of country and ranges of mountains hitherto undiscerned. The French front could be packed away in a corner of this long battle line. The lack or abundance of supplies "up there" had been for days the subject of anxious talk. What to take was settled ruthlessly at last by stringent orders regarding the limit load for a mule. Officers and men might be unequally handicapped in this respect; both were equal in their desire for knowledge of what lay beyond the low, flat camping-ground where lizards crawled and bull-frogs croaked by night. Everything we had seen and experienced was to be outdone, men thought, in this new adventure. Yet, in setting forth from the Salonica zone, no one guessed how much of civilization he was leaving, or what a solitude lay beyond.

Details of each day's halt are still at hand, and the name of each locality passed through, but the tale of this journey must be given as it remains in the memory, a journey that will never be forgotten, at least by one. The whole of the Macedonian experience looms now, across the gulf of time, like a romantic dream. There are no lamp-posts in that part of the world, and to our Londoners that was a disgusting fact! Macedonia is a Kubla Khan country, and inhabitants are the least part of it. To wander about it by night is to appreciate by contrast the meaning of civilization. To be lost in it by night is to know fear. To see it by day is to know beauty, and grandeur, and desolation.

The first and second days' marches were long and uneventful. All went well, and it was novel to see the Battalion marching in single file. At present this was not a necessity, for the country was open, but the staff had wisely decided that practice in that formation was essential. Elaborate rules had been devised for the setting-up of the nightly bivouac, but they had to be modified in practice, to the annoyance of the regimental sergeant-major, whose status, somewhat on the wane in France and in the battle line, had swelled to something of its old home importance in the cooped-up tent-lines of Salonica! On this march everyone was starting the war again. The loss of field-kitchens, the packing and unpacking of bivouac tents and blankets, the reliance placed on long lines of mules, gave a sense of newness and beginning. These were, in fact, the first days of gipsy wandering, a period when the blessed word "billet" dropped clean out of use.

It is probable that survivors of this march have forgotten the names of the first two halting places—our first two nights in the wilderness—but Sarigol and Snevce are miserable memories, and the names remain. It is permissible, perhaps, to quote the Battalion versifier:—

"I have seen Sarigol, and if I see it twice
May the soles of my field boots be eaten by mice.
I have twice been to Snevce, if I go again,
May I miserably drown in a puddle of rain."

The way was lost, and found again, and before our long straggling line reached Sarigol the weather broke. Sarigol is no town, but a sugar-loaf hill, without a blade of vegetation on it, as bare as your knee, and as you stand on it with a staff-captain, parcelling it out for battalions and companies for the night, you feel a bitterly cold wind and chilly rain. A shack or two existed somewhere in the neighbourhood, where one or two human beings, left over from various Balkan wars, drank vile coffee and gazed at you with apathetic suspicion. The I-talians had made a muck-heap of Sarigol's hill long before we were thought of, as Jock

Mackay, bemused with "C" Company's rum, discovered suddenly, to his undoing. But Sarigol, all running with water though it was, boasted a dump, and an officer in a fur coat in charge of it, who was persuaded to produce a rum ration the Battalion long remembered. The next morning the weather cleared, and we marched all day, arriving in the evening at Gramatma, a very pleasant bivouac by a broad stream. The evening was so fine that we bathed, racing up and down on the sandy shallows. This was on January 13th. Half-an-hour later those who could get the wood were glad to light fires, as the sun sank and the night wind came.

Next day we reached Snevce. The mountains were before us; at their feet this ruinous village. Here, leaving heavy artillery on our left, we broke off to the right, bivouacking in a field, near a mountain stream whose waters were melted ice. Here, presaging, it may be supposed, a rough time, Colonel Watney made an impassioned speech, the substance of which Time has unkindly stolen. But Time makes few inroads in the memory of what followed.

It was rather fun, at first, leaving Snevce next morning, and starting to climb those mountains in single file; it was amusing to see the men of one's company passing backwards and forwards, above and below, as the tracks wound this way and that, ever searching an easier way. But as the day wore on, packs and kits, heavy at the start, grew cruelly heavier, the men began to wonder how long the ascent would last and where night would cover us. Arrived at length, in the late afternoon, at a halting place somewhere in the clouds, efforts were made to get the men not to disclose their whereabouts, though we were miles from anywhere, and the Bulgars were remotely hidden whole English counties away, on a much higher sky line of their own. But now a great vagueness reigned about such matters, and we were not much better than little boys lost. Such an expression may be resented by one who would rather paint a picture of soldiers, strong and masterly, conquerors in a strange land. But in Macedonia the true picture is in other colours. Here the country itself was always the compelling factor. Here the landscape was on such a scale that several hole-and-corner wars could easily be lost on it. And it bore on its face the scars of many such wars; most buildings were ruined, most villages desolate. We visited later many utterly abandoned places, plundered years ago, empty, forgotten. For the present we were in the mountains.

Roads, in this part of Macedonia, are to be avoided. Baked hard in the dry weather, they become in the winter troughs of dark mud in which a man can almost be lost if he falls down. The rain of the previous days had caused our foot-track to fall into a doughy consistency; moreover, the trees were so thick, and the track itself so deeply scored and narrow, that supervision on the part of officers and N.C.O.'s was impossible. Night came on as men and mules slowly moved forward in our ever lengthening line that stretched for miles, though none knew the length of it. How anxious were the officers when touch was lost over and over again in a blanketing darkness as the men stumbled on and on, round bend upon bend on the downward course! It had been rumoured that at a certain place below, the 12th Lancashire Fusiliers, whom we were to relieve, had kindly and thoughtfully arranged to light fires for us, as a final guide to our bivouac ground for that night, yet the hours passed, and not a glimmer was visible. At length, far below, we beheld points of flame. These, acting as a lure, drew us, one by one, almost throughout the night, down that long twisting track, across, in the final stages, a tract of open country, across the small sluggish river that always turns up in that country to quench your last hopes, and so to the terraced and sparsely treed rocky flats, where the beacons flamed. Our colonel stood watching us as we passed. A group, a space, a few more, a solitary stumbling figure; then more, in that last hour before the dawn. Daylight showed that only one or two in the whole Battalion had had the strength to pitch their bivouacs. Many had fallen asleep on them, while in the act.

The place of bonfires was pleasant enough when the sun came out and helped forgetfulness of the night. A clear streamlet gave us drinking water, there were oak trees and good flat places among the rocks for the bivouac tents. But though we would fain have lingered, late afternoon saw us moving still onward towards the line, leaving Mahmudli—delectable name—a place to be revisited by companies when in reserve. No one thought this last lap would daunt him when so much of discomfort lay behind, but Macedonia has plenty of surprises up her sleeve, and the last stage proved the worst. It lay through the roughest country anyone had ever imagined; its features were that of a wild dream. We went up in the night and down in the night, followed the rocky banks of a torrent, picked our way through a wood, stumbled over rocky boulders. The guide lost his way four times. Finally, after much descent, we ascended, and after many halts and misadventures, were dimly aware in the deep darkness of a large fort or earthwork on a ridge of foothills mostly covered by oak scrub. This was our objective, "the line," and the half underground fort was our head-quarters, "Dover Tepé."

It was 2.30 on the morning of January 17th before the relief was effected, and many more hours, and even days, elapsed before the details and complications of the interchange were cleared up. The night had been a misery of wandering, but daylight discovered to our newly-posted sentries a panorama superb beyond their dreams. It was revealed to them as the mists of morning rolled away that they were on the lower slopes of a range of mountains cleft by ravines. In front and below them, to the sight line in either direction, stretched a great flat valley, several miles across, now hidden by mists, but cut by torrents the composite murmur of whose many voices rose to the sentries' posts. The mists, clearing, disclosed the top of the minaret of a distant ruined township, later known to us as Palmis. Beyond this, flushed with the dawn and capped with snow, the Bulgarian frontier, over a mile high, impassively displayed pine forests that looked like pocket handkerchiefs, and tremendous masses of rocky headlands down which rushed waters to join those murmuring in the plain. And on our side, at first imperceptible, our sentries could distinguish a single ruined railway track, and here and there certain tiny objects, trucks, abandoned on that line. Such was the position with which we were to make ourselves familiar in the days that followed.

3.

At Dover Tepé.

It seems almost unbelievable, looking back on that period, that we only held the line at Dover Tepé for about six weeks. For though the sole event of military importance was the Palmis raid, the varieties of weather we experienced and the vastness of the front we occupied, and the bitterness of the discomforts of that chilly season, have made our sojourn appear six months. The weather, which had steadily grown worse since our departure from Salonica, became, as always in Macedonia, our worst enemy; the Bulgar was a bad second—had he been let alone it is probable he would not have bothered about our presence at all. But war is kept alive by the higher commands, who from time to time devise plans that make each side healthily inimical. Signs of war on our arrival at this vast theatre were few and futile. At midday, when the weather was fine, the sun would melt a little of the snow on the great mountain barrier beyond the plain, and keen eyes could pick out the Bulgarian wire, like a black snake, far way up near the peaks. Sometimes from those heights invisible mountain guns would shoot at us, and small shells would drop seemingly out of nowhere round and about the fort. Almost all of them failed to explode, but once one man was killed and two wounded. Soon after our arrival we learned to name Bergerie Wood, and our first small adventure was a visit by Lieut. Southin, our scout officer, after several of the enemy had been seen in it. The smallness of our numbers and the length of our line made the nights an anxious time for officers who knew how easy it would be for the enemy to march through at any point, thoughts that were checked by the supposition that he could not continue or make good such an advance without the support of troops and material he did not appear to possess. So scattered were we, so loosened the units of command, that platoon officers lorded themselves in areas usually allotted to company commanders, who in their turn had terrains more suited to a battalion, while our colonel, lodged in the Fort Dover Tepé—a most malodorous and undesirable headquarters—seemed, in respect to the lands under his care, a veritable divisional general. Far to our right, in even more shadowy and unknown regions, the King's Own Yorkshire Light Infantry, old hands at the game, and settled down with their own flocks and herds, amused themselves by the sporadic shelling of a place in the plain called Peroi.

The weather, bad enough on our arrival, speedily grew worse, and the brigade commander, visiting the line two days afterwards, found a miserable and rain-soaked infantry and condemned them for their want of zeal. It was difficult to muster any up in a place where the war seemed more than usually futile and the stage set for all time. The mere act of keeping one's end up was enough to exhaust the strength and spirits of the strongest. The days speedily grew darker and shorter, rain turned the ground into a sponge, and in the middle of the second week came a blizzard of snow. Severe penalties were threatened against any officer who might inadvertently allow any of his men to suffer "trench foot." How the complaint was avoided by wretches who perforce remained soaked day after day is a miracle to look back upon. The long nights were for the most part unillumined even by a candle—for candles were unbelievable luxuries, and the apportioning of the one or two that came our way gave rise to much quarrelling and disputing. In the spring or summer the position we occupied must have been pleasant enough, but the leafy Arcadian arbours we inherited indirectly from the Italians were poor shelter in winter time.

Towards the end of the month two deserters from Palmis gave much information regarding the disposition of the enemy in that ruined town and on the heights beyond, and a few days later the brigade-major came to the fort to discuss plans for a raid. Nearly a week was taken up in preparations, and at the end of it the weather cleared up. The object of the raid was to kill or capture enemy outposts in Palmis, a town on the far side of the valley at the foot of the Beles, the huge mountains that constituted the Bulgarian frontier. Our strength consisted of nine officers and one hundred and fifty-eight men; two parties of two officers and thirty men formed the striking force, the others were in support and reserve. The enterprise was extremely hazardous, if there are considered the difficulties of crossing by night a ravine-intersected plain, and of effecting a successful retreat. Forays of this nature depend for their success very largely on luck; the most that can be counted on is to give the enemy a shake-up; if fair numbers are killed or captured it is generally by good fortune, nor is it easy afterwards to construct a plain story out of the various versions of the combatants, whom, with bayonets blackened and steel helmets covered with cap-comforters, you may now imagine descending the curved track from the Fort, crossing the railway line, and being swallowed up in the plain. The plan was for the first party, led by Lieut. Southin, to march round the eastern side of Palmis and cut the telephone wire on the north. The second party, officered by Lieuts. Smith and Hoskyns-Abrahall, was to creep into a pre-arranged position, and at a given time both parties would attack simultaneously.

The plan was upset at the outset by the first party marching into the relief to a sentry post. Lieut. Southin shot one man, one was bayoneted, one taken prisoner, and two escaped. We were then fired on, and one man was killed. We then charged into the village, and two more men were wounded. The village was empty. Our party then retired, as arranged, to the rallying post.

Our second party, on attacking a sentry-post, found it vacant. Advancing to a mill we met seven men outside a hut. One ran inside and was shot by Lieut. Smith. The rest ran away down a ravine. Rifleman Denyer threw a bomb at them and four fell. We pushed on, gained a ledge at the foot of a hill, and were nearly surrounded by the enemy. At this point Hoskyns-Abrahall was severely wounded, and we retired to another position, where one man was killed and several wounded. A fight ensued. The enemy were driven up the hill, where they were caught by shrapnel from our guns on the other side of the valley. We then successfully withdrew, but despite the fine efforts of Sergeant Sergeant, who, himself wounded, helped to bring in several wounded men, had to leave one dead and one wounded behind. The raid was considered a success, and Sergeant Sergeant was rewarded with the Military Medal, and Lieut. Southin with the Military Cross.

Little of moment happened during the rest of February. About the middle of the month Captain Everest went sick with rheumatism. One of the earliest officers to join the Battalion, he now went to Salonica, where he remained for the rest of the war, unfit for service in the line. Lieut. Levy had left us the previous month for the flying corps, and Puckle was to leave us a few days later. The transport was taken over by Coyle, known as "Paddy Coyle," whose great merit was that he could speak to mules in their own language. Yet, even with these changes, the Battalion retained much of its old personnel. Macdonald, that capable Scot, still exercised a thinly-veiled authority at head-quarters, where Sergt.-Major Jennings dwelt, lamenting the utter impossibility of close-order drill in our part of Macedonia. Capt. Walter still quietly commanded his company; Bloy was the ostentatious lord of "A"; Coldicott dwelt apart with "C" Company, building houses and making roads. Utter peace reigned in the line, but we beheld sometimes, afar off, signs of war. The Yorkshires, early one morning, attacked Lower Peroi. Standing on some rocky platform, one could see it all in miniature—see the shells bursting, little eggs of flame and puffs of blue smoke. Then rifle fire crackling, and the small empty sound of bombs exploding. Then the artillery lengthened its range, and we knew the Yorks were attacking. But it was like looking on at another war. All very far away.

Domestic cares, as usual in remote theatres of war, loomed larger than war itself. The three spies who attempted (vainly in that hard weather) to penetrate the Beles, went forth unremarked in a general lament that no provision had been made for the re-soling of boots. Capt. Bloy's reconnaissance of Palmis and report that no one was there, passed unnoticed in a general demand for candles. The men made unto themselves cabins and shelters out of what they might, and spent the remnants of their energies in grubbing out the roots of scrub-oaks for fuel. Small adventurous unofficial parties of officers and men would, on moonlit nights, go down to the railway station and hack pieces of wood away, and bring them back for fuel. One of the marvels of our position was a railway carriage, hidden half-way up the hill, used by us as a sleeping place for the men. How did the wonderful I-talians put it up there? None knew. Down at Mahmudli, by the picturesque but awful route our pack-mules traversed with difficulty every day, the company in reserve generally managed to have a good time. The duties were to provide logs for the bakery in distant Snevce, and to mend a road—the latter task as obviously hopeless as those the mythic heroes attempted in Olympian times. But Mahmudli was a pleasant haven, with food and water and plenty of fuel, and cabins to live in "of clay and wattle made"—reared in the first place by the I-talians who long had passed away. Rarely the brigade staff penetrated to Mahmudli—to that high slope of it inhabited by the reserve battalion, where the air was thin, and men panted if they walked quickly.

> "Mahmudli, thy name's like the rivers and rills
> That murmur at night amid Macedon's hills,
> Or talk from the plain to the plateau on high
> And hide the patrol passing fearfully by."

March followed February in much the same uneventful way. Several patrols went out, but did not meet with any fresh adventure. It was remarkable that, although the enemy fired sixty-three shells at Lieut. Antrobus's patrol, which went out to recover some telephone wire, no one was wounded. One or two deserters came in during the earlier part of the month, probably because they were half starving. A day or so before a patrol occupied Globostica news somehow filtered through that before long we should be on the move again, and this caused the usual excitement and speculation. "Box respirators"—the latest means of defence against gas—were issued, and we were ordered to practise with them daily. Awful rumours began to be current concerning our destination. A real war area this time, it was hinted, with massed artillery on either side, going for each other hammer and tongs; somewhere on the extreme left of our front—beyond Lake Doiran. It made the boldest feel a little nervous—attenuated and tired as we were by our eight weeks' struggle against rain and snow and cold. To the accompaniment of the howling of packs of the wild dogs of those regions that ranged the foot hills nightly on the chance of finding out where we stored our rations, little parties, sitting over a brazier or grouped round a solitary candle, would discuss the possibility of gas shells, and wonder if they had actually come into use and were as noxious as was darkly supposed. Most were ready to be on the move again, few were sorry to be bidding farewell to our landscape panorama, however wildly magnificent. The actual relief, this time by the 1st Yorks and Lancs, took place on the 26th. A, B, and D Companies were in the line, C was at Mahmudli in reserve. The Yorks and Lancs was a happy, easy-going crowd, who took life far more sensibly than we, who could never get more than a respectful distance from regulations. Many's the good time we could have enjoyed, and the war carried on just as well, had certain in authority amongst us imparted a spice of devil-may-care into their somewhat thin and fearful habits of strict observance. One remembers with joy the delightful arrival of these military nomads. A tinkling of many bells preceded them—the noise of the cattle they drove before them like the patriarchs of old. One company owned goats, and a goat carried the company commander's home-made chair, which took to pieces. Cows were soon picking up what provender they could down near the transport lines in Mahmudli. These Yorkshiremen were charcoal burners, too, as befitted wanderers in such regions, and they had large copper cauldrons with them, and dump upon dump of articles you simply could not do without if you wished to be comfortably at war; while we, we actually were short of lashings to tie our scanty goods upon our mules, the day we set forth on our eventful journey.

4.

The Vardar Valley.

"Over the hills and far away" would have been a suitable tune to lead off with on this recommencement of our wanderings. Here there was no tune to play or anyone capable of playing it. Those route marches in England when the band made us for a time soldiers indeed—that highwater-mark of our achievement when actually we could produce two bands (the allusion is to Major Wright's drum and fife adventure at Sutton Veney), even those comparatively recent days when we marched to our own music Sommewards—those bygone inspiriting experiences had now become to us the happenings of a faded dream. No one was happy at the start of this new journey; no one had begun to forget that nightmare of a march up, when the bonfires were lit in Mahmudli. Packs were as heavy now, and the goat-track we were to follow would be worse after the past week's blizzards and rains. There was a feeling amongst the officers that a mistake had been made in not sending the transport mules in advance. These mules carried the men's bivouac sheets as well as officers' valises, and, as it was intended we should camp on our arrival at Snevce, it was obvious that there would be an uncomfortable wait at the end of this first night's march.

The light was failing when the column tailed off in Indian file and began the climb. The weather was just fine, but heavy rain-clouds impended, looking as if they would break down upon us at any moment. Miserable as many days at Dover Tepé had been, we had had our sunny ones, too, and were not so terribly glad to go now that we were streaming away. For Mahmudli had always been a haven, and it was a sorrow to leave it to the comfortable K.O.Y.L.I.S.—to call them by the name they loathed. Even now the place could be looked down upon from a different level, and now a turn hid it, and there was nothing left but to plunge and scramble upwards and on. "Soldiers —that's what they call them"—one loves to quote again the dramatic, ironical phrase of that Napoleon of sergeant-majors, R.S.M. Jennings.

Darkness came swiftly, and by the time the first fatigues of the march were felt the rain began. By the time we had reached the summits we were in the middle of it. It seemed to be raining from us to the places below. The windows of heaven were opened, and we were walking through them. Impenetrable darkness wrapped us about. Exalted persons who, by the waterproofing aid of such far-away firms as *Thresher and Glenny,* had never been properly wetted through since the beginning of this miserable war, got properly wetted through now. The horses snorted to get rid of it, the men moved without speaking under the increased burden of their packs, the rain continued and the night wore on. Intermittently we wondered how the transport was getting on; it was certain that Paddy Coyle would have exhausted his vocabulary by now. But thought could not be tempted away from our wet selves. Billets do not exist in Macedonia. There was nothing to look forward to. And no way led out of the rain.

After long hours the column became disjointed, and halts were made from time to time by officers to collect up bunches of their men. Once or twice on the downward slopes the track was called into dispute, but, turning to left and right upon itself in its efforts to negotiate us down, it remained generally the only practicable road. At last it became fairly certain that we were coming down into Snevce, that most wretched of places; and after further lapses of time we were groping on amongst houses black as the night we moved in. There is no street in Snevce, or in any such embryo Macedonian township, but the stone-built hovels roughly group themselves along and about some stony track. This one, as it flattened out at the bottom end, became, or ran into a wide and rapidly increasing brook—the inevitable aforementioned rivulet, final dampener of one's hopes. Somehow this was floundered across. It is still raining heavily as guides lead us on to a soggy wet field, no one knowing why. Enquiries reveal the horrid truth that this is our bivouac-ground—in fact, we have arrived. This is where we are to pass the short—ah! happily short—remainder of the night. Meanwhile the mules wander in the mountain passes. Bivouac sheets and shelters are things to dream of for to-morrow—if you can dream. Or, if you cannot—go on walking about!

The remarkable fact about that depressing bivouac was that most of the men went to sleep for the remainder of the night. Utterly tired out, they lay down on the wet ground. Others—officers mainly—paced to and fro, waiting the transport mules, which arrived in ones and twos just before daybreak. Day brought us one of those remarkable changes of weather common in Macedonia, though the first beginnings were cheerless enough. The behaviour of a certain N.C.O. on wakening typifies the resiliency of the men. He at once started to sing the chorus of a music-hall song, joking and making witty remarks as he roused the others. One beheld the like in Syria when a football match was started after an exhausting day. Easily depressed, quick to cheer up again, it was not easy to foretell the passing moods of this small composite society. Amongst the weaker ones it was the jesters who towered spiritually aloft, and with the officially recognized, equally deserved decorations.

Dawn revealed several large marquees in the corner of one of the fields. Some few officers had discovered them during the night. Rations arrived from nowhere and were pitched down on the ground. The sun came up, and almost at once the weather began to be hot. We washed and took an interest in life once more. The pitiful, tired cries of the transport men: "Two-Twenty-first, where are you?" as they had drifted in at the end of the night—were already forgotten. All that was past and over. We began to look forward to what would happen to-day. Everyone grew cheery—the weather was so very fine. But a little wind now suddenly blew up—a little puff of wind. A minute or two and we were hanging on to the ropes of the marquees to save them. More wind—furious now. And now torrents of rain, the whole earth steaming with it. Misery for everyone. And now, when it is at its worst, behold the sun again! In a few minutes everyone is getting hot. A further experience of Macedonia.

The afternoon passed uneventfully, and just before dusk the Battalion assembled to continue the march. Instructions had been received on our departure from Mahmudli the day before, that our progress to the Vardar was to be made by night, to deny information that might be gathered by enemy aircraft. The rank and file and most of the officers thought the precaution unnecessary, for though it was generally known that owing to the inferiority of our machines we played a bad second fiddle to the Hun in the Balkans, no one had ever seen an enemy aeroplane, and we seemed extremely remote and secure in these almost uninhabited wilds. Of bombing from the air the Battalion had had no experience. The appearance of a 'plane just as we moved off caused no surprise until it swooped down and began to drop bombs. A scene of confusion followed, complicated by the death agonies of thirteen mules—for the brunt of the attack fell upon the transport. One transport man was killed and three wounded, and Lieut. Bull was slightly wounded in the head. Seventeen men were also wounded. Shaken by the unexpectedness of this attack, the Battalion pushed off as rapidly as possible. Its destination was a small place in a tract of plain country called Hirsova. It had once been fortified, and was occupied by a heavy battery. A small advance party, mounted, had left early in the afternoon to find a bivouac ground, not only for our own Battalion, but for brigade head-quarter details, a trench mortar transport, and machine-gun transport. The column, therefore, with two platoons of "B" Company, under Lieut. Capes, as advanced guard, and two platoons of "C" Company, under Lieut. Cowper, as rear guard, was heterogeneous, long, and unwieldy, as it moved off in a hurry, led by guides into an almost trackless piece of open country, intersected at irregular intervals by deep clefts or hollows.

The events of that unhappy night are too deeply scored in the memory of surviving members of the Battalion who may read this narrative to make necessary a vivid reconstruction, and those whose interest is at second-hand must remember that the impersonality which in a record of this kind must perforce shroud the narrator, covers up, too, to some extent, such vivid events as brought personalities into sharp conflict. To one at least the doings of that night were presented at a sharp angle; others might recognize the tale told thus only by its general outline. Personal experiences differ so much in war that two persons affected by the same event often give widely varying accounts of it. But all will remember roughly what happened. And, roughly, on this occasion, this was the way of it.

A composite column moving over difficult country by night needs very skilful leadership, otherwise it will break into pieces and be lost. When at about four next morning the commander of this column arrived at the wrong side of the stream that marked Hirsova, it was evident to an observer that only a small fraction of his troops was behind him. The rest, in fact, had split up, and were either postponing the attempt to find Hirsova until day-dawn, or were still searching for a way out of the puzzle of clefts and baby chasms that characterized that part of Macedonia. A footbridge led half-way over the stream and broke off abruptly in the middle. Someone had hung a lantern on the end of it, for the night was dark. The track that led down to the stream had swampy ground on either side. Further along, a large bridge looms in one's memory, totally smashed. Somewhere, too, there was a railway line. To this place fragments of the Battalion drifted throughout the night in total ignorance of the direction of the enemy, who, in fact, was many miles away. The event at dusk made him seem still very much at hand. The camping place lay on rising ground beyond. As the sun rose everyone fell asleep. One remembers only the colonel's tent pitched perfunctorily at a rakish angle, and a hot sun looking down on a caravansary of exhausted soldiery.

The colonel wanted to make an early start. This, however, was out of the question, as the Battalion was utterly exhausted. Finally the colonel went off with his mess people, his tent, a corporal, and a few men. Later in the day the Battalion followed. Hirsova behind us, all went well. After some hours' marching we actually found a road, and the men were able, after many months, to march in fours again. It is astonishing what a tonic effect this had on their spirits. By the light of a fine full moon, to the accompaniment of the croaking of millions of raucous bullfrogs—dwellers in the swamps on our left—we marched along in fine style, singing that famous ditty, "We haven't seen the Kaiser for a very long time." This time we bivouacked in a steep ravine at the foot of some hills. A very small stream of water trickled there, just sufficient for our needs. Next morning revealed two observation balloons tethered not very far from us, and before long one of them was attacked by an enemy 'plane and brought down in flames. The two observers floated off in parachutes and descended unharmed. The remaining "sausage" boldly continued observing, feeling very uncomfortable, no doubt.

The final day's march was performed in a blazing heat which proved very trying to the men, who could only keep going with extreme difficulty. The time factor became of importance. Authority seemed to be very anxious that we should arrive at a certain hour. Eventually Thornhill Camp was reached on the evening of March 30th. By April 1st we were in the line.

There were evidences enough on our final march to the line that Vardar Valley warfare would bear some faint resemblance to France. This was an artillery sector: here the guns were dominant. The road to the line was pitted with large shell holes; the countryside bore silent witness of having been battered about. No one who accompanied the Battalion to this peculiar place can ever have forgotten it, but it is part of the purpose of this history to enrich such recollection. There is magic in names, and the mention of "Bates Ravine," "Chapeau de Gendarme," "Glen Smol," "Happy Valley," "Morgan Gully," will at once call up pictures for those who were there. However various the experiences of individuals, the sluggish Vardar river itself that flowed through the lines on the left of the 24th, the white ruins of the village of Mackukovo gleaming by night in the moon, our shallow trenches blasted in the rock, and the hilly mounds of reddish coloured earth on the reverse side, where we passed our somewhat insanitary days—these pictures remain for everyone, whether he lived fearfully in sector "L4," was happy in the comparative security of "L8," or dwelt under the wing of battalion head-quarters in "LLG."

It was a curious affair, this stalemate by the Vardar. Here was the key to the whole position in the Balkans, and yet, from month to month, the official reports never varied. Always there was "Artillery activity at the Mackukovo Gap." On our left across the river, the French took, lost, and re-took positions almost at right-angles to our own, but our line never changed, and no one on our side thought it probable that the position of our immediate enemy could be stormed, so formidable was that hill, so bare and exposed to gun-fire the wide and down-like No Man's Land, whose broad bosom heaved at intervals almost imperceptibly into mounds, named on the map by French and English—"Petit Piton," "Double Hill," "Stony Hill"—but very difficult to identify, gazed on from afar. One position of our own, "L4," ran right out into this disputed territory, and was connected to our main line by fences of wire only, and thus it was left almost like a beleagured fortress. The main enemy position, which it was rumoured the Germans had fortified, was a hill that rose up close to the river, bare and forbidding, bristling with wire, and apparently untakeable. The passage of the river itself at the inception of this period of warfare, had been elaborately blocked by wire by both combatants. By day both sides almost ceased from war; by night the guns spoke, and the space of hilly down country between us was roamed over by bands of fearful men, who sometimes bumped up against each other by accident, and fought.

The one curious fact about our trenches that stands out is that they were almost uninhabited by day. The reason for this was that portions of them were in full view of the enemy, partly because it had not been possible to blast them deep enough in the rock. Passages ran from the trenches to the reverse side of the hill, on whose upper slopes we dwelt, and even could pitch a tent. Our precarious security rested on the fact that it was a very difficult spot for enemy guns to search, but this security was highly localized, and a few yards further down one was by no means safe. There were gun positions far in the rear that were bombarded daily, and sometimes a battery would be knocked right out. Several howitzers were set in the open just on the reverse of the hills the front line held. It was, as we were shortly to experience, a place of many guns.

Our first week passed quietly enough. The weather, now becoming hot, was glorious, the nights cold, but magnificently fine. On the 6th an elaborate artillery demonstration began, and after a short period of dead silence, the enemy replied. For the first time we heard the horrid wobble of shells filled with liquid that, when they burst, turned into the colourless gas that resembles rotten vegetables in smell and is called di-phosgene. Apart from the dark hints dropped by our battalion commander while we were at Dover Tepé, and the issue of the horrid box-respirators, pamphlets lately put into our hands gave us information about various gases, and included a chilling paragraph which stated that, though no immediate effects might be felt, death might, nevertheless, ensue later. Everyone loathed this latest form of frightfulness. Apart from this and the ghastly night walks in No Man's Land, the Vardar was a pleasant place in this delightful spring-time. By day we could live lazily enough, cooped up, it is true, but still more or less at rest, doubly pleasant for a while after our wanderings. For here we were contracted into a small sector, cramped almost, after our life on the great mountainous slopes we had outposted only a few days since. Here rocks outcropped at intervals from the reddish soil; the oak scrub, lately so familiar, was absent entirely. This place had recently seen agriculture. Fields of currant bushes existed in the rear of our line, breaking down at their edge into sandy areas, good hiding places for troops, well known to us in a few days as our reserve positions, where, owing to the extremely irregular formation of the ground, drilling or military exercise of any kind was absolutely impossible.

Into that Elysium of sloth the Battalion moved after a fortnight in the line—a fortnight in which nothing had happened but gas shells and heavy gun-fire. We had grown accustomed to our new rock-hewn trenches, to looking by moonlight at Mackukovo, all white and seemingly solid, habitable, and real, but in reality the battered shell of what was once a village. Some of us could distinguish Double Hill from Petit Piton after much practice. A few had wandered through our series of somewhat sketchy wire aprons into our undulating No Man's Land, a piece of country that had apparently never been cultivated, except on the extreme left, where some pieces of land automatically reproducing vegetables were a sufficient warning on a dark night that Mackukovo was not far off. At this end, too, was a shell-smitten hollow tree in which dwelt certain large birds—ravens, perhaps—that would fly out noisily at nights on the approach of a patrolling group. To this tree once some Bulgars ventured, though it was right at the foot of our lines, and left a cloth hanging there to daunt us. And this of itself was a proof that patrolling, useless and dangerous though it seemed, was absolutely necessary if we were to maintain our prestige. Our support positions "A" in Gun Hollow, "B" in "LL4," "C" in Bates Ravine, "D" in Morgan Gully and Carlisle Kloof—precluded as aforementioned, activity on our part, but stimulated apparently that of the enemy. It appears that Germany had lent the Bulgars at this point a special squadron of bombing aeroplanes. One afternoon while some of us were arranging a little tactical exercise for Lewis guns on the banks of the

Vardar near our bathing place, a number of planes appeared, flying low, backwards and forwards over our heads. Some new squadron of our own we surmised, until we saw the Imperial Eagle on them and were deafened by the explosion of their bombs. They probably mistook the iron bathing sheds for our ammunition dump. No one was hit, but they did considerable damage either on this or on a later occasion to rail-head, where trucks containing ammunition were set fire to. It was only the day before that Battalion headquarters had been warned of the possibility of an advance on our part, but the news never percolated down to the men. Two or three days later the division staged a tremendous bombardment, which lasted five days, and in the course of which we were counter-bombarded by every sort of projectile, including quantities of gas shells, which, though they caused no casualties, had a most harassing effect on the men's nerves, for they were aimed and timed with such skill that they searched with success even so difficult a place as Bates Ravine, where the shells spilt their detestable liquid at the very entrances of the dug-outs. Enemy gun-fire was throughout extremely accurate; it was evident that the Bulgars or their German gunners were well served with information from the air. One of our batteries in the rear had every gun knocked out of action. In fact, in every respect the Vardar was proving a much more lively place than lonely Dover Tepé.

On May 1st the Battalion went back into the line, relieving the 2/22nd, and two days later a patrol action took place—the only one during our Vardar Valley period. As usual in patrol actions, the story of what occurred is confused, but the main facts are as follows:—At 22.00 hours, Lieut. Antrobus, of "C" Company, went out from "L6" to reconnoitre Stony Hill and Double Hill, purposing to return through "L4." An hour and a quarter later Lieut. Capes left "L4" with his sergeant on duty to visit a post on the band of wire at Mackukovo Gap. When he was about fifty yards from the post he heard some men whispering. Lieut. Capes went straight to the sentry post, picked up four men, and came into contact with several of the enemy about fifteen yards from the wire. On seeing us they threw a bomb, opened rapid fire, and then bolted. At the same time bombing and rifle fire were heard from Stony Hill.

Meanwhile Lieut. Antrobus had received a report from Corporal Lockie, one of our scouts, that the enemy were on Stony Hill. The patrol was in the neighbourhood of Stony Hill when it was attacked from the rear, with the result that two men were killed and nine men wounded. Lieut. Antrobus, though himself wounded, prepared to charge, but the enemy escaped in the darkness. Later the ground was searched but no one discovered.

The result of this patrol action was entirely negative. On a dark night the issue of an affair of this nature is largely a matter of luck. It seems that our patrol ran into an enemy attack on "L4," the advance party of which was discovered by chance by Lieut. Capes. Lieut. Antrobus acted with considerable gallantry. The Brigade and the Division were not enthusiastic about the incident, for they were thirsting for information about the enemy, and it was continually being dinned into our ears that, come what may, we, or some other battalion must somehow get hold of a prisoner. On the next day a large enemy 'plane suddenly swept down on "L8" and flew along our line of trenches, escaping unharmed before our frantic Lewis gunners could tear the dust-coverings off their guns and open fire. Half a minute too late dozens of Lewis guns and machine-guns spoke, and the whole front was in an uproar, but the Germans had caught us napping. On the 7th "L4" and "L6" were badly shelled. The next day Colonel F. D. Watney, who had never been really well, went sick, and though he returned unexpectedly at a later period for a few days, he may be said at this moment to have severed his connection with the Battalion. On the 11th we were enabled to watch a most spectacular assault and capture of a hill by the French on the other side of the Vardar. On the same day we obtained at last the delighted thanks of the Brigade and the Division, for we managed to capture a prisoner, who turned out to be a Saxon of the 13th Jäger Regiment, who came to this front from France a month previously.

The remainder of our stay in the line was uneventful, and on May 17th the Battalion went into divisional reserve at Gully Ridge. A scheme of intensive training was drawn up, but on the 25th, after a period of uncertainty, the Battalion moved to Caussica. A few days previously Lieut.-Col. W. Gibson, 2nd Battalion, Northumberland Fusiliers, assumed command, and soon became very popular. On the 27th the Battalion moved to a place near Galavanci, better described as being in the middle of the Ardzan Plain. In this extraordinary place, in a kind of large open cleft or "wadi" on the bare earth, the Battalion began to settle down to a programme of training in wiring, lectures, and tactical exercises, while every day parties marched over the plain to Lake Ardzan, thoroughly enjoying the rare delight of a good swim. The plain was very swampy and inhabited by countless bull-frogs, frightful creatures that blew themselves out to an immense size, while from millions of throats came the same volume of raucous noise that inspired Aristophanes to write the most famous of his comedies. In the lake there were water-snakes. Between the long, poisonous-looking grasses of the plain, buzzed and flitted horrible painted flies, very brightly coloured and very nasty looking. It was a bad place for any troops to camp, but drafts continued to arrive, until by June 2nd we numbered thirty-two officers and 944 other ranks. It soon became generally known that the Battalion was once more off on its travels, and would never see the Vardar Valley again. On June 4th Captain Coldicott, who had been in command of "C" Company since our departure from England, was evacuated to Salonica with malaria. Next day the Battalion started on its backward journey, this time performed uneventfully and in perfect weather, first to Sarigol (of dismal memory), then to Amberkeny, thence to Narish, and finally, on the 8th, to Ushanta Camp, Salonica, whence we had originally set out. Here we re-equipped. Lieut. Liddiatt returned with a further draft of twenty-three other ranks, and took over command of "C" Company. Leman, Levy, and Antrobus returned with a smaller draft the next day. Before long the great rumour began to get about that we were destined to join General Allenby's army in Palestine. On the 15th we were under twenty-four hours' notice to embark. On the 16th and 18th respectively the Battalion embarked: head-quarters, nineteen officers, and some 500 other ranks on the *Minnetonka*; fourteen officers and over 400 other ranks on the *Huntspill,* one of a German line of ships captured by us. Macedonia, as if to express to the last its thorough dislike of us, provided a torrential downpour at the moment of embarkation. And so we bade farewell to a front where the chief enemy was the climate, and our chief experiences the joys and sorrows of a gipsy life.

CHAPTER IV.—PALESTINE.

1.

Before Beersheba.

> A thousand days, a thousand nights,
> Essayed to set the world at rights;
> But all in vain. The battle-line
> Ran kindling on, up Palestine.
> And we, poor straws in that fierce blaze,
> Were driven, warfare's waifs and strays,
> A thousand nights, a thousand days.

The news that we were to visit Egypt had been good news to a battalion wearied of much wandering in a land where civilization seemed to have reached only the fringes, and, even on the shores—those opulent shores of the Mediterranean—to have failed completely, dragging on a down-at-heel, third-rate, miserable cheap-jack kind of existence. We were glad to be going to the Egyptian field of operations, whence news from time to time had blown across the sea to us in little gusts, and thoughts were frequent of possible leave to Alexandria; it was felt, too, that even to be ill in hospital in such a place would be in the nature of a treat! And we longed to walk on pavements again, to see good shops and have a good meal.

It was disappointing, therefore, that on our arrival at that eagerly expected place, we were instantly entrained for a small French town called Ismailia, a very clean, and neat, and quiet little settlement on the shores of Lake Timsah, part of whose inland waterways connected with the Suez Canal. Disappointing, but good for us, for instead of the garish amusements and excitements attendant on a camp outside a great city, we found here exactly what we needed, sufficient time and opportunity in a pleasant backwater to refit and recondition ourselves. No member of the Battalion will ever think of Ismailia except in the light of a happy memory. No one will forget Lake Timsah and the avenue of trees that led down to it—trees whose trunks were of the grey, ancient colour of dusty elephant skin. It was a real oasis. Beyond and about it were fleckless sand-dunes and illimitable deserts.

A week after our arrival Colonel Gibson went sick, and about the same time Regimental Sergeant-Major Jennings was awarded the Meritorious Service Medal. It is impossible to speak too highly of this potentate—the absolute monarch of the non-commissioned officers. The welfare of the Battalion was to him his very being. A technical expert in close-order drill, he held the secret many officers could never learn—of making men jump to him. Without at long last the goodwill of the rank and file, feats such as his are impossible, and the fact that he held the confidence of the men is his best and most valuable testimonial. As we had never known any other sergeant-major, the exceptional nature of his gifts and service was probably not appreciated —until towards the end of the history of the Battalion, when he became established as a still mightier lord at famous Kantara, that transitory city of tents, where he was wont to range up other regimental sergeant-majors and make them jump about like recruits. Another came, one faintly remembers, to take his place : then we knew what he had been.

A few days afterwards, Lieut. Macdonald, our zealous and industrious adjutant, went sick, and though he came back for a few days a fortnight later, he was not really well until the middle of August. His temporary capitulation deserves mention, for this officer had not spared himself since the commencement of the war, and it had become habitual for him to shoulder most of the work at headquarters. A difficult post to fill, he never seemed to tire, and we had grown accustomed to rely on his steady hard work and powers of organization. Shortly after his illness he left us for the Brigade, but returned later and remained in his old place until the end. Surely a remarkable record, but he was a remarkable man.

On July 5th we were inspected by General Bulfin. Our strength was thirty-three officers and 976 other ranks. It may be noted here that almost exactly a month after this inspection General Bulfin became a corps commander, and was succeeded by General Shea. Our general had been much liked. He was one of those old-fashioned, hard-working, personally brave ones. He and his son were known as "The Bing Boys." The private code-word by which battalions signalled his sudden arrival was "Beryl." Every general has his fad—his was to penetrate into the kitchens and sample the men's food. General Shea, who led us henceforward, could be very kindly, and sometimes almost disconcerted us with the unconventional friendliness of his methods.

On July 8th, entirely re-equipped, we left Ismailia, and marched to Ferdan, thence to El Ballah, and on the 10th to

Kantara, then rapidly growing into a huge city of tents. Once across the canal the Battalion entrained for Deir el Belah, where camel transport arrived, and nearly three uneventful weeks was spent at this place, remarkable chiefly for a good deal of sickness amongst officers and men, and for the desultory beginnings of training in open warfare. At the end of the month the Battalion again moved, this time to a name on the map, "Hisea," a short journey from Shellal, which was in those days our rail-head.

These movements of the Battalion have been but briefly epitomized because they were in no sense important considered in conjunction with the events that followed. The place we had now arrived at—this "Hisea"—was simply an expanse of absolutely bare country. It was like living on a plain of fuller's earth. Sand-hills could be seen in the distance, and there were one or two nearer mounds or undulations, but of vegetation not one sign. Unbroken as the country appeared, it was evident, as one scanned it more carefully, that it was scored in places by wadis differing widely in their characteristics—sometimes surprising you when almost at their edge, narrow and deep rifts in the earth scarce a dozen yards wide, sometimes great open spaces at a lower level like gravel pits, but leading away into deeper and narrower clefts and forks; and sometimes on a vaster scale, regular geographical features, of which the great Wadi Ghuzze was our nearest example. The ground itself was not a sand, but a fine grey earth as dry as powder. Every day was exactly the same. Clouds in the sky were utterly unknown. The sun would begin to lift its large red disc above the horizon, and in the chilly last remains of night we would get up and parade. All the work was done in these early hours or towards nightfall. By ten in the morning the heat would be tremendous, and until the middle of the afternoon progressively overpowering, making any kind of military exercise absolutely impossible. Officers' messes were square holes dug in the ground and covered with rush mats, though it was difficult to come by anything in that desert. Life at mid-day was a torment. Flies, the curse of the East, hung about each man, and clustered on our food up to the last moment before it was consumed. They settled on our lips as if on cattle. Though the middle part of the day was almost breathless, the fine, gritty dust was always in movement; nothing could keep it out of our food or our clothing. Later in the afternoon a cold wind would get up, gradually increasing in strength and blowing thin clouds of dust with it. Then one could choose between lying sweltering in a closed tent, or cool and dust-swept with the sides looped up. It was a place exasperating to the nerves. Everyone hated it, and everyone gradually came to know that the Turks had stayed us in this barren area and that they inhabited far more delectable regions.

Our days were spent in training for the campaign which, though nothing was said, we dimly felt was bound to come upon us. Gaza, in Turkish hands, was about eleven miles away to our front; Beersheba was on our right rear, distanced about twenty miles. The Turks held a loosely defined line between these two places, and their horsemen sometimes met our mounted infantry on reconnaissances. Ours was purely a training area, out of the fighting zone, but a place called Kent Fort, into which we moved on August 15th, was part of a system of defences nobody understood or took very seriously. Little was done in August. On the last day of the month, General Shea inspected the Battalion. But from September onwards training began in earnest. On the 7th there was a brigade night exercise, one of the most trying and boring experiences we had yet come across. Battalions marched by compass to a preconceived meeting-place in absolute silence and in clouds of dust. At dawn—an extraordinary natural spectacle, with sun and moon mingling their light in the sky—the men kindled small fires and made a meal. In some ways we were re-approaching the kind of training we had had in England in the early days. Here we marched in fours again, a great and welcome change for the men, but with the files opened out by reason of the dust. But new practices were introduced among us. Companies, as well as battalions, now had their "head-quarters"—runners, servants, cooks, signallers, and what not—machinery immediately behind the company commander, who thus had a small staff of his own. Now, too, the Lewis gunners (under Lieut. Cowper) were trained again and brought into prominence. These still depended on mules for their transport. Camels, with native attendants, transported in large nets the bulk of our belongings. Officers still rode their horses. We wore but little. A shirt, open at the neck and with the sleeves rolled up, a pair of scanty "shorts," a pair of puttees ending at the bare knee, a sun helmet— this completed our attire.

>   "Bare to the elbows, brown and lean,
>   Behold them as they go—
>   'The Londons', desperately keen,
>   Doggèd and firm and slow."

But we were not on the move yet, though daily becoming browner and harder and leaner; held as yet by the Turk on this detestable training ground, this area of baked friable soil of lightest quality, a desert of dust to all seeming, waiting, however, the touch of rain's lightest finger to break into life in a night-born shimmer of green.

During the whole of September training progressed, tempered at the end of the month by sports to keep us in good fettle. In spite of the minor torments climate and the flies provided, the Battalion had not for months been so well or so keen on work. One wondered, looking at the men at football or on parade, that these magnificently fit people had once been those pallid undersized Londoners who had come to us, many of them mere boys, at the outbreak of war. For, despite casualties and some changes, our rank and file were still very much the same personnel that entrained at Warminster and suffered at La Marguerette. Now, in this last training period, after many false starts and much wandering, we were being got ready for a final something that would be worth while. So, day by day we imagined for ourselves schemes of attack, advanced as once of old "by short rushes," fought complicated mock battles in the great Wadi Ghuzzi (as once, how differently! over Beverley Brook) and enjoyed a magnificently staged series of field firing exercises planned most realistically on a grand scale. The men entered into it all and were in splendid spirits. But for certain officers life held for the moment something finer—nothing less than a mounted reconnaissance of Beersheba—known more correctly as Bir El Saba. How can one in an epitome such as this, on so scanty a page, set forth the excitement and romance of that outriding?

Beersheba lay roughly about eighteen miles as the crow flies on our right flank. It was not, however, possible to progress by any means in a straight line, for the ground was rift asunder by two great clefts or wadis—the Wadi Ghuzze and the Wadi Mirtaba. Moreover, as one approached the neighbourhood of Beersheba itself, sand gave place to barren limestone rocks, complicated into a mass of little hills and valleys, irregular beyond belief. Our first reconnaissance into this district, by a small group of mounted officers led by Colonel Gibson, necessitated the establishment of a temporary base at Gamli in the bed of a wadi. Thence we penetrated into the country destined to be invested secretly by the whole desert column in days that were now at hand. Face to face in the late afternoon with those white limestone summits, whose wired approaches were just visible before rapidly approaching twilight plunged the whole strange territory into shadows, we realized how difficult would be the secret movement of large bodies of troops to this region by night. For night increases enormously earth's apparent heights and depths, and only the most resolute pacing and confidence in a compass can ensure the keeping of direction. A wild ride over a wild country.*

Shortly after this reconnaissance, the Battalion moved into "Kent Fort." It was known that the "push" would have to take place soon, for the season of rain was near, and once the rains began movement would become impossible. Already once, in the night, the quiet pattering of a few drops had been heard, and lo! by morning our arid waste of grey dust had produced a shimmer of green. A few serious showers and we should be helpless in a sea of mud. Moreover, a ride to railhead disclosed one morning a cage, erected to accommodate Turkish prisoners yet to be. Then came an instruction from the Brigade to officers to send away all superfluous kit. As a week elapsed and we were still in "Kent Fort," doubts began to arise, but on October 20th the Battalion was relieved by the 1st Hereford Regiment, and on the 21st marched to Tel El Fara, a barren bump in the desert, and there sat down. Changes had been wrought in the command. On September 27th Major S. B. Smith joined us from the Loyal North Lancs as second in command, displacing Major Leman, who took over "B" Company and shortly afterwards went sick. On October 1st the Rev. S. G. McMurtree, our popular padre, left us. To the regret of all Colonel Gibson left us in the early days of October, and Colonel Watney reappeared, only, after a few days, to retire to the Base, leaving in command Lieut.-Col. J. A. Jervois, sent from the King's Own Yorkshire Light Infantry. This young, able, and gallant officer commanded us henceforth until the end. His influence was entirely good, and the Battalion was fortunate to secure, on the eve of an important campaign, so competent and energetic a commander.

At Tel-el-Fara we still further divested ourselves of our possessions, and company messes hurriedly drank up their stocks of drink. General Shea, our divisional commander, came to this place to address us, and shortly after dusk on the following day we moved further eastward. To our left front lay miles of open country, flat at first, then mildly

---

* For a detailed account of the taking of Beersheba, described from the point of view of an officer of the 2/21st Battalion, see *The Cornhill Magazine* for November, 1918.

undulating till one again struck wadis and the confused masses of rock-strewn hills and valleys which, far away, concealed Beersheba. The march was an anxious one, for there was a thick mist, and we had to feel our way along a wadi edge. At length we found our way down into a wide part of the wadi. Hidden thus we remained several days, while bombs, flares, and wire-cutters were issued. Aeroplane photographs of the Beersheba defences were passed round. Interest in the coming attack quickly rose. Immense preparations were going on all round us. Great square areas, where the camel transport of various units waited the signal to advance, showed, no less than the haste with which the railway was being pushed forward, that large bodies of troops were about to be on the move. And all these preparations were made in secret. The attack on Beersheba, though it involved the movements of a complete column (the "Desert Column" was the name given to us) was prepared as a complete surprise to the Turks, now leisurely lapping up their porridge on the hidden side of the hill "1070."

The advance began at nightfall. We assembled in darkness and absolute silence; our march this first night was to the clefts and hollows of a great wadi, a wild place marked by one ruined building and called Rashid Bek. We moved slowly in a long, snake-like column, raising from the powdery soil clouds of fine dust that almost hid the camel transport swinging deliberately beside us. The moon was by this time up: it was intolerably cold. For a long time we halted—other troops were passing our front. At length the flat plain bosomed slightly, and we found ourselves marching on a slight incline. Then the ground dipped. Our twelve-mile march was over; we had arrived at Rashid Bek.

By this time we knew the part we had to play in the attack. We had arrived at this intermediate hiding-place at one in the morning. We remained quietly hidden during the day. Orders were issued at five in the afternoon by dictation, nothing on paper was to be taken beyond. The order of attack was briefly as follows: The 2/21st, less three platoons "D" Company, who were acting under Major Smith as convoy to the water camels ("Train C"), were to form an outpost line. Through this line the other three battalions of the brigade were to advance one and a half hours before midnight and take up positions in Shropshire and Pembroke Wadis, immediately in front of enemy works, but hidden from view. At dawn, after an hour's wire-cutting, these battalions would attack and take the enemy's advanced works. The 2/21st would advance under cover of the bombardment to Pembroke Wadi, and closely support the 2/22nd, the directing battalion. In the second phase the 2/21st, accompanied by the 2/23rd and 2/24th, would pass the 2/22nd and attack the main position. Each battalion would finally send forward one company to establish themselves on the Beersheba track.

We left Rashid Bek soon after the issue of orders. The sun soon dropped low on the horizon, and by the time we approached the outpost position the light was failing. Each company was now marching independently to its position in the outpost line. Horses and grooms trailed away to a hollow in the rear—battalion head-quarters. Midway on our miniature landscape of rock-strewn hills and valleys, each company had its head-quarters, and in front in the darkness that made the work difficult, subalterns were establishing sentry groups even as in England in the far-away training period. Great pains had been taken to impress on the men the necessity for absolute silence. In the event of a chance encounter with an enemy patrol, the bayonet alone was to be used. Were we to betray ourselves prematurely the success of the whole operation would be imperilled. But all went well. The line was established, the other battalions passed through. We collected ourselves together, and in Shropshire Wadi, just before dawn, once more settled ourselves down to wait.

Dawn was heralded by the appearance of various stray officers from other units and formations. They all seemed lost. Then the artillery on both sides woke up, and it was only a matter of seconds before Shropshire Wadi became a very dangerous place. We lay "in artillery formation," seeking what cover we could. By this time it had become light. The famous hill "1070," a very formidable position, was now completely hidden by the dust raised by our considerable artillery fire. A certain amount of time was lost owing to a slight change of programme. At half-past eight, a ten minutes' intense bombardment was ordered Though the attacking battalions were ready to "go in" three-quarters of an hour before, it was not until 10 o'clock that the advance began. Half-an-hour later we followed.

We had lost some men by enemy shell fire in the hours of waiting, but the actual advance—taken at the double—was achieved without casualty, and when we came to the base of the famous hill all the wire was smashed, and no one remained to defend it. We climbed up and sat down on our side of the hill-top. Only wounded or dead Turks remained. Our guns had done their work. The first phase was at an end.

Between the two phases much valuable time was lost before the Division gave the word to proceed. Our artillery had moved up into their second position with great skill and speed. We were ready to advance by 11 o'clock, but the attack was ordered for 12.15 p.m. We advanced eventually under cover of an intense bombardment, and so eagerly that we almost ran into our own barrage. Here, as before, on the furthermost ridge of the hill we found that we had arrived too late. The Turks were in flight. They could be seen scurrying away in the plain below. But some had turned and were sweeping our new position with fire. Hurriedly we formed an outpost line. Here Lieut. Aldis, second in command of "C" Company, met his death, shot through the head by a chance bullet.

We spent the remainder of the day on these white limestone summits, a day of burning sun, physical exhaustion, and filthy smells. The men discovered in the Turkish stores quantities of gay-coloured garments woven like tweeds, in beautiful greens and yellows. These they donned, and thus gave colour to a scene that already was sufficiently fantastic. So surprised were the Turks that they left great cauldrons of porridge behind—their untasted breakfast of that morning —but they took with them what was much more important —their guns. Had the attack been a complete success, not one of the enemy would have escaped. We delayed too long between the attacks, and the mounted troops were not quick enough in getting round to the back of the enemy's position.

The usual chilly night followed this glamorous day. We were short of water, dead tired, and extremely dirty. The next day was spent in burying the dead and cleaning up as far as possible this evil-smelling place. A dense dust-storm followed, making life even more miserable. And so, perforce, we tarried. Half left, below us, past the cliffs of a whitely gleaming ravine, Beersheba lay, a collection of huddled buildings, mostly mud huts. To the white ravine some of our men ventured, unbidden, and found water to bathe in. Four days the dust-storm raged, and saved the Turkish forces, but on the morning of November 3rd, while it was still in progress, we marched to a barren slope among some low hills south of Beersheba. Our halt was only for a few hours, and in the afternoon we passed through

Beersheba itself. It lingers faintly in the memory, a place of mud and ruins, dirty, desolate, and malodorous, shadowed over by the vivid happenings of the events that preceded and followed that entry.

2.

To Jerusalem.

The country in the neighbourhood of Beersheba is little more than a mass of volcanic rock, very barren and very desolate. The map marks most of it "impracticable for wheeled traffic," we found it as we forged slowly onward, nearly impracticable for foot passengers, too ! In all the history of our wanderings in Macedonia and Palestine we never struck such a stony wilderness as the tract between Beersheba and the region of Kanwakah defences. We were now heading north-west in the direction of Gaza. One remembers passing a group of engineers busily engaged in tapping some well and spreading out a canvas tank in which to store water, now a precious commodity. Little else, except dust and heat and fatigue, remain of that march. The first night we halted and bivouacked on a good piece of ground near the railway. The weather was perfect, the dust-storm over. The next day, November 4th, we continued the march to Abu Irgeig and relieved the 10th Battalion, the Buffs. The relief took place in pitch darkness, and we passed through a wadi where there was much congestion. Morning found us holding our extended line on a flattish piece of country, easy to move about on by day, but terribly difficult at night. Far in front of us figures could be seen, horsemen, moving about near a well. We fired at them with Lewis guns, but the range must have been too great, or our shooting bad, for they did not take any notice. In all probability they were Bedouins. All day long we lay flat with nothing whatsoever to do, and in utter ignorance of our exact position on the map or of what was toward. During the day some staff officers of another brigade came up, and there was much spreading of maps and discussion as to our position, without any conclusion being reached. The night of the 5th will long be remembered by the commanders of "C" and "D" companies, who were ordered to "move out to get into touch with the left flank of the 74th Division," who were supposed to be attacking at dawn a system of trenches across our front. As the night was another pitch dark one, and as no one had seen any trenches or the 74th Division, and as the country we were in was almost featureless and apparently illimitable, the difficulty and danger of complying with such an order are obvious. All night long we crept about in the dark, and just as dawn was breaking reassembled. It soon became known that an attack would shortly take place on the Kanwakah defences, and that the 181st Brigade would be in reserve. We marched until three in the afternoon, when we halted in a sandy wadi in the stifling heat. There had been a good deal of gun-fire and rifle-fire all day. After resting for some time we heard that the attack had been successful, and that we were to push on. Accordingly, we streamed off on the march again in pursuit of the Turk, who was now well on the run.

We marched for the remainder of the afternoon, and at the end of it, just before twilight, halted. The pace had been pretty hot, no one knew exactly where we were or where the Turks were, and it transpired later that higher commands were equally befogged. At the moment of halting, a message came for battalion commanders to confer with the brigade commander, and so our C.O., together with the O.C. 2/22nd, went off, expecting to return shortly. Night was approaching, but did not herald the return of the battalion commanders. Orders, however, had earlier been promulgated that the Battalion was to take up an outpost line north of Wadi Sheria to form a bridge-head over water supply, and just before night fell Captain Coldicott, being senior officer present, took the responsibility of moving the Battalion off in parallel columns on a compass bearing in search of Wadi Sheria, the 2/22nd Battalion coming along behind, and in rear of them the Brigade Ammunition Column and two sections 181st Machine Gun Company. The whole proceeding was risky in the extreme, as the only map available was a sheet of white paper stamped with innumerable forked lines representing Wadis. No one knew exactly where we were, and the exact location of Sheria was hazy in our minds, but it would obviously have been a criminal proceeding to have left two battalions resting in column of fours at night within touch of the enemy, whose precise whereabouts remained unknown. A forward policy is the best when a war is on, so on we went. As we disappeared, a member of the brigade staff galloped up and shouted out, "You are going into the blue." But into the blue we went, and anxious indeed were the scouts who marched screening the two columns, and gradually went slower and slower as darkness became more intense. The distance had been roughly estimated at the start, and, by the counting of paces, it seemed that a dip in the ground was the wadi in question.

In this dip the whole force halted, the 2/22nd disengaging to the left, and "C" and "D" Companies forming an outpost line. All this took some time, and in the meanwhile a party was sent along the dip to the left to reconnoitre the left flank, but ran into what they reported to be an enemy outpost, but which was probably a collection of natives fugitive from Sheria. Two hours before dawn Captain Coldicott, who was not at all certain that the battalions were far enough advanced, or were in the Wadi Sheria at all, scouted in front of the outpost line with Rifleman Francis, and discovered (the moon was up) that the Wadi Sheria yawned like a gravel pit in front of us, a pit with deep sides, but with one easy way down into it. At the same time a movement was heard on the right, and up crawled a staff-officer of the 74th Division, who were supposed to be coming up on our right. This officer engaged to bring troops up to the wadi before daybreak if we could move our outpost line forward to make good the wadi. This with all speed was accomplished, thanks chiefly to the loyal way in which Lieuts. Capes and Carr (in charge of the outpost line) co-operated with Captain Coldicott. Exhausted though the men were they pushed forward, and just before dawn were in position on the enemy side of the wadi, while the remainder of the column moved forward into the wadi. It had been evident during the latter part of the night that considerable confusion reigned in Sheria, which lay on our left, and towards dawn the explosion of a mixed dump of ammunition and signal rockets added to the picturesqueness of the scene. As dawn broke, rifle-fire became more intense, and as the light grew stronger it gradually became apparent that the other two battalions of the brigade were attacking at some distance, and that we were admirably placed to assist them by enfilading the enemy, which we accordingly did. After a short time our advance was ordered, and it was while we were proceeding to the high ground in front of us, under a rain of bullets—for the Turk had had to disengage a portion of his troops to deal with this diversion—that Colonel Jervois reappeared, walking unconcernedly from the direction of Sheria, in front of our attacking line. Pushing on, we gained the top of the hill and found an enemy gun, for the capture of which, a few moments previously Colonel Boughton was awarded the V.C. A platoon of "C"

Company with a Lewis gun had just time to throw themselves in front of it before a fresh Turkish gun-team appeared over the crest from the right and galloped down to retake the gun. It was broken up easily, and a prisoner taken. The attacking companies of the Battalion then moved forward, and, with their left flank pushed up, got across the railway line, in touch with the right wing of the other battalions, whose attack, held in the early stages, had now proved successful. Lying thus, the outpost companies, especially on the left of the line, came under heavy gun-fire from the direction of Huj. Scouts working in front of the line soon spotted a complete battalion of the enemy at no great distance, being reformed for a counter-attack by an officer on a white horse. It looked for a few moments as if our position was desperate, for our right flank (under Lieut. Carr) was hopelessly in the air, the 74th Division having failed to materialize—in fact, we never saw them south of Jerusalem. But two things happened in the nick of time. The enemy battery that had been ranging on us suddenly packed up, and the 181st Machine-gun Section—one gun in particular from a position on the railway line—opened fire on the adversary Turks with such admirable effect that the mass of men melted and broke and was lost in various wadis. At the same time, word was sent to the line by our adjutant, "Expect some mounted troops shortly," and a few minutes afterwards a brigade of cavalry charged through our lines to the country beyond—as fine a sight as any man can hope to witness. We remained in position, still worried by hostile machine-gun fire, and during this period, Sergeant Andrews, of "C" Company, who had been continuously with the company since the Battalion left England, was mortally wounded. At dusk more mounted troops rode through to clear the country. They came in line, riding knee to knee, swept down into the railway cutting, rose like a billow in ordered confusion out of it, and charged on like a gigantic human wave. Throughout the day we had been unsupported by artillery, for the horses were so exhausted for want of water that they could not pull the guns. And only by difficult degrees that afternoon could water-bottles be passed up to the troops holding the line. So ended the battle of Sheria, a very important episode in the history of the advance to Jerusalem. For Sheria, half-way between Gaza and Beersheba, was an enormous store-house of munitions of war for the Turks, and the great dump there had taken the Turk six months to accumulate. In this battle the 2/21st, by appearing on the enemy's flank at the critical moment, played no small part.

The night was an unquiet one for the outpost companies, who remained in position and started up time and again on a series of false alarms. Early next morning the Battalion assembled and pushed off in the direction of Huj, which is some ten miles east of Gaza. Huj was being strongly defended by the Turks, and it was from this direction that the hostile gun-fire had come that had so worried us the day before. The march was intensely monotonous, but was rendered spectacularly memorable by the fact that the brigade moved intact over these dusty, level plains, with ambulance, guns, and transport all in view. Half-way through the day's march a rise in the ground allowed us to see in the distance Gaza, a hazy mass of buildings with a few trees. It was late in the afternoon before the nature of the ground changed, a few trees were passed, and then, winding on a sudden to the left among some low hill-lands, we came upon a dramatic scene. A Turkish battery had been charged by the Warwicks and the Worcesters, and the gunners put to the sword. Our arrival was but shortly after the event. Prisoners were being led away; dead men and horses covered with blood sprawled left and right. But the minutes were few before darkness would come rushing down; our thoughts were all for our bivouac ground, and our eyes for any small bits of wood that could be grabbed to make a fire. The day had been intolerably hot—flies were always with us—we were doomed to carry them from place to place on our packs, and now the water question was becoming as burning as our thirsts. There was just time to pitch the tents and sink to rest.

We made a late start next morning, bound for a place called Jemmameh. Major Smith, who had made a mild reconnaissance on a fresh horse, gave us high hopes for this day's march, for he said that "Jemimer" was quite near and that it was downhill all the way. The distance was not, in fact, far, but the march was exhausting in the extreme. The first part of our way lay over a bare earthen expanse, littered with odds and ends the Turk had rid himself of in his retreat. Later we passed through a native village—the first we had seen since we quitted Beersheba. The country then became utterly desert. We crossed a wadi and then panted on over a plain—our course marked only by the bodies of horses and the whitened ribs of camels that had been. The hours that followed were overcome one by one by successive feats of endurance on the part of an already exhausted soldiery. Someone has said that Palestine is the most difficult country in the world to fight over. Our townsmen, overladen with heavy packs, not too well nourished, and exhausted by the rigours of the preceding days, found the path to "Jemimer" almost too much for them. At length a building appeared, set by a low bridge. This bucked the men up, it looked as if we were coming to some place. Then the country began to change, and presently we were following a track that led gradually upward and wound in and out amongst large stones. There was quite a hint of Macedonia about it. At last we knew that we had arrived, for here was a village, and there, slightly to the left, were the wells, the hope and desire of which had lured us onward through the day's long heats.

The men had not rested for more than a few minutes before news arrived that a Turkish corps was reported to be moving in our direction, and that the Battalion was to form an outpost line. So exhausted company commanders had vague stretches of hill country allotted them by a tired C.O., and in due course the Battalion spread itself out over a very uneven and broken-up terrain, and faced North. There was not much time to organize the line before night fell. It was moonless, and so pitch black that no operations of any kind could have taken place in it. Luckily, nothing untoward happened. The supposed Turkish corps changed its intentions, and the morn was tranquil.

We stayed five days at Jemmameh. The Battalion had a thorough rest. It was at this place that a light sudden shower occurred one night—the first rain we had seen in Egypt excepting a freakish five minutes at Sheikh Nuran. Our Sheria performance had pleased the Brigade—the brigade commander visited us and was affable; and the divisional commander liked the 181st Brigade, referring to it as "priceless." Our field ambulance was with us here, and we had an opportunity of seeing something of that ever-popular unit. Our departure on the fifth day was leisurely, and the march easy. No one knew where we were going. We bivouacked in a bare stubble-field near a small stream—a most welcome object. So far relaxed were we that it was supposed another wait would be made in this place. We were leisurely improving our camping site the next morning when orders came to march at once.

This order, and our destination, were equally unexpected, for we soon learnt that we were actually on the march to Sheria—the very place we had set out from little more than a week before; we were, in fact, doubling on our tracks. Our route lay alongside the railway, and we passed about mid-day a fine stone viaduct broken in half. This was the only feature on the landscape, and long before nightfall we halted outside where Sheria had been, on a very bare and barren expanse of dry dirt, intently watched by a small encampment of Bedouins. One remembers the place by the quantity of litter that lay about, in particular a painted and grained washstand—an incongruous object to come across, standing by itself in a desert. The next day we marched to Hareira, *en route* for Gaza. At Hareira there was one tree, a meat issue, a gentle shower of rain, and a supply of serge tunics, which set us guessing once more. For the present we could not speculate beyond Gaza, which was reached the following day after a march full of interest, for we passed many evidences of the recent fighting: in particular, some dummy guns made of wood, with shell-holes all about them. The scenery gradually changed as we drew nearer: green grasses and deep red poppies were welcome after the deserts we had left behind. We camped, together with other troops, on a low, flat piece of ground. In front of us were sand-hills covered with barbed-wire and dark cactus compounds. These hid, for the most part, Gaza itself. To our left was the welcome sight of the blue Mediterranean. Gaza had, of course, fallen about the time we were fighting at Sheria; the town was but a forsaken husk. Some of us, exploring it on the afternoon of our arrival, found the place wrecked and almost completely deserted. It was a melancholy spectacle, made more melancholy yet by the relentless approach of the first of the long-delayed rains: no shower this time, but a steady downfall. Everyone was more or less soaked that night, for our camping ground had been badly chosen, and the whole place speedily grew swampy. It cleared up at dawn, and was tolerably fine as we set out and left Gaza behind us. Nor was the going bad, for a night's rain had not yet turned the bone-dry earth to mud.

Before we started, Colonel Jervois treated us to one of his rare and brief speeches, from which we gathered that much marching was in front of us. Our route lay to the East of Gaza: the Battalion as a whole never entered the city. All went well until shortly after mid-day, when a drizzle turned into a second instalment of the same steady rain. The men, weighed down with sodden packs and slipping on the mud, were soon in miserable plight. The march went on and on, the pace got slower and slower. Finally, just before dark, the companies disengaged to the left into a barley field soaked with rain, and settled down for the night to make the best of it. We were in the neighbourhood of Esdud. It will always be a place of hateful memory to the Battalion.

Next morning everyone set off in bad humour to the accompaniment of a general "ticking-off" from the top downward. One remembers how miserable the mules were on that occasion—for they turned up caked all over with mud. Yet after an hour or two the weather cleared and the men's spirits revived. Song broke out on the march. We passed through a native village inhabited by a wretched low type of beings, the women very dirty, with matted hair. At nightfall we bivouacked in a field very much like the one before, but the night was fine. Here women came with sacks and sold us large Jaffa oranges. Here, too, there was wood and warmth.

This again was but a night's halting-place. Next day we set out for El Kustine, and soon ran into the back area of the corps commanded by General Bulfin, our old divisional commander. It was pleasant to find that our resting place that night was not a rain-soaked field, but a fine, dry, well-drained piece of land just to the left of the road. It was rumoured that we were to spend several days at El Kustine, but next morning saw us once more on the march. We started with the conviction, somehow gained about this time, that we were bound for Jerusalem. Our wanderings to no purpose in the Sheria district had shaken our faith as to our ultimate destination, but now we were certain. We had not marched far before we passed a railway-line scientifically smashed by the Turk, a station, and some smashed houses. Captured stores lay about, including a damaged aeroplane. Later we traversed some broken country and passed a pool full of dead oxen, flung in to contaminate the water. Near the pool some Turkish prisoners were working. A cut across country, very stony, took us to the road again, and we marched for hours, always on the upward trend. The weather was cloudless, hot, but not oppressive; we seemed to have left the rains behind. At the halts natives offered us nuts and oranges, bought by us after much bargaining. Gradually, as we passed onward, the face of the country changed. The land on either side now appeared cultivated, and it varied much in quality, reminding us irresistibly of the good and stony ground of the parable. This first foretaste of hills gave place after a time to open fields. The road, late a track that twisted on itself, now straightly entered upon a slow descent. At length, as we topped a slight rise, we saw in front of us, in the distance, the veritable hill country, a mass we should have called mountainous had we never seen Bulgaria's frontier. At the foot of the dark hills some buildings lay—houses, and one apart, with three poplars near it. Close as they seemed, an hour elapsed and we were still marching, the men very fatigued, for it had been a long day. The road branched right and left. We took the right. There was a regular traffic jam at this place owing to an ambulance convoy having attempted to push past us as we were crossing a bridge. At last we got clear. Plough-lands of a rich chocolate-brown merged on our right into rocky highlands; over our left shoulders we caught a glimpse of the road we had lately left, curving up Jerusalem-way between two great hills. Slightly below us on our right, among reeds and grasses, trickled a stream of precious water—the first running water we had seen since we had set foot in Egypt. Our final bivouac was on a kind of ledge, covered with flat, loose pieces of rock, half-way up the hill. From it the whole brigade could be seen—the camels, with their blue-gowned attendants, the sand-carts of the ambulance, the long train of mules just arriving. The scene was full of beauty; it was a lovely evening; everyone felt tired and happy. The name of the place was Latrun. We stayed several days and enjoyed a thorough rest, troubled by no one. The flies had left us. There were oranges to eat, to supplement our rations of dates and raisins, and we could wash. The weather continued perfect; we demanded, for the moment, no more.

Such interludes are rare. It was upon a Tuesday that we "packed up," soon to find ourselves marching on a road sunken deep between two heights. This gorge persisted for some time, but at length we rested in a space where some olives were growing. The road still ran uphill, but after a while the cliffs on the left fell away, and taking a great sweep in that direction, it opened out a wide vision before us—the hills among which we had ascended, the plain we had journeyed over on our way to Latrun, and, on the uttermost verge, the grey haze of the far Mediterranean. On the right was another scene—rocky formations, ravines that intermingled, the misty tops of hillsides unapproached.

We learned at the end of the fourth hour of the march that we were to go straight into the line that night and relieve the Scots, who, after much fighting, had been held up upon Nebi Samwil. The line was still many miles away, no one speculated over where it was or how long we should take to get there. Sufficient unto us the immediate scene and the appeasements of our march weariness. Half an hour brought us to a place where we halted—it was mid-day —for several hours. Stone-built houses were visible in the far distance. Everywhere, at every level, stone terraces added their blue-grey tones to the dark metallic greens of the olive. At a distance, hills lifted their shadowy masses. Near us and above us a white building flew a Red Cross flag. The hours of rest passed, and, falling in at last in a hurry, we pressed on, topped the hill, caught sight of the stone walls of a monastery, and turned off the road, leaving En Nab behind. We had descended, but now, passing a plantation, began to climb again, and soon were in the middle of a wilderness of rock. The going began to be very difficult. Slabs and fragments of rock jutted out on or lay a-tilt across our twisted path. This told upon the men, already weary with the day's long climb. At length we arrived at some buildings, and saw some of the Scots' transport near a well. Our own transport remained here. We moved off again, and in a few minutes the light had gone and we were marching under a pale moon.

We now began a descent. The ground became more open; loose stones lay about. Presently the valley opened out, and we were dimly aware that we had come into a great space. On our right we passed the bodies of dead camels, great mounds of pallid flesh, horrid to look at in the moonlight. Guided by an unintelligible Scot, we somehow arrived at the back of what appeared to be the line, a ridge consisting of a series of rocky terraces piled up upon each other in every sort of confusion. Here, after the usual delays, we managed to supplant the weary Scots, taking over an outpost line on the further side of the ridge, and sitting down amongst a battery of light guns that seemed to inhabit the very bivouac-places of the infantry.

We stayed in this position for several days, in the very midst of gunfire, but suffering no casualties. Nebi Samwil rose on our right and slightly to the rear of us, a gun-broken building on its summit, the centre of most of the noise. The twenty-pounders stationed in our midst spoke often, their small shells just clearing our bivouacs. Here we tasted the heavy red wine of Palestine, a most intoxicating drink. Our position was a responsible one, but nothing happened.

We moved suddenly one night, crossing the valley in our rear, climbing the steep terraced slopes beyond, passing through a village, and so on, and down into a second valley, not smooth and pleasant, but rugged and desolate, a veritable wilderness. Luckily there was a moon. We picked our way amongst huge boulders, and finally gained a hill that lay across the valley. On a series of rocky terraces the Battalion spread itself out. Head-quarters was near a compound which concealed a battery. We stayed two days in this inhospitable place. From it we got our first look at Jerusalem, lying spilt, as it were, among the hills, a mass of buildings with one tall shaft standing by itself away on the left. Our next position proved to be on a hog's back of broken boulders somewhere between the village of Beit-Iksa and Nebi Samwil. The companies moved independently to this place, the scene of recent bitter fighting. On a steep hill on the other side of the valley, it was possible to make out in the dusk the Turkish trenches—an irregular dark line. Our business was to guard the valley and re-take Nebi Samwil if anything went amiss. At last we were on the top of the Turks again, our advanced posts could hear them talking. Our first night in this position was an anxious one, for not long after the troops we had relieved departed, a wet, cold, impenetrable mist arrived, making supervision impossible. We were shelled, but still remained without casualties. On the third day our position was shifted again, and during the move the rains recommenced. Still clad in khaki shorts, we had found the Judea hills uncomfortably cold; rain completed our discomfort. After much wandering on the part of the companies, each of which had an entirely separate set of misadventures that night, the Battalion came together, wet to the skin, in a kind of plantation. It was not till dawn that the last company arrived. Morning showed that we were in the hollow of two hills, and on a track which ran up the valley for about three-quarters of a mile and then took a sudden detour to the left and joined (our maps told us) the main Jerusalem road. The track swerved to avoid a hill, on the top of which a few stone buildings huddled together, and looked like a castle. This was Kustul, our position for the night, an outpost line through which the other brigades were to pass at dawn to assault the main Turkish trenches. The division had orders to sweep north-eastwards towards Jerusalem on a two-miles front, touch the fringes of its eastern outskirts, and, crossing the Lifta road, wheel gradually to the north astride the Nablus road. The attack was timed to coincide with the arrival of the 53rd Division at Jerusalem's southern outskirts. This was to be the work of a day.

The night of December 7th was a wet one, and will long be remembered even among other wet ones, by the survivors of the 2/21st. For the windows of heaven were opened, and of shelter there was practically none. Battalion headquarters was ensconced just to the left of the track, behind a mass of rock. One of the companies was in Kustul itself, expecting at dawn to be blown to pieces—for the place was a landmark. But though the attacking troops passed through—how they found their way in that night of blinding rain was a miracle—the bombardment never came. The Turk was taken by surprise. Only Allenby's command would have thought of continuing a war in such weather; most of the Turks were rolled up in greatcoats at the bottom of their trenches.

The Battalion assembled on the morning of the eighth in a soggy field on the left of the road—a mixture of weeds, grasses, and rocks, on a general background of wet day. A wintry sun peered forth, and working together with a keen wind, dried us, but did not enliven. After a time the road silted up with transport going Jerusalem-way. Then a battery of sixty-pounders opened up on the other side of the road. Everybody had grown tired of waiting, and it was only gradually that we learned that we were in reserve, and that the soggy field was our night's bivouac. Rations arrived very late, and most of the night was taken up in getting them distributed. At about 3 o'clock on the morning of the 9th, we moved off, treading the road to Jerusalem. Company officers did not know how far the attack had progressed; the fog of war had closed down on us. As a matter of fact, a mile or so in front of us on this very road, Izzet Bey's letter, surrendering Jerusalem, was being handed over at Lifta by a Turkish official. We did not continue, however, in that direction, but turned right at some stone houses that marked the beginnings of Kulonieh on to a track that led downward into a wonderfully beautiful gorge. Orchards lay at the entrance. We followed the track for miles, a twisted course, crossing again and again the bed of a torrent. At length the path led upward, and we climbed into one of the streets of Ain Karim, a Russian colony. It was a beautiful place, but we had little time to admire. The Battalion formed up in column of fours and moved on, on a good road now, still on the climb.

We had not been long on the march before an order came to halt and leave the road clear. Accordingly we packed ourselves by companies into a series of stone-walled compounds on the left. A long ridge formed our skyline, and the road ran up to the base of it and then ran along that base to the left, and so over the ridge and out of sight. To the right of us on the other side of the road, a rock-face shut out the view; the whole of the ground to the left beyond the compounds was a great open depression. Just as we had settled down for a long rest, important orders arrived, and then Colonel Jervois and the four company commanders pounded up the road together. At the top bend these five climbed the hill. Topping the crest two things burst on them —a bitterly cold wind and a magnificent close view of Jerusalem from the most spectacular side. For the city could not extend in this direction, but was bounded by its wall, owing to the fact that the whole plain between us and it was a medley of rock—one vast stone quarry. Over this we had been ordered to attack, wheeling left before we reached the city itself. The plan of attack was arranged, the companies given their objectives. Meanwhile the adjutant had brought the Battalion up to the top bend of the road. There, then, we lay, waiting the signal. And so we waited. Presently the brigade-major arrived. We formed up on the road. Gradually it became known that the brigade commander had decided the road was safe—we were to march in as a brigade. Time passed, and the 179th Brigade went by. At last we moved. The road ran like a ribbon through the rocky waste. At one point we were checked by the wreck of two guns of a Turkish field battery, knocked out by shell-fire in the act of galloping away. Some peasants in a garden on the left watched us as we passed. One held a large crucifix, taken from some church. Now we were approaching Jerusalem's suburbs. The nearest houses were hung with white flags. In a few moments we were passing through a street fringed with a nondescript crowd that stared curiously. We halted, then plunged on, hemmed in on both sides by sightseers, like troops in a London crowd. The men marched badly, the pace was too great, and they seemed exhausted; yet, as we at last got clear and came on to and across a large square whose centre was virgin rock, the Battalion pulled itself together. Again we plunged into streets. Then, suddenly, halted.

A short period followed, during which we held ourselves in readiness for whatever might befall. For a while nobody knew anything. Then, suddenly, the brigade commander appeared, and we got our orders. The colonel was standing with his back to a wall where a narrow passage gave on to a rocky slope. At this point the suburb came to an abrupt end, and bare hillside began. In front lay a valley with a mass of stone houses almost at the bottom, which, as the ground dropped somewhat suddenly on the lowest slope, was not visible. Further, the terrain sloped up to a great ridge of rock and earth. On the right of this ridge a dark clump looked like trees; on the left a little stone hut could be picked out on the skyline. "That's the front the Battalion will attack," said our C.O. "Order of attack as before. 'A' and 'D' will form the firing line, 'C' and 'B' support." Off, therefore, we went, in successive extended lines, as if on home manœuvres.

By this time the Turk, though in retreat, was hanging on to the skirts of the city, and was certainly in possession of the German Hospice, a building with a tall tower that lay to the right of our objective. Had the 53rd Division been absolutely up to time it is probable that the enemy would have found the ridge untenable. However, there they were, firing furiously at us as we emerged from the stone houses near the bottom of the slope. The advance on the whole went well. The enemy did not stay to contest the ridge itself, except on our extreme right, where they had to be turned out of a large white building known as Sir John Grey Hill's house. This was accomplished by a platoon of "C" Company under Lieut. Hockey, who was later awarded the M.C. A bitterly cold storm of rain and hail arrived, and the whole Battalion spent a most uncomfortable night. Several casualties took place during our advance, the company on the right, in particular, being enfiladed from the German Hospice. Captain Coldicott, who had commanded "C" Company since the Battalion left England, was shot in the garden of the white house, and carried off by two of his men in the darkness. Four of our N.C.O.'s were killed, and fifteen rank and file wounded. Sergeant Gillard and Lance-Corporal Austin were awarded the Military Medal. The enemy suffered heavy casualties. So ended a long and memorable day.

3.

The Jordan Valley.

The last section of the history of the 2/21st Battalion is composed of the events that led to the expedition into the Jordan Valley, an expedition that can be taken as the climax of the long series of experiences briefly chronicled in the foregoing pages. With that unhappy raid this history properly should end. The second expedition was of no account, and shortly afterwards news reached our unit of its impending dissolution. Up to this point this narrative, though sketchy and incomplete, has been that of an eye-witness. The following account of the last and most exciting of our adventures, is perforce, eked out by bare extracts from that dry document, the official war diary. No one has been forthcoming to describe these events except Lieut. Capes, who was ill during the earlier part of the period, and wounded in the final catastrophe. All that is of interest now comes from his pen; our "eye-witness" was out of the fighting, and all he can do is to round off the picturesque fragments contributed by Lieut. Capes.

* * * * *

The Battalion remained holding the ridge until the morning of the 13th, when a surprise attack was launched at dawn on the enemy position, Tower Hill. "B" and "D" Companies, under Lieut. Leman, captured the hill and took a machine-gun in action and seven prisoners. "C" Company was pushed forward, under Lieut. Carr, to protect the right flank, and came under heavy machine-gun fire. Lieut. Carr was killed. Later the enemy attempted to dislodge "C" Company, but the line was maintained and consolidated after dusk. 2nd.-Lieut. Evans was killed, and five rank and file, and fifteen were wounded.

The next day the Battalion was relieved by the 2/23rd, and was in support until the 18th, when we were relieved by the 12th Cheshires, and marched to billets in Jerusalem in torrents of rain. On the 20th we marched to Beit Sorik to support 2/24th and 2/22nd, and there we remained, sometimes in support and sometimes in the line, until the 28th, when we moved forward and bivouacked for the night behind Jedirah. The next day we moved to Ra Fat to support an attack by 2/22nd and 2/23rd on Bireh Ridge. The attack was successful, and late that night two companies moved through the 2/22nd and held Hill 2,735, El Balua, where the Battalion remained with two companies in the line and two in support. The weather was extremely wet and cold. On January 3rd (1918), we relieved the 10th Buffs, and on the 4th, "A," "C," and "D" Companies attacked at dawn Hill 2,635, "B" Company protecting the right flank. On the 5th we were relieved by the 1/4th and 1/5th Welsh Regiment, and marched to billets in Jerusalem, and there stayed until the 15th, bathing and disinfecting. On the 16th we went into brigade reserve at Er Ram, and spent a fortnight, mainly in the rain, making a new road to Jeba. On the last day of the month the Battalion made a very successful reconnaissance of the enemy's position at Ras el Tawil

o

from the direction of Mukhmas. The Battalion moved along the Jeba track, turned west, and went down the track leading to the Wadi Netif. After turning off at Jeba it was necessary to march in single file. Luckily it was a bright moonlit night. During the advance one of our men stumbled; this aroused the enemy, and 2nd-Lieut. Linfoot, with "B" Company's scouts, encountered about fifty Turks on the forward slope of Tel Es Suwan. All ran away except two, who remained with rifles levelled at Lieut. Linfoot. He drew his revolver. One put up his hands and was captured; the other tried to escape and was shot dead. "C" Company captured Mukhmas after little opposition. "B" Company occupied Tel Es Suwan, was counter-attacked, and took a prisoner. We immediately withdrew to Er Ram, having sustained no casualties.

The first fortnight of February was spent in brigade reserve, in the pleasant pastime of road-making. The weather was, as usual, extremely wet. During some of the time "D" Company was in a part of the line known as "X8." On the 14th the Battalion, with one section 181st Machine-gun Company, attacked and seized Mukhmas. Patrols pushed out to occupy Tel Es Suwan and Round Hill, east of Suwan. "C" Company remained at Mukhmas in reserve. The attack was a success, and one officer and eleven rank and file were taken prisoner—without any casualties on our side. The enemy then shelled Round Hill and were repulsed, but at the expense of the lives of 2nd-Lieut. Redway and five rank and file, while twenty-four rank and file were wounded.

The next day we were relieved by the 2/24th. On the 17th we returned to the line, and on the 18th the 2/23rd moved through us to Round Hill. On the 17th, "D" Company moved to protect the right flank of the brigade. The Battalion assembled in brigade reserve and then moved to Ras El Tawil early in the afternoon, and took up an outpost line. We were, in fact, covering the assembly of the brigade. Next day we were in touch with the Turkish rearguard, and came under heavy machine-gun fire. The C.O. is remembered to have been particularly active on this occasion, crawling about with his single field-glass, and it was during this engagement that he pointed out to his second-in-command the disadvantages he laboured under in being followed about "by such a damned long fellow as you are, Smith." We suffered fourteen casualties, and were relieved at night by the 10th King's Shropshire Light Infantry.

After the Turkish retirement from Jericho, the Battalion remained near Ras El Tawil till the 27th, when they returned via Mukhmas to Ramah, in pouring rain and hail and bitter cold, and bivouacked by the side of the track south-west of the village, but found better quarters and better weather next day at a rest camp within sight of liberated Jerusalem. Here no tasks fell to their lot heavier than the mounting of guards at the gates of the City and the Church of the Holy Sepulchre. On March 5th a move was made into the Jordan valley via the Wady El Kelt, and for the next few days reconnoitring parties were busy opening up the way for a further advance to cover Jericho, and, as it proved, to form a jumping-off point for the raid by which it was hoped to enable the Arabs under Lawrence to join forces with us. On the night of the 8th the Wadi Aujah was occupied, and our right flank was resting upon the Jordan; resistance was slight and mainly confined to spasmodic shelling. In a very brief time the Wadi Aujah, so recently a mysterious objective, which none but night patrols could hope to gaze on, had become a prosaic front line camping ground, which even the well-directed Turkish "pip-squeaks" could hardly touch with more than a momentary thrill of adventure; and our Jordan flank was robbed alike of danger and romance by the establishment of "Jones' Post," a detached group overlooking the junction of the Aujah and the Jordan, and accessible only by night by way of a seemingly endless plain without a single landmark of any kind, except one cow, dead, long dead, from which a compass bearing could be taken to enable the wanderer eventually to arrive at his objective. No one was ever known to find Jones' Post unless they had previously paid their respects to the shades of the departed cow, but, fortunately, it was not to the eye alone that she made her presence felt, and on favourable nights it was possible to accomplish the preliminary part of the journey by simply (as the saying is) following one's nose. From this post, as well as from "A" Company's "O.P.," we could see the enemy's positions on the opposite bank, and a fair amount of minor movement was reported from day to day. Did he suspect a further movement on our part? But for the moment he was left in peace, while plans were brewing in Jerusalem which were to result in the last adventure the Battalion as a unit was to undertake.

* * * * *

No contrast can be imagined more complete than that between the first and the last battle fought in Palestine by the 2/21st. Our part in the turning of the Turkish line at

Beersheba was the result of weeks of eager preparation and anxious counsel : every detail had been arranged, discussed, perfected : every contingency had (we hoped) been provided for. We had maps which showed every Turkish trench—we had allotted every section of the enemy's line to its appointed captors. Every "wadi" was named, and every hill was numbered : every man had been acquainted with his task, and no one would have dared admit the slightest doubt as to the whereabouts of those mysterious objectives, the red, the blue, and the green line. The result was a success so rapid and complete that the illusion was produced of wasted effort and excessive preparation : "We might as well have marched up 1,070 and down again. The Turk would have 'packed up' just the same." Even Sheria and Nebi Samwil had not quite freed us from this idea. All our battles—however fierce and harassing at the time—had ended up somewhat after the traditional style of the nursery tale—"So he ran away, and we trekked happily ever after."

But a different tale has to be told of the final dash into the mountains of Moab, away from our heavy guns, far from our bases, and finally passing even beyond the top right-hand corner of our last and most imaginative maps, where the little purple arrows indicated vaguely the direction of a "Metalled road to Amman." This last phase began with a sudden outbreak of curiosity on the part of the authorities concerning the possibilities of crossing the Jordan. Battalion intelligence officers were instructed to proceed to various points where the staff had decided the Jordan was fordable. Map references were supplied to guide the young officer in his wanderings. Those who have seen the often-quoted sheet XXI., or "composite," will know what it is like to attempt to identify any spot in that fantastic work of imagination with any feature on the (equally fantastic) face of Palestine.

On March 9th the Battalion moved to Wadi Aujah in support to 2/22nd. During this night-march everyone was so utterly exhausted that the whole Battalion went to sleep for an hour at a ten minutes' halt. We took up a position on some low hills—it seemed that we were almost surrounded by Turks, for when we flashed a helio back to brigade, the enemy fired at battalion head-quarters. Lieut. Cowper and 2nd.-Lieut. Linfoot were wounded, but remained at duty. Shelling continued for several days. On the 17th all wheeled transport was sent to the dump—a significant move, indicating that a serious push was contemplated. For the moment reconnaissance was the order of the day.

The Mandesi Ford fell to the lot of the 2/21st; it proved impracticable for a crossing, but was selected as an excellent scene for a "demonstration." El Ghoranye and Makhadet Hajla were more favourably reported on.

In due course the Battalion was relieved from the Aujah, and found its way back to Jericho by comparatively easy stages. While it rested in bivouac on the 20th, Lieut.-Col. J. A. Jervois found time to be presented with the M.C. at Jerusalem.

An unexpected fine day in mid-winter is known in the North of England as a "weather breeder," and storms are expected to follow. Army conditions are curiously meteorological in their instability. Experts in both cases attempt equally elaborate forecasts, and are equally liable to be taken unawares. The day at Jericho was a "weather-breeder."

The Battalion, after an early march, lay quietly concealed among the scented orange-groves which surround the little whitewashed town; companies settled down beneath the trees on either side of a pleasantly flowing, shallow stream; the hostile planes which had hovered over the column in the early hours had disappeared. The gaily-painted act-drop was down: the illusion was perfect. We had learnt by now not to speculate too curiously on what scenes were being set behind, but to enjoy the effect while it lasted.

It was not for long. "Be ready to move by sunset," came unexpected orders. In a few hours we had left the sunny gardens of Jericho; our swimming party, in the blackness of a Syrian night, was struggling to carry across the rain-swollen stream at El Ghoranye, the rope which would make a beginning of the pontoon bridge, by which the Battalion was to cross, to form the bridge-head covering the general advance.

The original bridge of wood had been destroyed by the Turks about ten days previously; but they were suspicious of the road—the only one from Jericho—and had a standing patrol on their side of the river, supported by machine-guns and field artillery. (We discovered their blockhouse and trenches, well concealed in the undergrowth, next day.) Our attempt was to be covered, if necessary, by a machine-gun barrage, as there was little possibility of crossing unobserved. The most we could hope was that the "demonstration" further up the river at Mandesi and the attack at Makhadet Hajla by the 2/19th would distract the defenders. The reverse proved to be the case, and our attack, though carried out in grim earnest, served only to attract the enemy's attention to ourselves and turn his attention from the operations further South. The stream was swollen by winter rains, and the current was too fierce for our strongest swimmers. The Turkish guard had the ford under rifle-fire, and a brisk little field battery shelled the road down to the ford with an accuracy sufficient to render it useless except as a guide to our whereabouts in the darkness. The swimming party, under cover of our machine-guns, made repeated efforts, but man after man was swept down-stream, and was pulled ashore, exhausted, many yards below. Sergeant Holmes, in charge of the party, received wounds from which he died next day. Meantime, the rest of the Battalion stood-to in silence under cover of the wadi, where they had halted after their hurried evening march over the bare and trackless plain. But the word to advance never came, and daybreak found us still on Jordan's nearer bank; the brisk little field battery lengthened its range in hopes of taking revenge for lost sleep. Luckily a wadi is a very efficient shelter against the briskest of field batteries, and our breakfast was undisturbed. Before mid-day the success of the 2/19th had compelled the Turks to retire from all the Jordan crossings, and the Battalion passed over the pontoons unmolested in broad daylight, on the very scene of last night's struggle. Bivouacs were pitched that night in the bare, tumbled country at the foot of the hills of Moab in readiness for an advance next day, with Es Salt as final objective. The Turks were not willing to retire further without a struggle, and on the morrow a battle developed on the most approved "Infantry Training" principles, with artillery formations, directing companies, lines of skirmishers, and all the orthodox delights of war. By evening we had captured the enemy's position at El Haud, covering the way to Es Salt, together with some German prisoners and machine-guns, and were advancing in column of route along a road which almost deserved the description of "metalled," bestowed upon it by the ever-charitable "composite." We continued our march next day in streaming rain, through country which grew more and more rugged and beautiful, and after a few stray shots at sundown we found Es Salt abandoned to us by the soldiers, and the civilians professing the warmest delight at our appearance. On March 26th we remained quiet outside the town, basking in warm sun after the previous day's soaking. The following morning, after a hurried and unexpected start in the early hours, we passed through the outskirts of Es Salt and set off post-haste on the track of the Turk towards Amman and our final adventure. Signs were not wanting that the enemy's retreat had been hastier than he had expected—we passed a dozen abandoned motor lorries stuck fast in the atrociously muddy road—its promise of metal had not been maintained—and noted the German Eagles painted on their sides, to the exclusion of the Crescent. They seemed to contain chiefly irrelevant maps from some orderly room, which probably parted from them without regret; but the sight gave us a pleasant sense of chivvying the retreating foe. "D" Company was dropped in the course of our march at Sweileh, to keep peace between Cross and Crescent, disturbed by some casual murder. The inhabitants on the route were curious and friendly, but any advances on the part of their women-folk were sternly repressed, and the young lady who cast kindly eyes on the adjutant during a roadside halt, disappeared with remarkable speed when her husband passed along, and gave his wife—and the gallant officer—a glance full of the silent eloquence of the East. We began to hope for more such amusing incidents when we marched into Amman in the course of a day or two, though we rather expected a rearguard action to develop on the morrow to cover the evacuation of the town. With this idea in view, we deployed next day over the skyline below which our night's rest had been taken, undisturbed. Our objectives were allotted—on the ground, as maps of the country, if there were any, did not reach company officers—and we prepared to push our way over the undulating country into the still invisible town. Hardly fifty yards had been covered when we found ourselves up against an efficient barrage of machine-guns and field guns, and casualties came thick and fast. "B" and "C," our two leading companies, made stoutly for their objectives, and head-quarters, with the reserve company, followed on to their appointed position; but further advance was impossible: our left-hand company was isolated by fire, and could not regain touch with the company on its right, who were hard put to it to retain their own position on a steep, rounded hill, in face of continuous shelling. Head-quarters was little better off, forming practically part of the line and joining on to the left of the 2/23rd with some difficulty. An indiscreet machine-gun, which operated from the shelter of Battalion head-quarters, drew upon itself an amount of attention which nearly proved too much for itself and its temporary resting-place. At night attempts were made with what reserves were available in the Battalion, to extend our left flank to meet the Australian Mounted Rifles, who were supposed to be in touch with us; but our fifteen men and two Lewis guns found a gap of a quarter of a mile from their left, even after extending to the utmost possible limits. The brigade commander visited the front line during the night with words of encouragement, but there was nothing for us to do at the moment but hang on, and hang on we did through the whole of that endless Good Friday, "waiting to be surrounded," and under intermittent fire from well-placed machine-guns and field guns, which methodically registered our position. Later on our own mountain artillery turned up and found a few of the most offensive of the Turks' machine-guns. We had a stiff struggle to retain our hold on the round hill, and could find no traces of our left-hand company. During the day came orders that the 17th and 18th were to pass through our lines that night in an assault on Amman, and the word was given that the Turk was expected to make his usual retirement. But the relieving troops, waited for in the dark and rain, made no appearance, and next morning found us still holding the same positions. Shortly after daylight an intensive bombardment started, and our position on the round hill—enfiladed by field guns—was heavily shelled and then assaulted in force. After a hand-to-hand struggle the enemy gained the crest. A counter-attack was launched and our position regained by a bayonet charge, and twenty prisoners taken. But our casualties were heavy, and reinforcements were asked for.

The brigade ordered up "D" Company, but by this time the enemy had regained the crest with a strong force. This made "D" Company's position untenable, and Battalion head-quarters had to retire to the next ridge to cover the retirement of the remnants of "B" and "C" Companies.

These companies returned with all their officers casualties. They came back with the remnants of two companies of the 2/23rd, all under the command of Captain Entwistle of the 2/23rd, who had gallantly kept the enemy engaged till dark, and had managed to bring in his casualties. It transpired that the first line of "B" Company had been cut off, together with Captain D. W. Leman, who was killed, and Lieut. H. M. Justice. Our losses, killed, wounded, and missing, amounted to about 215.

On the last day of the month the brigade group commenced to extricate itself from this valley of death. It was evident that the enemy was present in overwhelming numbers, and that further advance, over one of the most difficult terrains in the world for an attacking force, was impossible. The withdrawal was carried out in good order, and we were accompanied by half the native population.

By April 7th the remnant of the Battalion was installed once again in corps reserve, on that ridge by Jerusalem near Sir John Hill's house, with a fine view of the volcanic and inhospitable region which had denied it passage.

4.

Last Days.

It was a battered and tattered Battalion our "eye-witness" found camped within a few hundred yards of the very scene of that afternoon assault when the Turks were squeezed out of Jerusalem. He brought with him a batch of new officers, trained mostly in Egypt, for supplies were running low in these latter days. Enquiring for his company, he found that the remains of it—a weak platoon—had been absorbed by another company. The conduct sheets, which modern units guard with almost a religious care, were discovered after much enquiry in the pocket of one of the cooks ! Even the mess kit was missing. Thus we emerged, extricated with difficulty, from that unhappy expedition.

A few days later the brigade commander, who had long since become most popular with the battalions, gave a garden party, an effort to pull us all together again and to make us gay. There were certain sports and contests, and the brigade concert party performed.

> "But the greatest discovery
> Was when you discovered me
> And I discovered you—ou."

Tunes play no small part in recalling scenes; had this history been longer, many would have been noted, many war-time ballads recited. This party, held in such strange surroundings, and on a lovely day, brought the brigade together again. We were, in fact, about to move, and on the 16th marched *en route* for corps reserve at Balua, a pleasant enough spot amongst the lavender-grey rocks now dotted with flowers. Brigade head-quarters was in a flat-topped house in Ram Allah. Here the usual activities grew up. Sports were arranged. The Battalion, making a tremendous effort, gave a splendid dinner furnished from Egypt, in a large tent on a bitterly cold night. It was an occasion on which colonels became even as boys. It was felt that things were settling down—after all, there was no reason why this interminable war should ever get finished. The brigade was beginning to get interested (fumigations finished) in musketry.

When all was most secure, a message came on the 'phone from Corps that the brigade was to get ready to move at once—down to that familiar heat bath, the Jordan Valley. No heavy baggage was to be taken, so a large brigade dump was formed on a flattish piece of ground near Lake Balua. On May 2nd the Battalion moved to Bethany. Here it was unexpectedly packed into motor lorries and dumped two miles east of El Ghoranye. The Jordan was crossed that night, and on May 4th we were holding an outpost position in the neighbourhood of Wadi Nimrin. Our departure had not been without haste. One remembers certain auxiliary units passing along the road through Ram Allah by ones and twos, obviously having set out in the order of getting ready.

We did not take part in any fighting in this last expedition. From the 7th to the 13th we were in reserve, digging trenches, and on the 14th went to a bivouac area at Talet-el-Dumm. This was but prelude to our return, and by the 20th we were back at Balua.

Seven days later everyone received a great shock. Orders had come for the Battalion to be disbanded.

It appeared that further reinforcements from England were not forthcoming, and that it had been determined to re-organize the brigade. Troops from India were on the way; the reconstituted white units were to be the stiffening. To most of us this order was a tragedy, for the Battalion was our other home. Many of the men had been with it since the beginning of the war. A great depression fell upon every-one. It was hard luck that we should have travelled so far and for so long and not be permitted to survive as an entity until the end. But lamentations are vain against official edicts, and there was nothing to do but to await dissolution. On June 2nd the Battalion was formed into drafts, four officers and 173 other ranks to join the 2/13th; six officers and 229 other ranks to the 2/19th; six officers and 245 other ranks to the 2/22nd. The remaining seventeen officers were to go to the Base.

Next day these drafts were paraded and marched to join their units. The scene resembled the depatriation of a people. Our adventures had come to an end untimely. We had ceased to exist. Official business went on for some days. On June 4th the transport went to Ludd under "Paddy" Coyle, to hand in stores. Yet a few clerks lingered, a few bell tents remained. By June 12th even these had gone. Nothing was left but the lavender-coloured rocks and the dusty track that wound towards Ram Allah.

APPENDICES

AND

INDEX.

BATTLE HONOURS

OF

THE FIRST SURREY RIFLES.

SOUTH AFRICA, 1900-02,
Aubers,
FESTUBERT, LOOS, SOMME, 1916-18,
Flers-Courcelette, Le Transloy,
MESSINES, 1917,
Ypres, 1917,
CAMBRAI, 1917,
St. Quentin,
BAPAUME, 1918,
Ancre, 1918, Amiens,
ALBERT, 1918,
Pursuit to Mons, France and Flanders, 1915-18,
Doiran, 1917, Macedonia, 1916-17, Gaza, El Mughar,
Nebi Samwil,
JERUSALEM, JERICHO, JORDAN,
Tell 'Asur, Palestine, 1917-18.

Honours printed in capital letters are those carried on drums and bugles.

HONOURS LIST,

1915—1919.

The following is the list of honours awarded and mentions in despatches for services with the 1/21st and the 2/21st Battalion (FIRST SURREY RIFLES) London Regiment. The dates given are those of the *London Gazette*. In many cases, however, especially in the case of immediate awards, the date is that of the authority for the award received at Divisional Head-quarters, and corresponds more nearly with that of the act of gallantry recognized.

In cases where the award of bars only to the D.S.O., M.C., and M.M. are recorded, the decoration itself was won before the holder joined the FIRST SURREY RIFLES.

ORDER OF ST. MICHAEL AND ST. GEORGE.

COMPANIONS.

Kennedy, H. B. P. L. (K.R.R.C.), Brig.-Gen. 3/6/18

DISTINGUISHED SERVICE ORDER AND TWO BARS.

Dawes, G., M.C. (S. Staffs Regt.),
Lieut.-Col. ... ... D.S.O. 7/1/18
                                  1st Bar 3/3/18
                                  2nd Bar 30/9/18

DISTINGUISHED SERVICE ORDER.

Kennedy, H. B. P. L. (K.R.R.C.),
  Major (Temp. Lieut.-Col.) ... D.S.O. 3/6/16
Pidsley, W. G., Capt. ... ... D.S.O. 3/6/18
Hemsley, H., Capt. ... ... D.S.O. 1/1/18

BREVET PROMOTIONS.

Kennedy, H. B. P. L. ... ... Com. 21st London,
                                  B. Lieut.-Col. ... 3/6/17
Kennedy, H. B. P. L. ... ... Com. 140th Inf.
                                  Bd., B. Col. ... 1/1/19

MILITARY CROSS AND THREE BARS.

Gilkes, H. M., Lieut. ... ... M.C. 11/7/17
                                  Bar 20/1/18
                                  2nd Bar ... 13/4/18
                                  3rd Bar ... 13/10/18

MILITARY CROSS AND ONE BAR.

Jackman, I. H., Lieut.	M.C.	11/7/17
	Bar	3/6/18
Lawes, J., 2nd Lieut.	M.C.	29/5/18
	Bar	13/10/18
McKay, G. M., 2nd Lieut.	M.C.	8/6/16
	Bar	6/10/16
Taylor, N. A., 2nd Lieut.	M.C.	8/6/16
	Bar	6/11/16

MILITARY CROSS.

Barker, F. C., 2nd Lieut.	M.C.	17/9/17
Bird, E. T., 2nd Lieut.	M.C.	24/6/16
Catton, E. C., 2nd Lieut.	M.C.	11/1/19
Chambers, P. E. H., Lieut.	M.C.	1918
Charman, A. E., C.S.M.	M.C.	11/1/19
Coldicott, H. R. S., T.A./Capt.	M.C.	19/3/18
Corby, S. W., T/Capt.	M.C.	14/1/16
Coyle, J. P., Capt.	M.C.	31/12/18
Crowther, C., 2nd Lieut.	M.C.	15/2/18
Eastwood, C. S., Capt.	M.C.	3/6/18
Edmunds, J., Lieut.	M.C.	15/2/18
Elkington, H. G., Capt.	M.C.	26/7/18
Harry, C. F., 2nd Lieut.	M.C.	23/7/18
Hitch, J. O. B., 2nd Lieut.	M.C.	22/4/18
Hockey, A. L., 2nd Lieut.	M.C.	4/2/18
Hutchence, A., Capt.	M.C.	14/1/16
Jackman, H. E., 2nd Lieut.	M.C.	9/1/18
Laing, J. O. C., C.S.M.	M.C.	24/6/16
Martin, R., Lieut. & Q.M.	M.C.	25/5/17
O'Connell, C., 2nd Lieut.	M.C.	24/6/16
Pidsley, W. G., Capt.	M.C.	1/1/18
Roberts, C. H. H., 2nd Lieut.	M.C.	4/11/18
Ruthven, H., Capt.	M.C.	24/6/16
Smith, H. T., Capt.	M.C.	25/11/16
Snell, J., C.S.M.	M.C.	24/6/16
Southin, C. A., 2nd Lieut.	M.C.	17/4/17
Stickland, A. L., Capt.	M.C.	26/7/18
Stone, F. N., 2nd Lieut.	M.C.	22/4/18
Tidd, R. R., Capt.	M.C.	11/1/19
Turner, G. C., Capt.	M.C.	3/6/18
Underhay, C. T., Lieut. (A/Capt.)	M.C.	25/4/18
Walter, A. J., Capt.	M.C.	16/1/18
Webb, J. A. N., 2nd Lieut.	M.C.	29/11/18
Wickes, E. L., C.S.M.	M.C.	31/10/18
Wray, C. R., 2nd Lieut.	M.C.	11/1/19

ORDER OF THE BRITISH EMPIRE.

Tomlin, M. J., Lieut.-Col.	O.B.E.	30/5/19

DISTINGUISHED CONDUCT MEDAL.

Biggs, H., Rfn.	D.C.M.	3/6/19
Burley, W., Sgt.	D.C.M.	16/1/19
Buss, J., Sgt.	D.C.M.	5/12/18
Charman, A. E., Sgt.	D.C.M.	28/3/18

Coe, H. C., C.S.M.	D.C.M.	5/5/18
Cole, A. H., Rfn.	D.C.M.	15/3/16
Day, W. A., C.S.M.	D.C.M.	3/6/18
Downer, J. C., C.S.M.	D.C.M.	3/6/19
Eastlake, F. W., L/Cpl.	D.C.M.	14/1/16
Ellis, W., L/Cpl.	D.C.M.	15/3/16
Fenner, A. H., Sgt.	D.C.M.	5/12/18
Jackson, F. C., R.S.M.	D.C.M.	20/6/16
Laing, J. O. C., T/R.S.M.	D.C.M.	3/9/18
Martin, F., Rfn.	D.C.M.	31/5/16
Marsters, R. H., Cpl.	D.C.M.	16/11/15
Nethersole, G., Sgt.	D.C.M.	3/6/19
Parkinson, B., C.S.M.	D.C.M.	28/3/18
Peachey, C. B., L/Cpl.	D.C.M.	14/11/16
Rawlinson, G. F., Sgt.	D.C.M.	3/6/18
Rowe, R. A., Rfn.	D.C.M.	3/6/19
Shellard, R. S., Cpl.	D.C.M.	5/8/15
Silvester, H. A., Sgt.	D.C.M.	6/8/18
Smith, O. G., Sgt.	D.C.M.	3/6/18
Tidmarsh, S., Sgt.	D.C.M.	5/12/18
Wickes, E. L., C.S.M.	D.C.M.	3/6/18
Wigzell, H. K., Cpl.	D.C.M.	14/1/16

MILITARY MEDAL AND ONE BAR.

Browett, A. A., Cpl.	M.M.	31/12/16
	Bar	13/2/18
Edwards, J. N., L/Cpl.	M.M.	10/8/16
L/Sgt.	Bar	21/12/16
Harris, W. E., Cpl.	M.M.	4/2/18
	Bar	13/9/18
Newman, J., Sgt.	M.M.	3/6/16
	Bar	10/8/16
Palmer, H., Rfn.	M.M.	12/12/17
	Bar	14/5/19
Taylor, T. H., Cpl.	M.M.	14/9/16
	Bar	20/10/19
Tidmarsh, S., L/Sgt.	M.M.	10/8/16
	Bar	13/3/18
Wakefield, E., Cpl.	M.M.	28/7/17
	Bar	13/3/18

BAR TO MILITARY MEDAL.

Weisberg, T., Rfn.	Bar	14/5/19

MILITARY MEDALS.

Adams, F., A/L/Cpl.	M.M.	5/5/18
Alexander, D., L/Cpl.	M.M.	12/9/16
Appleford, J. D., Rfn.	M.M.	10/5/16
Austen, P. W., Rfn.	M.M.	19/6/19
Austin, R. S., T/L/Cpl.	M.M.	4/2/18
Austin, G. W., Rfn.	M.M.	11/2/19
Baker, E., Sgt.	M.M.	11/2/19
Barker, F. J., Sgt.	M.M.	11/2/19
Barnes, D. S., Bglr.	M.M.	28/7/17
Billing, G., A/Cpl.	M.M.	23/7/19

P

Blanchflower, V. G., Rfn.	M.M.	11/2/19
Blood, G. W., Rfn.	M.M.	25/4/18
Boddy, H., Cpl.	M.M.	10/8/16
Boughton, A., Sgt.	M.M.	13/3/19
Boult, A. F., Sgt.	M.M.	21/12/16
Brooks, H. W., Sgt.	M.M.	13/3/19
Brown, B. R., Sgt.	M.M.	21/12/16
Brown, W., Rfn.	M.M.	11/2/19
Bunn, E. C., L/Sgt.	M.M.	14/9/16
Burgess, A., L/Cpl.	M.M.	30/12/16
Burley, W., Sgt.	M.M.	16/1/16
Butler, W., Sgt.	M.M.	10/8/16
Carpenter, P., L/Cpl.	M.M.	14/2/18
Charman, A. E., L/Cpl.	M.M.	3/6/16
Chantler, A. W., Sgt.	M.M.	21/12/16
Chester, H. T., Rfn.	M.M.	9/12/16
Chivers, J. A. T., Rfn.	M.M.	13/3/18
Christian, C., C.Q.M.S.	M.M.	21/12/16
Clark, S., Cpl.	M.M.	11/2/19
Clarke, C. V., Rfn.	M.M.	14/2/18
Clarke, F. C., L/Cpl.	M.M.	3/6/16
Coleman, A., Rfn.	M.M.	11/2/19
Collingwood, G., Rfn.	M.M.	14/2/18
Connor, T., L/Cpl.	M.M.	21/12/16
Cooper, F. G., Rfn.	M.M.	11/9/16
Cooper, T. R., Sgt.	M.M.	6/8/18
Cox, P. H., Rfn.	M.M.	3/6/16
Dann, E. J., Rfn.	M.M.	11/2/19
Davies, C., Cpl.	M.M.	21/12/16
Dawson, E. S., Rfn.	M.M.	14/9/16
Dew, F. G., Sgt.	M.M.	14/9/16
Donovan, P., C/Sgt.	M.M.	21/12/16
Dunster, H., L/Cpl.	M.M.	14/9/16
Dyer, J. W. J., Rfn.	M.M.	11/2/19
Eastwood, W. J., L/Cpl.	M.M.	6/3/17
Eden, E., Sgt.	M.M.	13/3/19
Ellis, W., C.S.M.	M.M.	11/2/19
Faithful, L., Rfn.	M.M.	28/7/17
Fitzgerald, A. R., Sgt.	M.M.	13/3/18
Flinn, A., Sgt.	M.M.	14/6/19
Foreman, W., Rfn.	M.M.	24/1/19
Francis, H. W., Rfn.	M.M.	19/3/18
Friend, A., Rfn.	M.M.	13/3/19
Fry, J. P., Cpl.	M.M.	3/6/16
Gillard, E. F., Sgt.	M.M.	4/2/18
Goldsmith, B., S/Q.M.S.	M.M.	9/12/16
Gush, E. C., L/Cpl.	M.M.	10/8/16
Hackett, J., Sgt.	M.M.	14/9/16
Hales, H., L/Cpl.	M.M.	3/6/16
Henderson, G., Sgt.	M.M.	14/9/16
Heslewood, A., Rfn.	M.M.	6/8/18
Hills, L. G., L/Cpl.	M.M.	29/4/16
Hocking, P. S., Sgt.	M.M.	28/7/17
Holloway, R., Rfn.	M.M.	18/7/17
Hopkins, P., Bglr.	M.M.	21/12/16
Howse, J. S., L/Cpl.	M.M.	19/3/18
Huckstepp, A. R., Rfn.	M.M.	21/12/16

James, T., Sgt.	M.M.		29/5/18
Jannaway, W. H., Rfn.	M.M.		27/3/19
Johnson, H. R., Sgt.	M.M.		11/2/19
Jones, A. J., Cpl.	M.M.		21/12/16
Jones, F. J., Sgt.	M.M.		14/9/16
Kelly, F., L/Cpl.	M.M.		14/9/16
Kemp, J. A., L/Cpl.	M.M.		21/12/16
King, W. C. T., Sgt.	M.M.		14/9/16
Kingston, A. H., Sgt.	M.M.		11/2/19
Lambert, B., Cpl.	M.M.		14/9/16
Lambert, H. W., L/Cpl.	M.M.		21/12/16
Lancaster, C., Rfn.	M.M.		19/11/17
Lane, J. H., Rfn.	M.M.		27/4/18
Lay, H. J., Cpl.	M.M.		21/12/16
Longman, S., Rfn.	M.M.		11/2/19
Marsh, C. W. F., Rfn.	M.M.		10/8/16
Middleton, R. A., Rfn.	M.M.		17/8/18
Mills, J. R., L/Cpl.	M.M.		28/7/17
Moss, E., Rfn.	M.M.		13/3/18
Mullins, W., L/Cpl.	M.M.		28/7/17
Murril, W. H., Rfn.	M.M.		19/9/18
Newman, W. J., Cpl.	M.M.		21/12/16
Oakey, A., Rfn.	M.M.		13/3/19
Odams, F., A/L/Cpl.	M.M.		27/10/18
Owen, N. G., Cpl. A/Sgt.	M.M.		6/8/18
Page, F. G., Rfn.	M.M.		27/10/18
Paroissien, F., L/Cpl.	M.M.		21/12/16
Parrott, A. H., Sgt.	M.M.		28/7/17
Pipe, J. W., Sgt.	M.M.		6/8/18
Powell, A., Cpl.	M.M.		9/12/16
Price, B., Sgt.	M.M.		11/5/17
Reddick, G. P., Rfn.	M.M.		10/8/16
Reid, J. C. B., Sgt.	M.M.		19/3/18
Ribbits, A. W., Rfn.	M.M.		13/3/19
Richardson, F., Cpl.	M.M.		21/12/16
Ridley, R. H., Rfn.	M.M.		11/2/19
Rushbrook, O. E., Rfn.	M.M.		11/2/19
Sagar, H., Rfn.	M.M.		28/7/17
Sainsbury, F. A., Sgt.	M.M.		13/3/18
Sargeant, A. J., Sgt.	M.M.		18/6/17
Seale, W., Rfn.	M.M.		11/2/19
Sexton, H. J., Cpl.	M.M.		21/12/16
Sexton, G., Cpl.	M.M.		28/7/17
Silvester, H. A., Sgt.	M.M.		6/8/18
Simons, A., A/Cpl.	M.M.		23/7/19
Smith, R., L/Sgt.	M.M.		17/6/19
Souster, A., Rfn.	M.M.		17/6/19
Spooner, J., Sgt.	M.M.		14/9/16
Stringer, E. O., Rfn.	M.M.		19/8/16
Tarr, W. R., L/Sgt.	M.M.		11/2/19
Tattersall, F. C., Rfn.	M.M.		19/3/18
Taylor, F. A., L/Sgt.	M.M.		10/8/16
Tubb, J., A/L/Cpl.	M.M.		19/3/18
Ward, A. J., Rfn.	M.M.		21/12/16
Warner, G. S., Bglr.	M.M.		8/12/16
Watts, F. C., L/Cpl.	M.M.		17/9/17
Watts, V. B., L/Cpl.	M.M.		9/12/16
Watson, F., Rfn.	M.M.		21/12/16

Watkins, L. A., Rfn.	M.M.	28/7/17
Whitehead, P., Sgt.	M.M.	10/8/16
Williams, S., L/Cpl.	M.M.	13/3/18
Williams, S., Cpl.	M.M.	6/8/18
Youell, F., Rfn.	M.M.	2/4/18

MERITORIOUS SERVICE MEDAL.

Burkmar, G., Bde.Q.M.S.	M.S.M.	17/6/18
Cobley, E. H., Cpl.	M.S.M.	3/6/19
Cooper, E. E., Cpl.	M.S.M.	3/6/19
Eason, W. C., L/Cpl.	M.S.M.	3/6/19
Hall, F. J., A/Sgt.	M.S.M.	13/8/19
Jennings, A., R.S.M.	M.S.M.	18/6/17
Lidstone, L. G., Sgt.	M.S.M.	12/12/19
Martin, R., R.Q.M.S.	M.S.M.	1/8/19
Masters, R. H., Sgt.	M.S.M.	18/1/19
Oram, R. B., A/Q.M.S.	M.S.M.	3/6/19
Webb, W. C., C.Q.M.S.	M.S.M.	3/6/19

FOREIGN DECORATIONS.

FRENCH CROIX de GUERRE WITH PALMS.

Kennedy, H. B. P. L., Lieut.-Col. (Brig-General) ... 3/6/18

FRENCH CROIX de GUERRE.

Baker, E., Sgt.	1/5/17
Bowers, F. L., Sgt.	17/8/18
Dawes, G., Major	27/1/19
Middleton, R. A., Rfn.	17/8/18
Perver, J. R., 2nd Lieut.	10/8/18
Pidsley, W. G., Capt.	26/11/18

BELGIAN.

CHEVALIER de L'ORDRE de LEOPOLD.

Tidmarsh, S., Sgt. ... 7/4/19

CROIX de GUERRE.

Boughton, A., Sgt.	2/2/18
Butler, R. A., Sgt.	2/2/18

ITALIAN.
CROCE di GUERRA.

Pidsley, W. G., Capt. ... 29/11/18

PORTUGUESE.
GRAND OFFICER ORDER OF AVIS.

Kennedy, H. B. P. L., Col. (Brig.-General) ... 11/11/18

GRAND OFFICER TOWER AND SWORD.

Kennedy, H. B. P. L., Col. (Brig.-General) ... 3/6/19

ROUMANIAN.
MEDAILLE BARBATIE SI CREDINTA.

Hocking, P. S., C.S.M. ... 10/3/19

ROYAL HUMANE SOCIETY.
BRONZE MEDAL AND CERTIFICATE.

Davis, G. W., A/Cpl. ... 23/11/18

MENTIONED IN DESPATCHES.
SEVEN MENTIONS.

Kennedy, H. B. P. L., Lieut.-Col.	3/6/16
Lieut.-Col.	1/1/17
Lieut.-Col. (Brig.-General)	3/6/17
Lieut.-Col. (Brig.-General)	1/1/18
Lieut.-Col. (Brig.-General)	3/6/18
Colonel (Brig.-General)	1/1/19
Colonel (Brig.-General)	3/6/19

THREE MENTIONS.

Hutchence, A., Capt.	First Mention	1/1/16
	Second Mention	2/1/17
	Third Mention	3/7/19
Pidsley, W. G., Capt.	First Mention	3/1/16
	Second Mention	2/1/17
	Third Mention	28/5/18

TWO MENTIONS.

Dawes, G., A/Lieut.-Col.	First Mention	27/12/18
	Second Mention	11/1/19
Dew, F. G., Sgt.	First Mention	15/6/16
	Second Mention	11/2/19
Macdonald, A. C., 2nd Lieut.	First Mention	21/7/17
	Second Mention	18/11/17

MENTIONED IN DESPATCHES.

Alexander, W. F., Sgt.	16/1/18
Barker, F. A., C.Q.M.S.	25/5/17
Blow, A. W. F., Capt.	16/1/18
Boughton, A., Sgt.	24/12/17
Brett, R. W., T/Capt.	3/6/19
Burrows, W. C., C.S.M.	1/1/16
Cavell, W. H., L/Cpl.	10/7/19
Chambers, P. E. H., Lieut.	30/12/18
Chivers, G. H.	25/5/17
Clark, G., Cpl.	10/7/19
Coe, H. C., C.S.M.	14/6/18

Coldicott, H. R. S., T/Capt.	2/1/17
Collihole, V., Sgt.	23/3/17
Corby, S. W., Capt.	1/1/16
Cox, C. A., R.Q.M.S.	23/3/17
Coyle, J. P., A/Capt.	11/6/18
Downes, J. C., C.S.M.	24/12/17
Fisher, A. L., 2nd Lieut.	30/12/18
Fletcher, B., Lieut.-Col.	7/7/16
Gilkes, H. M., Lieut.	1/1/16
Hamilton, C. P., Lieut.	23/10/18
Hollands, F. R., Lieut.	30/12/18
Howard, W. F., A/Sgt.	10/7/19
Hozier, A. F., Cpl.	25/5/18
Huish, E. C., Sgt.	10/7/19
Jackson, F. C., Lieut.	25/5/17
Jennings, A., R.S.M.	14/6/18
Johnson, A. R., Sgt.	20/5/18
Leman, H. C., Capt.	3/6/19
Liddiatt, A. W., T/Lieut.	2/1/17
Lockie, E. C., Rfn.	29/3/17
Lowry, A. J., 2nd Lieut.	30/12/18
Martin, R., R.Q.M.S.	25/5/17
Nethersole, G., Sgt.	30/12/18
Nutbrown, L. A., 2nd Lieut.	27/12/18
Pape, F., R.Q.M.S.	24/12/17
Persse, S. H., 2nd Lieut.	1/1/16
Perver, J. R., 2nd Lieut.	30/12/18
Richards, H. P., Major	15/6/16
Roberts, C. H. H., 2nd Lieut.	1/1/16
Ruthven, H., Capt.	15/6/16
Salmon, R. S., Rfn.	30/11/15
Stickland, A. L., Capt.	4/10/18
Stubbs, J. R., Rfn.	10/7/19
Taylor, F. A., Rfn.	30/11/15
Taylor, N. A., 2nd Lieut.	1/1/16
Terry, R, V., Sgt.	10/7/19
Tidd, R. R., Capt.	25/5/18
Tubb, J., A/Cpl.	16/1/18
Walter, A. J., Capt.	15/1/18
Walford, Q., Major	25/5/17
Ward, A. J., Sgt.	16/1/18
Watney, F. D., Lieut.-Col.	21/7/17
Wright, W. E., Sgt.	14/6/18

THE ROLL OF HONOUR OF THE FIRST SURREY RIFLES, 1914—1918.

OFFICERS.

Richards, H. P., Major
Robinson, H. H., Major (M.C. and Bar).
Heppell, F. R., Capt.
Hunter, R. J., Capt.
Leman, D. W., Capt.
McDougall, L. M., Capt.
Messervy, E. O., Capt.
Perkins, F. A., Capt.
Roberts, C. H. H., Capt. (M.C.)
Taylor, N. A., Capt. (M.C. and Bar).
Balfour, B., Lieut.
Carr, W. P., Lieut.
Edmunds, C. H., Lieut.
Hull, L. H. R., Lieut.
Hunt, L. H., Lieut.
Martin, C. B., Lieut.
Reynolds, C. E., Lieut.
Richmond, H. B., Lieut.
Savell, H. R., Lieut.
Walton, J. L., Lieut.
Jackson, F. C., Lieut. & Q.M.
Morrison, C., Lieut. & Q.M.
Aldis, R. H., 2nd Lieut.
Balfour, A. C., 2nd Lieut.
Bradley, H. M., 2nd Lieut.
Chance, F. M., 2nd Lieut.
Clare, M. V., 2nd Lieut.
Cohen, M., 2nd Lieut.
Coombes, H. V., 2nd Lieut.
Dickson, J., 2nd Lieut.
Edkins, H., 2nd Lieut.
Edmunds, G., 2nd Lieut.
Evans, D. L., 2nd Lieut.
Frolick, J. C. C., 2nd Lieut.
Garner, R. L., 2nd Lieut.
Geary, R. F. M., 2nd Lieut.
Hodge, F. C., 2nd Lieut.
Hotchkin, L. A., 2nd Lieut.
Hunter, A. F., 2nd Lieut.
Jones, F. J., 2nd Lieut.
Joel, H. W., 2nd Lieut.
Joseph, C. T. A., 2nd Lieut.
Kendal, B., 2nd Lieut.
Lack, F. C., 2nd Lieut.
Lloyd, D. M. A., 2nd Lieut.
Lloyd, G. L., 2nd Lieut.
McCourt, C. D., 2nd Lieut.
Morton, A. D., 2nd Lieut.
O'Connell, C., 2nd Lieut (M.C.).
Pragnell, A. E., 2nd Lieut.
Redway, F. M., 2nd Lieut.
Roberts, O. H. S., 2nd Lieut.
Sadler, W. H., 2nd Lieut.
Southin, C. A., 2nd Lieut. (M.C.).
Townend, 2nd Lieut.
Ward, C. B., 2nd Lieut.
Warren, C. G., 2nd Lieut.
Woodruff, G. N. C., 2nd Lieut.

NON-COMMISSIONED OFFICERS AND RIFLEMEN.

EXPLANATION OF ABBREVIATIONS.

"b." ... "born."	"k. in a." ... "killed in action."	
"e." ... "enlisted."	"F. & F." ... "France and Flanders"	
"d." ... "died."		(including Italy).
"d. of w." ... "died of wounds."	"E.E.F." ... "Egyptian Expeditionary Force."	

N.B.—When the place of enlistment is followed by the name of another place in brackets, the latter indicates the soldier's place of residence.

Abel, Hender Arthur, b. Kennington, e. Camberwell, 5247, Rfn., k. in a., F. & F., 6/11/16.
Adams, Joseph Edwin, b. Walham Green, e. Camberwell (Battersea), 654641, Rfn., k. in a., F. & F., 30/8/17.
Adaway, John, b. Vauxhall, Warwick, e. Bodmin (Birmingham), 652587, Rfn., k. in a., F. & F., 8/10/16, formerly 23377, D. of Cornwall's L.I.
Addis, George Henry, b. Lambeth, e. London, 652948, Rfn., k. in a., F. & F., 10/12/17.
Alexander, Douglas, e. Camberwell (Clapham), 2953, Sgt., k. in a., F. & F., 12/9/16.
Alexander, Frederick, b. Marlborough, Wilts., e. Wimbledon (Sandhurst, Berks.), 653189, Sgt., k. in a., F. & F., 9/12/17, formerly 4030, E. Surrey Regt.
Allcorn, John, b. Crowborough, Sussex, e. Wimbledon (Ashstead, Surrey), 653290, Rfn., d., Home, 9/5/18, formerly 3755, East Surrey Regt.
Allen, Walter, b. Walworth, London, e. Camberwell, 655947, Rfn., d. at Sea, 30/12/17.
Alleyne, George Albert, e. Camberwell (Forest Gate), 3067, Rfn., k. in a., F. & F., 23/5/16.
Amos, Harry, b. Towcester, e. Camberwell, 654380, Rfn., k. in. a., F. & F., 7/6/17.
Anderson, Charles, b. Royston, Herts., e. Woolwich (Woolwich), 652043, Rfn., k. in a., F. & F., 15/9/16.
Anderson, Walter, e. Camberwell (Camberwell), 2766, Rfn., k. in a., F. & F., 15/9/16.
Anderson, William Charles, b. W. Norwood, e. Camberwell (W. Norwood), 3337, Rfn., k. in a., F. & F., 4/10/16.
Andrews, Joseph Stapleton, e. Camberwell (Camberwell), 650590, Sgt., d. of w., E.E.F., 9/11/17.
Andrews, William, b. Leytonstone, e. Stratford (Stratford), 654316, Rfn., d., F. & F., 13/10/18.
Andrews, William Horace, e. Camberwell (E. Dulwich), 651188, L/Cpl., k. in a., F. & F., 7/6/17.
Anson, Albert Henry, e. Camberwell (Forest Hill), 652392, Rfn., k. in a., F. & F., 8/10/16.
Apalyras, Francis Pericles, b. Liverpool, e. Camberwell (Chiswick), 1664, Rfn., k. in a., F. & F., 9/5/15.
Aplin, Harry Walters, b. Lambeth, e. Camberwell (E. Dulwich), 655942, Rfn., d. of w., F. & F., 24/3/18.
Arnett, Ernest, b. Camberwell, e. Whitehall, 5789, Rfn., d. of w., F. & F., 12/7/16, formerly S/15296, Rifle Brigade.

Ashby, Arthur Robert, b. Camberwell, e. Camberwell, 651393, Rfn., k. in a., F. & F., 17/8/17.
Aston, Lessey, b. St. Albans, Herts., e. London, W.C. (Fulham), 7568, Rfn., k. in a., F. & F., 15/9/16, formerly 5289, 12th London Regt.
Austin, Frank Thomas, e. Camberwell (Leyton), 2890, Cpl., d. of w., Home, 15/10/16.
Avery, Richard, b. Huntingdon. e. Camberwell (Westminster), 650602, Rfn., k. in a., E.E.F., 9/12/17.
Ayling, Walter Edward, b. Croydon, Surrey, e. Bodmin (Menherriot, Cornwall), 5740, Rfn., d. of w., F. & F., 26/9/16, formerly 24391, D.C.L.I.
Ayres, George Henry John, e. Camberwell (Westminster), 3631, Rfn., d. of w., F. & F., 17/9/16.
Baber, Frank Gilbert, e. Camberwell (Tooting), 3671, Rfn., k. in a., F. & F., 21/7/16.
Baker, Albert John, b. Peckham, e. Camberwell (Clapham), 2035, Sgt., k. in a., F. & F., 8/10/16.
Baker, Charles Anthony, b. Wandsworth, e. Kingston-on-Thames (South Norwood), 654346, Rfn., d. of w., E.E.F., 25/7/18.
Baker, Charles Thomas, b. Woolwich, e. Woolwich, 656022, Rfn., d., E.E.F., 30/12/17.
Baker, Frederick Albert, b. Bow, E., e. Camberwell (Old Ford), 3755, Rfn., k. in a., F. & F., 23/5/16.
Baldry, Alfred, b. Stoke Newington, e. Stratford (Walthamstow), 4791, Rfn., d. of w., F. & F., 18/9/16.
Baldwin, Ernest, b. Flamstead, Herts., e. London, W.C. (Hammersmith), 7577, Rfn., k. in a., F. & F., 15/9/16, formerly 5634, 12th London Regt.
Ball, Albert John, b. Lee, Kent, e. Camberwell (Lee), 653521, Rfn., d. of w., E.E.F., 13/5/18.
Ball, Horace William, b. Rotherhithe, e. Camberwell, 650102, Rfn., k. in a., F. & F., 24/5/16.
Ball, Richard, b. St. Pancras, e. Whitehall (Camden Town), 652921, Rfn., k. in a., F. & F., 16/8/18.
Ball, Robert, b. Bermondsey, e. Camberwell, 652177, Rfn., k. in a., F. & F., 15/9/16.
Bamford, Leslie George, b. Stratford, e. Camberwell (Forest Gate), 2025, Rfn., k. in a., F. & F., 12/9/16.
Banfield, Frederick Jack, e. Camberwell (Brixton), 2141, Rfn., k. in a., F. & F., 27/12/15.
Bannister, Henry Walter, e. Camberwell (Welling, Kent), 650462, Rfn., d. of w., F. & F., 6/4/18.
Barker, Charles, e. Camberwell, 651166, Rfn., d., E.E.F., 7/10/18.
Barker, Frank James, b. Bow, E., e. Bodmin (Bow, E.), 652614, Sgt., k. in a., F. & F., 1/9/18. formerly 24690, D. of C. L.I., M.M.
Barkman, Charles Stuart, b. Bow., E., e. Camberwell, 678049, Rfn., d. of w., F. & F., 15/6/18, formerly 452670, 11th London Regt.
Barnes, George Henry, b. Dorchester, Dorset, e. Winchester (Portsmouth), 653181, Rfn., d. of w., F. & F., 21/12/17.
Barnes, John Henry, b. Shoreditch, e. Whitehall (Hackney), 652280, Rfn., k. in a., E.E.F., 30/3/18.
Barnes, William, e. Camberwell, 651214, Rfn., k. in a., F. & F., 1/9/18.
Barrell, Charles William, b. Birmingham, e. Whitehall (Peterborough), 7570, Rfn., d. of w., F. & F., 23/9/16.
Barrett, Reginald William, e. Kensington, 678028, L/Cpl., k. in a., F. & F., 6/4/18, formerly 490532, 13th London Regt.
Bass, Frederick Edward, b. Islington, e. Whitehall (Holloway), 653854, Rfn., d., Home, 22/4/17.

Batten, Sidney Percy, e. Camberwell, 651950, Rfn., d. of w., E.E.F., 29/3/18.
Baxter, Henry Frederick, b. Peckham, e. West London, 675046, Rfn., k. in a., F. & F., 1/9/18, formerly 616207, 19th London Regt.
Bazinsky, Solomon, b. Shoreditch, e. Stratford, 654317, Rfn., k. in a., F. & F., 26/8/17.
Beazley, Charles Arthur, b. Streatham, e. Wimbledon (Streatham), 6686, Rfn., k. in a., F. & F., 24/12/16, formerly 2547, E. Surrey Regt.
Beaton, Stanley, b. Peckham, e. Camberwell, 1556, Rfn., d. of w., F. & F., 22/5/16.
Beaty, Walter, e. Camberwell, 3842, Rfn., k. in a., F. & F., 23/5/16.
Bellman, Weedon Douglas, b. Kennington, e. Camberwell (Herne Hill), 1839, Rfn., d. of w., Home, 14/6/15.
Belton, George Henry, e. Deptford, 651814, Rfn., k. in a., F. & F., 15/9/16.
Bennett, Charles Edward, e. Camberwell (Streatham), 2674, Rfn., k. in a., F. & F., 15/9/16.
Bennett, Ernest, b. Bermondsey, e. Camberwell (Bermondsey), 1239, Rfn., k. in a., F. & F., 30/3/16.
Bennett, William, b. Battersea, e. Camberwell (Battersea), 678039, Rfn., d., Home, 6/4/18, formerly 452795, 11th London Regt.
Bennett, William Ernest, b. Clerkenwell, e. Bodmin (Clerkenwell), 652628, Rfn., k. in a., F. & F., 15/9/16, formerly 25463, Duke of Cornwall's L.I.
Bertoglio, Hector Peter, b. Whitechapel, e. Whitehall, 653834, Rfn., k. in a., F. & F., 8/10/16.
Bidgood, Frank William, b. Brixton, e. Camberwell, 716, Cpl., k. in a., F. & F., 25/5/15.
Bidwell, Albert Cecil, b. Camberwell, e. Camberwell, 651781, Rfn., d. of w., E.E.F., 10/12/17.
Billingsley, Sydney Walter, b. Bethnal Green, e. Camberwell, 4001, Rfn., k. in a., F. & F., 12/9/16.
Binks, Albert Alexander, b. Bow, E., e. Stratford, 652040, Rfn., k. in a., F. & F., 8/10/16.
Birch, Edward John, b. Peckham, e. Camberwell, 655980, Rfn., d., At Sea, 30/12/17.
Bird, Frederick Joseph, e. Camberwell (Merton), 650581, Rfn., k. in a., F. & F., 23/5/16.
Birlo, John Reginald, b. Paddington, e. Islington (Paddington), 5803, Rfn., k. in a., F. &. F., 15/9/16.
Bishop, Frederick, b. Wandsworth, e. Mitcham, 6824, Rfn., d. of w., F. & F., 10/10/16, formerly 1417, E. Surrey Regt.
Black, William Alexander, b. Hammersmith, e. Camberwell (Tooting), 651791, Rfn., k. in a., E.E.F., 13/12/17.
Blackman, George Dullam, b. Beverley, Yorks, e. Camberwell (Wallington), 1656, Sgt., k. in a., F. & F., 23/5/16.
Blackmore, John Freeman, b. Penge, e. Wimbledon (Chiswick), 653279, Rfn., k. in a., F. & F., 8/10/16.
Bloomfield, Edgar, b. Maidenhead, e. Reading, (Maidenhead), 5721, Rfn., k. in a., F. & F., 15/9/16.
Bolding Walter Robert, b. Haggerston, e. Stratford (Bethnal Green), 655755, Rfn., k. in a., F. & F., 24/8/18.
Bolland, Frederick James, b. Devizes, Wilts, e. Oxford (Tring), 652528, Rfn., k. in a., F. & F., 10/6/17.
Bond, Arthur Joseph, b. Lambeth, e. Camberwell, 656005, Rfn., d., At Sea, 30/12/17.

Bone, George William, b. Lee, Kent, e. Kingston-on-Thames (Bermondsey), 656485, Rfn., k. in a., F. & F., 2/9/18.
Boorman, Alfred Edward, b. Barnes, Surrey, e. West London (Fulham), 654502, Rfn., k. in a., F. & F., 25/3/18.
Booth, Harry Owen, b. Hendon, e. Bunhill Row, E.C. (Winchmore Hill), 652739, Rfn., d., E.E.F., 1-31/7/18.
Borley, Harnwell Jackson, b. London, e. Camberwell, 1929, Rfn., d., Home, 10/3/15.
Bostwick, Ernest, e. Camberwell, 3386, Rfn., d. of w., F. & F., 28/5/16.
Boucher, Douglas Brunskill, e. Camberwell (Palmer's Green), 650943, Rfn., d. of w., F. & F., 9/6/17.
Boulter, William, b. Walthamstow, e. Camberwell, 650195, Rfn., d. of w., F. & F., 25/1/17.
Boulter, William John, e. Camberwell, 4403, Rfn., d. of w., F. & F., 25/5/16.
Bowden, Stanley Charles, e. Camberwell, 650721, Rfn., d. of w., Balkans, 25/4/17.
Bowdery, Sidney Charles, b. Mitcham, e. Wimbledon (Mitcham), 653210, Rfn., k. in a., F. & F., 8/10/16, formerly 3239, E. Surrey Regt.
Bowen, Henry, e. Camberwell, 3265, Rfn., k. in a., F. & F., 9/5/15.
Bowles, William Thomas, b. Poplar, e. Whitehall (Clerkenwell), 678040, Rfn., k. in a., F. & F., 8/4/18, formerly 452202, 11th London Regt.
Bowman, Alfred James, e. Camberwell (Beckenham, Kent), 2938, Rfn., k. in a., F. & F., 1/10/15.
Boxall, Thomas, e. Camberwell (Wandsworth), 650832, Cpl., k. in a., F. & F., 7/6/17.
Boyack, William Hood Hill, b. Dundee, e. London, W.C. (Hammersmith), 653833, Rfn., d. of w., F. & F., 12/12/17.
Bracey, Humphrey Alfred, b. Stoke Newington, e. Camberwell (Ilford), 1768, L/Cpl., k. in a., F. & F., 25/5/15.
Braddick, Henry James, b. Clapham, e. Wimbledon (S. Lambeth), 653293, Rfn., k. in a., F. & F., 8/10/16, formerly 2752, East Surrey Regt.
Bradley, John Donald, e. Camberwell, 3066, Rfn., k. in a., F. & F., 25/5/15.
Bradshaw, Charles, e. Camberwell (Catford), 652391, Rfn., k. in a., F. & F., 13/4/17.
Bramble, Walter, b. Camberwell, e. Camberwell, 651440, Sgt., d., E.E.F., 23/8/18.
Brand, Percy Charles, b. Greenwich, e. Woolwich (Greenwich), 5180, Rfn., k. in a., F. & F., 15/9/16.
Bray, Frederick William, e. Camberwell (W. Norwood), 2124, L/Cpl., k. in a., F. & F., 25/5/15.
Breakspear, Vincent, b. Dulwich, e. Camberwell, 651106, Rfn., k. in a., F. & F., 23/5/16.
Brewer, Harry, b. Peckham, e. Camberwell, 652339, Rfn., k. in a., F. & F., 30/4/17.
Brewis, Errington, e. Camberwell (Enfield, Middx.), 2891, Rfn., d., Home, 24/3/15.
Bridges, Stanley Hart, b. Gillingham, Kent, e. Camberwell, 650245, Cpl., k. in a., F. & F., 7/6/17.
Bright, James, e. Camberwell, 651668, Rfn., d. of w., F. & F., 29/3/18.
Bright, Joseph Charles George, b. Kentish Town, e. St. Paul's Churchyard (Southend-on-Sea), 5695, Cpl., k. in a., F. & F., 15/9/16, formerly 11260, Duke of Cornwall's Light Infantry.
Brokenshire, Herbert, b. Brixham, Devon, e. Bodmin (Fowey, Cornwall), 5769, Rfn., k. in a., F. & F., 15/9/16, formerly 24718, Duke of Cornwall's Light Infantry.

Bromley-Smith, Walter, e. Camberwell (West Norwood), 650593, Cpl., k. in a., E.E.F., 14/2/18.
Brooker, Alfred John Claude, b. Deptford, e. London, W.C. (Deptford), 7554, Rfn., k. in a., F. & F., 15/9/17.
Brooks, Archibald, b. Walthamstow, e. Camberwell, 1738, Rfn., k. in a., F. & F., 25/5/15.
Brooks, Alfred Edward, b. Merton, Surrey, e. London, W.C. (Willesden), 653836, Rfn., k. in a., F. & F., 15/9/16.
Brooks, Charles Ernest, b. Peckham, e. Camberwell, 653121, Rfn., d. of w., F. & F., 19/6/17.
Brooks, George J. F., b. Islington, e. Whitehall (Holloway), 652869, Rfn., k. in a., F. & F., 25/4/17.
Brooks, Harold John, b. Ipswich, e. Whitehall (Barnsbury), 7553, Rfn., k. in a., F. & F., 15/9/16.
Brooks, Walter Stephen, b. Peckham, e. Camberwell, 651494, Rfn., d. of w., F. & F., 9/6/17.
Brown, Andrew Louis, e. Camberwell (Stockwell), 4076, Rfn., k. in a., F. & F., 15/5/16.
Brown, Arthur Norman, b. Southwark, e. Whitehall (Borough, S.E.), 655917, Rfn., k. in a., F. & F., 24/3/18.
Brown, Frank, b. Woolwich, e. Woolwich, 653882, Rfn., k. in a., F. & F., 2/9/18.
Brown, Frederick William, e. Camberwell (Westminster), 2198, Rfn., k. in a., F. & F., 25/5/15.
Brown, Joseph William, e. Camberwell, 651401, Rfn., k. in a., F. & F., 16/7/17.
Bryant, Albert Edward, b. Bermondsey, e. Camberwell (Bermondsey), 1495, L/Cpl., k. in a., F. & F., 25/5/15.
Buck, Donald William, e. Camberwell (Clare, Suffolk), 653674, Rfn., k. in a., F. & F., 12/10/17.
Buck, Spencer Samuel, b. Kilburn, e. West London, 655964, Rfn., k. in a., F. & F., 2/9/18.
Buckham, Joseph Thomas, b. Hoxton, e. London, W.C. (Stoke Newington), 653851, Rfn., k. in a., F. & F., 15/9/16.
Budd, Ernest, b. Bethnal Green, e. Wimbledon (Epsom), 653207, Rfn., k. in a., F. & F., 8/10/16. formerly 2708, East Surrey Regt.
Budd, William Frank, b. Lambeth, e. Camberwell, 678048, Rfn., k. in a., F. & F., 28/8/18, formerly 452654, 11th London Regt.
Bull, Arthur Edward, b. Walworth, e. Camberwell, 1702, Sgt., k. in a., F. & F., 9/5/15.
Bunker, Edward Arthur, b. Kensington, e. Camberwell (Battersea), 5271, Rfn., d., F. & F., 29/7/16.
Bunn, George, b. Bermondsey, e. Camberwell (Southwark), 653133, Rfn., d. of w., F. & F., 18/4/17.
Burgess, Albert, b. Lewes, Sussex, e. Camberwell (Walworth), 1577, L/Cpl., k. in a., F. & F., 23/5/16.
Burley, Archer, b. Belcham, Essex, e. Camberwell (Plaistow), 652159, Rfn., k. in a., F. & F., 8/10/16.
Burrell, Oswald, b. Aldershot, e. Bunhill Row, E.C. (Hackney), 652730, Rfn., k. in a., Balkans, 12/5/17.
Burrows, Charles Ephraim, e. Camberwell (Herne Hill), 2385, Sgt., k. in a., F. & F., 15/9/16.
Bursnoll, William, b. Tring, Herts., e. London, W.C. (W. Croydon), 7549, Rfn., k. in a., F. & F., 15/9/16.
Burt, James, b. Islington, e. Whitehall (King's Cross), 653481, L/Cpl., k. in a., F. & F., 26/5/18.
Burtenshaw, Arthur William, e. Camberwell (Fulham), 2298, Rfn., k. in a., F. & F., 26/5/15.

Buse, John Francis, b. St. Minver, Cornwall, e. Bodmin (St. Minver, Cornwall), 5770, Rfn., k. in a., F. & F., 15/9/16, formerly 24719, Duke of Cornwall's Light Infantry.
Bush, Charles George, b. Limehouse, e. Whitehall (Stepney), 7574, Rfn., k. in a., F. & F., 11/9/16.
Bush, Sidney Charles, e. Camberwell (Wandsworth), 3999, Rfn., k. in a., F. & F., 23/5/16.
Bushell, George, e. Camberwell (Sydenham), 651409, Rfn., k. in a., F. & F., 30/4/17.
Byrne, Alexander James, b. Balham, e. Whitehall (Islington), 656044, Rfn., k. in a., F. & F., 23/3/18.
Campbell, Sydney George, e. Camberwell (New Malden, Surrey), 650569, Rfn., d. of w., E.E.F., 9/12/17.
Cannon, Thomas, b. Brixton, e. Wimbledon (Brixton), 6729, Rfn., k. in a., F. & F., 6/11/16), formerly 3050, East Surrey Regt., M.M.
Capel, Edward Albert, e. Shaftesbury St., N. (Tottenham), 653870, Rfn., k. in a., F. & F., 7/6/17, formerly 3306, 4th London Regt.
Carne, Martin, e. Camberwell, 2603, Rfn., d. of w., F. & F., 2/10/15.
Carpenter, Arthur, b. West Ham, e. Stratford, 654279, Rfn., k. in a., F. & F., 20/9/18.
Carpenter, Alfred George, e. Camberwell, 651934, Rfn., k. in a., E.E.F., 28/3/18.
Carr, Lionel Hubert, e. Camberwell (Romford), 650706, Rfn., k. in a., E.E.F., 31/10/17.
Carter, Bert, b. Redruth, Cornwall, e. Bodmin (Redruth), 652617, Rfn., d. of w., F. & F., 1/9/17, formerly 24715, Duke of Cornwall's L.I.
Carter, William, b. Longworth, Berks, e. Reading (Farringdon, Devon), 653198, Rfn., k. in a., F. & F., 8/10/16.
Case, John, e. Bodmin (Par Station, Cornwall), 652568, Rfn., k. in a., F. & F., 15/9/16, formerly 19080, Duke of Cornwall's Light Infantry.
Catling, John Charles, b. Battersea, e. St. John's Hill S.W., 653930, Rfn., d., At Sea, 30/12/17, formerly 3849, 23rd London Regt.
Chalkley, Joseph Frank, b. Finsbury Park, e. Camberwell (New Cross), 1410, Rfn., d., F. & F., 10/11/15.
Chambers, Charles Edward, b. London, e. Westminster (Stratford), 678008, Sgt., k. in a., F. & F., 1/9/18, formerly 2510, 2nd Bn. Royal Fusiliers.
Chaplain, Edward, b. Felixstowe, Suffolk, e. Norwich (Foxley), 5565, Rfn., d., F. & F., 10/8/16, formerly 2370, 2nd E.A. Field Ambulance, R.A.M.C.
Chapman, Edward, b. Bermondsey, e. London, 675064, Sgt., k. in a., F. & F., 3/9/18, formerly 681847, 22nd London Regt.
Chatting, Leonard Harry, b. Battersea, e. Bunhill Row, E.C. (Clapham), 652728, Rfn., d., F. & F., 15/10/18, formerly 3144, 5th London Regt.
Chave, Percy, b. Bermondsey, e. Camberwell, 652420, Rfn., k. in a., F. & F., 18/5/17.
Checketts, Harry James, b. Pershore, Worcester, e. Woolwich, 4905, Rfn., d. of w., F. & F., 4/11/16.
Chelton, Alfred William, b. Walworth. e. Camberwell, 1453, Rfn., k. in a., F. & F., 25/5/15.
Cheshan, Harry Charles, b. Islington, e. Whitehall (Holloway), 678054, Rfn., k. in a., F. & F., 1/9/18, formerly 452274, 11th London Regt.
Chettleburgh, Claude Arthur, b. Norwich, e. Norwich, 652479, Rfn., k. in a., F. & F., 23/3/18, formerly 2694, 4/1st East Anglian Field Ambulance.
Chiles, Walter Frederick, b. Hanwell, e. Camberwell, 678238, Rfn., k. in a., F. & F., 24/8/18, formerly 616035, 19th London Regt.

Chinchen, Frederick John, b. Swanage, Dorset, e. Stratford (Barking), 678055, Rfn., k. in a., F. & F., 1/9/18, formerly 473591, 11th London Regt.

Chinn, Sidney James, b. Bridgewater, Somerset, e. Taunton (Bridgewater), 652820, L/Cpl., k. in a., F. & F., 10/6/17, formerly 21570, Somerset Light Infantry.

Christie, John, e. Camberwell (Dulwich), 650834, Rfn., k. in a., F. & F., 15/9/16.

Claridge, William Edward, e. Shaftesbury St., N., 678255, Rfn., d. of w., F. & F., 20/7/18, formerly 282230, 4th London Regt., posted 8th Bn. East Surrey Regt.

Clark, Frederick James, b. Brixton, e. Camberwell, 1753, Rfn., k. in a., F. & F., 15/9/16.

Clark, Lewis, b. Blackfriars, e. Camberwell, 2063, L/Cpl., k. in a., F. & F., 23/5/16.

Clark, Reginald Charles, b. St. Andrew's the Great, Cambridge, e. Cambridge, 678275, Cpl., k. in a., F. & F., 7/5/18, formerly 2740, 1st, East Anglian F.A., R.A.M.C., posted 8th Bn. East Surrey.

Clark, William, b. Stepney, e. Whitehall (Mile End), 7560, Rfn., k. in a., F. & F., 15/9/16, formerly 5570, 12th London Regt.

Clarke, Albert, b. Adstock, Bucks, e. Oxford (Winslow, Bucks), 652503, Rfn., k. in a., F. & F., 8/10/16, formerly Ox/17107, Ox. and Bucks Light Infantry.

Clarke, James Thomas, b. Bromley, Kent, e. Woolwich (Bromley, Kent), 652113, Rfn., k. in a., F. & F., 15/9/16.

Cleaver, William Albert, b. Lewis, Kent, e. Stratford, 5139, Rfn., k. in a., F. & F., 15/9/16.

Clee, Albert Frederick, b. Camberwell, e. Camberwell, 650390, Rfn., k. in a., Balkans, 9/4/17.

Clee, Frederick James, e. Camberwell, 2561, L/Cpl., d. of w., F. & F., 24/5/16.

Clements, David Frederick, b. Greenwich, e. Woolwich, 675019, Rfn., k. in a., F. & F., 6/4/18. formerly 616175, 19th London Regt.

Clewley, William Joseph, b. Peckham, e. Camberwell, 678200, Rfn., k. in a., F. & F., 24/8/18, formerly 615962, 19th London Regt.

Cockram, Arthur Herbert, b. Tooting, e. Camberwell (Norwood), 1546, d. of w., F. & F., 22/9/16.

Coffin, Cecil James, b. Southampton, e. Winchester (Southampton), 6788, Rfn., k. in a., F. & F., 4/11/16.

Cole, Douglas, e. Camberwell (Brentwood), 2847, Rfn., k. in a., F. & F., 25/5/15.

Cole, George Frederick, b. Cambridge, e. Wimbledon (Mitcham), 653248, Rfn., k. in a., F. & F., 25/3/18, formerly 2716, East Surrey Regt.

Coles, John, b. Ashwater, Devon, e. Bodmin (Saltash, Cornwall), 652618, Rfn., k. in a., F. & F., 10/6/17, formerly 24721, Duke of Cornwall's Light Infantry.

Collins, Arthur, e. Camberwell, 4307, Rfn., k. in a., F. & F., 13/9/16.

Collins, Frederick Edward, b. Clapham, e. Camberwell, 1377, Rfn., d., Home, 12/3/15.

Collins, William George, e. Camberwell, 651881, Rfn., k. in a., Balkans, 12/5/17.

Comber, Ernest Charles, b. Marylebone, e. Camberwell (Tooting), 654411, Rfn., d. of w., F. & F., 5/7/17.

Compton, Edward, e. Camberwell, 2207, Cpl., k. in a., F. & F., 18/5/16.

Connolly, Stanley Arthur, b. Dublin, e. Wimbledon (Clapham), 653283, Cpl., k. in a., F. & F., 8/10/16, formerly 2756, East Surrey Regt.

Constable, Thomas, b. Wimbledon, e. Camberwell, 1516, Rfn., k. in a., F. & F., 25/5/15.
Cook, Edwin Maitland, b. Bow, E., e. Stratford, 653563, Rfn., k. in a., F. & F., 30/4/17.
Cook, Sydney Henri Frederick, e. Camberwell (Clapham), 2398, Rfn., k. in a., F. & F., 15/9/16.
Cook, William, b. Mitcham, Surrey, e. Wimbledon, 653242, Rfn., k. in a., F. & F., 5/6/17, formerly 2513, East Surrey Regt.
Coomber, Alfred Ernest, b. Croydon, e. Camberwell, 656055, Rfn., k. in a., F. & F., 22/8/18.
Cooper, Arthur Sydney, e. Camberwell (Forest Hill), 650685, L/Cpl., k. in a., F. & F., 24/8/18.
Cooper, Lewis, e. Camberwell (Kensington), 651033, Rfn., k. in a., F. & F., 23/5/16.
Cooper, Reginald Saterley, b. Camberwell, e. Camberwell (Dulwich), 1312, Rfn., d , F. & F., 30/6/15.
Cooper, Thomas Ernest, b. Hoxton, e. Camberwell, 655983, Rfn., d., At Sea, 30/12/17.
Coppard, Francis Charles, e. Camberwell (Dulwich), 651760, L/Cpl., k. in a., F. & F., 28/8/17.
Corby, Frederick Ernest, b. Croydon, e. Wimbledon (Croydon), 653208, Rfn., k. in a., F. & F., 8/10/16, formerly 2718, East Surrey Regt.
Corn, Harold Frank, b. Stoke Newington, e. Bunhill Row, E.C. (Ewell), 652738, Rfn., k. in a., E.E.F., 13/12/17, formerly 3147, East Surrey Regt.
Corner, Sidney William, b. Brixton, e. Camberwell (Battersea), 6406, Rfn., d. F. & F., 11/1/17.
Cossins, Ernest, b. Camberwell, e. Whitehall (Loughborough Junction), 652643, Rfn., k. in a., F. & F., 30/8/17.
Cotmore, Harold Arthur, b. Peckham, e. Brixton, 1212, Cpl., k. in a., F. & F., 9/5/15.
Cowper, Edward, b. Tottenham, e. Camberwell, 1823, L/Cpl., k. in a., F. & F., 25/5/15.
Cox, James Charles, b. Shoreditch, e. London, W.C. (Edmonton), 653840, Rfn., k. in a., F. & F., 15/9/16, formerly 5292, 12th London Regt.
Cox, Robert William Braddon, b. Lambeth, e. Penton St., N. (Dalston), 678013, Sgt., k. in a., F. & F., 1/9/18, formerly 450051, 11th London Regt.
Craig-Vincent, Sidney George, b. Deptford, e. Camberwell (Brockley), 656191, Rfn., k. in a., F. & F., 22/8/18, posted 1/23rd Bn. London Regt.
Crane, Samuel William, b. Palgrave, Suffolk, e. Stratford (West Ham), 652650, Rfn., d. of w., F. & F., 11/6/17.
Crawford, Edward, b. Camberwell, e. Camberwell, 651394, Rfn., d., E.E.F., 22/1/18.
Crawley, Frank Short, e. Camberwell (Streatham), 652405, Rfn., d. of w., F. & F., 9/9/18.
Crawley, John Frederick, b. London, e. Stratford, 652647, Rfn., k. in a., F. & F., 26/8/17.
Crompton, Percival, b. Greenwich, e. Woolwich, 652046, Rfn., d. of w., F. & F., 16/8/17.
Cromwell, George, b. Upper Norwood, e. Camberwell (Penge), 4280, Rfn., d., Home, 24/5/15.
Cross, Francis, e. Camberwell (Kentish Town), 3058, Rfn., k. in a., F. & F., 15/9/16.
Cross, Ralph Leslie, b. Camberwell, 650961, Rfn., d. of w., Home, 5/4/18.

Crowe, Edward, e. Camberwell, 651533, Rfn., k. in a., F. & F., 8/10/16.
Crowther, Alfred Edward, b. Lambeth, e. Camberwell (Clapham), 654591, Rfn., d., At Sea, 30/12/17.
Cuff, Francis Arthur, e. Camberwell, 2272, Rfn., k. in a., F. & F., 25/5/15.
Cullom, Clement Charles, b. Camberwell, e. Camberwell, 1891, Rfn., k. in a., F. & F., 15/9/16.
Curness, William Henry, e. Camberwell, 3519, Rfn., d. of w., Home, 10/10/16.
Curtis, William Alfred, b. Stepney, e. Stratford, 654327, Rfn., k. in a., F. & F., 7/6/17.
Cushway, Harry, e. Camberwell (Bethnal Green), 650719, Cpl., k. in a., F. & F., 7/6/17.
Cutting, Edmond, b. Lambeth, e. Camberwell (Battersea), 5066, Rfn., d. of w., F. & F., 12/9/16.
Daines, Bernard Thomas, b. Brixton, e. Camberwell (Lee, S.E.), 652224, Rfn., k. in a., F. & F., 7/6/17.
Dalgleish, Henry, b. Lambeth, e. Camberwell, 1433, Rfn., k. in a., F. & F., 15/9/16.
Dalton, Frederick James, b. Peckham, e. Camberwell, 652345, Rfn., k. in a., F. & F., 8/10/16.
Danbury, Alfred John, b. Camberwell, e. Camberwell, 1518, Sgt. k. in a., F. & F., 15/9/16.
Daniel, Frederick John, e. Camberwell (Romford), 650913, L/Cpl., k. in a., E.E.F., 30/3/18.
Darbyshire, George Ernest, b. S. Norwood, e. Camberwell, 4839, Rfn., k. in a., F. & F., 15/9/16.
Darling, Walter, e. Camberwell, 650587, Rfn., d., Balkans, 28/1/17.
Davenport, Frederick George, e. Camberwell, 652239, Rfn., k. in a., F. & F., 25/2/17.
Davey, Harry, b. Crythole, e. Bodmin (St. Germans, Cornwall), 5775, Rfn., k. in a., F. & F., 12/9/16.
Davies, Alfred Edward, b. Peckham, e. Camberwell, 651222, Rfn., k. in a., F. & F., 26/8/17.
Davies, John, b. Llanfair, Cardiganshire, e. Bunhill Row (Crouch End), 5954, Rfn., k. in a., F. & F., 20/7/16.
Davis, Daniel, b. Bermondsey, e. Camberwell, 651783, Rfn., k. in a., F. & F., 5/4/18, posted 1/23rd Batt. London Regt.
Davis, Edward James, b. Walworth, e. Camberwell, 651503, Rfn., k. in a., F. & F., 15/9/16.
Davis, Horace Charles, b. Brixton, e. Camberwell, 1786, L/Cpl., k. in a., F. & F., 15/9/16.
Davis, Henry George, b. Kennington, e. Camberwell, 1588, Rfn., d. of w., F. & F., 22/5/16.
Davis, John Percy, e. Camberwell, 3501, Rfn., d. of w., F. & F., 25/5/16.
Davis, William, e. Camberwell, 651257, Rfn., k. in a., F. & F., 23/5/16.
Dawe, Ernest, b. Goldsithney, Cornwall, e. Bodmin (Goldsithney), 5779, Rfn., k. in a., F. & F., 12/9/16.
Dawes, John Thomas, b. Kentish Town, e. Bodmin (King's Cross), 5732, Rfn., k. in a., F. & F., 15/9/16.
Deeth, Arthur Edwin, e. Camberwell, 650556, Rfn., k. in a., F. & F., 15/9/16.
De Levante, Frederick Robert, b. Camberwell, e. Camberwell, 60, L/Sgt., k. in a., F. & F., 25/5/15.
Dellar, Arthur, b. Lambeth, e. Hounslow, 656654, Rfn., d., Home, 8/12/18, posted 3rd Batt. East Surrey Regt.

Denny, William John, e. Winchester (Vauxhall), 5826, Rfn., k. in a., F. & F., 15/9/16.
Desaleux, Frederick John, b. Lambeth, e. 27 St. John's Hill, 653511, Rfn., k. in a., F. & F., 25/2/17, formerly 1831, 23rd London Regt.
Dewdney, Ernest Henry, b. Bayswater, e. Whitehall, 4980, Rfn., d. of w., F. & F., 21/9/16.
Dickerson, George, b. Canning Town, e. East Ham (N. Woolwich), 652396, Rfn., k. in a., F. & F., 7/6/17.
Diver, Harold Thomas, b. Forest Hill, e. Camberwell (Sydenham), 653472, Rfn., k. in a., F. & F., 23/3/18.
Dobson, William John, e. Camberwell, 651281, Rfn., k. in a., F. & F., 23/5/16.
Dodds, James Charles, b. Deptford, e. Camberwell (Rotherhithe). 653430, Rfn., k. in a., F. & F., 15/5/17.
Dodgson, William, b. Colne, Lancs, e. Woolwich (Belvedere, Kent), 653885, L/Cpl., k. in a., F. & F., 2/9/18.
Dodsley, James Henry, b. Leyton, e. Walthamstow, 653565, Rfn., k. in a., F. & F., 7/6/17.
Doig, David Taylor, b. Forfar, N.B., e. Camberwell (Stoke Newington), 650536, L/Sgt., k. in a., E.E.F., 28/3/18.
Dommett, Herbert, b. Staines, e. Camberwell (Staines), 2054, L/Cpl., k. in a., F. & F., 4/5/16.
Donovan, John, e. Camberwell (Herne Hill), 4116, Rfn., d., Home, 25/6/15.
Dorrington, Charles Percy, b. Lambeth, e. Camberwell, (Clapham), 654468, Rfn., d., Home, 24/2/17.
Downham, Frederick Frank, b. Ashton, Essex, e. Whitehall (Borough), 656013, Rfn., d., At Sea,, 30/12/17.
Downing, Norman, b. Durgan, Cornwall, e. Bodmin (Fowey), 652602, Rfn., k. in a., F. & F., 8/10/16.
Downs, Murray Stephen, b. Horsell, Surrey, e. Hounslow (Marylebone), 678219, Rfn., k. in a., F. & F., 2/9/18, formerly 616396, 19th London Regt.
Drake, Henry, e. Camberwell (Peckham), 3537, Rfn., k. in a., F. & F., 23/5/16.
Draper, Ernest, b. Stepney, e. Stratford (Wanstead), 652093, Rfn., k. in a., 7/6/17.
Duck, Leslie Sidney, b. Lewisham, e. Camberwell (Brockley), 650022, Sgt., k. in a., F. & F., 23/5/16.
Dudley, William Henry, b. Srinsbury, Oxon, e. Oxford (Banbury), 5656, L/Cpl., k. in a., F. & F., 15/9/16, formerly 22184, Ox. & Bucks L.I.
Duerdin, William, b. Fulham, e. Wimbledon (Wimbledon), 653201, Rfn., k. in a., F. & F., 7/6/17, formerly 3039, East Surrey Regt.
Duffell, Edward James, b. Walthamstow, e. London (Leytonstone), 652583, Rfn., k. in a., F. & F., 6/4/18, formerly 21693, Duke of Corn. L.I.
Dundridge, Richard, e. Kingston-on-Thames (Deptford), 656397, Rfn., d., Home, 13/7/18.
Dunford, Raymond Stanley, e. Camberwell (West Acton), 650771, L/Cpl., k. in a., E.E.F., 30/11/17.
Dutton, Archibald, b. Summerstown, Surrey, e. Wimbledon (Tooting), 653148, Rfn., k. in a., F. & F., 8/10/16, formerly 3055, East Surrey Regt.
Dyke, Harold Frederick, e. Camberwell (Stevenage, Herts), 650949, Cpl., k. in a., E.E.F., 31/3/18.
Earthrowl, Walter Thomas, b. Bermondsey, e. Camberwell, (Bermondsey), 652123, Rfn., k. in a., F. & F., 8/6/17.

Q

East, George, e. Camberwell (Camberwell), 3098, Rfn., k. in a., F. & F., 25/5/15.
Eastlake, Frank Wootton, e. Camberwell (Peckham), 2121, L/Sgt., k. in a., F. & F., 23/5/16, D.C.M.
Edwards, Horace, b. Freemantle, Southampton, e. Winchester (Free mantle), 653296, Rfn., k. in a., F. & F., 8/10/16.
Eggleton, Edwin, b. Dorking, Surrey, e. Wimbledon (Epsom), 653359, Cpl., k. in a., F. & F., 8/10/16, formerly 2818, East Surrey Regt.
Elder, Arthur, b. Islington, e. St. Pancras (Islington), 5830, Rfn., d. of w., F. & F., 16/9/16.
Elger, Marshall, e. Camberwell (Croydon), 651462, Rfn., k. in a., F. & F., 23/5/16.
Ellis, Arthur Henry, b. Greenwich, e. Camberwell (Deptford), 655790, Rfn., k. in a., F. & F., 25/10/17.
Ellis, Arthur Sydney, e. Camberwell (Norbury), 2689, Rfn., k. in a., F. & F., 25/5/15.
Ellis, Charles John Henry, b. Limehouse, e. Stratford (Mile End), 653591, Rfn., k. in a., F. & F., 7/6/17.
Ellwood, Edward Albert, b. Peckham, e. Camberwell (East Dulwich), 650170, Rfn., k. in a., F. & F., 23/5/16.
Elphick, Douglas, e. Camberwell (East Dulwich), 2540, Sgt., d. F. & F., 16/1/17.
Elsdon, George Edward, e. Woolwich (Plumstead), 652060, Rfn., k. in a., F. & F., 15/9/16.
Elsworth, William Arthur, b. Manor Park, e. Camberwell (Manor Park), 651357, Rfn., k. in a., F. & F., 7/6/17.
Embery, Alfred William, b. Peckham, e. Camberwell (Peckham), 650036, Rfn., k. in a., F. & F., 24/8/18.
Evers, Frederick, e. Camberwell (East Dulwich), 3509, Rfn., k. in a., F. & F., 15/9/16.
Fairburn, George, b. Lambeth, e. Whitehall (St. Lukes), 652285, Rfn., k. in a., E.E.F., 30/3/18.
Falconer, Henry Edward, b. Poplar, e. St. John's Hill (Tooting), 653902, Rfn., d. of w., F. & F., 5/9/18, formerly 3969, 23rd London Regt.
Faulkner, Edward Robert, b. Barnsbury, e. Camberwell (Brixton), 1977, Rfn., d. of w., F. & F., 27/9/16.
Favell, Arthur, b. Walworth, e. Camberwell (Bermondsey), 1081, Sgt. k. in a., F. & F., 18/5/16.
Fenn, Harold George, b. Valetta, Malta, e. Camberwell (East Dulwich), 1990, L/Cpl., d. of w., F. & F., 6/6/15.
Fenwick, John Robert, b. Bermondsey, e. Camberwell (Bermondsey), 655898, Rfn., k. in a., F. & F., 4/12/17.
Ferebee, Henry, b. Chelsea, e. W. London (Chelsea), 652899, Rfn., d., Home, 13/9/18.
Field, Cyrus, b. Birmingham, e. Birmingham (Birmingham), 652501, Sgt., k. in a., F. & F., 24/3/18, formerly 9511, Ox. and Bucks L.I.
Field, Oscar, b. Finsbury Park, e. Camberwell (Brixton), 1813, Rfn., k. in a., F. & F., 25/5/15.
Findlay, James Lewis, e. Camberwell (Rotherhithe), 650795, Rfn., k. in a., F. & F., 14/4/17.
Findlay, Walter Charles, b. Epsom, e. Wimbledon (Wimbledon), 653136, Sgt., k. in a., F. & F., 23/1/17, formerly 2296 East Surrey Regt.
Finn, Edgar, b. Chertsey, e. Camberwell (Walworth), 653873, Cpl., k. in a., F. & F., 25/3/18.
Fisher, Arthur, b. Battersea, e. Clapham Junction (Battersea), 653455, L/Cpl., d. of w., E.E.F., 15/12/17, formerly 1864, 23rd Battalion London Regt.

Fisher, John Herbert, e. Camberwell (Clapham), 2602, Rfn., d. of w., Home, 3/6/15.
Fitch, Frederick Arthur, e. Camberwell (Upper Norwood), 651277, Rfn., k. in a., F. & F., 23/5/16.
Fiveash, Arthur Sidney, e. Camberwell (Walworth), 3289, Rfn., k. in a., F. & F., 26/9/15.
Fleming, William Thomas, b. Plumstead, e. Stratford (London, E.), 655804, Rfn., k. in a., F. & F., 3/11/17.
Ford, William, b. Penryn, Cornwall, e. Bodmin (Penryn, Cornwall), 5738, Rfn., k. in a., F. & F., 15/9/16, formerly 24389, Duke of Cornwall's L.I.
Fountain, John William, b. Charterhouse, e. Camberwell (Camberwell), 1696, Rfn., k. in a., F. & F., 15/5/16.
Fowler, George, e. Endell Street, W.C. (Kentish Town), 8/678259, Rfn., k. in a., F. & F., 1/9/18, formerly 2642, 1/1st London Regt., posted 8th Battalion, East Surrey Regt.
Fox, Edward James, e. Fulham (Fulham), 652664, Rfn., k. in a., F. & F., 15/9/16.
Franks, Charles Alfred, e. Whitehall (Stockwell), 4796, Rfn., k. in a., F. & F., 15/9/16.
Freeman, William George, e. St. Pancras (London, N.), 652663, Rfn., d., F. & F., 1/11/17, formerly P/7, Rifle Brigade.
Frey, Leonard, e. Camberwell (Westminster), 3097, Rfn., k. in a., F. & F., 25/5/15.
Fricker, George, b. Dartford. e. Woolwich (Dartford), 652129, Rfn., k. in a., F. & F., 7/6/17.
Frost, Charles William, e. Camberwell (Camberwell), 651966, L/Cpl., k. in a., E.E.F., 31/3/18.
Frost, George Henry, e. Camberwell (West Norwood), 651830, Rfn., k. in a., E.E.F., 31/10/17.
Fulbrook, Ernest Croydon, b. St. Martins, e. Camberwell (Camberwell), 1358, Sgt., k. in a., F. & F., 13/9/16.
Fuller, Edwin John, e. Camberwell (East Dulwich), 650486, Cpl., d. of w., F. & F., 9/3/17.
Gadd, Arthur Edward Hale, b. St. Leonards, Sussex, e. Whitehall (Stoke Newington), 4995, Rfn., d., F. & F., 30/8/16.
Gaiger, Ernest Evelyn Keith, b. Chiswick, e. Wimbledon (Wimbledon), 653375, Rfn., k. in a., F. & F., 8/10/16, formerly 2485, E. Surrey Regt.
Galley, Victor Alphonso, b. Ridgwell, e. Camberwell (Peckham), 652955, Rfn., k. in a., F. & F., 20/5/17.
Gapper, James, e. Camberwell (East Dulwich), 4424, Rfn., k. in a., F. & F., 17/7/16.
Gaydon, Frederick John, b. Southwark, e. London (London, S.E.), 652796, Rfn., d. of w., F. & F., 27/8/18.
Gaydon, Henry Alfred, b. Clerkenwell, e. Whitehall (London, E.C.), 652831, Rfn., d., Home, 21/5/18.
Gentleman, Bert, b. Leyton, e. Leyton (Leyton), 7277, Rfn., k. in a., F. & F., 28/12/16, formerly 5651, 11th London Regt.
Geolot, Charles, b. Hampstead, e. Camberwell (Lambeth), 650347, Rfn., k. in a., E.E.F., 28/3/18.
George, Stephen Penry, e. Camberwell (Brixton), 2426, L/Cpl., k. in a., F. & F., 23/5/16.
Gibbons, Charles William, b. Waltham St. Lawrence, Berks, e. Oxford (Marlow), 5688, Rfn., d. of w., F. & F., 31/12/16, formerly 22689, Ox. and Bucks L.I.
Gibbons, Leslie William, e. Camberwell (Forest Hill), 650973, Rfn., k. in a., E.E.F., 14/2/18.

Gibson, Everett Charles, b. Harrietsham, Kent, e. Camberwell (Brixton Hill), 656006, Rfn., d., At Sea, 30/12/17.
Giddings, Wilfred Henry, e. Camberwell (Herne Hill), 2817, Rfn., k. in a., F. & F., 16/8/16.
Gilbert, Arthur, b. Lower Bigston, Cornwall, e. Wimbledon (Wandsworth), 653243, Cpl., k. in a., F. & F., 24/8/18, formerly 2723, E. Surrey Regt.
Giles, Herbert, b. Stanton, Fitzwarren, Wilts, e. Swindon (Highworth), 675060, Rfn., k. in a., F. & F., 4/9/18, formerly 2050, R.A.M.C., posted 12th Battalion, East Surrey Regt.
Gillard, William, e. Sun St., E.C. (Shepherds Bush), 678289, Rfn., k. in a., F. & F., 22/8/18, formerly 3974, 7th Battalion, London Regt., posted 8th Battalion, East Surrey Regt.
Godwin, John, b. St. Pancras, e. Whitehall (St. Pancras), 653490, Rfn., k. in a., F. & F., 30/4/17.
Godsland, George Baker, b. Lambeth, e. Camberwell (Brixton), 182, Sgt. k. in a., F. & F., 9/5/15.
Goldston, Lionel Emanuel, e. Camberwell (New Cross), 2130, Rfn., k. in a., F. & F., 30/5/15.
Goldsworth, Archibald, b. Battersea, e. Clapham Junction (Battersea), 653519, Rfn., d. of w., F. & F., 5/7/17, formerly 1284, 23rd London Regt.
Goode, James, b. Newent, Glos, e. Camberwell (Catford), 653103, Rfn., d. of w., F. & F., 4/12/17.
Goodman, Joseph William, b. Silvertown, e. Stratford (Silvertown), 652667, Rfn., k. in a., F. & F., 15/9/16.
Gosham, George Ernest, b. Deptford, e. Camberwell (New Cross), 652118, Rfn., d., F. & F., 6/2/18.
Gray, Albert, b. Newington Butts, e. Camberwell (Newington Butts), 3327, Rfn., k. in a., F. & F., 15/9/16.
Gray, William George, b. Windsor, e. Windsor (Windsor), 653297, Rfn., k. in a., F. & F., 7/6/17, formerly 3227, East Surrey Regt.
Green, Arthur Alfred, b. Peckham, e. Camberwell (Peckham), 650386, Rfn., d., E.E.F., 12/12/17.
Green, Frank, b. Maidstone, e. Whitehall (London, S.E.), 5840, Rfn., d. of w., Home, 7/10/16, formerly S/15149, Rifle Brigade.
Greenwood, Joseph Robert, b. London, e. Camberwell (Kennington), 650330, Rfn., d. of w., F. & F., 9/6/17.
Gregory, Percy Sidney, e. Camberwell (Norwood, S.E.), 650935, Cpl., k. in a., E.E.F., 30/3/18.
Grellier, Peter, e. Camberwell (Stockwell), 3760, Rfn., k. in a., F. & F., 15/12/15.
Griffiths, Robert Bodvan, b. Ireland, e. Camberwell (Catford), 1662, Rfn., k. in a., F. & F., 25/5/15.
Gurney, John Arthur, e. Camberwell (Cricklewood), 2946, Rfn., k. in a., F. & F., 25/5/15.
Hall, Ernest Albert, e. Camberwell (Camberwell), 651134, L/Cpl., k. in a., F. & F., 15/9/16.
Hall, Ernest Richard, b. Westminster, e. Camberwell (Kennington), 1232, Cpl., F. & F., 10/9/16.
Hall, Henry Herbert, b. Southwark, e. Camberwell (Camberwell), 652259, L/Cpl., k. in a., F. & F., 9/12/17.
Hall, Stanley, e. Camberwell (Camberwell), 3257, Rfn., k. in a., F. & F., 25/5/15.
Hannen, John Vernon, e. Camberwell (Camberwell), 651808, L/Cpl., k. in a., F. & F., 6/4/18.
Hambling, Henry John, b. Reading, e. Reading (Reading), 653184, Rfn., k. in a., F. & F., 9/7/17.

Hammond, Herbert Frederick, b. Lambeth, e. Camberwell (Deptford), 652967, Rfn., k. in a., F. & F., 7/6/17.
Hancock, George Henry, b. Camberwell, e. Camberwell, 1287, Rfn., k. in a., F. & F., 15/9/16.
Hand, Thomas, e. Camberwell, 3520, Rfn., k. in a., F. & F., 15/9/16.
Hannett, Charles Robert, b. Marylebone, e. Camden Town (Camden Town), 675010, Rfn., k. in a., F. & F., 24/8/18.
Hanrahan, Richard, b. Dulwich, e. Camberwell (East Dulwich), 650358, Rfn., k. in a., F. & F., 23/5/16.
Hanson, Frederick John, e. Camberwell (Nunhead), 651939, Rfn., k. in a., E.E.F., 28/3/18.
Hardiman, Arthur William, b. Peckham, e. Camberwell (Hither Green), 654437, Rfn., d. of w., F. & F., 4/11/17.
Hares, Harry Henry, b. Bristol, e. Bristol (Bristol), 652823, Rfn., d. of w., F. & F., 1/11/18.
Harland, Thomas William, b. Bourne End, Bucks, e. Camberwell (Fulham), 1422, Rfn., k. in a., F. & F., 25/5/15.
Harlock, Edward Arthur William, e. Camberwell (Lewisham), 2951, Cpl., k. in a., F. & F., 23/5/16.
Harlow, Charles Henry, b. Bermondsey, e. Camberwell (Peckham), 655984, Rfn., k. in a., F. & F., 5/4/18.
Harman, Jack Pennington, e. Camberwell (Clapham Common), 651358, Rfn., k. in a., F. & F., 23/5/16.
Harrington, Robert James, b. Bermondsey, e. Camberwell (Camberwell), 652322, Rfn., k. in a., F. & F., 7/6/17.
Harris, Melville George, b. Scorner, Cornwall, e. Bodmin (Liskeard), 5751, Rfn., k. in a., F. & F., 15/9/17.
Harris, William Edward, b. Paddington, e. Camberwell (Queen's Park, W.), 650328, Cpl., k. in a., F. & F., 1/9/18, M.M. and bar.
Harris, William, e. Camberwell (Peckham), 2688, Rfn., k. in a., F. & F., 11/5/15.
Hart, Edward Samuel, e. Clapham Junction (Wandsworth), 653886, Rfn., k. in a., F. & F., 3/12/17, formerly 4101, 23rd London Regt.
Hart, Stewart William, e. Camberwell (Brighton), 651005, L/Sgt., k. in a., F. & F., 23/5/16.
Harwood, Joseph, b. West Ham, e. Stratford (West Ham), 653939, Rfn., k. in a., F. & F., 23/3/18, formerly 210856, 25th T.F. Rifle Brigade, posted 1/23rd Bn. London Regt.
Haselden, Albert Charles George, e. Camberwell (Norbury), 650430, Sgt., k. in a., F. & F., 16/7/17.
Haslett, Arthur, e. Camberwell (Peckham), 653995, Rfn., d., At Sea, 30/12/17.
Hawkins, William Dudley, b. Stoke Newington, e. Whitehall (Holloway), 656007, Rfn., d., At Sea, 30/12/17.
Hawes, Cecil Alfred, e. Camberwell (Clapham Junction), 650561, Rfn., k. in a., Balkans, 9/4/17.
Hawken, William Henry, b. Kentish Town, e. St. Pancras (Camden Town), 652672, Rfn., d. of w., Home, 1/8/17, formerly P/896, 16th Rifle Brigade.
Hayman, Henry John, e. Camberwell (Denmark Hill), 2173, L/Cpl., k. in a., F. & F., 4/5/16.
Hayward, Alfred, e. Camberwell (Peckham), 653926, Rfn., d., At Sea, 30/12/17.
Haywood, John, b. London, e. Whitehall, (Finsbury, E.C.), 652673, Rfn., k. in a., F. & F., 15/9/16.
Hazell, James, b. Malton, Yorks, e. Camberwell (Loughborough Junction, S.E.), 651380, Cpl., k. in a., F. & F., 7/6/17.

Hazle, Joseph John, b. Camberwell, e. Camberwell (Camberwell), 650184, Rfn., k. in a., F. & F., 1/9/18.
Heal, Walter, b. Shoreditch, e. Bunhill Row (Forest Gate), 5962, Rfn., k. in a., F. & F., 17/7/16.
Healey, James Henry, e. Camberwell (Camberwell), 651918, Rfn., d. of w., E.E.F., 8/6/18.
Healy, James Joseph, e. Camberwell (Peckham), 2195, Rfn., k. in a., F. & F., 25/5/15.
Heavingham, Arthur Ernest, e. Camberwell (Goodmayes), 650823, Rfn., k. in a., E.E.F., 30/3/18.
Helmer, Frank Sidney, b. Deptford, e. Camberwell (Peckham), 678085, Rfn., k. in a., F. & F., 21/3/18, formerly 452730, 11th London Regt.
Hemens, Albert Clement, b. Peckham, e. Wimbledon (Tooting), 653300, Rfn., k. in a., F. & F., 10/3/17, formerly 2917, 5th Bn. East Surrey Regt.
Henderson, George Henry, b. Westminster, e. Whitehall (Southwark), 7099, Rfn., d. of w., F. & F., 28/12/16, formerly 6039, 23rd London Regt.
Hensman, Ernest Alfred, b. Bradwell, Bucks, e. Oxford (Stantonbury), 652541, k. in a., F. & F., 15/9/16, formerly 22542, Oxford and Bucks Light Infantry.
Herbert, Frederick James, b. Hanslope, Bucks, e. Bletchley (Wolverton), 652517, Rfn., k. in a., F. & F., 8/10/16, formerly 21834, Oxford and Bucks Light Infantry.
Heritage, Charles, b. Tooting, e. Camberwell (Tooting), 651383, Rfn., k. in a., F. & F., 7/6/17.
Heron, Joseph Solomon, b. Camberwell, e. Camberwell (New Cross Gate, S.E.), 1926, Rfn., k. in a., F. & F., 25/5/15.
Hesketh, Percy, b. Westminster, e. Whitehall (Westminster), 652128, Rfn., k. in a., F. & F., 23/3/18.
Hewlitt, Frederick John Lindsell, b. Camberwell, e. Camberwell (Denmark Hill), 654671, Rfn., d., At Sea, 30/12/17.
Higgins, Edward, b. Wimbledon, e. Wimbledon (Tooting), 653151, Rfn., k. in a., F. & F., 8/10/16.
Higgs, Percy, b. Camberwell, e. Camberwell (Byfleet), 2143, Rfn., k. in a., F. & F., 26/5/15.
Higham, Samuel Montaigne, b. Highgate, e. Camberwell (Tufnell Park), 650376, L/Cpl., d. of w., F. & F., 29/4/17.
Hilderbrando, Ernest, b. Sandwich, Kent, e. Woolwich (Woolwich), 4908, Rfn., d. of w., F. & F., 10/7/16.
Hill, George William, b. Camberwell, e. Camberwell (Camberwell), 1982, Rfn., k. in a., F. & F., 25/5/15.
Hill, Harry Calverley, e. Camberwell (Peckham), 651649, Rfn., k. in a., Balkans, 6/2/17.
Hill, Percy Gordon, b. Wembley, e. Camberwell (Peckham), 2076, L/Cpl., k. in a., F. & F., 8/10/16.
Hill, William James, e. Camberwell (Peckham), 3715, Bglr., k. in a., F. & F., 15/9/16.
Hills, Alfred, b. Sudbury, Suffolk, e. Woolwich (Romford), 5847, Rfn., k. in a., F. & F., 15/9/16.
Hines, Claude Horace, b. Windsor, e. Windsor (Windsor), 653301, Rfn., k. in a., F. & F., 8/10/16.
Hitchcock, Frederick George, b. Highgate, e. Clapham Junction (Earlsfield), 653921, d., At Sea, 30/12/17, formerly 3716, 23rd London Regt.
Hitchcock, William Lord, b. Camberwell, e. Camberwell (Peckham), 653399, Rfn., k. in a., F. & F., 2/9/18, posted 2/23rd London Regt.

Hobbs, George, b. Peckham, e. Camberwell (Kennington), 653462, Rfn., k. in a., F. & F., 16/8/18.
Hobbs, Sidney, e. Camberwell (East Dulwich), 3436, Rfn., d. of w., F. & F., 23/5/16.
Hockey, Albert James, e. Camberwell (Westminster), 2654, Rfn., k. in a., F. & F., 25/5/15.
Hogfress, Charlie Mears, b. Tooting, e. Wimbledon (Merton), 653245, Rfn., d., At Sea, 30/12/17, formerly 2639, 5th East Surrey Regt.
Hogger, Edward Albert, b. Camberwell, e. Camberwell (Camberwell), 650286, L/Cpl., d. of w., E.E.F., 29/3/18.
Holcombe, Alfred George, e. Camberwell (Vauxhall), 2910, Rfn., d. of w., F. & F., 26/9/15.
Holden, Horace Hadden, b. Bloomsbury, e. Kingston-on-Thames (Wimbledon), 652557, Sgt., k. in a., F. & F., 15/9/16, formerly 10456, Duke of Cornwall's Light Infantry.
Holl, Edward, b. Yorkoll, Herd, e. Wimbledon (Clapham), 653246, Rfn., k. in a., F. & F., 8/10/16.
Hollands, Harold Evan, e. Camberwell (Camberwell), 650850, Cpl., k. in a., E.E.F., 20/2/18.
Hollox, Frank Robert, b. Clacton-on-Sea, e. Camberwell (Deptford), 652310, Rfn., k. in a., F. & F., 8/10/16.
Holmes, George Harvey, e. Camberwell (Camberwell), 653729, Rfn., k. in a., F. & F., 24/8/18.
Holmes, Joseph, e. Camberwell (Camberwell), 4064, Rfn., d., Home, 27/11/15.
Holmes, Worthy George, e. Camberwell (Stratford), 651080, L/Sgt., d. of w., E.E.F., 23/3/18.
Holwill, Edward Charles, b. Bridport, Dorset, e. Camberwell (East Dulwich), 678025, Rfn., k. in a., F. & F., 21/3/18, formerly 452736, 11th London Regt.
Honey, William James, e. Camberwell (Paddington), 650724, Rfn., d., E.E.F., 18/12/17.
Horning, Charles Frederick, b. Grays, Essex, e. Woolwich (Dartford), 655816, Rfn., k. in a., F. & F., 31/3/18.
Horth, John Thomas, b. St. George's-in-the-East, Essex, e. Stratford (Canning Town), 678092, Rfn., d. of w., F. & F., 3/9/18, formerly 452518, 11th London Regt.
Houghton, John, b. Camden Town, e. Whitehall (Camden Town), 652705, Rfn., d., F. & F., 30/9/18.
Howard, alias Bergman, George James, b. Haggerston, e. Camberwell (Peckham), 1846, Rfn., k. in a., F. & F., 25/5/15.
Howard, Percy Albert, b. Hoxton, e. Whitehall (Islington), 653975, Rfn., k. in a., F. & F., 21/3/18, formerly 210733, 25th Rifle Brigade.
Howell, George Albert, b. Kennington, e. Camberwell (Nunhead), 651336, Rfn., k. in a., F. & F., 23/5/16.
Howman, Joseph Chad, b. Fakenham, Norfolk, e. Camberwell (Kentish Town), 650417, Sgt., k. in a., F. & F., 8/10/16.
Huckstepp, Henry, e. Camberwell (Walworth), 651485, Rfn., d. of w., F. & F., 27/9/17.
Hudson, William John, b. Homerton, e. Stratford (Homerton), 655987, Rfn., d., At Sea, 30/12/17.
Hudspith, Harold Baron, b. St. John's Wood, e. Camberwell (Streatham), 544, Sgt., k. in a., F. & F., 25/5/15.
Hughes, James, b. Bethnal Green, e. Whitehall (Bethnal Green), 652668, Rfn., d. of w., F. & F., 6/4/18.
Hull, Walter, e. Huntingdon (Godmanchester, Hunts), 678262, Rfn., d. of w., F. & F., 2/8/18, formerly 225501, 1st London Regt., posted 8th Bn. East Surrey Regt.

Hunt, Cecil George, b. Highgate, e. Woolwich (Dartford), 652194, Rfn., k. in a., F. & F., 8/10/16.
Hunt, Ernest, e. Camberwell (Kennington), 651858, Rfn., k. in a., Balkans, 6/2/17.
Hunt, Percy Henry Hart, b. Chelsea, e. Camberwell (Dulwich), 1426, L/Sgt., d. of w., F. & F., 28/5/15.
Hunter, Alfred George, b. Hoxton, e. London (Upper Holloway), 678093, Rfn., k. in a., F. & F., 1/9/18, formerly 452223, 11th London Regt.
Hurlin, Thomas William George, b. Hoxton, e. Whitehall (Hoxton), 5208, Rfn., k. in a., F. & F., 4/10/16.
Hurrell, Sidney Walter, e. Camberwell (Tulse Hill, S.W.), 2942, Rfn., d. of w., 2/6/16.
Hurst, Charles William, b. Norbiton, Surrey, e. Oxford (Slough), 652550, Rfn., k. in a., F. & F., 15/9/16, formerly 22671, Ox. and Bucks L.I.
Hutchings, Harry Edgar, e. Camberwell (Lewisham), 2706, Rfn., k. in a., F. & F., 11/6/15.
Hyde, Arthur Allison, e. Camberwell (South Hampstead), 2527, L/Cpl., d. of w., F. & F., 12/6/15.
Hughes, Idris, e. Camberwell (Aberdare), 3068, Rfn., d., F. & F., 22/3/15.
Inge, Henry Leonard, b. Walworth, e. Camberwell (Walworth), 651168, Rfn., k. in a., F. & F., 15/9/16.
Irons, Herbert Walter, b. Walworth, e. Camberwell (Herne Hill), 652937, Rfn., d., F. & F., 12/2/17.
Isaacs, Elias, b. Westminster, e. W. London (South Hampstead), 655918, Rfn., d. of w., E.E.F., 5/4/18.
Izzard, William Jesse, b. Reading, e. Wimbledon (Wimbledon Park), 653303, Rfn., k. in a., F. & F., 8/10/16, formerly 3214, 2/5th E. Surrey Regt.
Jacob, Edgar, e. Camberwell (Camberwell), 3476, Rfn., k. in a., F. & F., 4/5/16.
Jacobs, Phillip, b. Edmonton, Middx., e. Stratford (Mile End), 675025, Rfn., d. of w., F. & F., 29/8/18, formerly 613697, 19th London Regt.
Jacobs, Herbert, b. Clapham, e. Camberwell (Peckham), 653192, Rfn., k. in a., F. & F., 8/10/16, formerly 4406, E. Surrey Regt.
Jackson, Charles Frederick, b. Walthamstow, e. Stratford (Walthamstow), 653270, Rfn., k. in a., F. & F., 8/10/16, formerly 4328, E. Surrey Regt.
Jackson, Frederick, b. St. Lukes, London, e. Camberwell (Stamford Hill), 2778, Rfn., k. in a., F. & F., 5/5/16.
Jackson, Thomas Henry, e. Camberwell (Stamford Hill), 2769, L/Cpl., k. in a., F. & F., 23/5/16.
Jakeman, Henry, b. Camberwell, e. Camberwell (East Dulwich), 651180, Rfn., k. in a., F. & F., 15/9/16.
James, Ingley Cynon, b. Holloway, e. Whitehall (Holloway), 653798, Rfn., k. in a., F. & F., 8/10/16, formerly 5203, 19th London Regt.
James, Frederick Charles, b. Dorking, e. Bunhill Row (Walton-on-Hill), 652766, Rfn., d. of w., E.E.F., 8/4/18, formerly 3344, 5th London Regt.
James, Herbert Franklin, b. King's Cross, e. Camberwell (Maida Vale), 1861, Rfn., d. of w., F. & F., 9/5/15.
Jameson, Harold Riseborough, b. Norwood, e. Camberwell (Purley), 1931, Rfn., d. of w., F. & F., 4/4/15.
Janes, Arthur George, e. Camberwell (Westminster), 2257, Rfn., d. of w., F. & F., 29/5/15.

Janaway, Frederick Samuel, b. Camberwell, e. Wimbledon, 653305, Rfn., k. in a., F. & F., 8/10/16.
Jardine, Thomas Henry, b. Lambeth, e. Newark (Brixton), 1259, L/Cpl., k. in a., F. & F., 25/5/15.
Jeffs, Alfred, b. Penge, e. Camberwell (West Norwood), 3783, Cpl., k. in a., F. & F., 15/9/16.
Jenkins, Leonard, e. Camberwell (Battersea), 2655, Rfn., d. of w., Home, 15/8/15.
Jenner, Arthur James, b. Islington, e. Bodmin (Hoxton), 652615, Rfn., k. in a., F. & F., 8/10/16, formerly 24692, Duke of Conwall's L.I.
Jenner, Bertram Ewart, b. Newington, e. Camberwell (Clapham), 650643, Rfn., F. & F., 8/10/16.
Jennings, Percy Frederick, b. Camberwell, e. Camberwell (Lee Green), 652157, Rfn., k. in a., F. & F., 23/1/17.
Jesset, Joseph Richard, b. Cardiff, e. Camberwell (Peckham), 1708, Sgt., k. in a., F. & F., 23/5/16.
Johnson, Harold Reuben, e. Camberwell (St. George's, S.W.), 650862, Sgt., d. of w., F. & F., 21/10/18, att. 142 T.M.B., M.M.
Johnson, Henry Thomas, e. Camberwell (Camberwell), 650908, Cpl., k. in a., E.E.F., 28/3/18.
Johnson, Lionel, b. Mile End, e. Whitehall (Stepney), 653188, Rfn., d. of w., F. & F., 5/10/18, formerly 4244, 5th E. Surrey Regt., posted 1/23rd Bn. London Regt.
Jones, Alfred, e. Camberwell (Camberwell), 3864, Rfn., k. in a., F. & F., 15/9/16.
Jones, Albert George, b. Walworth, e. Camberwell, 653695, Rfn., k. in a., F. & F., 12/10/17, posted 8th Bn. E. Surrey Regt.
Jones, Charles Samuel, b. Deptford, e. Camberwell (Deptford), 678099, Rfn., k. in a., F. & F., 24/8/18, formerly 453010, 11th London Regt.
Jones, Frank, b. London, e. Bodmin (Bedminster), 5744, Rfn., k. in a., F. & F., 15/9/16, formerly 24413, D. of Corn. L.I.
Jones, Francis William, b. Marylebone, e. W. London (Marylebone), 653953, Rfn., k. in a., F. & F., 5/4/18, formerly 211281, Rifle Brigade, posted 1/23rd Bn. London Regt.
Jones, Henry John, e. Camberwell (Camberwell), 651719, Rfn., d. of w., F. & F., 3/5/17.
Jones, Joseph, b. W. Norwood, e. Camberwell (West Norwood), 651397, Rfn., k. in a., F. & F., 7/6/17.
Jones, John George, b. Camberwell, e. Camberwell (Camberwell), 2138. Sgt., k. in a., F. & F., 31/10/15.
Jones, Leslie Oscar, b. Lambeth, e. Camberwell (Bromley), 1659, L/Cpl., k. in a., F. & F., 5/5/16.
Jones, Robert, b. Lambeth, e. Whitehall (Bethnal Green), 5861, Rfn., d. of w., F. & F., 18/9/16, formerly S/15684, Rifle Brigade.
Jones, William, b. Aberystwyth, e. Camberwell (Battersea), 653423, Rfn., d. of w., F. & F., 18/5/17.
Jones, William Gray Frank, e. Camberwell (Peckham), 652367, Rfn., k. in a., F. & F., 8/10/16.
Jordan, John, b. Beereferers, Devon, e. Bodmin (Liskeard), 5736, Rfn., k. in a., F. & F., 15/9/16, formerly 24357, D. of Corn. L.I.
Joyce, Frank Stanley, b. Stoke Newington, e. Bunhill Row, E.C. (Stoke Newington), 652783, Rfn., k. in a., Balkans, 6/2/17.
Judd, Frederick, e. Ealing (Acton), 678293, Cpl., k. in a., F. & F., 24/8/18, formerly 4243, 8th Bn. Middlesex Regt.
Judge, Edward Stanley, e. Camberwell (Watford), 650953, L/Cpl., k. in a., F. & F., 20/7/17.

Juniper, John Henry, e. Harrow Road, W. (Notting Hill), 678274, Rfn., k. in a., F. & F., 25/10/18, formerly 4475, 3rd London Regt.
Jupp, Thomas Frederick, b. Tolworth, Surrey, e. Wimbledon (South Wimbledon), 653222, Rfn., k. in a., F. & F., 8/10/16, formerly 3031, 5th E. Surrey Regt.
Jury, Frederick Ernest, b. Camberwell, e. Camberwell (Camberwell), 651100, Rfn., k. in a., F. & F., 23/5/16.
Kemp, Albert Henry, e. Woolwich (Greenwich), 4822, Rfn., k. in a., F. & F., 15/9/16.
Kemp, Charles Albert, b Camberwell, e. Camberwell (Walworth), 650149, Sgt., d. of w., F. & F., 8/9/18. M.M.
Kemp, William Thomas Franklin, b. Marylebone, e. Camberwell (Camberwell), 650110, Bugler, k. in a., F. & F., 5/6/17.
Kent, Alfred, b. Camberwell, e. Camberwell (Peckham), 5093, Rfn., k. in a., F. & F., 15/9/16.
Kidd, William Leonard, b. Poplar, e. Stratford (Poplar), 652677, Rfn., k. in a., F. & F., 8/10/16, formerly S/15801, Rifle Brigade.
Killick, Alfred Andrew, b. Sutton, Surrey, e. Wimbledon (Sutton), 6939, Rfn., k. in a., F. & F., 8/10/16, formerly 3077, 5th E. Surrey Regt.
Kimish, Alfred, b. Southwark, e. Whitehall (Islington), 653573, Rfn., k. in a., F. & F., 10/6/17, formerly 5543, 11th London Regt.
King, George Edward, b. New Cross, e. Camberwell (New Cross), 650154, Rfn., k. in a., F. & F., 15/9/16.
King, William Henry, b. Poplar, e. Stratford (Plaistow), 6793, Rfn., d., F. & F., 6/11/16, formerly 4222, 2/5th E. Surrey Regt.
Kirby, John, b. Sheffield, e. Camberwell (Purley), 653896, Rfn., d. of w., F. & F., 5/12/17.
Kirch, William Dominique, b. Camberwell, e. Camberwell (Camberwell), 1603, Rfn., d. of w., F. & F., 23/1/16.
Kitteridge, Robert Francis Freeman, b. Hackney, e. Stratford (Stoke Newington), 652980, Rfn., k. in a., F. & F., 7/6/17.
Knight, Harry Herbert, b. Lambeth, e. Camberwell (Camberwell), 650199, Cpl., k. in a., E.E.F., 28/3/18.
Knight, Morlington Nicholls, b. Wandsworth, e. Camberwell (East Dulwich), 3569, Rfn., d. of w., F. & F., 24/5/16.
Kottman, Frederick, b. Stepney, e. Stratford (Stepney), 678232, Rfn., k. in a., F. & F., 1/9/18.
Lacey, William, e. Camberwell (Brockley), 3610, Rfn., k. in a., F. & F., 15/9/16.
Lack, Lovell William, b. Brixton, e. Camberwell (Brixton Hill), 1764, Rfn., k. in a., F. & F., 25/5/15.
Lambe, Thomas Herbert, e. Camberwell (Nunhead), 2818, Rfn., k. in a., F. & F., 25/5/15.
Lambert, Stanley Edward, b. Catford, e. Camberwell (Catford), 653987, Rfn., k. in a., F. & F., 22/8/18.
Lamude, Edward Alfred John, e. Camberwell (East Dulwich), 651907, Rfn., d. of w., E.E.F., 2/4/18.
Lamude, Henry Edward, b. Bow, e. Stratford (Bow), 654303, Rfn., k. in a., F. & F., 2/9/18. posted 2/23rd Bn. London Regt.
Lane, Henry Richard, e. Whitehall (St. Pancras), 653799, Rfn., d. of w., F. & F., 11/6/17, formerly 5245, 19th London Regt.
Lane, Thomas George, b. Bethnal Green, e. Whitehall (Bethnal Green), 656067, Rfn., k. in a., F. & F., 6/4/18.
Lane, William Albert, b. St. Pancras, e. Bodmin (Paddington), 5748, Rfn., k. in a., F. & F., 15/9/16, formerly 24446, Duke of Cornwall's Light Infantry.
Langley, Edward, b. London, e. West London (Notting Hill), 655894, Rfn., k. in a., F. & F., 23/3/18.

Langridge, Robert, b. Mitcham, e. Wimbledon (Mitcham), 653154, Rfn., k. in a., F. & F., 4/11/17, formerly 2423, 5th East Surrey Regt.
Langton, Alfred, b. Holloway, e. Whitehall (Finsbury Park), 7516, Rfn., d. of w., F. & F., 25/9/16, formerly 5371, 19th London Regt.
Larkin, Christopher John, e. London, N. (Hoxton), 678273, Rfn., k. in a., F. & F., 1/9/18, formerly 4441, 4th London Regt., posted 8th Bn. East Surrey Regt.
Lash, Robert Harold, e. Camberwell (Camberwell), 2329, L/Sgt., k. in a., F. & F., 11/9/16.
Last, Harry Arthur, e. Camberwell (Southfields), 2522, L/Sgt., d. of w., F. & F., 15/4/16.
Lawrence, Basil Bernard, b. Norwich, e. Stratford (Stratford), 652678, Rfn., k. in a., F. & F., 4/11/17.
Lawrence, Wilfred R., b. Remenham, Berks, e. Oxford (Henley), 652551, A/Sgt., k. in a., East Africa, 14/8/17, formerly 22685, Ox. and Bucks Light Infantry, posted 3/2nd King's African Rifles.
Layton, Eric William, e. Camberwell (East Dulwich), 650483, Rfn., k. in a., F. & F., 15/9/16.
Lazenby, David, b. Liverpool, e. Stratford (Stratford), 7511, Rfn., k. in a., F. & F., 15/9/16, formerly 5266, 19th London Regt.
Lea, Frederick, e. Northampton (Northampton), 652454, Rfn., k. in a., E.E.F., 31/10/17, formerly 2259, R.A.M.C.
Lecount, Alfred, b. Bow, e. Stratford (Walthamstow), 7539, Rfn., k. in a., F. & F., 15/9/16, formerly 5610, 19th London Regt.
Lee, Ernest Harold, b. Peckham, e. Camberwell (Peckham), 652366, Rfn., d. of w., F. & F., 3/9/18.
Lee, Ernest James, b. Islington, e. Whitehall (Islington), 7507, Rfn., k. in a., F. & F., 15/9/16, formerly 5216, 19th London Regt.
Lee, Thomas, b. Hampstead, e. Camberwell (Brixton), 3696, Rfn., k. in a., F. & F., 15/2/16.
Lee, William Alfred, b. Bethnal Green, e. Whitehall (Bethnal Green), 5864, Rfn., k. in a., F. & F., 15/9/16.
Lee, Wiliam David, e. Camberwell (Leytonstone), 651564, Rfn., k. in a., E.E.F., 28/3/18.
Lee, Walter George, e. Camberwell (Wood Green), 2132, L/Cpl., d., F. & F., 24/5/16.
Lees, William Thomas, b. Willesden, e. Bunhill Row (Harlesden), 652716, Rfn., k. in a., E.E.F., 31/10/17, formerly 3159, 5th London Regt.
Lemon, Frederick Reginald, b. Lambeth, e. Whitehall (Southwark), 653517, Rfn., d. of w., F. & F., 15/10/18, formerly R/18525, K.R. Rifle Corps.
Lench, Charles, e. Camberwell (Peckham), 651260, Rfn., k. in a., F. & F., 8/10/16.
Lenton, William Augustine, b. Tottenham, e. West London (Dalston), 675043, Rfn., d., F. & F., 20/10/18, formerly 616193, 19th London Regt.
Leonard, Thomas, e. Camberwell (Tooting), 651430, Bugler, d. of w., F. & F., 27/9/17.
Leuillette, Sidney, b. Edmonton, e. Bunhill Row (Billinghay, Lincs), 652745, Rfn., d. of w., Balkans, 17/5/17, formerly 3160, 5th London Regt.
Lever, Albion Herbert, b. E. Dulwich, e. Reigate (Purley), 653373, Rfn., d. of w., F. & F., 7/10/17, formerly 3843, 5th East Surrey Regt.
Lewis, Charles Henry, b. Bath, e. West London (Fulham), 7145, Rfn., k. in a., F. & F., 14/11/16, formerly 6424, 23rd London Regt., posted 1st Bn. Royal Irish Rifles.

Lewis, George Michael, e. Camberwell (Clerkenwell), 651865, Rfn., k. in a., Balkans, 4/5/17.
Lewis, Leon Edgar, b. Rotherhithe, e. Whitehall (Rotherhithe), 678106, Rfn., d. of w., F. & F., 4/4/18, formerly 468015, 2/11th London Regt.
Lewis, Norman Charles Thomas, b. Clapham, e. Camberwell (South Norwood), 650161, Rfn., d. of w., F. & F., 6/4/18.
Lidgley, John Charles, b. Hounslow, e. London (Hounslow), 652630, Rfn., k. in a., F. & F., 15/9/16, formerly 3/4647, Duke of Cornwall's Light Infantry.
Line, Percy Alfred, b. Camberwell, e. Camberwell (Peckham Rye), 3107, Sgt., k. in a., F. & F., 24/9/16.
Linsell, Francis Joseph, b. Bermondsey, e. Camberwell (Romford), 2752, Rfn., d., F. & F., 23/5/15.
Lister, Ernest, e. Chenies St., W. (King's Cross), 653844, Rfn., d. of w., F. & F., 7/6/17 ,formerly 3730, 12th London Regt.
Lister, William, b. York, e. Whitehall (London, N.W.), 678107, Rfn., k. in a., F. & F., 2/9/18, formerly 322771, 6th London Regt.
Lock, Frederick Charles, e. Camberwell (Camberwell), 652368, Rfn., k. in a., F. & F., 8/10/16.
Lock, Stanley Thomas, b. Walworth, e. Camberwell (Herne Hill), 163, Sgt., k. in a., F. & F., 25/5/15.
Long, Alfred Henry, b. Hoxton, e. Whitehall (Islington), 654485, Rfn., k. in a., F. & F., 17/11/17.
Longhurst, Ernest John, e. Camberwell (Bermondsey), 2666, Rfn., d. of w., F. & F., 11/5/15.
Longman, Cecil Theophilus, b. Hammersmith, e. Camberwell (Brockley), 652311, Rfn., d. of w., F. & F., 11/6/17.
Lovett, George Powell, b. Newton-Stewart, Co. Tyrone, e. West London (West Kensington), 6790, Rfn., d. of w., F. & F., 14/10/16.
Lovett, Walter, b. Battersea, e. Camden Town (Finsbury Park), 653797, Rfn., k. in a., F. & F., 22/8/18, formerly 4679, 19th London Regt., posted 1/23rd Bn. London Regt.
Lucken, William Joshua, b. Kennington, e. Camberwell (Camberwell), 652143, Rfn., d., F. & F., 11/8/18.
Lugar, Clifford, b. Kennington, e. Frinton-on-Sea (Peckham), 652884, Rfn., k. in a., E.E.F., 28/3/18.
Mace, James, b. Stepney, e. Whitehall (Shadwell), 653806, Rfn., k. in a., F. & F., 15/9/16, formerly 5378, 19th London Regt.
MacGregor, Frederick Alexander, e. Camberwell (Kennington), 3285, Rfn., d. of w., F. & F., 3/10/16.
Macro, Albert Walter, e. Camberwell (Camberwell), 3491, Rfn., d. of w., F. & F., 1/9/16.
Maddox, Charles Albert, b. Islington, e. Whitehall (Camberwell), 678111, Rfn., k. in a., F. & F., 11/2/18, formerly 452157, 11th London Regt.
Maggs, Thomas Frederick, e. Camberwell (Brixton), 652376, Rfn., k. in a., F. & F., 19/1/18.
Maggs, Walter William, e. Camberwell (Brixton), 652377, L/Cpl., d. of w., F. & F., 23/1/18.
Mann, Harold Arthur, e. Camberwell (Deptford), 651768, Rfn., k. in a., F. & F., 2/9/18.
Manson, Magnus Murray, b. Norwood, e. Camberwell (Finchley), 1999, Rfn., k. in a., F. & F., 10/4/15.
Mapley, James Joseph, e. Camberwell (Peckham), 651199, Rfn., k. in a., F. & F., 28/8/17.

Marks, George, b. Wandsworth, e. Clapham Junction (Clapham Junction), 653549, Rfn., k. in a., E.E.F., 14/2/18, formerly 1849, 23rd London Regt.
Marr, Charles Wesley, b. Lambeth, e. Camberwell (Brixton), 2288, Rfn., k. in a., F. & F., 11/9/16.
Marsden, Charles Frederick, b. Camden Town, e. Camberwell (Bermondsey), 4870, Rfn., k. in a., F. & F., 15/9/16.
Marson, William Arthur, b. Putney, e. Wimbledon (Putney), 6746, Rfn., k. in a., F. & F., 22/12/16, formerly 3769, 5th East Surrey Regt.
Martin, Frank, b. Walworth, e. Camberwell (Camberwell), 650164, L/Cpl., d. of w., F. & F., 22/1/17, D.C.M.
Martin, Theodore Leonard, e. Camberwell (Wandsworth), 2948, Rfn., d. of w., F. & F., 6/4/15.
Martin, William, b. Dartford, e. Woolwich (Dartford), 652309, Rfn., k. in a., F. & F., 30/4/17.
Mason, Harold Charles, b. Brixton, e. Camberwell (Camberwell), 653767, Rfn., d., F. & F., 31/12/17.
Mason, John, b. Greenwich, e. Woolwich (Greenwich), 7526, Rfn., k. in a., F. & F., 10/6/17, formerly 5448, 19th London Regt.
Massingham, William George, e. Camberwell (Brixton), 653734, Rfn., k. in a., F. & F., 9/12/17, formerly 820878, 31st London Regt.
Matcham, Ernest James, b. Lambeth, e. Camberwell (Tooting), 650782, Rfn., k. in a., Balkans, 4/5/17.
Mathers, Alfred James, b. Islington, e. Stratford (Walthamstow), 654333, Rfn., k. in a., F. & F., 22/8/18, posted 1/23rd Batt. London Regt.
Matthews, Frederick, b. Summerstown, Surrey, e. Wimbledon (Enfield), 653155, Rfn., k. in a., F. & F., 8/10/16.
Matthews, Thomas, b. Shoreditch, e. Whitehall (Hoxton), 655839, Rfn., d., At Sea, 30/12/17.
May, Herbert Charles, b. Lambeth, e. Camberwell (Brixton), 651230, Sgt., k. in a., F. & F., 2/9/18.
McCabe, James, b. Bethnal Green, e. Whitehall (Bethnal Green), 675049, Rfn., k. in a., F. & F., 9/6/18, formerly 616204, 19th London Regt.
McDonald, George, b. Stepney, e. Stratford (Mile End), 655795, Rfn., k. in a., F. & F., 1/9/18.
McMillan, Alfred, b. Hackney, e. Stratford (Hackney), 678120, Rfn., k. in a., F. & F., 1/9/18, formerly 324045, 6th London Regt.
McPherson, Mark, b. Marylebone, e. London (Clerkenwell), 652934, Rfn., k. in a., F. & F., 4/11/17.
Meaghan, James, b. Brixton, e. Camberwell (Long Acre, W.C.), 650323, Cpl., k. in a., F. & F., 8/10/16.
Mears, Arthur Alfred, b. Peckham, e. Camberwell (New Cross), 1988, Rfn., k. in a., F. & F., 11/5/15.
Mears, Frederick, e. Camberwell (New Cross), 2845, Rfn., d. of w., F. & F., 16/5/15.
Meek, Joseph George, b. Shoreditch, e. Whitehall (Kingsland), 652281, Rfn., k. in a., F. & F., 1/9/18.
Merkett, James, b. Clewer, Berks, e. Reading (Windsor), 653180, Rfn., d. of w., F. & F., 30/5/18, formerly 22390, Somerset L.I.
Merralls, Walter George, e. Camberwell (Ulcombe), 651081, L/Sgt., k. in a., E.E.F., 28/3/18.
Merryweather, Charles Samuel, b. Camberwell, e. Camberwell (Peckham), 650131, Rfn., k. in a., F. & F., 23/5/16.
Merryweather, George Thomas, e. Camberwell (Westminster), 2675, Rfn., k. in a., F. & F., 30/10/15.
Merryweather, William John Edward, b. Chelsea, e. Clapham Junction (Chelsea), 653775, Rfn., k. in a., F. & F., 10/12/17, formerly 2669, 23rd London Regt.

Middleton, Bertram, b. Rotherhithe, e. Woolwich (Woolwich), 652047, Rfn., d. of w., E.E.F., 4/5/18.
Miles, William Frederick, b. New Cross, e. Camberwell (Dulwich). 650418, Sgt., k. in a., F. & F., 7/6/17.
Mills, Henry, b. Peckham, e. Camberwell (Peckham), 653400, Sgt., k. in a., F. & F., 10/12/17.
Milne, George Sidney, b. Exning, Cambs, e. Hertford (Newmarket), 652576, Rfn., k. in a., F. & F., 15/9/16, formerly 21316, Duke of Cornwall L.I.
Milson, Henry Joseph, b. Deptford, e. Camberwell (Deptford), 651818, Rfn., k. in a., F. & F., 10/6/17.
Milverton, William Alfred, b. Holloway, e. Camberwell (Peckham), 653037, Rfn., k. in a., F. & F., 10/6/17.
Mitchell, Charles Leonard, b. Peckham, e. Camberwell (East Dulwich), 678155, Rfn., k. in a., F. & F., 25/8/18, formerly 452905, 11th London Regt.
Mobley, Alfred, b. Gt. Rollright, Oxon, e. Oxford (Chipping Norton), 5669, Rfn., k. in a., F. & F., 15/9/16, formerly 22481, Ox. and Bucks Light Infantry.
Moir, William Sutherland Dickie, b. Brechin, N.B., e. Hounslow (West Kensington), 656320, Dmr., k. in a., F. & F., 22/8/18, posted 1/23rd Batt. London Regt.
Mole, Arthur Francis, b. Rotherhithe, e. Camberwell (Camberwell), 5169, Rfn., k. in a., F. & F., 15/9/16.
Molony, Arthur, b. Clapton, e. Stratford (Clapton), 653336, Rfn., k. in a., F. & F., 7/6/17.
Moody, William, b. Knightsbridge, e. Camberwell (Camberwell), 650273, Rfn., k. in a., F. & F., 17/7/17.
Moore, Douglas Henry, b. Lambeth, e. Wimbledon (Wimbledon), 653227, Rfn., k. in a., F. & F., 8/10/16, formerly 2643, East Surrey Regt.
Moreton, Harold, e. Camberwell (West Dulwich), 650633, Rfn., k. in a., F. & F., 4/7/17.
Morgan, Bertie Thomas, e. Camberwell (Peckham), 2762, L/Cpl., d. of w., Home, 6/10/16.
Morley, Hubert Adrian, b. Bromley, e. Camberwell (Brixton Hill), 652258, Rfn., k. in a., F. & F., 15/9/16.
Morrison, Frederick John, b. Fulham, e. W. London (Fulham), 653277, Rfn., d. of w., F. & F., 4/7/17, formerly 4295, 5th East Surrey Regt.
Mortimore, Stanley Wilfred, b. Dulwich, e. Camberwell (Dulwich), 1157, Cpl., k. in a., F. & F., 15/9/16.
Mullins, Arthur Ernest, e. Camberwell (Holloway), 2715, Rfn., k.in a., F. & F., 29/5/15.
Munford, William, b. Bermondsey, e. Camberwell (Bermondsey), 653429, Rfn., k. in a., F. & F., 23/3/18.
Myers, Edwin Bertram, e. Camberwell (Kennington), 2259, Cpl., k. in a., F. & F., 15/9/16.
Myers, Judah, b. Mile End, e. Whitehall (Long Acre, W.), 652298, Sgt., k. in a., F. & F., 2/9/18.
Nagle, Sidney Ernest, b. Pembroke, S. Wales, e. Woolwich (Portsmouth), 652183, Rfn., k. in a., F. & F., 7/6/17.
Narraway, William Henry, b. Bedford, e. W. London (Fulham), 7177, Rfn., k. in a., F. & F., 15/11/16, formerly 6427, 23rd London Regt., posted 1st Batt. Royal Irish Rifles.
Nash, Frank Edward, b. Maidenhead, e. Reading (Maidenhead), 653256, Rfn., k. in a., F. & F., 10/12/17, formerly 4027, East Surrey Regt.
Neal, John Henry, b. Peckham, e. Camberwell (Peckham), 650263, A/L/Cpl., d. of w., F. & F., 26/3/18.

Neale, Arthur Henry Thomas, b. Kentish Town, e. Whitehall (Kentish Town), 653287, Rfn., k. in a., F. & F., 8/10/16, formerly 5709, 19th London Regt.
Neale, Stanley Arthur, e. Camberwell (Brixton), 651620, A/L/Cpl., k. in a., F. & F., 14/2/18.
Nelson, Leonard, b. Bermondsey, e. Camberwell (Newington), 650235, Rfn., k. in a., F. & F., 23/5/16.
Nesbitt, Robert, b. Shield Field, Northumberland, e. Winchester (Newcastle-on-Tyne), 5874, Rfn., k. in a., F. & F., 15/9/16, formerly S/15849, Rifle Brigade.
Nesling, Ernest, b. Bethnal Green, e. London (Bethnal Green), 652105, Rfn., d., F. & F., 24/12/17.
Neve, Charles Walter, b. Walworth, e. Camberwell (Camberwell), 4865, Rfn., d. of w., F. & F., 2/10/16.
Newman, George Alfred, b. Bermondsey, e. Camberwell (Bermondsey), 652981, Rfn., k. in a., F. & F., 10/6/17.
Newman, George Sidney, b. Dulwich, e. Wimbledon (Beckenham), 6767, Rfn., k. in a., F. & F., 8/10/16, formerly 2661, 5th East Surrey Regt.
Newman, Walter John, e. Camberwell (Champion Hill), 651119, Cpl., d. of w., F. & F., 3/9/18, M.M.
Newstead, Arthur, b. Norwich, e. Norwich (Norwich), 652474, Rfn., d. of w., Balkans, 8/2/17, formerly 1916, R.A.M.C.
Nichols, Edward, e. Camberwell (Bermondsey), 651381, Cpl., d. of w., F. & F., 15/10/18.
Nicholson, Arthur, b. Battersea, e. Stratford (Barking), 654325, Rfn., k. in a., F. & F., 21/3/18.
Nightingale, Charles, b. Marylebone, e. Whitehall (St. Pancras), 7508, Rfn., k. in a., F. & F., 15/9/16, formerly 5237, 19th London Regt.
Nightingale, Leonard Edward, b. Woolwich, e. Woolwich (Woolwich), 4845, Rfn., k. in a., F. & F., 14/9/16.
Norrie, Ernest Walter, e. Camberwell (Nunhead), 2819, Rfn., k. in a., F. & F., 25/5/15.
Nowne, Frederick, e. Camberwell (Peckham), 2153, Rfn., k. in a., F. & F., 25/5/15.
Nudd, William, b. Deptford, e. Stratford (Cubitt Town, E.), 5875, Rfn., k. in a., F. & F., 15/9/16, formerly 15775, Rifle Brigade.
Nunn, Alfred Thomas, b. Rotherhithe, e. Stratford (Rotherhithe), 5709, Rfn., d. of w., F. & F., 4/12/16, formerly 19625, Duke of Corn. L.I.
Nunn, Walter Frederick Francis. b. Charlton, Kent, e. Camberwell (Balham), 1951, Rfn., k. in a., F. & F., 30/3/16.
Nunney, Henry Edward, b. Lambeth, e. Lambeth (Brixton), 7079, Rfn., k. in a., F. & F., 15/11/16, formerly 6021, 23rd London Regt., attached 8th Batt. Royal Irish Rifles.
Oakley, Bertram Thomas, b. Woolwich, e. Woolwich (Old Charlton, Kent), 7522, Rfn., k. in a., F. & F., 15/9/16, formerly 5426, 19th London Regt.
Oliver, Thomas Charles, b. Mile End, e. London (Mile End), 653801, Rfn., k. in a., F. & F., 15/9/16, formerly 5274, 19th London Regt.
Onslow, Leonard James, e. Camberwell (Thames Ditton), 651746, L/Cpl., k. in a., E.E.F., 31/10/17.
Opher, George William, b. Lambeth, e. Camberwell (Clapham), 685, Sgt., k. in a., F. & F., 26/5/15.
Oram, John Marshall, b. Camberwell, e. Camberwell (Camberwell), 1809, Rfn., k. in a., F. & F., 23/1/16.
Orriss, Robert Edward, e. Camberwell (Balham), 3435, Rfn., k. in a., F. & F., 15/2/16.

Osborne, Frederick, b. Norwich, e. Whitehall (Southwark), 653814, Rfn., k. in a., F. & F., 23/3/18, formerly 5463, 19th London Regt.
O'Shea, Maurice, b. London, E., e. Camberwell (Camberwell), 651656, Rfn., k. in a., F. & F., 28/8/17.
Owen, Francis Victor, b. Lambeth, e. Camberwell (Brixton), 974, L/Cpl., d. of w., F. & F., 24/10/15.
Oxlade, Frank, e. Camberwell (Dulwich), 650606, Rfn., k. in a., F. & F., 23/5/16.
Pacey, Reginald, e. Ipswich (Northampton), 652487, Rfn., k. in a., E.E.F., 31/3/18, formerly 2597, R.A.M.C. .
Packer, Frederick, b. Peckham, e. Camberwell (East Dulwich), 652207, Rfn., d. of w., E.E.F., 10/12/17.
Page, Ernest Edward, b. Whetston, e. Camberwell (Clapham), 653413, Rfn., k. in a., F. & F., 7/6/17.
Page, Frederick John, b. Camberwell, e. Camberwell (Brixton), 678188, Rfn., k. in a., F. & F., 23/3/18, formerly 452688, 11th London Regt.
Page, George, e. Camberwell (Waltham Cross), 2734, Rfn., k. in a., F. & F., 22/4/15.
Page, Henry John, e. Camberwell (Hammersmith), 2709, Rfn., d. of w., F. & F., 22/5/16.
Page, William Charles, b. Oxford, e. Camberwell (East Dulwich), 3396, Rfn., k. in a., 15/9/16.
Palmer, Donald Maurice, b. Deptford, e. Kingston-on-Thames (New Cross), 656548, Rfn., k. in a., F. & F., 7/10/18.
Palmer, George, b. Hammersmith, e. W. London (Fulham), 5879, Rfn., d. of w., F. & F., 23/9/16, formerly 15799, Rifle Brigade.
Park, John, b. Camberwell, e. Camberwell (Peckham), 653072, Rfn., k. in a., F. & F., 24/11/17.
Parke, George Victor, b. Battersea, e. Camberwell (Brixton), 1942, Rfn., k. in a., F. & F., 15/9/16.
Parker, Charles, e. Camberwell (Nunhead), 651089, Rfn., k. in a., F. & F., 8/10/16.
Parker, Edward Ernest, b. Greenwich, e. Camberwell (Lee, S.E.), 653081, Rfn., d. of w., F. & F., 7/7/17.
Parkin, Frederick Harold, b. Camberwell, e. Camberwell (Peckham). 651211, Rfn., k. in a., F. & F., 23/3/18.
Parkinson, Bertram, e. Camberwell (Peckham), 651006, C.S.M., d. of w., F. & F., 29/3/18, D.C.M.
Parossien, Albert Frederick Ernest, b. Dulwich, e. Camberwell (Dulwich), 1923, Rfn., d. of w., F. & F., 23/9/15.
Parry, Albert, b. Pimlico, e. Whitehall (Fulham), 653096, Rfn., k. in a., F. & F., 15/10/18.
Parsons, Arthur, e. Camberwell (Forest Hill), 651259, Rfn., d. of w., F. & F., 1/12/17.
Parsons, Albert Edward, b. Lambeth, e. Camberwell (Brixton), 653411, Rfn., k. in a., F. & F., 7/6/17.
Partridge, William, b. Camberwell, e. Camberwell (East Dulwich), 651330, Rfn., k. in a., F. & F., 23/5/16.
Passey, George Leonard, b. Cuddlesdon, Oxon, e. Camberwell (Oxford), 650404, L/Cpl., k. in a., F. & F., 23/5/16.
Patmore, Zachariah, b. Lewisham, e. Camberwell (New Cross), 653350, Rfn., k. in a., F. & F., 23/1/17, formerly 4192, 5th E. Surrey Regt.
Payne, Harry Henry Frederick, b. Deptford, e. Camberwell (Deptford), 655934, Rfn., k. in a., F. & F., 7/12/17.
Pearce, Ernest, b. Forest Hill, e. Camberwell (Forest Hill), 678130, Rfn., d. of w., F. & F., 27/4/18, formerly 452635, 11th London Regt.
Pearce, George, e. Camberwell, 4226, Rfn., d., Home, 18/3/16.

Pearson, John Henry, b. Walthamstow, e. Stratford (Walthamstow), 5878, Rfn., k. in a., F. & F., 15/9/16, formerly S/15732, Rifle Brigade.
Peart, Stanley Brace, e. Camberwell (Peckham), 2436, Rfn., k. in a., F. & F., 25/5/15.
Pengelly, William Arthur, b. Camden Town, e. Whitehall (Camden Town), 653818, Rfn., k. in a., F. & F., 15/9/16, formerly 5497, 19th London Regt.
Pennell, Daniel Archibald, b. Mitcham, e. Wimbledon (Mitcham), 653228, Sgt., k. in a., F. & F., 24/8/18, formerly 13279, 5th E. Surrey Regt.
Perring, Ernest John, b. Torquay, Devon, e. Exeter (Torquay), 5745, Rfn., k. in a., F. & F., 15/9/16, formerly 24423, D. of Corn. L.I.
Perry, Arthur Alfred, b. Clerkenwell, e. Whitehall (Highbury), 4989, Rfn., k. in a., F. & F., 8/10/16.
Perry, George James, e. Camberwell (Battersea), 650427, Sgt., k. in a., F. & F., 10/6/17.
Peters, George, b. Camberwell, e. Camberwell (Nunhead), 651441, Cpl., k. in a., E.E.F., 9/12/17.
Petty, Albert, b. Islington, e. London (Kingsland, N.), 652559, Rfn., k. in a., F. & F., 8/10/16, formerly 12615, D. of Corn. L.I.
Phillips, Mark Aubrey, e. Clapham Junction (Balham), 653913, Rfn., k. in a., F. & F., 10/12/17, formerly 2194, 23rd London Regt.
Phillpott, Victor James, e. Kennington (Loughborough Junction), 652712, Rfn., d., E.E.F., 4/3/18, formerly 3102, 24th London Regt.
Pile, Ivor, e. Camberwell (Brixton), 651301, Rfn., k. in a., F. & F., 23/5/16.
Pitt, William, e. Camberwell (Camberwell), 651911, Rfn., k. in a., F. & F., 25/10/17.
Platt, Albert Thomas, b. Rotherhithe, e. Camberwell (Rotherhithe), 653022, Rfn., k. in a., F. & F., 7/6/17.
Playle, Wallace Edward George, e. Camberwell (Belvedere, Kent), 651466, Cpl., k. in a., F. & F., 8/10/16.
Plummer, Frank Aloysius, e. Camberwell (Peckham), 652004, Rfn., k. in a., F. & F., 11/2/18.
Pooley, Frederick Bowler, e. Camberwell (Camberwell), 2642, Rfn., k. in a., F. & F., 23/1/16.
Potter, William Frederick, b. King's Cross, e. Camberwell (Camberwell), 1255, Rfn., k. in a., F. & F., 25/5/15.
Powell, Alexander William, b. Camberwell, e. Holland Rd., Brixton (Camberwell), 1213, L/Cpl., k. in a., F. & F., 25/5/15.
Power, John Joseph, b. Paddington, e. W. London (Paddington), 653946, Rfn., k. in a., F. & F., 5/4/18, formerly 211124, Rifle Brigade.
Poynter, Frederick, b. Mortlake, e. Wimbledon (East Sheen), 6671, Rfn., k. in a., F. & F., 8/10/16, formerly 2496, 5th E. Surrey Regt.
Pratt, Robert Frederick Wilton, b. Islington, e. Bodmin (Leyton), 652627, Rfn., k. in a., F. & F., 12/6/17, formerly 24858, D. of Corn. L.I.
Prettejohn, Edgar Edwin, b. Bow, E., e. Stratford (Bow, E.), 652974, Rfn., k. in a., E.E.F., 9/3/18.
Pullen, William James, b. Bow, E., e. Mill Hill (Poplar), 656351, Rfn., d. of w., F. & F., 25/8/18.
Pursey, William, b. E. Croydon, e. Whitehall (Shaftesbury Avenue, W.C.), 655875, Rfn., d. of w., F. & F., 6/4/18.
Puttock, Robert, e. Camberwell (Camberwell), 651687, Rfn., k. in a., F. & F., 7/6/17.
Pye, William, b. St. Pancras, e. Camberwell (Walworth), 651382, Rfn., k. in a., F. & F., 12/6/17.

R

Pyke, Albert George, b. Bradfield, Berks, e. Reading (Newbury, Berks), 653666, Rfn., k. in a., F. & F., 8/10/16, formerly 4015, 5th E. Surrey Regt.
Radley, Christopher Septimus, e. Camberwell (South Norwood), 2842, Rfn., d., Home, 28/9/14.
Rae., Charles Edward, b. Watton, Norfolk, e. Norwich (Watton), 652453, Rfn., k. in a., E.E.F., 28/3/18, formerly 2698, R.A.M.C. (T.F.).
Ramsell, George, b. Swanley, Kent, e. Camberwell (Peckham), 651325, Rfn., k. in a., F. & F., 8/10/16.
Rand, Frederick Ernest, e. Camberwell (Kennington), 2242, Rfn., d., F. & F., 27/4/15.
Randall, Ernest Albert, b. Camberwell, e. Camberwell (Peckham), 653556, Rfn., k. in a., E.E.F., 28/3/18, formerly 6260, 23rd London Regt.
Randle, Donald, b. Wood Green, e. Camberwell (Wood Green), 2916, Rfn., k. in a., F. & F., 25/5/15.
Ransford, Charles, e. Farringdon St. (London Rd., S.E.), 651854, Rfn., d., At Sea, 30/12/17, formerly 3939, 3rd London Regt.
Rapley, Thomas, b. Lambeth, e. Camberwell (Kennington), 655999, Rfn., d., At Sea, 30/12/17.
Redman, John William, e. Camberwell (Brixton), 651566, Rfn., k. in a., F. & F., 15/9/16.
Redmond, Peter Thomas, b. West Ham, e. Canning Town (West Ham), 652025, Rfn., d. of w., F. & F., 3/5/17.
Reeves, Percy Frederick, b. Wimbledon, e. Wimbledon (Merton), 653315, L/Cpl., k. in a., F. & F., 23/3/18, formerly 3207, 5th East Surrey Regt.
Restall, William Henry, e. Camberwell (Brixton), 3102, Rfn., k. in a., F. & F., 21/12/16.
Richardson, Frederick Reginald, b. Camberwell, e. Camberwell (Camberwell), 1275, L/Cpl., k. in a., F. & F., 15/9/16.
Rickwood, Walter William, e. Paddington (Peckham), 653583, Rfn., k. in a., F. & F., 7/6/17, formerly 5703, 9th London Regt.
Riddington, David, b. Lambeth, e. Camberwell (Brixton), 652257, Rfn., k. in a., F. & F., 10/6/17.
Riley, Ernest Albert, b. Walthamstow, e. Stratford (Walthamstow), 654335, Rfn., k. in a., F. & F., 7/6/17.
Rissone, Eugene, b. Dublin, e. London (Soho), 653464, Rfn., k. in a., F. & F., 28/3/18, formerly 5231, 23rd London Regt.
Rist, Walter, b. Camberwell, e. Camberwell (Peckham), 651546, L/Sgt., k. in a., F. & F., 24/8/18.
Rivers, Harry, b. Camberwell, e. Camberwell (Walworth), 2023, Rfn., d., Home, 10/1/15.
Rixon, John William Henry, b. Hampstead, e. Hounslow (Kensal Rise), 656347, Rfn., d. of w., F. & F., 2/9/18.
Robbins, Richard Edward, b. Lambeth, e. Camberwell (East Dulwich), 1767, Rfn., k. in a., F. & F., 25/5/15.
Roberts, Arthur, b. Wimbledon, e. Wimbledon (Wimbledon), 653230, Rfn., k. in a., F. & F., 24/8/18, formerly 2644, 5th East Surrey Regt.
Roberts, Albert Henry, b. Peckham, e. Camberwell (Peckham), 1775, L/Cpl., k. in a., F. & F., 15/9/16.
Roberts, Dai, b. Kennington, e. Camberwell (Kennington), 651420, Rfn., k. in a., F. & F., 7/6/17.
Roberts, Henry Thomas, b. Holborn, e. Whitehall (Kennington), 653017, Rfn., d. of w., F. & F., 5/3/17.

Robinson, Alfred James, e. Camberwell (Tooting), 3978, Rfn., k. in a., F. & F., 23/12/15.
Robinson, Frederick George, b. Battersea, e. Camberwell (South Lambeth), 651486, Rfn., k. in a., F. & F., 4/12/17, attached 8th Bn. Royal Innis. Fusiliers.
Robinson, Richard, e. Camberwell (Peckham), 4517, Rfn., k. in a., F. & F., 2/8/16.
Robson, Thomas Henry, b. Battersea, e. Camberwell (Loughborough Junction), 1793, Rfn., k. in a., F. & F., 25/5/15.
Rodwell, Edwin William, e. Kennington (Wandsworth), 652714, Rfn., d., E.E.F., 14/11/17, formerly 3299, 24th London Regt.
Roe, Frederic Harrison, b. South Hackney, e. Camberwell (Forest Gate, E.), 2893, Rfn., k. in a., F. & F., 25/5/15.
Rogers, William Alban, b. Littlehaven, Pembrokeshire, e. Camberwell (Peckham), 653437, Rfn., k. in a., F. & F., 7/6/17.
Roofe, Albert Ernest, b. Kentish Town, e. London (London), 652555, Rfn., k. in a., F. & F., 15/9/16, formerly 10112, Duke of Cornwall's Light Infantry.
Roos, Ernest Frederick, b. London, e. Camberwell (Peckham), 650159, Rfn., d. of w., F. & F., 29/8/17.
Rosenberg, John, b. Whitechapel, e. Hackney (Hackney), 653584, Rfn., k. in a., F. & F., 13/3/17, formerly 5695, 9th London Regt.
Roser, Albert Henry Francis, e. Camberwell (East Dulwich), 651785, Rfn., k. in a., E.E.F., 30/3/18.
Rothon, Walter Frank Sydney, e. Camberwell (Camberwell), 651556, Rfn., k. in a., F. & F., 15/9/16.
Rudd, Frederick John, b. Middleton, Norfolk, e. Reigate (Wimbledon), 653778, Rfn., d. of w., F. & F., 4/5/17, formerly 3839, 5th East Surrey Regt.
Ruffey, Leonard, b. Camberwell, e. Camberwell (Brockley), 3624, Rfn., d. of w., F. & F., 28/9/16.
Ruggles, William James, b. Wimbledon, e. Wimbledon (Wimbledon), 653232, Rfn., d., F. & F., 29/7/18, formerly 3770, 5th East Surrey Regt.
Rumble, Eric Exton, b. Peckham, e. Camberwell (Peckham), 2052, Rfn., d. of w., Home, 8/10/16.
Rundle, Albert Thomas, b. Peckham, e. Camberwell (Peckham), 1330, Rfn., k. in a., F. & F., 23/5/16.
Rushton, Frederick, e. Oxford (Birmingham), 5649, Rfn., k. in a., F. & F., 14/9/16, formerly 22162, Oxford and Bucks Light Infantry.
Russell, Albert, b. Camberwell, e. Camberwell (Southwark), 651688, Rfn., d. of w., F. & F., 2/9/18.
Russell, Cecil Edward, e. Camberwell (Herne Hill), 3111, Rfn., k. in a., F. & F., 13/9/16.
Russell, Ernest Alfred, b. Stepney, e. Whitehall (Bethnal Green), 5007, Rfn., k. in a., F. & F., 15/9/16.
Russell, Edward Thomas, b. Bermondsey, e. Camberwell (Peckham), 650267, L/Cpl., k. in a., F. & F., 15/9/16.
Ryan, William, b. Bermondsey, e. Camberwell (Peckham), 4869, Rfn., k. in a., F. & F., 15/9/16.
Sabine, George, e. Camberwell (Kennington), 651418, Rfn., k. in a., F. & F., 23/3/18.
Sainsbury, Frederick Albert, b. Lewisham, e. Camberwell (Walworth), 650077, Sgt., k. in a., F. & F., 23/3/18, M.M.
Salmon, Ernest William, e. Sawbridgeworth, Herts (Sawbridgeworth), 4036, Rfn., k. in a., F. & F., 15/9/16.
Salmon, Ronald Stuart, e. Camberwell (High Wycombe), 3061, Rfn., k. in a., F. & F., 25/5/15.

Sams, Alfred Wheatley, b. Canning Town, e. London, W.C. (Upper Manor), 653846, Rfn., k. in a., F. & F., 31/8/17, formerly 355, 12th London Regt.
Sanders, Albert William, b. Camberwell, e. Camberwell (Peckham), 652352, Rfn., k. in a., F. & F., 7/6/17.
Sanders, Robert Howard, b. Poplar, e. Stratford (Poplar), 652688, Rfn., k. in a., F. & F., 30/11/17, formerly 15805, Rifle Brigade.
Saunders, Archibald Sidney Harry, b. Brighton, e. Stratford (Hackney), 653368, Rfn., d. of w., Home, 22/3/18, formerly 4340, 5th East Surrey Regt.
Saunders, Henry James, e. Camberwell (Camberwell), 651550, Rfn., k. in a., F. & F., 7/6/17.
Savager, Timothy Joseph, b. Bermondsey, e. Camberwell (Southwark), 653271, Rfn., k. in a., F. & F., 25/4/17, formerly 4419, 5th East Surrey Regt.
Sawyer, Charles Louis, b. Battersea, e. Camberwell (Battersea), 653491, Rfn., k. in a., F. & F., 4/11/17, formerly 5207, 23rd London Regt.
Sawyer, Frederick Charles, b. Battersea, e. Camberwell (Walworth), 1649, Rfn., k. in a., F. & F., 23/5/16.
Scarbrough, Edwin, b. Walworth, e. Camberwell (Walworth), 650723, Rfn., k. in a., F. & F., 15/9/16.
Scantlebury, Edwin Horsman, b. Liskeard, Cornwall, e. Bodmin (Liskeard), 652621, Rfn., k. in a., F. & F., 26/8/17, formerly 27430, Duke of Cornwall's Light Infantry.
Scarlett, Frederick James, b. Windsor, e. London (Mayfair, W.), 652126, Rfn., k. in a., F. & F., 15/9/16.
Schleider, George James William, b. East Dulwich, e. Camberwell (West Norwood), 1882, Rfn., k. in a., F. & F., 25/5/15.
Schofield, Herbert, e. Camberwell (Borough, S.E.), 651437, Rfn., k. in a., F. & F., 23/5/16.
Schwarz, George, b. Beckenham, e. London, E.C. (Beckenham), 678160, Rfn., k. in a., F. & F., 24/8/18, formerly 322062, 6th London Regt.
Scott, Arthur James, e. Camberwell (Kensal Rise), 3012, Rfn., k. in a., F. & F., 23/1/16.
Scott, Charles Edward, b. St. Luke's, e. London, N. (Islington), 678149, Rfn., d. of w., F. & F., 28/5/18, formerly 3438, 11th London Regt.
Scott, George Rupert, b. Kennington, e. Camberwell (East Dulwich), 652885, Rfn., k. in a., E.E.F., 28/3/18, posted 2/23rd Bn. London Regt.
Seach, Henry Arthur, e. Camberwell (Surbiton), 3046, Rfn., k. in a., F. & F., 25/5/15.
Searle, William Joseph, b. Battersea, e. Camberwell (Battersea), 653655, Rfn., d. of w., F. & F., 23/4/18.
Searles, Frederick, b. Lambeth, e. Camberwell (Camberwell), 3764, Rfn., k. in a., F. & F., 19/5/16.
Sharman, John Robert, e. Camberwell (Stratford), 650426, Sgt., k. in a., F. & F., 7/2/18.
Sharp, William James, b. Lambeth, e. Camberwell (Clapham), 656082, Rfn., k. in a., F. & F., 22/8/18, posted 1/23rd London Regt.
Sheaf, Gilbert Halford, e. Camberwell (Blackwell Stour, Worcs), 3045, L/Cpl., k. in a., F. & F., 15/9/16.
Shepherd, William James, b. Charlton, Oxon, e. Oxford (Charlton), 5652, Rfn., k. in a., F. & F., 15/9/16, formerly 22173, Ox. and Bucks L.I.
Shepphard, George John, e. W. London (Westbourne Park, W.), 653558, Rfn., k. in a., E.E.F., 7/11/17, formerly 6458, 23rd London Regt.
Sherlock, Archibald Henry, e. Camberwell (Hanwell), 2309, Rfn., k. in a., F. & F., 10/4/15.

Shinkfield, James Edward, e. Camberwell (Peckham), 650954, L/Cpl., d. of w., F. & F., 29/8/17.
Shinn, Leslie Victor, b. Brockley, e. Camberwell (Forest Hill), 654001, Rfn., d. of w., F. & F., 6/4/18.
Shipston, John Henry, b. Woolwich, e. Woolwich (Woolwich), 654728, Rfn., d. of w., F. & F., 14/10/18.
Shoobert, George Frederick, b. London, e. Wimbledon (South Norwood), 653160, Rfn., k. in a., F. & F., 26/8/17, formerly 3747, E. Surrey Regt.
Shorter, Alfred Arthur Richard, b. Newington, e. Camberwell (Camberwell), 1308, Rfn., d. of w., Home, 27/10/15.
Silvester, Frederick John, e. Camberwell (Herne Hill), 2834, L/Cpl., k. in a., F. & F., 23/5/16.
Silverman, Harry, e. Whitehall (Mile End), 652667, Rfn., k. in a., F. & F., 4/11/17.
Simmons, Charles, b. W. Norwood, e. Wimbledon (Norwood), 653333, Rfn., k. in a., F. & F., 8/10/16, formerly 3208, 5th E. Surrey Regt.
Simpson, Arthur Henry, b. Reading, e. Winchester (Basingstoke), 6910, Rfn., k. in a., F. & F., 8/10/16, formerly 4140, 5th E. Surrey Regt.
Simpson, Charles Edward, e. Camberwell (Canonbury), 3866, Rfn., k. in a., F. & F., 23/5/16.
Simpson, Hugh Fitzjohn, e. Camberwell (Kennington), 2119, Rfn., d., Home, 14/8/14.
Skudder, Ernest Thomas, e. Camberwell (Clapham), 651604, Rfn., d., F. & F., 18/2/18.
Slade, Ernest Thomas, b. Westbury-on-Tyne, e. Reading (Horfield, Bristol), 653267, Rfn., k. in a., F. & F., 8/10/16, formerly 4143, 5th E. Surrey Regt.
Slater, Henry Thomas, e. Camberwell, 651453, Bugler, d., F. & F., 6/5/17.
Slipper, William Daniel Thomas, b. Hammersmith, e. W. London (W. Kensington), 653346, Rfn., k. in a., F. & F., 8/10/16, formerly 4341, 5th E. Surrey Regt.
Small, Maurice John, e. Camberwell (Peckham), 2513, Rfn., k. in a., F. & F., 15/9/16, posted 1/23rd London Regt.
Smart, Herbert Arthur, b. Edmonton, e. Kingston-on-Thames (Camberwell), 656442, Rfn., k. in a., F. & F., 22/8/18.
Smith, Albert George, e. Camberwell (Brixton), 4636, Rfn., k. in a., F. & F., 17/7/16.
Smith, Alfred Charles, b. Winchester, e. Winchester (Eastleigh), 653183, Rfn., k. in a., F. & F., 8/10/16, formerly 4071, 5th E. Surrey Regt.
Smith, Alfred Donaldson, b. Camberwell, e. Camberwell (Nunhead), 652220, L/Cpl., k. in a., F. & F., 7/6/17.
Smith, Alfred George, b. Leatherhead, Surrey, e. Woolwich (Plumstead), 5183, Rfn., k. in a., F. & F., 15/9/16.
Smith, Arthur Alfred, e. Camberwell (Dulwich), 651181, Drmr., k. in a., F. & F., 26/9/17.
Smith, Arthur Charles, b. Lambeth, e. Lambeth (Lambeth), 653487, Rfn., k. in a., F. & F., 7/6/17, formerly 6203, 23rd London Regt.
Smith, Charles Henry, e. Camberwell (West Norwood), 3004, Cpl., d., F. & F., 24/10/16.
Smith, David John, e. Camberwell (Camberwell), 651574, Rfn., k. in a., F. & F., 4/11/17.
Smith, Dudley, b. Battersea, e. Whitehall (Knightsbridge), 655836, Rfn., k. in a., F. & F., 6/4/18.
Smith, Edward, e. Camberwell (Nunhead), 651235, Rfn., k. in a., F. & F., 23/5/16.

Smith, Edwin Ernest, b. Dulwich, e. Camberwell (Sydenham), 652918, Rfn., k. in a., F. & F., 7/6/17.
Smith, Emanuel, e. Camberwell (Peckham), 651916, Rfn., k. in a., Balkans, 9/4/17.
Smith, Frederick, e. Camberwell (Dulwich), 651741, Rfn., d., F. & F., 1/4/17.
Smith, George, b. Blackfriars, e. Camberwell (E. Dulwich), 653036, Rfn., k. in a., F. & F., 7/6/17.
Smith, Gerald Banks, e. Camberwell (Sutton, Isle of Ely), 2692, Rfn., d. of w., F. & F., 27/4/16.
Smith, Gilbert Edgar, b. Heyshott, Sussex, e. Camberwell (Peckham), 652155, Rfn., k. in a., F. & F., 10/12/17.
Smith, Harry Benson, b. Calgary, Canada, e. Bodmin (London, E.), 5783, Rfn., k. in a., F. & F., 15/9/16, formerly 24447, D. of Corn. L.I.
Smith, Henry, e. Camberwell (Walworth), 3941, Rfn., k. in a., F. & F., 15/9/16.
Smith, Henry Lott, b. Camberwell, e. Camberwell (Peckham), 651370, Rfn., d. of w., F. & F., 17/8/17.
Smith, Leonard Henwood, b. Camberwell, e. Stratford (East Ham), 655919, Rfn., d., At Sea, 30/12/17.
Smith, Martin John, b. Mile End, e. London (Mile End), 652689, Rfn., k. in a., F. & F., 7/6/17, formerly 15115, Rifle Brigade.
Smith, Ralph, b. Bath, e. Taunton, Somerset (Bath), 652821, L/Sgt., d. of w., F. & F., 3/9/18, formerly 21256, Som. L.I.
Smith, Sidney Edward, b. Lambeth, e. Camberwell (Stockwell), 654295, Rfn., d. of w., E.E.F., 29/3/18, formerly 8031, 23rd London Regt.
Smith, Thomas, b. Lambeth, e. Whitehall (Walworth), 5001, Rfn., k. in a., F. & F., 15/9/16.
Smith, William, e. Camberwell (Bermondsey), 3634, Rfn., k. in a., F. & F., 15/9/16.
Smith, William, b. Stony Stratford, Bucks, e. Reading (Newbury, Bucks), 653193, Rfn., k. in a., F. & F., 17/5/17, formerly 4142, E. Surrey Regt.
Smith, William George, e. Camberwell (Camberwell), 651231, Rfn., k. in a., F. & F., 4/12/17.
Smith, William James, e. Camberwell (East Dulwich), 651338, Rfn., d. of w., Home, 12/7/17.
Sneath, Charles Valentine, b. Camberwell, e. Camberwell (Herne Hill), 652245, Sgt., k. in a., F. & F., 24/8/18.
Snell, George, b. Wimbledon, e. Wimbledon (Wimbledon), 653356, L/Sgt., k. in a., F. & F., 5/10/18, formerly 2741, E. Surrey Regt.
Soper, Stanley, b. Brixton, e. Camberwell (Sutton, Surrey), 651219, Rfn., k. in a., F. & F., 23/5/16.
Spalding, Edwin Samuel, e. Camberwell (Dulwich), 650441, Rfn., k. in a., F. & F., 23/5/16.
Speer, Joseph Percy, b. Bermondsey, e. Camberwell (Bermondsey), 678155, Rfn., k. in a., F. & F., 24/8/18, formerly 495650, 13th London Regt.
Spencer, Edwin William, b. Camden Town, e. W. London (Fulham), 6882, Rfn., k. in a., F. & F., 8/10/16, formerly 4301, 4/5th E. Surrey Regt.
Spiller, Leonard Allen William, b. Tooting, e. Camberwell (Lee, S.E.), 652412, Rfn., d. of w., F. & F., 27/3/18.
Spite, Henry William, b. Holborn, e. Whitehall (Goswell Road, E.C.), 652932, Rfn., k. in a., F. & F., 1/9/18.
Stainer, Ernest Henry, b. Lambeth, e. Camberwell (Dulwich East), 1700, Rfn., k. in a., F. & F., 26/5/15.

Stahl, Ernest Frank, e. Camberwell (Kennington, S.E.), 2685, Rfn., k. in a., F. & F., 25/5/15.
Stanbridge, Frederick Joseph, b. St. Albans, e. Camberwell (Battersea), 653129, Rfn., k. in a., E.E.F., 28/3/18, posted 2/23rd London Regt.
Stanton, John Tate, e. Camberwell (Denmark Hill), 2517, Rfn., d. of w., F. & F., 17/6/17.
Stanton, William Baker, e. Camberwell (Denmark Hill), 2488, Rfn., k. in a., F. & F., 9/5/15.
Stapleton, Sidney Thomas, b. Walworth, e. Southwark (Kennington), 654524, Rfn., d. of w., F. & F., 7/6/17, attd. 14th Bn. Royal Irish Rifles.
Stenning, Richard, e. Camberwell (Merton), 2573, Rfn., d. of w., F. & F., 1/6/16.
Stevens, Ernest Harry, e. Camberwell (Sutton, Surrey), 2176, Rfn., k. in a., F. & F., 25/5/15.
Stimson, Henry Charles, b. King's Cross, e. Camberwell (Southgate), 7589, Rfn., d. of w., F. & F., 8/10/16.
Stinton, Kennedy, b. Hammersmith, e. Camberwell (Peckham), 652409, Rfn., k. in a., F. & F., 7/6/17.
Stringer, Ernest William, e. Camberwell (Camberwell), 3458, Rfn., k. in a., F. & F., 15/9/16.
Stringer, Philip Charles, b. Plaistow, e. Stratford (Plaistow), 6875, Rfn., k. in a., F. & F., 22/12/16, formerly 4227, 5th E. Surrey Regt.
Style, William John, e. Camberwell (Leyton), 651186, Rfn., k. in a., F. & F., 23/5/16.
Suter, George Frederick, b. Lee, S.E., e. Camberwell (Lewisham), 650014, Sgt., k. in a., F. & F., 23/5/16.
Swann, Ernest Arthur, b. Warmington, N'ton, e. W. London (St. John's Wood), 5885, Rfn., d. of w., F. & F., 16/9/16, formerly 15773, Rifle Brigade.
Symonds, Robert Arthur Richard, b. Norwich, e. Norwich (Norwich), 653742, Rfn., k. in a., F. & F., 23/8/18, formerly 2595, R.A.M.C. (T.F.).
Symons, Edgar Chubb, b. Paignton, Devon, e. London (Aldermanbury), 678158, Rfn., k. in a., F. & F., 23/3/18, formerly 452814, 11th London Regt.
Talbott, Harry Chrichly, b. Whitechapel, e. Camberwell (Southwark), 650229, Rfn., d., E.E.F., 6/12/17.
Tamblyn, William Henry, e. Bodmin (Liskeard), 652594, Rfn., d. of w., F. & F., 19/9/17, formerly 24359, Duke of Cornwall's Light Infantry.
Tancock, Arthur Charles, b. Sheldon, Devon, e. London (Exeter), 5690, L/Cpl., k. in a., F. & F., 16/9/16, formerly C/7808, Duke of Cornwall's Light Infantry.
Tapp, Walter Ernest, e. Whitehall (Bermondsey), 678163, Rfn., d. of w., F. & F., 10/4/18, formerly 452236, 11th London Regt.
Tarr, William Robert, e. Camberwell (Peckham), 650659, L/Sgt., d. of w., F. & F., 1/9/18, M.M.
Taylor, Sydney Clarence, b. Kennington, e. Camberwell (Camberwell), 651192, Rfn., k. in a., F. & F., 7/1/18.
Taylor, Ernest Edward, b. Bromley, E., e. Stratford (Bromley), 652973, Rfn., k. in a., F. & F., 10/6/17.
Taylor, Frederick, b. Peckham, e. Bunhill Row, E.C. (South Norwood), 652791, L/Cpl., d., E.E.F., 30/11/17, formerly 3203, 5th London Regt.
Taylor, Harry Sylvester, b. Camberwell, e. Camberwell (Camberwell), 651160, Rfn., k. in a., F. & F., 8/10/16.
Taylor, Percy, b. Camberwell, e. Camberwell (Camberwell), 651331, Rfn., d. of w., E.E.F., 3/4/18.

Taylor, Walter William, b. Lambeth, e. Camberwell (Herne Hill), 604, Rfn., k. in a., F. & F., 25/5/15.
Telling, William James, b. Hatcham, e. Camberwell (West Norwood), 1629, Rfn., k. in a., F. & F., 23/5/16.
Teverson, George Frederick, b. Buckhurst Hill, Essex, e. London, W.C. (Buckhurst Hill, Essex), 5953, Rfn., k. in a., F. & F., 2/8/16, formerly 3132, 5th London Regt.
Thatcher, Reginald, b. Chelsea, e. Camberwell (Clapham Junction), 5266, Rfn., k. in a., F. & F., 11/9/16.
Thomas, Reginald, b. Cardiff, e. Wimbledon (Tooting), 653165, Rfn., k. in a., F. & F., 8/10/16, formerly 3753, 5th East Surrey Regt.
Thomas, Victor George, b. Camberwell, e. Camberwell (Peckham), 651332, Rfn., k. in a., F. & F., 23/5/16.
Thompson, Albert, e. Camberwell (East Dulwich), 3383, Rfn., k. in a., F. & F., 15/9/16.
Thompson, Charles Henry, b. New Cross, S.E., e. Camberwell (Catford), 652189, Rfn., k. in a., F. & F., 30/4/17.
Thorne, Frederick, e. Camberwell (Vauxhall), 2360, Cpl., d. of w., F. & F., 11/10/16.
Throsby, Alfred, b. Heeley, Yorks, e. Camberwell (Peckham Rye), 1173, Rfn., k. in a., F. & F., 23/5/16.
Thwaits, Leonard Henry, e. Camberwell (Denmark Hill), 3899, L/Cpl., k. in a., F. & F., 18/5/16.
Tibblé, Albert, b. Fulham, e. West London (Fulham Rd., Chelsea), 678169, Rfn., k. in a., F. & F., 24/3/18, formerly 452208, 11th Bn. London Regt.
Tippetts, Clifford, b. Carrington, e. Taunton (Stawell, Somerset), 6097, Rfn., k. in a., F. & F., 20/7/16, formerly 20412, Somerset Light Infantry.
Tipping, Alfred Edward, b. Wimbledon, e. Wimbledon (South Wimbledon), 6755, Rfn., k. in a., F. & F., 4/11/16, formerly 3280, 5th East Surrey Regt.
Tondeur, Frank, e. Camberwell (Kennington), 651616, Rfn., k. in a., F. & F., 15/9/16.
Townrow, Gerald Claud, b. Huntingdon, e. Huntingdon (Huntingdon), 652842, Rfn., k. in a., E.E.F., 14/2/18, formerly 507, Hunt's Cyclist Bn.
Trueman, Frederick Joseph, b. Herne Bay, e. Whitehall (Camberwell), 652692, Rfn., k. in a., F. & F., 18/10/16, formerly S/14681, Rifle Brigade.
Trythall, Leonard James, b. Longsdon, Staffs, e. Camberwell (Herne Hill), 652152, Rfn., k. in a., F. & F., 15/9/16.
Tue, Joseph Stanley, b. St. Pancras, e. Bodmin (Holloway), 652612, L/Cpl., k. in a., F. & F., 7/6/17, formerly 24686, Duke of Cornwall's Light Infantry.
Tudor, Thomas, b. Bristol, e. West London (Kilburn), 654735, Rfn., k. in a., F. & F., 24/8/18.
Turk, Rupert Charles, b. Dalston, e. London, E.C. (Wanstead), 652751, L/Cpl., d., E.E.F., 3/5/18, formerly 3133, 5th London Regt.
Turley, Alfred, b. Lambeth, e. Camberwell (Brixton), 652244, Rfn., d. of w., F. & F., 9/6/17.
Turner, Alfred Thomas, e. Camberwell (Brixton), 3064, Rfn., k. in a., F. & F., 25/5/15.
Turner, James Thomas, b. Brixton, e. Camberwell (Herne Hill), 650225, Rfn., k. in a., F. & F., 21/3/18.
Turtill, James John, e. Bodmin (Upton Park), 652626, Rfn., d. of w., F. & F., 3/9/18, formerly 24854, Duke of Cornwall's Light Infantry.

Underwood, William Arthur, e. Camberwell (Buckingham Palace), 2523, Sgt., k. in a., F. & F., 18/5/16.
Vail, Alexander, b. Bethnal Green, e. Whitehall (Hackney), 5899, Rfn., k. in a., F. & F., 15/9/16, formerly S/15689, Rifle Brigade.
Vallis, William George, b. Streatham, e. Wimbledon (Tooting), 653320, Rfn., k. in a., F. & F., 8/10/16, formerly 3160, 5th East Surrey Regt.
Varney, Bernard Fielding, b. Sheffield, e. Wimbledon (Merton Park), 653374, Rfn., k. in a., F. & F., 31/8/17, formerly 2419, 5th East Surrey Regt.
Vassay, George Alfred, e. Camberwell (Brixton), 651724, Rfn., k. in a., F. & F., 8/10/16.
Vaughan, David Victor, b. Canning Town, e. Stratford (Walthamstow), 655855, Rfn., d., F. & F., 22/4/18.
Vaughan, Harold, e. Camberwell (Dulwich, S.E.), 2177, Rfn., k. in a., F. & F., 25/5/15.
Vickery, Frank, b. Kennington, e. Camberwell (Kennington), 1590, Rfn., k. in a., F. & F., 25/5/15.
Vigor, Frank, e. Camberwell (Battersea), 3249, Rfn., k. in a., F. & F., 28/12/15.
Vincent, Arthur, b. North Heigham, Norwich, e. Norwich (Norwich), 5575, Rfn., k. in a., F. & F., 13/9/16, formerly 2384, R.A.M.C. (T.F.).
Vincent, Frederick, b. Lambeth, e. Camberwell (Lambeth), 654451, Rfn., d., At Sea, 30/12/17.
Vint, Gerald, b. Croydon, e. Camberwell (E. Dulwich), 651355, Rfn., k. in a., F. & F., 23/5/16.
Wade, Alfred George, b. Battersea, e. Wimbledon (New Wandsworth), 653321, Rfn., k. in a., F. & F., 8/10/16, formerly 3691, 5th East Surrey Regt.
Wager, Joseph, b. Stratford, e. Stratford (Plaistow), 652095, Rfn., d. of w., F. & F., 31/8/17.
Walker, Alfred Stamford, b. Walsall, e. Bodmin (Walsall), 5760, Rfn., k. in a., F. & F., 15/9/16, formerly 24683, Duke of Cornwall's Light Infantry.
Walker, Frank, b. Islington, e. Whitehall (Hoxton), 652127, Rfn., k. in a., F. & F., 7/6/17.
Walker, Frederick Samuel, b. Bow, e. Camberwell (Brixton), 653747, Rfn., k. in a., F. & F., 4/11/17.
Waller, Henry Guy, b. Wandsworth, e. Clapham Junction (Battersea), 653876, L/Cpl., k. in a., F. & F., 22/8/18, formerly 3487, 23rd London Regt., posted 1/23rd Bn., London Regt.
Wallinger, Leonard John, b. Bermondsey, e. Rotherhithe (Bermondsey), 653395, Rfn., k. in a., F. & F., 7/6/17.
Wallis, Charles William Wynn, b. Camberwell, e. Camberwell (Crystal Palace), 1192, L/Cpl., k. in a., F. & F., 25/5/15.
Walsh, Henry Herbert, b. Hackney, e. West London (Paddington), 653059, Rfn., k. in a., F. & F., 26/8/17.
Walsh, Thomas, e. Camberwell (Camberwell), 651565, Rfn., k. in a., F. & F., 23/5/16.
Walters, Leonard George William, b. Camberwell, e. Camberwell (Camberwell), 651673, Rfn., d., At Sea, 30/12/17.
Warburton, Arthur John Egerton, e. Camberwell (East Molesey, Surrey), 650435, Rfn., d., Balkans, 14/8/17.
Ward, George Frederick, b. New Cross, e. Camberwell (Nunhead), 1466, Rfn., k. in a., F. & F., 23/1/16.
Ward, Henry Sidney, e. Camberwell (Peckham), 651176, Rfn., k. in a., F. & F., 23/5/16.

Ward, James Gorbell, e. Camberwell (Kennington), 3299, Rfn., k. in a., F. & F., 15/9/16.
Wareham, William Samuel, b. Walthamstow, e. Camberwell (Peckham), 651182, Rfn., d. of w., F. & F., 13/12/17.
Warrier, Harry, b. Dulwich, e. Camberwell (East Dulwich), 3647, Rfn., d. of w., F. & F., 20/6/16.
Waterhouse, Arnold Middleton, b. Watford, e. Camberwell (Watford), 1801, Rfn., k. in a., F. & F., 25/5/15.
Watkins, Benjamin Eugine, e. Camberwell (Peckham), 2374, Rfn., d., Home, 1/4/16, attached 107, Prov. Bn.
Watkins, Richard, e. Kennington (Blackfriars), 675067, L/Cpl., k. in a., F. & F., 30/9/18, formerly 3956, 2/24th London Regt., posted 12th Bn. East Surrey Regt.
Watson, Archibald William, e. Camberwell (West Norwood), 651328, Rfn., k. in a., F. & F., 23/5/16.
Watson, William, b. Newington, e. Camberwell (Camberwell), 655979, Rfn., d., At Sea, 30/12/17.
Watts, Eric, e. Camberwell (Peckham), 4562, Rfn., k. in a., F. & F., 16/8/16.
Watts, Joseph Charles, b. Bermondsey, e. Camberwell (Bermondsey), 650148, Cpl., k. in a., F. & F., 15/9/16.
Weaver, Henry Leonard, b. Cheltenham, Glos, e. Bristol (Cheltenham), 6154, Rfn., k. in a., F. & F., 20/7/16, formerly 2655, Gloucester Regt.
Webb, Arthur, b. Stockwell, e. Camberwell (Stockwell), 651657, Sgt., d. of w., F. & F., 31/8/18.
Webb, Edgar Dorrington, b. Streatham, e. Camberwell (Streatham), 1161, Sgt., k. in a., F. & F., 5/5/15.
Webb, Reginald Howard, b. Lambeth, e. Camberwell (Brixton), 4213, Rfn., k. in a., F. & F., 15/9/16.
Weedon, George, b. Plumstead, e. Woolwich (Plumstead), 6906, Rfn., k. in a., F. & F., 8/10/16, formerly 4231, 5th East Surrey Regt.
Weight, Walter Anthony, b. Plumstead, e. Woolwich (Woolwich), 652185, Rfn., d. of w., F. & F., 7/7/17.
Welch, James, e. Camberwell (Camberwell), 651139, Rfn., d. of w., E.E.F., 8/4/18, posted 2/23rd London Regt.
Welford, James, b. Holloway, e. Camberwell (Finsbury Park), 678181, Rfn., k. in a., F. & F., 23/3/18, formerly 321599, 6th London Regt.
Wells, Reuben Edgar, b. Poplar, e. Bodmin (Poplar), 5767, Rfn., k. in a., F. & F., 15/9/16, formerly 24695, Duke of Corn. L.I.
Wenham, George Joseph, b. Mitcham, e. Wimbledon (Tooting), 653382, Rfn., k. in a., F. & F., 4/12/17, formerly 2682, 5th East Surrey Regt.
West, George William, b. Bradwell, Bucks, e. Oxford (Wolverton), 5675, Rfn., d. of w., F. & F., 18/9/16, formerly 22541, Ox. and Bucks L.I.
West, Reginald Albert, e. Camberwell (Upper Tooting), 2532, Rfn., k. in a., F. & F., 23/1/16.
Westcott, Edgar Charles, b. Fulham, e. Clapham Junction (Battersea), 653155, Rfn., d. of w., F. & F., 4/7/17.
Wheeler, William Thomas Alfred, b. Bermondsey, e. Camberwell (East Dulwich), 653349, Rfn., k. in a., F. & F., 18/2/17, formerly 4426, 5th East Surrey Regt.
Wheeler, Walter Reginald, b. Ilfield, Sussex, e. Camberwell (Peckham), 652887, Rfn., d. of w., Balkans, 31/3/17.
Whenman, George Henry, b. Holborn, e. London (Gray's Inn Road), 7591, Rfn., k. in a., F. & F., 15/9/16, formerly 1922, 12th London Regt.

Whiffen, George, b. Lewisham, e. Camberwell (Catford), 5117, Rfn., d., Home, 12/5/16.
White, Edgar, e. Camberwell (Brixton), 651693, Rfn., k. in a., F. & F., 23/5/16.
White, Frederick, e. Camberwell (Camberwell), 3461, Rfn., k. in a., F. & F., 23/5/16.
White, Frederick Gordon, b. Nunhead, e. London, E.C. (Shepherds Bush Green), 652723, Rfn., d., E.E.F., 10/4/18, formerly 3111, 5th London Regt.
White, Walter Percy, e. Camberwell (Farnham, Surrey), 650891, Sgt., k. in a., E.E.F., 9/12/17.
Whitehall, Frederick, b. Northampton, e. Camberwell (Peckham), 651300, Rfn., k. in a., F. & F., 12/6/17.
Whitehead, Frederick Joseph, b. Stoke Newington, e. Camberwell (Camberwell), 652016, Rfn., d. of w., F. & F., 1/9/18.
Whitehead, Philip, b. Stepney, e. Camberwell (East Dulwich), 1373, Sgt., d. of w., F. & F., 13/9/16. M.M.
Whiting, Frank, b. Lambeth, e. Camberwell (Clapham), 653888, Rfn., d., Home, 10/6/18.
Whittick, Albert Edward, b. Mayfair, e. Whitehall (London, W.), 652696, L/Cpl., k. in a., F. & F., 2/9/18, formerly 15860, Rifle Brigade.
Wickham, Arthur, e. Camberwell (South Lambeth), 4369, Rfn., k. in a., F. & F., 11/9/16.
Wiggs, Alfred Harold, b. Peckham, e. Camberwell (Peckham), 650178, Rfn., k. in a., E.E.F., 31/3/18.
Wild, Herbert William, e. Camberwell (Brixton), 4023, Rfn., k. in a., F. & F., 15/9/16.
Willcocks, Kenneth Harding, b. Wimbledon, e. Wimbledon (Raynes Park), 653223, Rfn., k. in a., F. & F., 8/10/16, formerly 3231, 5th East Surrey Regt.
Willett, Mark, b. Loughton, Bucks, e. Oxford (Bletchley), 5673, Rfn., k. in a., F. & F., 15/9/16, formerly 22539, Oxford and Bucks L.I.
Williams, George Arthur, e. Camberwell (Herne Hill), 4084, L/Sgt., d., Home, 23/10/15.
Williams, Harry George, b. Tooting, Camberwell (Tooting), 1821, Rfn., k. in a., F. & F., 30/9/15.
Willicombe, William, e. Camberwell (Camberwell), 650567, A/Sgt., d. of w., E.E.F., 13/12/17.
Willis, Thomas Walter, b. London, e. Camberwell (Brixton), 652346, Rfn., k. in a., F. & F., 8/10/16.
Willoughby, Frank, b. Eastbourne, e. W. London (Fulham), 653343, Rfn., k. in a., F. & F., 7/6/17, formerly 4305, 5th East Surrey Regt.
Wilson, Ernest Sidney Leonard, b. Camberwell, e. Camberwell (Camberwell), 1321, Rfn., k. in a., F. & F., 23/5/16.
Wilson, George William, b. Hackney, e. Stratford (Canning Town), 653340, Rfn., k. in a., F. & F., 8/10/16, formerly 4233, 5th East Surrey Regt.
Wilson, Horace Septimus, e. Stratford (Ilford), 6273, Rfn., d., Home, 8/12/16.
Wingate, Alfred Thomas, b. Farningham, Kent, e. Woolwich (Farningham), 5358, Rfn., k. in a., F. & F., 21/12/16.
Winterflood, Edward, b. Southwark, e. Camberwell (Bermondsey), 654546, Rfn., k. in a., F. & F., 7/6/17.
Wolferstan, Charles Edward, e. Camberwell (Brixton), 650632, A/Sgt., k. in a., E.E.F., 30/3/18.
Wood, Charles Henry, b. Camberwell, e. Camberwell (Clapham Junction), 1530, Rfn., k. in a., F. & F., 11/5/15.

Wood, Harry, e. Camberwell (Kennington), 4146, L/Cpl., k. in a., F. & F., 15/9/16.
Wood, William, b. Brighton, e. Oxford (Stantonbury), 652545, Rfn., k. in a., F. & F., 15/9/16, formerly 22564, Ox. and Bucks L.I.
Wood, William George, b. Southwark, e. Kingston-on-Thames (Bermondsey), 656470, Rfn., k. in a., F. & F., 22/8/18.
Woodall, Samuel James, e. Camberwell (Long Lane, S.E.), 651512, Rfn., k. in a., F. & F., 15/9/16.
Woodward, Arthur George, b. Greenwich, e. Woolwich (Plumstead), 656024, Rfn., d., At Sea, 30/12/17.
Woolley, John Lewis, e. Camberwell (Peckham), 650848, L/Cpl., k. in a., F. & F., 7/6/17.
Worker, John, b. Castlethorp, Bucks, e. Oxford (Castlethorp), 652538, Rfn., k. in a., F. & F., 7/6/17, formerly 22538, Ox. and Bucks L.I.
Worsford, Harry Berry, b. Capel, Surrey, e. London, E.C. (Dorking), 652722, Rfn., d. of w., Balkans, 27/2/17, formerly 3178, 5th London Regt.
Worthy, Frank, e. Whitehall (Brixton), 4785, Rfn., k. in a., F. & F., 15/9/16.
Wright, Allan Hawksworth, b. Brixton, e. Kingston-on-Thames (Brixton), 656472, Rfn., k. in a., F. & F., 13/8/18, posted 1/23rd London Regt.
Wright, Bertie James, b. Walworth, e. Camberwell (Camberwell), 1575, Rfn., k. in a., F. & F., 15/9/16.
Wright, Frank, e. Camberwell (Brixton), 650560, Rfn., d. of w., F. & F., 7/4/18.
Wright, George Charles, b. Camberwell (Bermondsey), 652356, Rfn., k. in a., F. & F., 23/3/18, posted 1/23rd Batt. London Regt.
Wright, William Edward, b. Walworth, e. Camberwell (Camberwell), 651955, Rfn., d. of w., E.E.F., 22/2/18.
Wrigley, William, e. Camberwell (West Norwood), 3771, Rfn., k. in a., F. & F., 23/5/16.
Wyllie, John Malcom, e. Camberwell (Camberwell), 650447, Rfn., k. in a., F. & F., 23/5/16.
Young, Harry, b. Dulwich, e. Camberwell (East Dulwich), 654313, Rfn., d. of w., F. & F., 6/4/18.
Young, Henry Major, b. Marylebone, e. Camberwell (Cricklewood), 1857, Rfn., k. in a., F. & F., 22/4/15.
Young, Samuel George, b. Redcliffe, Bristol, e. Reading (Bedminster), 653261, Rfn., d., F. & F., 23/10/18, formerly 4165, 23rd London Regt.
Zoller, Herbert Sidney, b. Battersea, e. Camberwell (Catford), 653079, Rfn., k. in a., F. & F., 7/6/17.

INDEX.

Abbéville, 59, 64, 162
Abeele, 77
Ablain, 57
Abri Centrale, 150, 151, 159
Abri Mouton, 150, 159
Abu Irgeig, 195
Aeroplane bombing, 67, 76, 109, 178, 183
Agniers, 153
Ain Karim, 206
Alban, Col., 96
Albert, 60, 64, 91, 109
Aldis, R. H., 194
Alexander, F., 88
Alexandria, 186
Alison, J. M., 95, 106
Allouagne, 40, 44, 47
Amberkeny, 185
Americans, 92, 108, 109
Amiens, 106, 107
Amiens-Albert Road, 59, 108
Amman, 212, 214, 215, 216
Ancre, River, 105
Andrews, J. S., 198
Annequin, 27
Anneux, 83, 86
Antrobus, 2nd Lieut., 174, 183, 184, 185
Anzin, 148, 149, 159
Appleford, J. D., 104
Arabs, 211
Ardzan, Plain and Lake, 184
Armistice, 122
Army, 1st, 20, 28, 47, 56, 78
 ,, 2nd, 72
 ,, 4th, 109
Arneke, 70
Arques, 20
Arras, 49, 79, 147
Aryian Dump, 159
Auchel, 119, 123, 124
Aujah, Wadi, 211, 213
Austin, L/Cpl., 208
Australians, 106, 110, 113, 215
Austria-Hungary, 121
Autheuse, 161
Aveluy, 90, 105, 106

Avenue Anzin, 149, 152, 155
Avenue des Mortices, 150

Bailey, Brig.-Gen., 92, 95
Baisieux, 91, 109
Bajus, 58
Ballah, 187
Balua, 209, 217, 218
Balua, Lake, 218
Band, 14, 18, 59, 90, 91, 117, 139, 143
Bapaume, 81
Barastre, 82, 95
Barker, F. C., 98, 104
Barly, 58, 59
Barricade, The, 150
Barter, Sir C., 31
Bartle-Edwards, Capt., 144
Bates Ravine, 180, 183
Battle surplus, 57, 82
Battle Wood, 73, 74
Bavinchove, 78
Bazentin, 104
Beaulencourt, 104
Beaumetz, 82
Beauval, 106
Bécourt, 60
Bedfordshire Regt., 26
Bedouin, 195, 201
Beersheba, 186, 189, 190, 192, 194, 195, 212
Beetroot Factory, 94
Beit Iksa, 205
Beit Sorik, 209
Beles Mountains, 172, 173
Belgian Château, 66
Bergerie Wood, 171
Bermeuil, 162
Bertincourt, 90, 95
Bethany, 218
Béthune, 20, 23, 28, 32, 49
Beuvry, 27, 32
Beverley Brook, 133
Bidot, 150
Birdwood, Sir W. R., 111, 119, 121
Bireh Ridge, 209

Bir el Saba, 190
Bishops Stortford, 141
Black Watch, 20
Blogg, E. B., Major, 46
Bloy, A. W. F., 144, 173
Boeschepe, 65
Bois de Tailles, 109
Bombers, 46, 51, 52
Bonnal, 150, 151, 152, 153, 154, 158, 159, 160
Bottom's Buildings, 165
Bouchavesnes, 115, 117
Boughton, Lieut., 115
Boulogne, 64
Bourlon, 83, 85, 86, 89
Bouzincourt, 105
Boxing Day, 16, 17, 46
Box respirator, 66, 174
Boyau Charles, 150, 151, 152
Braintree, 16
Bray-Albert Road, 110, 111
Breastworks, 21, 22
Brett, Capt., 99
Brigade, 6th London, 31
,, 99th, 101
,, 140th, 60, 61, 62, 71, 73, 92, 101, 107, 109, 110, 115
,, 141st, 42, 43, 61, 73, 102, 114, 115, 117
,, 142nd, 23, 28, 43, 60, 65, 73, 98, 99, 115, 116, 122
,, 154th, 149
,, 179th, 145, 207
,, 181st, 196, 200
Brockwell Park, 132
Browett, A. A., 89
Browne-Wilkinson, A. R., Rev., 92, 113
Brunswick Park, 126
Buffs, 10th, 195, 209
Buigny l'Abbaye, 59
Bulfin, General, 144, 187, 202
Bulgaria, 170
Bull, Lieut., 137, 144, 178
Bully-Grenay, 56
Burley, W., 111
Burlington Arcade, 24
Bury, T. O., Major, 95
Bus, 101
Buss, J., 111
Butte de Warlencourt, 63

Cabaret Rouge, 49, 53
Cabaret Rouge Cemetery, 53
Cadre, 125
Café Vincent, 70

Calais, 64
Camberwell, 13, 131, 132, 134, 139
Camberwell, Mayor of, 126
Cambrai, 81
Cameroons, 80
Cameron Highlanders, 20
Canadians, 28, 160
Capes, Lieut., 178, 183, 184, 197, 209
Carcassone Camp, 162
Carency, 49, 50, 57
Carlisle Kloof, 182
Carnoy, 113
Carr, W. P., 197, 198, 209
Casualties, 22, 26, 31, 46, 55, 62, 75, 76, 87, 100, 114, 116, 117, 118, 150, 154, 160, 171, 184, 208, 209, 210, 216
Casualties, first in 1st Bn., 22
,, first in 2nd Bn., 150
Casualty Clearing Stn., 42nd, 157
Caterpillar, The, 73
Catlow, Lieut., 117
Caussica, 184
Cavalry, 46, 110, 198
Cavillon, 107
Chambers, P. E. H., 81, 98, 104, 110, 113, 115, 120
Chapeau de Gendarme, 180
Chaplains, 68, 76, 92, 93
Charman, A. E., 97, 102, 111, 115, 116
Château, Belgian, 66
,, Red, 95
,, Segard, 78
,, White, 76
Chelers, 153
Chemin Creux, 150
Cheshire Regt., 209
Chinese attack, 42
Chinese labour camp, 79
Chivers, J. A. T., 89
Choques, 119
Christmas Day, 16, 45, 67, 68, 90, 91, 125, 134, 166
Church of the Holy Sepulchre, 211
Church Parades, 18, 62, 63, 68, 76, 123
Civil Service Rifles, 83
Clacton, 143
Clark, Sgt.-Dmr., 104
Cléry, 117
Coggeshall, 139, 142, 143, 144
Coldicott, Col., 133, 143

Coldicott, H. R. S., 144, 173, 185, 196, 197, 208
Coldstream Guards, 20
Comines Canal, 72, 75
Commanding Officer, changes of, 25, 40, 71, 77, 122, 143, 161, 184, 191
Connaught Camp, 65
Contalmaison, 105
Corby, S. F., 14, 41
Cornet, 122
Corons, 56, 57
Corps, 1st, 20
Corsica, 163
Couillet Valley, 97
Cowper, Lieut., 178, 189, 212
Cow's Ear, 46
Coyle, J. P., 173, 218
Craters, 52, 54
Crowe, Capt., 133, 134
Crowther, C., 86
Cuinchy, 27

DaCosta, Brig.-Gen., 160
Dawes, G., 80, 82, 88, 101, 103, 114, 117, 119, 120, 122
Dawes, Miss, 90
Dead Cow Farm, 24
Decorations, 31, 52, 55, 85, 86, 90, 99, 107, 110, 111, 173, 186, 208, 213
Deir el Belah, 188
Demobilization, 124, 125
Denyer, Rfn., 172
Dessart Wood, 98
Dew, F. G., 60, 86
Dickebusch, 71, 76
Di-phosgene, 86, 181
Distinguished Conduct Medal, 31, 111
Distinguished Service Order, 99
Divion, 55
Division, 1st, 23, 60
,, 2nd, 79, 80, 81, 85, 90, 96, 101
,, 2nd London, 15, 20
,, 5th, 79
,, 7th, 121
,, 12th, 110, 112
,, 15th, 39
,, 16th, 47
,, 18th, 109
,, 23rd, 72, 94
,, 31st, 81
,, 35th, 159
,, 37th, 105
,, 41st, 72

Division, 47th, 20, 23, 41, 42, 56, 58, 63, 72, 85, 101
,, 51st, 149
,, 53rd, 205, 208
,, 56th, 85
,, 58th, 110, 112, 118
,, 60th, 131
,, 63rd (Naval), 56, 101
,, 74th, 115, 117, 195, 196, 197, 198
Doiran, Lake, 174
Double Hill, 181, 182, 183
Dover Tepé, 170, 171, 176
Dubs, Capt., 101
Dulwich College, 133
Dulwich, Ladies of, 134
Durham, G. A., 144
Durrant, A. W., 88
Dyer, —, 85

East Surrey Regt., 63, 77
Eastwood, C. S., 80
Eaucourt, l'Abbaye, 63, 104
Ecoivres, 146
Ecurie defences, 159
Edgware, 14
Edmunds, J., 86, 89
Education schemes, 124
Eecke, 78
Egypt, 186, 217
El Ballah, 187
El Balua, 209, 217, 218
El Ghoranye, 213, 218
El Haud, 214
El Kelt, Wadi, 211
Elkington, H. G., 81
El Kustine, 202
English, Capt., 144
En Nab, 204
Enquin-les-Mines, 47
Entwistle, F., 216
Epsom, 135
Equancourt, 95, 98, 99, 100
Erquinghem, 120
Er Ram, 209, 210
Erskine, Brig.-Gen., 83, 84
Escault, River, 122
Esdud, 202
Es Salt, 214
Essars, 25
Estrée Couché, 53, 55, 57
Etrée Wamin, 161
Etricourt, 91, 92
Etrun, 154, 160
Evans, D. L., 209
Everest, Capt., 173

Felixstowe, 126
Ferdan, 187
Ferfay, 125
Ferrières, 107, 108
Festubert, 23
Fielding, Lieut.-Col., 115, 117
Fins, 99, 100
Flesquières, 82, 94, 95
Fletcher, B., 144, 161
Fletcher, Sgt., 134
Flodden Road, 13, 134
Follies, 69, 80, 113, 125
Fontaine, 84
Foreign service men, 139
Fort Glatz, 43
Fosse No. 10, 56
Fouquières, 43
Fournier Camp, 162
Four Winds Farm, 101
Fowles, J., 17
Francis, Rfn., 197
French, Lord, 20, 144
Fricourt, 56
Fricourt, Bois de, 60

Galavanci, 184
Gallipoli, 56
Gamli, 190
Garner, R. L., 111, 113
Gas, 38, 41, 48, 49, 66, 76, 84, 96, 106, 109, 115, 117, 174, 181
Gavrelle, 79, 80
Gaza, 189, 195, 198, 199, 201
Génie Trench, 149
German Hospice, 208
Ghoranye, 213, 218
Ghuzze, Wadi, 188, 190
Gibson, Lieut.-Col., 184, 186, 190, 191
Gilkes, H. M., 79, 81, 87, 89, 90, 115
Gillard, E. F., 208
Givenchy, 21, 28, 31, 32, 33, 55
Glen Smol, 180
Globostica, 174
Godewaersvelde, 65
Godley, Gen., 113, 118
Gorell, Lord, 62
Gorhambury Park, 15, 17
Gorre, 26
Gorringe, Sir G. F., 79, 106
Gouzeaucourt, 83
Graincourt, 83, 87
Gramatma, 168
Grand Collecteur, 150, 151, 152, 159
Greenwood, Lieut.-Col., 82

Grimwood, Lieut.-Col., 102, 103, 104
Guards, The, 42, 81, 83
Gueudecourt, 104
Gully Ridge, 184
Gun Hollow, 182

Haillicourt, 40
Hairpin, The, 46
Haking, Sir R., 121
Halifax Camp, 65, 68, 69, 70
Hampshire Regt., 77
Hannay, T. N., 95, 105, 107, 116, 117
Happy Valley (Ancre), 110
Happy Valley (Macedonia), 180
Hardy, Rfn., 104, 115
Hareira, 201
Harpenden, 18
Harry, Capt., 133, 139
Hatter's Croft, 140
Haud, 214
Haut-Avesnes, 147, 153
Hâvre, 19, 126, 146
Havrincourt Wood, 94
Hazebrouck, 64
Heilly, 117, 119
Heksken, 76
Heliograph, 212
Helmet, Smoke, 48
Helmet, Steel, 50, 154
Hereford Regt., 191
Heslop, C. W. B., 21, 77, 78, 79, 80
Hessey, Sgt., 157
Highland Ridge, 94, 97, 98
High Wood, 60, 61, 63, 72
Hill 60, Ypres, 66, 68, 73
,, 70, Loos, 43
,, 1070, Palestine, 192, 193, 212
,, 2635, Palestine, 209
,, 2735, Palestine, 209
Hill's House, Sir John Gray, 208, 217
Hindenburg Line, 82, 83, 84, 87
Hirsova, 178, 179
Hisea, 188
Hitch, J. O. B., 105, 106, 114
Hockerill, 141, 142
Hockey, A. L., 208
Hohenzollern Redoubt, 45
Hollands, J., 80
Hollebeke, 72
Holmes, W. G., 214
Holy Communion in the line, 68
Holy Sepulchre, Church of, 211
Home Service Men, 139, 141

Honnerain, 122
Horlick, Capt., 144
Hoskyns-Abrahall, Lieut., 172
Houchin, 39, 46
Huish, E. C., 92, 116
Huj, 198, 199
Hull, L. H. R., 29
Hulluch, 43, 44
Hunt, L. H., 87
Hunter, R. J., 110, 111
Huntspill, S.S., 185
Hutchence, A., 21, 29, 30, 72, 77, 106, 107, 108, 113, 114
Hutted Camps, 65, 66
Hyde Park, 13
Hythe, 136

Indian Village, 24, 25, 27
Influenza, 107
Ireland, 77, 145
Ismailia, 186, 187
Italians, 167, 172, 174
Italy, Rumours of move to, 81, 119, 120
Ivernia, S.S., 162, 164, 166
Izel-les-Hameau, 161
Izzet Bey, 206

Jackman, I. H., 84, 115, 116
Jackson, F. C., 14, 76, 77
Jameson, H. R., 22
Japanese Rifles, 134, 136, 138
Jeba, 209, 210
Jedirah, 209
Jemmameh, 199, 200
Jennings, Reg.-Sgt.-Major, 140, 144, 161, 173, 176, 186
Jericho, 211, 213
Jerusalem, 131, 195, 198, 202, 205, 206, 207, 209, 211, 213, 217
Jervois, J. A., 191, 197, 201, 207, 213
Jones' Post, 211
Jordan Valley, 131, 208, 211, 214, 218
Judea, 205
Justice, H. M., 216

Kantara, 187, 188
Kanwakah, 195, 196
Kelvedon, 143
Kennedy Crater, 52
Kennedy, H. B., 14, 40, 44, 52, 61, 71, 72, 82, 83, 84, 95, 101, 104, 110, 113, 114, 117, 122
Kent Fort, 189, 191

King, Bandmaster, 14
King, H.M. The, 15, 109, 126, 145
King's Own Yorkshire L.I., 171, 173, 176, 191
King's Shropshire L.I., 210
Kit and Kat, 78
Kitchener, Lord, 15, 135
Kitchener's Army, 23
Kulonieh, 206,
Kustine, 202
Kustul, 205, 206

La Bassée, 28, 41
La Bassée Canal, 27, 28
Labeuvrière, 26
La Boisselle, 105
Lahoussoye, 59, 60
Laing, O., 54, 104
La Marguerite, S.S., 146
Lamotte-Buleux, 106
Lancashire Fusiliers, 169
Lapugnoy, 23
Lash, R. H., 156
La Tombe, 122
Latrun, 203
Laviéville, 64, 90, 106
Lawrence, T. E., Col., 211
Lealvillers, 105
Leave to England, 40, 56, 162
Lechelle, 92, 95, 101
Le Forest, 117
Le Maisnil, 120
Leman, D. W., 209, 216
Leman, H. C., 161, 191
Le Mesnil, 101
Lens, 41, 48, 56, 57
Le Quesnoy, 25, 26
Les Boeufs, 102, 103, 104
Les Brebis, 37, 41, 46
Les Facons, 25
Lestrem, 119
Le Touret, 25
Le Transloy, 101, 102, 103, 104
Levy, Lieut., 144, 173, 185
Lewis, Brig.-Gen., 47
Lewis Guns and Gunners, 51, 52, 75, 98, 99, 120, 184
Ley, Cpl., 100
Liddiatt, A. W., 145, 185
Liéramont, 117
Life in French villages, 20, 23, 26, 27, 28, 34, 37, 40, 47, 56
Lifta, 205, 206
Lille, 121, 122
Lillers, 44
Line, P. A., 156, 157

Linfoot, Lieut., 210, 212
Lockie, E. C., 183
Lomme, 121, 122
London Regt., 6th Battn., 95
,, ,, 7th Battn., 90
,, ,, 8th Battn., 31, 79, 85
,, ,, 15th Battn., 71, 83, 84, 98, 99, 101, 106, 109, 110, 112, 114, 115, 116, 117
,, ,, 17th Battn., 97, 98, 99, 101, 102, 105, 107, 110, 112, 115, 120, 122
,, ,, 18th Battn., 113, 119
,, ,, 19th Battn., 75, 106, 109
,, ,, 20th Battn., 54, 74, 102, 103, 104
,, ,, 22nd Battn., 23, 28, 41, 46, 55, 73, 110
,, ,, 23rd Battn., 23, 28, 29, 30, 42, 55, 63, 73, 80, 87, 88, 90, 98, 99, 100
,, ,, 24th Battn., 23, 28, 29, 30, 54, 63, 73, 80, 109
,, ,, 2/11th Battn., 95
,, ,, 2/13th Battn., 218
,, ,, 2/17th Battn., 216
,, ,, 2/18th Battn., 216
,, ,, 2/19th Battn., 213, 214, 218
,, ,, 2/22nd Battn., 141, 159, 183, 193, 196, 197, 209, 212, 218
,, ,, 2/23rd Battn., 141, 154, 193, 209, 210, 215, 216
,, ,, 2/24th Battn., 141, 193, 209, 210
London Rifle Brigade, 145
London Scottish, 20
Lone Tree, 43
Longpré, 162
Loos, 41, 46, 48, 58
Loos Crassier, 43
Lord Mayor of London, 126

Louez, 146, 147, 148
Louvencourt, 105
Love Crater, 52
Love, S. G., Major, 51
Lowry, A. J., 117
Loyal North Lancs Regt., 191
Lozinghem, 124
Ludd, 218
Luton, 18

Macdonald, A. C., 173, 187
Macedonia, 167, 168, 169, 176, 178, 179, 185
Machine Gun Company, 181st, 196, 198, 210
McKay, G. M., 29
Mackukovo, 180, 182
McMurtree, S. G., Rev., 191
Macnamara, T. J., Dr., M.P., 126
Madagascar Dump, 159
Maestre Line, 53
Mahmudli, 169, 174, 175, 176, 178
Mailly-Maillet, 82
Maisnil Bouché, 50, 57, 58
Maizières, 58, 59
Makhadet Hajla, 213
Malta, 163
Mametz Wood, 60, 62, 64
Mandesi Ford, 213
Manson, M. M., 22
Marles-les-Mines, 39, 119
Maroc, 33, 37, 46, 48
Maroeuil, 79, 153, 161
Marseilles, 162
Marshall, Rev., 92
Martin, R., 77, 80
Martin, T. L., 22
Martinsart, 106
Maurepas Ravine, 113, 117
Maxwell, Lieut.-Col., 99
Mazingarbe, 34, 37, 39, 43, 44
Mediterranean, 163, 201, 203
Meritorious Service Medal, 186
Merstham, 134, 136
Merville, 119
Messines, 72
Meteren, 75
Metz-en-Couture, 83
Metz Switch, 98, 100
Military Cross, 55, 62, 85, 86, 110, 111, 173, 208, 213
Military Medal, 52, 85, 90, 111, 173, 208
Millencourt, 63
Miller, Sgt., 54
Mills, Lieut., 133

Minenwerfer, 67, 111
Mining, 27, 45, 46, 50, 67, 155
Minnetonka, S.S., 185
Minotaur Dump, 159
Mirtaba, Wadi, 190
Moab, 212, 214
Moberly, A. H., 29
Mobilization, 13
Moeuvres, 83
Moislains, 115, 116, 117
Momber Crater, 52
Momber, E. M. F., Major, 51
Monro, Sir Charles, 20, 31
Mont des Cats, 65
Morgan Gully, 180
Moringhem, 77
Morlancourt, 109
Morland, Sir T. L. N., 119
Morris, W. F., 25, 40
Morton, A. D., 111
Moulle, 70, 71
Mukhmas, 210, 211

Nablus Road, 205
Narish, 185
Nebi Samwil, 203, 204, 205, 212
Netif, Wadi, 210
Neuve Chapelle, 21
Neuvillette, 161
Newman, W. J., 117
Newton, W. G., 100, 103, 104, 106, 117, 122
New Year's Eve, 1916, 68, 69
Nimrin, Wadi, 218
Nine Elms Sector, 108
Noeux-les-Mines, 43, 44
Norrent-Fontes, 20
North Staffordshire Regt., 106
Northumberland Fusiliers, 184
Nurlu, 115, 117

Oaf Lane, 73, 74
Oblinghem, 20
Old French Trench, 75
Olympus, 165
Ontario Camp, 76, 77
Oppy, 79
Orchard, The, 24
Ordnance House, 137
Oresdi-Bak, 165
Orival Wood, 94, 95
Ouderdom, 76
Ovillers, 105

Padres, 68, 76, 92, 93
Palestine, 131, 186, 199
Palmis, 170, 172, 173
Pantilotchi, 153

Parish, Lieut.-Col., 97, 100
Parsons, Brig.-Gen., 144
Pas de Calais, 57
Peel, Capt., 88
Pembroke Wadi, 192
Perkins, F. A., 75
Pernes, 126
Peroi, 171, 173
Persse, S., 30, 77
Petit Piton, 181, 182
Petticoat Lane, 70
Petrol Tins, Uses of, 38
Philosophe, 37
Picardy, 57
Picquigny, 107
Pike, Capt., 110, 111
Plumer, Lord, 72
Plumptre, B., Rev., 68, 76
Pollard, Dr., 92
Pont Fixe, 27
Pont Rémy, 64
Poperinghe, 68, 78
Pozières, 105
Puckle, Major, 144, 165, 173

Quarante Se(p)t, 69

Radinghem, 119
Ra Fat, 209
Ramah, 211
Ram Allah, 217, 218
Ras el Tawil, 209, 210, 211
Rashid Bek, 192, 193
Ravine Wood, 71
Recruiting, 13, 139
Red Château, 95
Redhill, 134, 137
Red House, 140
Redway, F. M., 210
Reed, Major, 103, 104
Regimental March, 14
Reid, J. C. B., 85
Reliefs, Organization of, 34, 154
Reninghelst, 65, 76, 77
Ribécourt, 92, 94
Richards, H. P., 21, 29, 47, 53
Richebourg St. Vaast, 21, 23
Richmond, H. B., 88
Ridge Wood, 75
Rippert, 150
Roberts, Lord, 15
Roberts, O. H. S., 79
Robinson, H. H., 25, 62, 75
Roclincourt, 151, 159
Rocquigny, 101, 102, 103, 104
Round Hill, 210
Routes Nationales, 58

Rowell, Lieut.-Col., U.S.A. Army, 108
Royal Berkshire Regt., 101, 102, 103
Royal Fusiliers, 90, 96, 100
Royal Scots, 149
Royal Welsh Fusiliers, 95, 98, 100, 105, 115, 116
Rue du Bois, 22, 24
Rue de Tilleloy, 119
Runners, 55, 74, 75, 91, 98, 99, 100
Ruskin Park, 132, 133
Russell, L. E., 139
Russia, Collapse of, 91
Ruthven, H., 42

Sablier, 150, 151, 155, 158
Sadler, W. H., 111
Saillisel, 96
Sailly-Labourse, 45
St. Acheul, 58
St. Albans, 13, 14, 18, 138, 139
St. Catherine, 154
St. Eloi (Arras Sector), 149
St. Eloi (Ypres Sector), 73
St. Hilaire, 20, 120, 121
St. Michel, 119
St. Omer, 20, 70, 77
St. Pierre Vaast, 96, 113, 114, 115
St. Pol, 119, 146
St. Riquier, 58, 59, 106
Salient, The, 64, 65
Salonica, 162, 164, 165
Sandbags, Uses of, 38, 39
Sardinia, 163
Sarigol, 167, 168, 185
Saumarez, Capt., 101
Savel, H. R., 29
Savy, 147, 153
Sawbridgeworth, 137, 139, 140
Scots Guards, 20
Scottish Camp, 65, 69
Scouts, 59, 102, 198
Seaforth Highlanders, 149
Segrave, Lieut.-Col., 83, 84, 100
Senlis, 106, 108
Sercus, 75
Sergeant, Sgt., 173
Sexton, —, 98, 117
Shea, Gen., 187, 189, 191
Sheikh Nuran, 200
Shellal, 188
Shellard, R. S., 31
Shenley Ridge, 14
Sheria, 197, 198, 200, 212
Sheria, Wadi, 196, 197

Sherlock, A. H., 22
Shropshire Wadi, 192, 193
Signallers, 55, 59, 75, 91
Sillitoe, Rev., 92
Sir John Gray Hill's House, 208, 217
Skating, 70
Smith, Lieut., 172
Smith, S. B., 191, 192, 199, 210
Snevce, 167, 168, 174, 177
Society Improved Entertainers, 96
Somme, 56, 58, 161
Somme, March to, 58, 59
Souchez, 48, 49
Souchez, River, 49
South Africans, 63
Southampton, 18, 126, 146
Southin, C. A., 156, 157, 158, 161, 171, 172, 173
South Staffordshire Regt., 80, 96
Squibb, Lieut., 79
Steenvoorde, 70, 71, 78
Stickland, A. L., 80, 82, 85, 87, 96, 97, 114
Stony Hill, 181, 183
Stretcher-bearers, 62
Strong Point 9, Ypres, 68
Suez Canal, 186
Summer Time, 70
Sunken Road, 159
Sutton Veney, 139, 143
Sweileh, 215
Sylvester, H. A., 97, 111

Talet el Dumm, 218
Tanks, 60, 82, 102, 110, 112
Taylor, N. A., 30, 31, 105
Tel el Fara, 191
Tel es Suwan, 210
Territorials, 2nd Line, 23
Thornhill Camp, 180
Tidd, R. R., 95, 104, 111
Tiddy, Lieut., 157
Tidmarsh, S., 79, 81, 89, 111, 120
Tidy, —, 85
Timsah Lake, 186
Tin Hat, 50
Tinques, 146, 147, 153
Toffee-apples, 154
Tolerton, R. H., 78, 80, 82, 87, 95
Tomlin, Morton, 13, 23, 25
Tooth, Lieut., 30
Tournai, 122
Toutencourt, 105
Tower Bridge, 43

Tower Hill, 209
Townend, Lieut., 156, 157
Transport, 14, 18, 59, 85, 95, 109, 141, 146, 154, 162, 166, 176, 178, 192
Trench-foot, 94, 171
Troop Trains, 19, 64, 146
Tunnelling Company, 176th, 51
Turner, Col., 80
Turner, G. C., 80, 86, 87, 106
Tyneside Troops, 56

Ushanta Camp, 165, 185

Vallulart Wood, 99
Vardar Valley, 178, 180, 182, 183
Velu, 90
Verbrandenmolen, 67
Vermelles, 45, 46
Vignacourt, 59
Villers-au-Bois, 49, 50, 53, 57
Villers Bocage, 59
Villers Plouich, 94, 96, 98
Villers-sous-Ailly, 162
Vimy Ridge, 49, 50, 53, 56, 57

Wadi Aujah, 211
,, El Kelt, 211
,, Ghuzze, 188, 190
,, Mirtaba, 190
,, Netif, 210
,, Nimrin, 218
,, , Pembroke, 192
,, Sheria, 196, 197
,, , Shropshire, 192, 193
Wakefield Camp, 81
Walford, Q., 21, 46, 77, 78, 99, 100
Walter, A. J., 144, 173

Ward, C. B., 160
Warlencourt, Butte de, 63
Warloy, 105, 106, 108, 109
Warminster, 143, 144, 145
Warwickshire Regt., 199
Water, Conveyance of, 38
Watney, F. D., 161, 163, 168, 184, 191
Watts, Brig.-Gen., 141
Welsh Regt., 209
Welsh Ridge, 94, 98
West, Capt., 108
Westhoek Ridge, 77, 78
White Château, 76
White City, 134
White Tower, 165
Willems, 122
Williams, Capt., U.S.A. Army, 108
Williamson, Rev., 93
Willows, The, 81
Wilson, R., 81, 85
Wilson, Sir Henry, 55
Wimbledon Common, 133
Winter, Lieut.-Col., 96, 100
Wippenhoek, 78
Wizernes, 20
Worcestershire Regt., 199
Works Battalion, 69
Wray, Lieut., 111, 117
Wright, S., 134, 138, 144, 145

York Camp, 77
Yorks and Lancs Regt., 175
Young, Major, 119, 120
Ypres, 64, 65, 66, 75, 78
Ytres, 101

Zouave Valley, 49

www.ingramcontent.com/pod-product-compliance
Lightning Source LLC
Chambersburg PA
CBHW031137160426
43193CB00008B/166